Hearing what God has spoken.

God

has spoken.

(Doctrine of Scripture).

To the reader.

The content of this book is entirely the work of the author unless otherwise indicated. The intention of this work is to help believers in their walk with Christ Jesus. Consequently the reader is free to make use of this work free from any copyright restrictions. The word of God is free. How then can I offer this work at any cost? I offer it for the benefit of all who chance to read it, and pray that in reading it they may be drawn into a deeper and closer communion with God the Father, Son and Holy Spirit.

Mike Viccary.

January 2017.

Contents:

Introduction and rationale.

We live in interesting times! Such a phrase stems, supposedly, from the English expression of a Chinese curse meant to enforce times of desperation and difficulty. I am not unaware of the difficulties and harsh realities that ordinary Christian folk face today as modern culture not only drifts, but accelerates towards anarchy and a rejection of all that is truly holy. It is tempting to consider that we need new approaches, and new ideas in order to combat this fall in society going on all around us. What can we do? Why are things getting so hard? Surely the answer is to try something new?

Not least of the difficulties that the Christian faces is that the world doesn't actually believe that it is falling or going astray. It would suggest that a better description for the recent history of the world is one of emancipation from the shackles imposed by a former authoritarian regime. The Christian faith is often charged with being a part of this former regime. Hence whenever we attempt to proclaim and declare the truths we love, we are doing so in a climate of rejection and hostility. Yet another difficulty we face is the whole "post-modern" milieu and ethos we are currently bathed in. There is a rampant rejection of "truth," but this is not a new thing for Christ Himself heard Pilate respond to His declarations with these hopeless words: "what is truth?"[1] The point Pilate was making was that to hold to an ideal "truth" is not really practical. The Romans, of course, were eminently practical or pragmatic. We live in similar days and times. Still another difficulty is the dreadful lack of certainty about such things as identity. Diversity is a great word and theme *if* we understand this in close connection with another essential theme, unity. From a Christian point of view all humans have been created in the image of God and so exhibit a deep and compulsive unity. However the Lord has not made all people equal. In fact Psalm 33v15 tells us that God has fashioned our hearts *individually*, hence the importance of diversity. But diversity is not a matter of personal choice. We are not autonomous and independent beings who have the right to self-determination. We cannot decide that we are male or female or whatever else we choose. We are created beings and dependent upon our Creator and one another for proper existence.

Given these and many other problems we encounter in this world, it might be tempting as I said at the start to think that our approach as Christians must change. What ought we to be doing that will help in our endeavour to reach this rapidly falling world? Well of course the response to such a question really depends on what we have been doing up to this point. If our efforts are

---

[1]   John 18v38.

wholly in accord with what the Lord requires of us then nothing needs changing. If, on the other hand, we reflect on our past and realise that in fact we have been doing things wrong, or we have been approaching the problems of witness and mission in the wrong way, then we will need to repent and turn back and do those things that God requires. The one great troubling thing that I have observed in recent years is what may be called a bifurcation of intention. The twentieth century is characterised from a Christian point of view by two distinct camps of Christians. There are the charismatics and there are the reformed. Now I do not want to suggest that such a simplistic division can be used to separate sheep from goats. There are godly people in both camps. There are misguided people in both camps. Some may lay claim to being in both, others in neither. My simple point here is that there has been a division into two modes of thought which I have observed as I have had the great privilege of travelling the country and visiting various churches. Thus on the one hand we have those who seem to understand clearly the need for solid doctrinal truth-based teaching. On the other hand we have those whose focus is on the experience of the Lord in a renewed heart and mind. The two ideas ought never to be separated. However go to a charismatic church and you will observe an emphasis on worship, experience and fellowship. The relational side is vital amongst these believers and this is a wonderful thing to witness. Their doctrine and their understanding is poor, but their love and fellowship is great. As an anecdotal piece of evidence I was at a meeting whilst writing this piece where several people independently brought a Scripture to the meeting to encourage the fellowship. It was the same Scripture and it was one you may be familiar with, and one which gets repeated often when the focus is on man and his world. The Scripture I am referring to is Jeremiah 29v11:

> *For I know the thoughts that I think toward you, says the Lord, thoughts of peace and not of evil, to give you a future and a hope.*

You don't often hear Scriptures like Jeremiah 7v8 or Jeremiah 23v16 quoted in meetings! Of course God does have a future for us. That is the great and wonderful thing about Christ coming into the world to die for sin and so on. However in many charismatic meetings the emphasis is always on making people feel positive and special. Now I do not want to be misunderstood here. I am all for the Scriptural truths which identify us being a royal priesthood, adopted and loved immensely by God. These are all necessary and extremely important. However there are many Scriptures that deal with the issues of on-going sin, of difficulties in relationships and of heresies and errors amongst the people of God. These factors are very rarely considered by our charismatic brethren.

Alternatively if you were to visit many evangelical or reformed fellowships your heart may be warmed as you hear the Scriptures faithfully expounded week by week. What you may not get very often is a warm welcome or a family feel. You may get a very traditional approach to worship, service and the Christian life. This may have been fine for a day when communities understood, to some extent, the Christian basis of life and so on. However in our day such luxuries are rare indeed. Most communities and settings are not just "post-modern" but anti-Christian, by which I mean that there is no thought of the true God in peoples minds. Now I am aware that this is a generalisation. However the kind of relational atmosphere where joy and heart-felt prayer of the saints is evident amongst charismatics is often lacking amongst those whose focus is solid Bible teaching.

Why is there this division, this bifurcation? What has happened? Well an answer to these two closely related questions would require a look into some history which we have not the time to develop here. However it is my deep conviction that a great part of the problem is a wholly wrong view of Scripture. Perhaps as a starting point it is worth noting the apostle Paul's perspective on his intention for teaching. Writing to the young Timothy the apostle makes this statement with regard to his purpose:

> *But the goal of our instruction is love from a pure heart and a good conscience and a sincere faith. (1Timothy 1v5, NASB).*

It is noticeable that the apostle Paul highlights the importance of "doctrine" in his epistles to Timothy and Titus, but he does not do this at the expense of love and precisely love of God and our fellow man.[2] In the verse above Paul sets out his prime intention to teach "love"! But this does not come about merely from having meetings where the family is the focus and where relationships are developed. These things are vital, of course, but they are not what Paul emphasises. Rather he points out that this love comes from something he describes in three ways. He speaks of a "pure heart," by which he means a cleansed mind and soul, or a renewed soul. He speaks of a "good conscience," by which he means again the inner being made perfect. He speaks of a "sincere faith," by which he means a genuine true and precious faith which looks exclusively to the Lord God. Now these things can only come about through the work of the Holy Spirit and His ministry through the word.

In my early days as a believer I was often shocked that older believers had trouble with creation, and consequently dabbled with some form of compromise with science, such as theistic evolution, or the gap theory and so on. I was shocked because I thought that such a simple thing had

---

2   The word "doctrine" can be found at: 1Timothy 1v3,10; 4v1,6,13,16; 5v17; 6v1,3; 2Timothy 3v10,16; 4v3; Titus 1v9; 2v1,7,10. The word "love" can be found at: 1Timothy 1v5,14; 2v15; 4v12; 6v10,11; 2Timothy 1v7,13; 2v22; 3v2,4,10; 4v8,10; Titus 1v8; 2v2,4; 3v4,15.

become so complex in these folk's minds. To me as a young Christian, who was also a scientist, it was a simple matter to recognise both the severe limitations of human enterprise (science), and the fact that what God had revealed was absolutely true and beyond reproach. When God stated how He created all things why ever would I doubt Him? When we factor in the motives behind mankind's approach to origins the case was simple: believe what God has revealed and understand the flaws in the modern scientific approach. Following this early development in my thought it became apparent that other problems people grappled with were not problems in themselves but problems people had with the Scriptures. In short the issue that really mattered was not the issues that people focused on (evolution, church growth techniques, ecumenism, psychology and so on), but the way in which people approached the problems, and the way in which people used Scripture or what they believed about Scripture. As a consequence of these ideas it became clear that the fundamental thing was to look closely and deeply at the doctrine of Scripture.

Early attempts at considering this wonderful subject centred on picking up the individual themes contained in Scripture such as the idea of it being "written," the concept of inerrancy, the breadth of Scripture, that it was the word of God, and so on. As I began to study these it became clear that there were ten separate themes which I developed as follows:

Writing	– Scripture means "writings"
Unity	– there is only one main message found throughout.
Revelation	– it all stems from God who always takes the initiative.
Inspiration	– how God makes known.
Preservation	– how God keeps His word.
Illumination	– how God makes known to us who believe.
Sufficiency	– that nothing else besides Scripture is needed (save the indwelling Spirit).
Scope	– that Scripture is broad and deals with everything necessary.
Efficacy	– that Scripture does its work very well.
Authority	– Scripture is the sole authority.

This present work builds on these themes but operates under a new structure. I have interacted with others who have written on Scripture and made use of their works, but largely I have attempted to draw from Scripture that which the Lord has to say about how He has communicated to us. In putting it like this it is vital that our chief view is about Christ and His coming into the world. The apostle John tells us that when the Word became flesh and dwelt amongst us, it was this very one who "declared" who God is.[3] Consequently our devotion and love for Christ ought always to be the central theme of our life and thought. Christ came into this world in order to communicate. He came to declare the very nature of God, since He was and is God. He came to teach us about our nature and about the gospel. But most of all He has come that we might know Him and fellowship with Him. In our studies we must not drift into an intellectual and academic mode which sucks the life out of that which we hold precious, even though we may need to exercise the muscles of our mind. All the while we do this we need to keep ourselves "in the love of God" as we build ourselves up on the "most holy faith, praying in the Holy Spirit."[4]

---

3   John 1v18.
4   Jude 1v20,21.

Part 1: The doctrine of Scripture considered under four key inter-related headings: Revelation, Inspiration, Preservation, and Illumination.

In a former attempt at writing on the doctrine of Scripture I worked on the principle that Scripture was a multi-faceted jewel. By taking this approach it meant that I could view Scripture in all its beauty from many different angles. However after some study and thought, it became apparent that whilst all the different facets had a certain connection to each of the others, there were four features which really demanded a connected approach. These follow in a logical order. Starting with revelation from God we proceed to the means and method that God chose to reveal (inspiration). Once the idea that it is God who brings His word to us through especial spokespersons is fully grasped, we are led naturally to consider how the word revealed to the prophets is kept through the ages, that is, how such revelation is preserved (preservation). Finally, once we recognise that God's word revealed is available for every generation, we are lead seamlessly to the idea of how such a revelation may be received by believing individuals (illumination).

Chapter 1.

The doctrine of Revelation.

Introduction: revelation and discovery.

We need to begin our study of the Bible by looking at two key words which are often used in normal speech and writing, but which have particular meanings in Scripture. The two words in question are: "revelation" and "discovery." One of these (revelation) is particularly important when considering Scripture. Discovery, on the other hand, is a word which is often used by scientists to describe the process by which new findings are uncovered. Although perhaps many modern scientists would not quite agree with Newton, the view he expressed about being like a boy on the seashore picking up pretty pebbles to consider seems as good as any to describe the idea behind discovery. Or perhaps you may remember playing "hunt the slipper." The game in which someone hides a slipper somewhere in a room whilst all the others playing the game are outside waiting expectantly, and when they return they have to look for the hidden footwear! These are both descriptions of discovery. Something that can be uncovered. It might take some finding (as in the game I described) or it may be plainly obvious, like the pebbles on the beach. The main point is that in discovery, things can be uncovered if you have a mind to look for them.

Revelation is something quite different to discovery. Thus, whilst discovery concerns the seeking and then finding or uncovering of something by human ingenuity and effort, revelation is that disclosure of something, or someone, which *cannot* ever be discovered, and which unless the person responsible for the unveiling does something to make what was unknown known, nothing would ever be disclosed. What is revealed cannot ever be discovered. What is discovered may be made known but only by effort (to varying degrees).

Having described the two ideas, our focus will be on revelation for this is the word that is used to describe what God has done in making Himself known.[5] It will be helpful to consider this idea of revelation under the following five headings:

[1] General and Special Revelation – an introduction.

[2] "Two books" and some history of science.

---

5   The concept of discovery forms a centre piece of the book of Ecclesiastes. The human "author" (Solomon) comes to the conclusion that discovery isn't really possible (Ecclesiastes 8v16,17).

[3] General revelation – some key texts.

[4] Special revelation (Scripture).

[5] Implications of the doctrine of revelation.

[1] General and Special Revelation – an introduction.

So, as we have established, revelation is that which is uncovered but could never be discovered. We shall begin our thoughts by considering one of the most wonderful things of all, namely, people. How does a person show forth their being? Before we answer this we may be tempted to think that others may "discover" things about a person. It is, of course, true that some thing about people may be discovered, but this is because the information is in the public arena. However a person can easily hide things about themselves and it isn't until they choose to reveal these things that they become available. Now there are two general ways in which a person may show forth who they are:

By what a person may say or write – by their words.[6]

By what a person may do or leave in their wake – by their by actions.[7]

In the same way, we can know God by His works and through His words. This leads to the splitting of revelation into its two separate divisions which we term: general and special. By the term **special** revelation we mean to focus on what God has said, (i.e. the Bible). By the term **general** revelation we mean to consider what God has done (usually not in the Bible but in creation, providence/history).[8] General revelation also includes that which the Lord gives by way of man's conscience.[9] Now it is vital that we grasp here that general revelation **must** be subordinated to special revelation as far as our understanding of these as human beings goes. God, of course, cannot lie nor contradict Himself. What he says (in Scripture) will never contradict what He "says" in creation, providence and history. Although this statement may not be true with respect to ordinary people (our words often contradict our actions sadly) it is eminently true with respect to God. What He says is not contradicted by what He does. Unfortunately, what God does may be interpreted by man using other than Biblical (God guided) ways. This means that general revelation may be made

---

6   An awful lot is spoken and written about "non-verbal" communication and symbolism. But these forms of communication, whilst important, cannot really be understood without some form of verbal explanation. If we go to a different culture where the hand gestures and body language is very different to ours, we will make many mistakes until someone takes the trouble to explain where we have misinterpreted them.

7   Think, for example, of the art world. The works of the great artists are easily recognisable.

8   Some Scriptures which highlight general revelation are: Romans 1v19,20; Psalm 19v1,2; Acts 14v17.

9   Ecclesiastes 3v11; Romans 2v14-16.

to say something which it was never meant to say.

The general distinction between general and special revelation got distorted through certain periods of church history into the concept of "two books" which we shall consider shortly.[10] As a brief interlude, we may consider the Reformers attitude. In this connection Louis Berkhoff is worth quoting at this point:

> Their view of the matter may be represented as follows: As a result of the entrance of sin into the world, the handwriting of God in nature is greatly obscured, and is in some of the most important matters rather dim and illegible. Moreover, man is stricken with spiritual blindness, and is thus deprived of the ability to read aright what God had originally plainly written in the works of creation. In order to remedy the matter and to prevent the frustration of His purpose, God did two things. In His supernatural revelation He republished the truths of natural revelation, cleared them of misconception, interpreted them with a view to the present needs of man, and thus incorporated them in His supernatural revelation of redemption. And in addition to that He provided a cure to the spiritual blindness of man in the work of regeneration and sanctification, including spiritual illumination, and thus enabled man once more to obtain true knowledge of God, the knowledge that carries with it the assurance of eternal life.[11]

These words are timely. They indicate the notion that what God actually says in and through creation and providence can be read aright. In other words, what God has "said" in general revelation is, in point of fact, clear. It is just that sin and human depravity has caused man to deviate from the clear truths that creation and providence elucidate and have opted for schemes and inventions of their own.[12] Consequently the Scriptures are given as the unfettered truth which can only be unlocked by the power of the Holy Spirit through His illuminating work in the heart of the regenerate saint.

[2] "Two books" and some history of science.

The teaching that God has spoken to us and given us two books, the first being his work of creation, and the second the Scriptures, has a long history. However the way in which this figure has been used and understood has varied significantly over time. In the earliest times following the apostolic era, the notion was simply that creation (nature) was a book which could be read by anyone with a mind to do so. In his paper on the two books before the scientific revolution, the catholic astronomer-theologian Tanzella-Nitti could write that:

---

10   Especially from the Middle Ages and the time of Thomas Aquinas, right up through the reformation era (fifteenth century), the scientific revolution (sixteenth century), and through to the enlightenment times (seventeenth and eighteenth centuries).
11   Louis Berkhof. Systematic Theology. Banner of Truth. 1988 printing. P38.
12   Ecclesiastes 7v29.

Among the Fathers of the Church, explicit references to the book of nature can be found in St. Basil, St. Gregory of Nyssa, St. Augustine, John Cassian, St. John Chrysostom, St. Ephrem the Syrian, and Maximus the Confessor.[13]

The early Christian era.

Although not in the list given by Tanzella-Nitti, Irenaeus (129 – 203) expresses a typical view which reflects the teaching of Scriptures such as Psalm 19 and Romans 1. Irenaeus spent time in Smyrna where he heard the famed Polycarp preach before eventually going to Lyons. We know of two written works by this man, namely a defence against the Gnostic heresies, and a work on Christian teaching which emphasised the idea that Christ was the fulfilment of the Old Testament prophecies. It is in his work, *"Against Heresies,"* that we find the idea of creation reflecting the Creator:

> For even creation reveals Him who formed it, and the very work made suggests Him who made it, and the world manifests Him who ordered it.[14]

Irenaeus does not use the term "book" but our second example, Anthony the Abbot (251 – 356) does. Anthony (also styled variously as "the great" and "the just"), was the first monk to retire into a desert life in Egypt (circa 270). According to one contemporary writer who observed this man, Anthony was a keen observer of God's creation. When asked by a philosopher "how can you endure being deprived of the comfort of books?" Anthony replied by saying: "My book, O philosopher is the nature of things that are made, and it is present whenever I wish to read the words of God."[15]

Moving forward to the fourth century we must consider the "golden mouthed" John Chrysostom of Antioch (347 – 407).[16] He was recognised as a "Doctor of the Church" because of the extent and value of his writings, of which some 600 sermons and 200 letters survive. From his *"Homilies on the Statutes,"* we can read about his thoughts on Scriptures such as Romans 1 and Psalm 19:

> The heavens may be silent, but the sight of them emits a voice, that is louder than a trumpet's sound; instructing us not by the ear, but through the medium of the eyes; for the latter is a sense which is more sure and more distinct than the former. [17]

---

13   G. Tanzella-Nitti, "The Two Books Prior to the Scientific Revolution," *Perspectives on Science and Christian Faith,* Volume 57, Number 3, September 2005. 235-248. P 237.
14   Irenaeus of Lyons. Against Heresies. Book II. Chapter 9.1. http://www.newadvent.org/fathers/0103209.htm.
15   Church History (Socrates Scholasticus).Book IV. Chapter 23. The Deeds of Some Holy Persons who devoted themselves to a Solitary Life. http://www.newadvent.org/fathers/26014.htm.
16   Chrysostom means "golden mouthed" and was the name given to John of Antioch because of his gift of preaching.
17   John Chrysostom. Homily IX.4. On the Statutes. http://www.newadvent.org/fathers/190109.htm.

... with respect to the heavens ... every man that walks upon the earth, shall hear this voice; for not by means of the ears, but through the sight, it reaches our understanding. ... Upon this volume the unlearned, as well as the wise man, shall be alike able to look; the poor man as well as the rich man; and wherever any one may chance to come, there looking upwards towards the heavens, he will receive a sufficient lesson from the view of them ... that the creation utters this voice so as to be intelligible ... to all mankind without exception, when he spoke on this wise; *There is no speech, nor language, where there voice is not heard.* What he means is to this effect, that there is no nation or tongue which is unable to understand this language; but that such is their utterance, that it may be heard of all mankind.[18]

In these words we learn that Chrysostom considers that the heavens speak for all to hear. It is not, to be sure, a truly audible word, but a sight which "speaks" more effectively than words. It is from "this volume" of the heavens that anyone may "receive a sufficient lesson," and it is this creation which utters a voice which is "intelligible" so that there is no one who is "unable to understand." But what is mankind meant to understand from the heavens and from creation? Chrysostom does not stray far from the apostle Paul's teaching stating:

[God] has placed His Creation in the midst, before the eyes of all men; in order that they may guess at the Creator from His works; which, indeed, another writer has referred to; *For from the greatness and beauty of the creatures, proportionably the Maker of them is seen.* [Wisdom 13:5].[19]

Turning to the famed bishop of Hippo, Augustine (354 – 430), we have a more definite expression of the idea of two books than we found in earlier Christian writings. In this first quote we note that Augustine makes a distinction between how we should interact with the two "books":

It is the divine page that you must listen to; it is the book of the universe that you must observe. The pages of Scripture can only be read by those who know how to read and write, while everyone, even the illiterate, can read the book of the universe.[20]

Scripture is for reading, listening to and heeding, but nature is for looking at. It would appear that literacy was low in Augustine's day, for he notes that whilst Scripture may only be read by the literate, the book of the universe can be read by all who can see.

Some people in order to discover God, read a book. But there is a great book: the very appearance of created things. Look above and below, note, read. God whom you want to discover, did not make the letters with ink; he put in front of your eyes the very things that

---

18   John Chrysostom. Homily IX.5. On the Statutes. http://www.newadvent.org/fathers/190109.htm.
19   As for footnote 18, IX.4.
20   Augustine, Enarrationes in Psalmos 45, 7 (PL36, 518) http://inters.org/Augustine-Book-of-Nature.

he made. Can you ask for a louder voice than that?[21]

Augustine explains that the book of the universe displaying created things, declares with a voice which is louder than any others the very being of God. We can see in these examples that it was a time when few could read the Scriptures for themselves. This was not just on account of widespread illiteracy, but also due to the cost of producing written texts.

The middle ages.

During the middle age era, the catholic scholar Tanzella-Nitti has claimed that:

> References to the book of nature can be found, with different nuances and to different degrees in St. Bernard of Clairvaux (1090–1153), Hugh of St. Victor (1096–1141), St. Bonaventure (1217– 1274), St.Thomas Aquinas (1224–1274), Thomas of Chobham (about 1255–1327), Dante Alighieri (1265–1321), Thomas of Kempis (1380–1471) and Raymond of Sebond (about 1385– 1436).[22]

The Saxon cleric Hugh of St. Victor (1096 – 1141) could describe the book of nature as something which requires a spiritual mind to read it:

> For this whole visible world is a book written by the finger of God, that is, created by divine power . . . But just as some illiterate man who sees an open book looks at the figures but does not recognize the letters: just so the foolish natural man who does not perceive the things of God outwardly in these visible creatures sees the appearances but does not inwardly understand the reason. But he who is spiritual and can judge all things, while he considers outwardly the beauty of the work, inwardly conceives how marvellous is the wisdom of the Creator.[23]

Hugh of St. Victor affirms creation both as being from the power of God and as a *text* which can be read. The world being visible for all is not however understood by all. It is only the spiritual who can grasp the meaning of the created world. Those who see outwardly admire the beauty but those who see with spiritual eyes can discern the greatness of God's wisdom. Here we can see the beginnings of a distinction between what general revelation actually reveals, and what man makes of it through his twisted mind and eye.

---

21   Augustine, Sermones 68, 6 (PLS2,505).   http://inters.org/Augustine-Book-of-Nature.
22   G. Tanzella-Nitti, "The Two Books Prior to the Scientific Revolution," *Perspectives on Science and Christian Faith,* Volume 57, Number 3, September 2005. 235-248. P 237.
23   Quoted by Jeffrey Turco in ENCYCLOPEDIC AESTHETICS: SCIENCE, SALVATION, AND STORYTELLING IN THE THIRTEENTH CENTURY, PhD thesis, Cornell University, August 2009. P15. Turco identifies the source as follows: "quoted in Gabriel Josipovici, The World and the Book (Stanford: Stanford University Press, 1971)." See also: Hugh of St Victor, *De tribus diebus* 4, in J.-P. Migne (ed.), *Patrologia cursus completus, series Latina,* Paris , (1857-1912) [PL], 122, 176.814 B-C.

The next most significant writer who uses this figure is the Catalan scholar, Raymond of Sebond (circa 1385 – 1436):

> God has given us two books: the Book of the Universal Order of Things (or, of Nature) and the Book of the Bible. The former was given to us first, from the origin of the world: for each creature is like a letter traced by the hand of God.[24]

This statement is concise and reflects a long history of use borne out of a reflection of Scripture. Raymond, however, has new ideas to add to the story. For him the book of nature is infallible, and, astoundingly, can teach about salvation!

> [God] made this visible world and gave it to us like a proper, familiar and infallible Book, written by his hand, in which the creatures are ranged like letters...so as to teach us the wisdom and science of our salvation.[25]

Not content with simply stating that the visible world speaks infallibility, Raymond works this out to teach that none can become a heretic through reading this volume:

> The Book of Nature cannot be corrupted nor effaced nor falsely interpreted. Therefore the heretics cannot interpret it falsely: from this Book no one becomes an heretic. With the Bible, things go differently.[26]

In Raymond of Sebond we see a significant change. Raymond went so far as to suggest that the book of nature was not just prior in time to the book of Scripture, but can provide all that is necessary in the knowledge of God and salvation. Although he did not advocate the abrogation of Scripture, his promotion of a natural theology effectively left Scripture as redundant.

It is essential that we make a few comments at this point. What Sebond is claiming must be taken in the context of the times. Today the modern world has a very different way of viewing things. General revelation has been twisted and distorted by the intelligentsia to such a degree that the average person considers not a created order which has fallen under the curse, but a natural and organic world which is always developing, but which is blighted by mankind's misuse. It is a world far removed from wonder – the wonder of the Creator – and instead invested with the wonders of human invention. Sebond's claim that heretics cannot misread the truths enumerated by general revelation is not just wide of the mark, but so wrong we need hardly point to the history which

---

24   Thomas Woolford, Natural theology and natural philosophy in the late Renaissance, PhD thesis, Trinity College, Cambridge, November 2011. P5,154.
25   As for footnote 24. P154.
26   As for footnote 24. P5,159.

teaches us this.

Revolution and renaissance.

The sixteenth century was a time of immense change. Not only do we see the beginning of the Christian Reformation following Martin Luther's challenge at Wurttemburg in 1517, but we see also the rise of the new natural philosophy (which we call "modern science") promoted by such men as Nicolaus Copernicus (1473 – 1503), Francis Bacon (1561 – 1626), Galileo Galilei (1564 – 1642), and Johannes Kepler (1571 – 1630). In the century following, the new science exploded with the work of such "greats" as Robert Boyle (1627 – 1691) and Isaac Newton (1643 – 1727). We cannot look at all these natural philosophers and must be content with considering just Francis Bacon, Galileo Galilei and Isaac Newton. We pass over Johannes Kepler and Robert Boyle whose Christian faith would appear to be formidable and strong, only because the intention here is to consider the decline and drift of modern thought. Whilst many early natural philosophers grew up within a strong Christian tradition, and many were true believers, their faith and stance was not enough to prevent the slide of modern science away from Biblical moorings. In Boyle, at least, we can see an attempt at reversing the great decline. Boyle was by no means perfect – he was a man of his time – but in his theological writings he argued against, for example, the vulgar notion of nature as he observed the loss of force of the Biblical doctrine of creation in his time.[27]

Francis Bacon.

In his 1605 work, *"The Advancement of Learning,"* Francis Bacon (1561 – 1626) made suggestion that students be diligent in the study of both books:

> To conclude therefore, let no man upon a weak conceit of sobriety or an ill-applied moderation think or maintain, that a man can search too far, or be too well studied in the book of God's word, or in the book of God's works; divinity or philosophy: but rather let men endeavour an endless progress or proficience in both; only let men beware that they apply both to charity, and not to swelling; to use, and not to ostentation; and again, that they do not unwisely mingle or confound these learnings together.[28]

Bacon speaks of the book of God's word and calls this "divinity" whilst the the book of God's works is termed "philosophy." His appeal for charity and humility is thoroughly Christian, but his

---

27   I would appeal to the Christian reader that whenever the world and universe around is being spoken of or referred to, the speaker use the term "creation" rather than "nature." I suggest this for two reasons. First to press hearers to consider that all things have truly come from the hand of God. Second to remove the ugly notion of "nature" which has served to separate in men's minds the created world from the Creator.
28   Francis Bacon The Advancement of Learning. Book 1.1.3.

recommendation is that these two "learnings" should not be confounded or mingled together. In this he is clearly calling for a separation of the two disciplines. In the same volume Bacon gives us a slightly different designation for the two books, namely, "the Scriptures" and "the creatures" which express God's power. By this latter term we take it that the whole of creation is meant.

> ... for our Saviour saith, YOU ERR, NOT KNOWING THE SCRIPTURES, NOR THE POWER OF GOD; laying before us two books or volumes to study, if we will be secured from error; first, the Scriptures, revealing the Will of God; and then the creatures expressing His Power; whereof the latter is a key unto the former: not only opening our understanding to conceive the true sense of the Scriptures, by the general notions of reason and rules of speech; but chiefly opening our belief, in drawing us into a due meditation of the omnipotency of God, which is chiefly signed and engraven upon His works. Thus much therefore for divine testimony and evidence concerning the true dignity and value of Learning.[29]

Bacon then goes on to explain his understanding of the relation between these two books. He states that the book of nature (creatures) is "a key" to the book of Scripture, for it helps us grasp the meaning and true import of what God has said in His word. This type of argument is one followed by many early Christian thinkers based on the premise that God created the world first and gave His written word much latter. Further, since we need language skills, an understanding of grammar, an appreciation of history and so on, these were inevitably considered as a precursor to coming to the Bible. Bacon stresses that the two books cannot be contrary to one another:

> But there is no such enmity between God's word and His works; neither do they give honour to the Scriptures, as they suppose, but much imbase them. For to seek heaven and earth in the word of God, (whereof it is said, HEAVEN AND EARTH SHALL PASS, BUT MY WORD SHALL NOT PASS,) is to seek temporary things amongst eternal: and as to seek divinity in philosophy is to seek the living amongst the dead, so to seek philosophy in divinity is to seek the dead amongst the living: neither are the pots or lavers, whose place was in the outward part of the temple, to be sought in the holiest place of all, where the ark of the testimony was seated. And again, the scope or purpose of the spirit of God is not to express matters of nature in the Scriptures, otherwise than in passage, and for application to man's capacity, and to matters moral or divine.[30]

In stressing this truth Bacon reinforces the idea that the two books speak separately and distinctly. It is wrong he suggests to seek truths about the created world in Scripture and it is equally erroneous to seek spiritual wisdom in philosophy. He continues with a figure drawn from the Old Testament and suggests that the purpose of the Scriptures is not to give us information about "nature" except

---

29   Francis Bacon The Advancement of Learning. Book 1.VI.16.
30   As for footnote 29. Book 2.XXV.16.

as it may be relevant to the application of the relevant passage.

In these three passages from *"The Advancement of Learning"* we can make the following two conclusions about Bacon's view. First, Bacon distinguishes sharply between Scripture and the natural created world. These two "books" are both given by God, as one is His revealed will, and the other expresses His Power. ***But*** the two must not be confused or mixed in any way. Second we learn that Bacon would set natural philosophy, (the learning we gather from creation), before Scripture as this is a key to understand what God has said. Before we continue and consider what Galileo had to say it is worth considering Bacon's stance. Is his use of the idea that creation preceded the word of God a legitimate vehicle for setting natural philosophy before Scripture? Consider the purpose of Scripture. It is not just a matter of knowing how to go to heaven. It is for a much greater purpose. In Genesis chapter 1, Adam and Eve are given the commission to multiply and subdue the earth. In Micah we read the prophet telling his contemporaries that God required them to, love mercy, to do justice, and to walk humbly with God.[31] The apostle Paul taught Timothy that the goal of instruction was that we should love.[32] The Lord gave the disciples the great commandment to teach the nations all that He had taught and to disciple them.[33] The two great commandments that the Lord Jesus spoke of, teach us that we should love God with everything we have, and that as a consequence we should love our fellow man.[34] These are just a few statements drawn from memory at the moment which clearly give us a far greater aim than simply to know how to be saved. If we consider the fact that revelation comes from a God whose nature is perfect, pure and holy, we must conclude that as such He cannot lie. Since the vehicle of revelation is the very history of the world, including, the created order (Genesis), the birth of the nation Israel and its subsequent history (Exodus through to Malachi), and then the story of God's kingdom as prophesied in Daniel and announced in the gospels, can it be that God revealed Himself to us in such a way as to subvert history, geography, knowledge, or other disciplines we may pursue?

Then what of the order that Bacon presupposes, namely that philosophy must precede the study of Scripture? Undoubtedly it derives in part from the medieval conception where the seven liberal arts, the Trivium of grammar, rhetoric and logic, and the Quadrivium of arithmetic, geometry, music, and astronomy, were the precursors to the study of philosophy and theology proper. It may even be an idea influenced by the church fathers who taught that God spoke first in creation and then latter on came the written word. However the Scriptures themselves give us the way in which we should consider things. Scripture must come first and all examination of the

---

31   Micah 6v8.
32   1Timothy 1v5.
33   Matthew 28v18-20.
34   Matthew 22v37-40.

created order must spring out of our understanding of the very oracles of God. We shall demonstrate this thought later on when we look further at the nature of the Bible.

Galileo Galilei.

Bacon did no scientific work and so is often considered irrelevant by some. However that he influenced his contemporaries is clear. His work and ideas were taken on board by many natural philosophers of his day and especially by those who formed the Royal Society.[35] But perhaps of greater influence for our era we should consider the words of the Italian scientist Galileo Galilei (1564 – 1642), whose advance in science was unsurpassed in his age. In two of the many letters that Galileo penned we are given an insight into this man's view of revelation. In this first quote from a letter written to Castelli (a monk, friend and a fellow mathematician), Galileo does not just reiterate the idea of two books from which we can drawn truth. Instead he gives us the origin of these books:

> For the Holy Scripture and nature both equally derive from the divine Word, the former as the dictation of the Holy Spirit, the latter as the most obedient executrix of God's commands.[36]

Galileo is a master with words. Note how he puts Scripture first and nature second, and describes Scripture with the prefixed appellation "Holy." Notice further how he considers both to come from the divine "Word" by which he means from God the Son. Galileo has made sure that he offends no one here. But his further elucidation of these two books leaves room for debate and discussion. For whilst Scripture is given by "dictation of the Holy Spirit," nature comes to us not as a mere message, but as "the most obedient executrix of God's commands" by which he wants to establish a priority and superiority for natural revelation. Galileo continues to describe the difference between these two books. Scripture is accommodating. It must reach down to the common tongue. Listen to how Galileo puts this:

> ... in order to adapt itself to the understanding of all people, it was appropriate for Scripture to say many things which are different from absolute truth in appearance and in regard to the meaning of the words.[37]

---

35   "His admirers in the Royal Society (an organization that traced its own inspiration and lineage to the Lord Chancellor's writings) viewed him as nothing less than the daring originator of a new intellectual era." http://www.iep.utm.edu/bacon/#H3
36   Taken from: The Essential Galileo. Edited and Translated by Maurice A. Finocchiaro. Hackett Publishing Company, Inc. Indianapolis/Cambridge. 2008. CHAPTER 41. Letters on Copernicanism and Scripture (1613–15). §4.1 Letter to Castelli (1613). P104,105.
37   As for footnote 36.

Thus Galileo believes that Scripture speaks about things which "are different from absolute truth" by which he means that the Scripture contains error and false information. Now consider how this is thought to contrast with nature. Galileo continues:

> ... on the other hand, nature is inexorable and immutable, and she does not care at all whether or not her recondite reasons and modes of operations are revealed to human understanding, and so she never transgresses the terms of the laws imposed on her [38]

Nature just is. It comes relentlessly and does not change. Galileo has not said that Scripture is mutable or changeable, but the contrast is established in the mind by claiming a permanence and stability for the natural order of things. Nature is a fixed law. The consequence of these assumptions is that the permanence and fixedness of natural revelation cannot be subverted or altered in any way by Scripture which admits of different meanings.

> ... therefore, whatever sensory experience places before our eyes or necessary demonstrations prove to us concerning natural effects should not in any way be called into question on account of Scriptural passages whose words appear to have a different meaning, since not every statement of Scripture is bound to obligations as severely as each effect of nature. [39]

Thus the Scriptures cannot govern study and research in the natural world. Galileo continues in this letter to describe why it is that the Scriptures are not to be controlling. These have been written to be understood by ignorant and common people, not the intellectual elite! Galileo points to the fact that God is given attributes akin to humans so that we can relate to Him. If this is the case and Scripture accommodates to the common man, surely the same is true when Scripture speaks of the created order? Here is how Galileo expresses this thought:

> Indeed, because of the aim of adapting itself to the capacity of unrefined and undisciplined peoples, Scripture has not abstained from somewhat concealing its most basic dogmas, thus attributing to God himself properties contrary to and very far from his essence; so who will categorically maintain that, in speaking even incidentally of the earth or the sun or other creatures, it abandoned this aim and chose to restrict itself rigorously within the limited and narrow meanings of the words? [40]

Elsewhere in this letter Galileo claims that Scripture has one purpose, to lead people to salvation. It

---

38   Taken from: The Essential Galileo. Edited and Translated by Maurice A. Finocchiaro. Hackett Publishing Company, Inc. Indianapolis/Cambridge. 2008. CHAPTER 41. Letters on Copernicanism and Scripture (1613–15). §4.1 Letter to Castelli (1613). P104,105.
39   As for footnote 38.
40   As for footnote 38.

does not give us accurate information about the heavens, only necessary information which serves to support the main aim of leading one to salvation. Galileo claims that God did not give us "senses, language, and intellect" if he did not mean us to use them and to discover for ourselves how the heavens go. The Scriptures teach us how to go to heaven, they do not teach us how the heavens go.[41]

> I should believe that the authority of the Holy Writ has merely the aim of persuading men of those articles and propositions which are necessary for their salvation … However, I do not think it necessary to believe that the same God who has furnished us with senses, language, and intellect would want to bypass their use and give us by other means the information we can obtain with them. … but if the first sacred writers had been thinking of persuading the people about the arrangement and the movements of the heavenly bodies, they would not have treated of them so sparsely, which is to say almost nothing in comparison to the infinity of very lofty and admirable conclusions contained in such a science.[42]

No one would object to the idea that God made sense, language and intellect for use, but the question remains: on what footing and foundation do we make use of them? Galileo's words hide the assumptions he is operating under. If we start from the authority of Scripture and base all endeavours on this foundation, then, I suggest, such a plan is the Christian way. Galileo, (and Bacon before him), wants us to base the foundation on reason and nature, for this must come first in their estimation.

Notice also in the last quote the passing comment about the lack of detailed information in Scripture on the heavens. By statements such as these Galileo sets out his stall in a very skilful manner. In answer to this it would, as John the apostle notes, make for an incredibly large not to say unwieldy book if all manner of detail were contained in Scripture. This fact does not mean much at all, for the important thing about Scripture is not so much the detail as the principles. The Scriptures encourage research and investigation into creation, but they do so with clear guidelines and principles. It is the lack of attention to these which has been the fault of the scientists of Bacon and Galileo's era, and it is the fault of the church in all ages for not demonstrating the efficacy of Scripture as a guide to studies in creation.

Galileo's letter to the Grand Duchess Christina, recounts very similar ideas but with some different expressions. One significant word he uses is "accommodating" in place of "adapt" when speaking of the nature of Scripture. The Scriptures accommodate to the "popular understanding"

---

41   Galileo Galilei. Lettere, Einaudi, Torino, 1978, pp. 128-135. http://www.oratoriosanfilippo.org/galileo-baronio-english.pdf.

42   Taken from: The Essential Galileo. Edited and Translated by Maurice A. Finocchiaro. Hackett Publishing Company, Inc. Indianapolis/Cambridge. 2008. CHAPTER 41. Letters on Copernicanism and Scripture (1613–15). §4.1 Letter to Castelli (1613). P106.

and they conceal "the most important truths" by use of such condescension.[43] It is clear that Galileo was aware of the reformers views on this topic of accommodation. Since they ascribe to God characteristics which are "very far from His essence" (i.e. that he has eyes or hands), Galileo asks candidly:

> who will categorically maintain that in speaking incidentally of the earth, water, sun, or other created thing Scripture has set aside such regard and has chosen to limit itself rigorously to the literal and narrow meanings of the words?[44]

The Scriptures then are limited and cannot be used where matters of the created order are under consideration. However such reasoning fails to take account of the basic understanding of Scripture. Whilst it is certainly true that God does not have eyes or hands, we are certain that He can see all and far more than we can and can do, touch and create infinitely more than we can too. Has not the God who created us with eyes and hands not got greater capacity and ability in these areas? Of course He has! So to push the principle of accommodation to teach that the Scriptures are not interested in creation or its workings is far from the truth. Galileo continues in this letter to Christina by repeating the notion that the aim and purpose of Scripture was for "the worship of God and the salvation of souls."[45] Galileo made his most forceful statement about Scriptural authority in this letter where he declares:

> Therefore, I think that in disputes about natural phenomena one must begin not with the authority of Scriptural passages, but with sense experiences and necessary demonstrations.[46]

Our experience and demonstrations of the natural world must guide not Scripture. Galileo continues with his view of the nature and origin of the two books but this time he derives them both from the "Godhead" not the "Word" and he speaks of God's "orders" rather than "commands."

> For the Holy Scripture and nature derive equally from the Godhead, the former as the dictation of the Holy Spirit and the latter as the most obedient executrix of God's orders.[47]

Galileo continues with his view that Scripture must necessarily contain error of material fact,

---

43   Taken from: The Essential Galileo. Edited and Translated by Maurice A. Finocchiaro. Hackett Publishing Company, Inc. Indianapolis/Cambridge. 2008. CHAPTER 41. Letters on Copernicanism and Scripture (1613–15). §4.2 Letter to the Grand Duchess Christina (1615). P109,110.
44   As for footnote 43.
45   As for footnote 43.
46   As for footnote 43.
47   As for footnote 43.

because it must accommodate to the common person:

> moreover, to accommodate the understanding of the common people it is appropriate for
> Scripture to say many things that are different (in appearance and in regard to the literal
> meaning of the words) from the absolute truth.[48]

Nature knows no such limitation, for it comes to us continually and without let up:

> on the other hand, nature is inexorable and immutable, never violates the terms of the laws
> imposed upon her, and does not care whether or not her recondite reasons and ways of
> operating are disclosed to human understanding.[49]

Galileo appeals to the church father Tertullian for corroboratory witness and concludes that
Scripture must not be arbiter of truth in the natural world.

> but not every Scriptural assertion is bound to obligations as severe as every natural
> phenomenon; finally, God reveals Himself to us no less excellently in the effects of nature
> than in the sacred words of Scripture, as Tertullian perhaps meant when he said, "We
> postulate that God ought first to be known by nature, and afterwards further known by
> doctrine—by nature through His works through official teaching" (Against
> Marcion, I.18); and so it seems that a natural phenomenon which is placed before our eyes
> by sense experience or proved by necessary demonstrations should not be called into
> question, let alone condemned, on account of Scriptural passages whose words appear to
> have a different meaning."[50]

Once again we must ask the question: how true are sense experiences and necessary
demonstrations? Of course Galileo is right to challenge the interpretation of Scripture. It may be
that they have been misunderstood. However **his** first port of call is to accept at face value the
experience of sense and the results of observations and experiment, (necessary demonstrations)..
These however may be interpreted too and this point has not be addressed by Galileo at all. It is
essential that the Scriptures come first, not reason and experiment.

Not content with merely stating his belief that Scripture cannot be guide and lead for natural
philosophy, he continues with some other testimonials:

> Among hundreds of instances of such testimony we have the following. Near the beginning
> of his work On Genesis Pererius asserts: "In treating of Moses' doctrine, one must take
> diligent care to completely avoid holding and saying positively and categorically anything

---

48   Taken from: The Essential Galileo. Edited and Translated by Maurice A. Finocchiaro. Hackett Publishing
Company, Inc. Indianapolis/Cambridge. 2008. CHAPTER 41. Letters on Copernicanism and Scripture (1613–15). §4.2
Letter to the Grand Duchess Christina (1615). P109,110.
49   As for footnote 48.
50   As for footnote 48.

which contradicts the decisive observations and reasons of philosophy or other disciplines; in fact, since all truths always agree with one another, the truth of Holy Scripture cannot be contrary to the true reasons and observations of human doctrines." And in St. Augustine (Letter to Marcellinus, section 7), one reads: "If, against the most manifest and reliable testimony of reason, anything be set up claiming to have the authority of the Holy Scriptures, he who does this does it through a misapprehension of what he has read and is setting up against the truth not the real meaning of Scripture, which he has failed to discover, but an opinion of his own; he alleges not what he has found in the Scriptures, but what he has found in himself as their interpreter."[51]

It is not a good thing to base an argument by bringing in supporting witnesses as though their word is the final say in the matter. The Christian appeals to the Word of God (Scripture) as the final authority because Scripture is God's word, and for mandate we have the Lord Jesus Christ Himself who used this same weapon in his temptation, declaring to Satan, "it is written"![52] Galileo makes the rather simplistic (philosophical) comment that "all truths always agree with one another." This is a truism, (it merely amounts to saying that whatever is "true" must be "true"), and he brings it in at this point to bring down Scripture from its exalted place of authority. He continues by stating that Scripture cannot be contrary to "the true reasons and observations of human doctrines." Now here he has laid bare his presuppositions. He accords the status of "truth" to Holy Scripture to begin with, but I suspect he could do no otherwise in the time in which he lived. However he has so framed his words to call Scripture into question against "the true reasons and observations of human doctrines" which are true without comment. What if we reverse the argument? What if we say that whatever is "observed" or "demonstrated" in natural philosophy cannot contradict what we know from Scripture? Would that be saying the same thing? At one level, maybe. But in reality by stating things the way he has, Galileo succeeds in calling Scripture into question. Certainly Galileo intends to challenge the interpretation of Scripture, but he forgets that the interpretation of whatever is sensed or demonstrated in nature may also be called into question too.

In the church fathers the problem of literacy and illiteracy lead these dear Christian folk to the notion that God has indeed spoken in creation. Those who could not read Scripture either through illiteracy or through poverty (the Scriptures were expensive) had no need to worry because God was near at hand and He has spoken in His creation. Now, however, we find that Galileo suggests that knowledge of nature must be gained through the use of the right language, and that language is mathematics. Scripture is accommodated to the common man and his low level understanding. Natural philosophy is only for the elite and skilful who are accomplished in

---

51   Taken from: The Essential Galileo. Edited and Translated by Maurice A. Finocchiaro. Hackett Publishing Company, Inc. Indianapolis/Cambridge. 2008. CHAPTER 41. Letters on Copernicanism and Scripture (1613–15). §4.2 Letter to the Grand Duchess Christina (1615). P120.
52   Matthew 4v4,6,7,10.

mathematics:

> Philosophy is written in this all-encompassing book that is constantly open before our eyes, that is the universe; but it cannot be understood unless one first learns to understand the language and knows the characters in which it is written. It is written in mathematical language, and its characters are triangles, circles, and other geometrical figures; without these it is humanly impossible to understand a word of it, and one wanders around pointlessly in a dark labyrinth.[53]

The catholic astronomer theologian, Tanzella-Nitti, sums up the situation we have come to with Galileo nicely:

> It is worthwhile pointing out that since the epoch of the early Fathers of the Church, the meaning of the metaphor is now surprisingly overturned. If St. Augustine could state that "everyone, even the illiterate, can read the book of the universe," in Galileo's view, people who are qualified to read it belong to a much narrower circle. Sebond's proposition that the knowledge of the book of nature is common to everyone, while the book of Scripture can be read only by the clerics, finds its mirror image here, but at the expense of the universality of the book of the world.[54]

Whatever man considers is tainted by the deceits and wicked intents of the heart.[55] It is only through regeneration of the Holy Spirit that man can come to any true understanding at all.

Thomas Browne.

The two letters of Galileo were written in the early part of the seventeenth century between 1613 and 1623. The year Bacon published his work, *"The Advancement of Learning"* (1605), saw the birth of a medic who was to write the following words in 1642:

> Thus there are two Bookes[56] from whence I collect my Divinity; besides that written one of God, another of his servant Nature, that universall and publike ManuScript, that lies expans'd unto the eyes of all; those that never saw him in the one, have discovered him in the other.[57]

Thomas Browne (1605 – 1682) had studied medicine at Oxford, Padua and Leiden before settling to

---

53   Taken from: The Essential Galileo. Edited and Translated by Maurice A. Finocchiaro. Hackett Publishing Company, Inc. Indianapolis/Cambridge. 2008. CHAPTER 7. The Assayer (1623). [§7.1 Comets,Tycho, and the Book of Nature in Mathematical Language]. P183.
54   G. Tanzella-Nitti, "The Two Books Prior to the Scientific Revolution," *Perspectives on Science and Christian Faith*, Volume 57, Number 3, September 2005. 235-248. Page 243,244.
55   Jeremiah 17v9; Genesis 6v5; Ecclesiastes 7v29.
56   Browne's original spellings have been retained as they were written.
57   Thomas Browne ,*Religio Medici* I.16. 1645.

practice in Norwich. His work, *"Religio Medici,"* sought to demonstrate how a medical doctor who followed natural philosophy (science), could also believe in the Christian faith. Like Bacon and Galileo before him, Browne advocates the same doctrine of the two books both of which stem from the same source. Nevertheless the book of nature is given special recognition as it is "universall and publike" and "lies expans'd unto the eyes of all" and it is possible to discover God through creation without recourse to Scripture.

Isaac Newton.

The year following Browne's words saw the birth of one of England's greatest scientists, Isaac Newton, (1643 – 1727). In Newton we find a new departure in the concept of the two books of revelation. Newton was not only a mathematician and scientist, but also a serious student of the Bible. Newton was committed to the idea that God had revealed through two books, Scripture and nature, but his writings are not always direct and straight forward. The clearest expression of his view, according to Snobelen, can be found in a work on the book of Revelation (Newton's favourite Bible book). In this treatise Newton is arguing that the simplest explanations are those which are the more reliable, a stricture which science has championed. This is how Newton expresses his view:

> As the world, which to the naked eye exhibits the greatest variety of objects, appears very simple in its internall constitution when surveyed by a philosophic understanding, & so much the simpler by how much the better it is understood, so it is in these visions. It is the perfection of God's works that they are all done with the greatest simplicity. He is the God of order & not confusion. And therefore as they that would understand the frame of the world must indeavour to reduce their knowledg to all possible simplicity, so it must be in seeking to understand these visions.[58]

Although Newton's choice of words does not follow the normal pattern, Snobelen contends that the great scientist was certain that God had "revealed Himself in both Scripture and Nature."[59] Having made such a commitment Newton believed that the same methods should be employed when looking for truth in either book.[60] Thus, like Galileo, Newton's view was that reason and observation of the natural world must come before theology. Snobelen writes of Newton that:

---

[58]   Stephen D. Snobelen, "To Discourse of God: Isaac Newton's Heterodox Theology and His Natural Philosophy," Chapter 3 of Science and Dissent in England, 1688-1945, ed. By Paul B. Wood (Aldershot, Hampshire, England: Ashgate Publications, 2004). https://isaacnewtonstheology.files.wordpress.com/2013/06/newtons-heterodox-theology-and-his-natural-philosophy.pdf
[59]   As for footnote 58. See also: Nature and Scripture in the Abrahamic Religions: Up to 1700. 2 Volumes. Edited by Jitse M. van der Meer and Scott Mandelbrote. Brill, Leiden & Boston. 2008. Chapter 16: Not in the Language of Astronomers: Isaac Newton, the Scriptures, and the Hermeneutics of Accommodation. Stephen D. Snobelen. PP491-530. P528.
[60]   As for footnote 58.

Although natural philosophy might help illuminate the Scriptures, Newton, like Galileo, believed that the formal teaching of natural philosophy is not part of the mandate of the inspired Word of God. Thus, in one manuscript he declares: "The system of the heavenly bodies is not at all taught in Scripture." This view allows Newton to reconcile phenomenalistic geocentric language in the Bible with the realist heliocentric view of the solar system he espoused. [61]

For Newton, then, natural philosophy is autonomous and may help in any understanding of the Scriptures. In contrast the Scriptures do not contain any germ of natural philosophy so that we cannot learn of how the heavens go from them. Again the idea that Scripture does not have detail about the heavens is taken to imply that it can have no authority on the subject of astronomy.

But the main fascination that comes from considering Newton is his departure from orthodoxy. Up until this point all the writers we have considered were orthodox Christian believers.[62] In Newton we find that this is no longer the case. The assessment of one writer (H. Floris Cohen) and contributor to an International Conference on Science and Religion on Newton and his faith, is particularly enlightening.

> The story of Newton and Christianity constitutes, in my perception of things, one chapter in the central drama of European civilization: the conversion of an originally Christian civilization into a scientific one.[63]

It is always tempting to consider one or another personality as the "moment" when things suddenly changed. A case can be made for Bacon or Galileo being such contenders. However Cohen's assessment comes from a consideration that Newton had departed from orthodoxy. Newton's heretical views were not widely known. He saw to it that few but an inner circle were privy to his essential ideas, but following his death the real situation of his faith could no longer be hidden. His departure was by no means trivial as Snobelen makes clear:

> The increasing availability of Newton's unpublished theological papers has allowed scholars to begin to reconstruct the nature of Newton's heresy. In addition to confirming what was suspected even by some in Newton's own day, namely, that he held to an antitrinitarian and generally Arian Christology, there have been a some unexpected revelations. On top of his denial of the Trinity, Newton also rejected the immortality of the soul and the literal

---

61   Taken from: Nature and Scripture in the Abrahamic Religions: Up to 1700. 2 Volumes. Edited by Jitse M. van der Meer and Scott Mandelbrote. Brill, Leiden & Boston. 2008. Chapter 16: Not in the Language of Astronomers": Isaac Newton, the Scriptures, and the Hermeneutics of Accommodation. Stephen D. Snobelen. PP491-530. P512.
62   At least in a nominal sense.
63   Proceedings of the International Conference "Science and Religion." Edited by Gianna Katsiampoura, Efthymios Nicolaidis 3 – 5 September 2015. Project NARSES – ARISTEIA Institute of Historical Research National Hellenic Research Foundation. H. Floris Cohen, Whose Myth-Making? Newton's Theology, Richard S. Westfall, and Westfall's Critics. PP305-312. P310.

existence of evil spirits.[64]

According to Snobelen Newton came to an anti-trinitarian view in the early 1670s. Such a belief ought to have meant that he could no longer hold his position at Cambridge but, as Snobelen explains, Newton was very fortunate:

> If his radical heresy had become known while he was Lucasian Professor, Newton would have been ignominiously extruded from the University – or worse. As it was, under the provisions of his Trinity College fellowship he was required to be ordained in the Church of England by 1675. His new-found heresy and rigid conscience would not allow this, and it was only a last-minute reprieve that came from Charles II in the form of an exemption from ordination for holders of the Lucasian Chair that allowed him to remain at Cambridge. Thereafter Newton lived the life of a Nicodemite, a secret heretic.[65]

The question that comes to mind at this juncture is, where did he get his unorthodox views from? Was there any influence or like-minded thinkers in his circles? Although there seems to be no direct evidence, Snobelen comments that recent research has identified close connections with heterodox folk on the continent:

> Until a few years ago little attention was paid to possible linkages between Newton's theology and that of contemporary radical dissent. Many scholars apparently believed Newton to be a self-taught heretic. More recently, Newton's heretical theology has been placed in the context of contemporary Continental and English heretical currents and a number of points of contact between Newton's theology and that of other heterodox believers have been confirmed. Thus his antitrinitarianism contains strong analogies not only to the Christology of the Continental Socinians and the German Arian Christopher Sand, but also to the polemical writings of late seventeenth-century English Unitarians. For example, Newton's late 1680s to early 1690s manuscript attacking Athanasius takes a very similar line as that adopted in an anonymous English Unitarian attack on the same fourth-century paragon of orthodoxy that dates, strikingly, from the same period as Newton's manuscript. Newton's mortalism is of a piece with that of several radical Civil War sectarians, including Richard Overton. His denial of a person[al] devil and ontologically real demons strongly resembles the position of the Radical Reformation thinker David Joris, along with that of some seventeenth-century English sectarians.[66]

Such connections has made some scholars conclude that Newton was in fact the first "Deist." Snobelen argues that whilst Newton was certainly anti-trinitarian and heterodox, nevertheless his

---

64   Stephen D. Snobelen, "To Discourse of God: Isaac Newton's Heterodox Theology and His Natural Philosophy," Chapter 3 of Science and Dissent in England, 1688-1945, ed. By Paul B. Wood (Aldershot, Hampshire, England: Ashgate Publications, 2004). https://isaacnewtonstheology.files.wordpress.com/2013/06/newtons-heterodox-theology-and-his-natural-philosophy.pdf
65   As for footnote 64.
66   As for footnote 64.

intentions were laudable and his desire was to find the truth:

> Westfall characterized Newton's theological tendencies as proto-deistic and as coming under the influence of encroaching scientific rationalism, whatever this might have meant in the early eighteenth-century. This proto-deist thesis allies nicely with the model of Newton as a stepping stone to Enlightenment sensibilities. But it will not do. One of its chief defects is that it assumes that Newton's theology looks forward to a putative secular future, rather than back to what Newton believed were the sources of true religion. Newton's God was the personal, all powerful Pantocrator[67] of the Bible. Concomitant with his Hebraic and profoundly biblical view of God, is Newton's characterization of God as a deity of unchallenged sovereignty, power and dominion.[68]

Snobelen's dismissal of Westfall's assessment is rash. Newton's views, even according to Snobelen, have significant links and connections to other false views found on the continent. These were precursors to the rise of Deism, so that to refer to Newton as a "proto-deist" is not really far from the mark.

Newton's view of interpreting Scripture borrows much from those who had advocated a doctrine of accommodation. Snobelen comments:

> In the short treatise on reconciling natural philosophy with biblical deScriptions of Earth and the heavens, Newton appeals directly to the principle of accommodation, arguing that those who want to use the Bible as an authority in disputes about the motion of Earth err, "the Scriptures speaking not in the language of Astronomers (as they think) but in that of ye common people to whom they were written." In this, he comes close to the earlier and similar positions of Augustine, Calvin, Galileo, and others—even though it is difficult to be certain how much he owed to previous thinkers on these matters.[69]

This idea of accommodation focuses on a distinction in the status of people. There are the elite like Newton, and then there are the common, and largely illiterate uneducated, people. Scripture, it is assumed, was written for the common people whose education and understanding were weak. Consequently the contents must be brought down, or accommodated, to their level. This meant, for Newton and others (Galileo, for example), that the Scriptures do not contain any information or principles necessary to aid natural philosophy.

Newton also expresses the view that Scripture speaks not in an absolute sense but in a

---

67   i.e. ruler of all.
68   Stephen D. Snobelen, "To Discourse of God: Isaac Newton's Heterodox Theology and His Natural Philosophy," Chapter 3 of Science and Dissent in England, 1688-1945, ed. By Paul B. Wood (Aldershot, Hampshire, England: Ashgate Publications, 2004). https://isaacnewtonstheology.files.wordpress.com/2013/06/newtons-heterodox-theology-and-his-natural-philosophy.pdf.
69   Taken from: Nature and Scripture in the Abrahamic Religions: Up to 1700. 2 Volumes. Edited by Jitse M. van der Meer and Scott Mandelbrote. Brill, Leiden & Boston. 2008. Chapter 16: Not in the Language of Astronomers": Isaac Newton, the Scriptures, and the Hermeneutics of Accommodation. Stephen D. Snobelen. PP491-530. P526.

relative one. Snobelen writes:

> Newton articulates his belief that it is both necessary to recognize the existence of relative language in the Bible and to avoiding committing a fundamental error by mistaking it for absolute language (which is what he believed Trinitarians do when they mistake the relative title 'God' used of Christ for a declaration that Christ is "very God" in a metaphysical sense). Thus, while Newton on the one hand seems to want to argue that one layer of the Bible is accessible to both the vulgar and the philosophers, while another layer is only accessible to the later, he also makes another social distinction. Some Scriptural texts have a deeper meaning at their core and thus the Word of God serves in part to challenge believers and to separate between the good and the bad. Ultimately, then, there were two types of people: those who get it and those who do not. Herein is seen an important social corollary to Newton's epistemological dualism.[70]

In many ways Newton and those who appeal to accommodationist views are promulgating a form of gnosticism. Only the elite and the educated, or only those "who get it" in the words of Snobelen can fully understand. In wonderful, and deeply stark, contrast the Scriptures present themselves as available for all and speak of deep and excellent things which we could never know by discovery of natural philosophy.[71] However, by 1794, Thomas Paine could declare these words:

> Do we want to know what God is? Search not the book called the Scripture, which any human hand might make, but the Scripture, called the creation.[72]

The figure of two books fell into disuse with the advent of the new geology and then with the rise of evolutionary ideas.

The story of the rise of modern geology with its evolutionary emphasis, which was coincidental with the removal from history of the contribution made by the "Scriptural Geologists" who were contemporary with well-known geological figures, charts another way of departure that borrows heavily from the ideas we have considered here.[73] We might also mention the effect of Kant, Hume and other rationalistic thinkers whose work showed increasingly significant departures from Biblical moorings. And then in 1859 Darwin published *"On the Origin of Species,"* which, together with the impetus from the rationalistic drift we have charted, forced the intellectual academic world into a secular mindset. Thus, taking the Royal Society as an example of this drift,

---

70   Taken from: Nature and Scripture in the Abrahamic Religions: Up to 1700. 2 Volumes. Edited by Jitse M. van der Meer and Scott Mandelbrote. Brill, Leiden & Boston. 2008. Chapter 16: Not in the Language of Astronomers": Isaac Newton, the Scriptures, and the Hermeneutics of Accommodation. Stephen D. Snobelen. PP491-530. P525.

71   Proverbs 22v20; Psalm 119v18; Jeremiah 33v3; Ecclesiastes 8v16,17.

72   Thomas Paine. The Age of Reason. 1794.

73   Mortenson, T.J. *British scriptural geologists in the first half of the nineteenth century.* PhD Thesis. Coventry: Coventry University in collaboration with Wycliffe Hall, Oxford. Available online at: https://curve.coventry.ac.uk/open/file/c2ca3d9b-4617-006a-3cba-cba9e86062f0/1/Mortenson1996.pdf.

we note that whilst it had its origins in Christian soil, by the early eighteenth century there was a significant faction within the Royal Society opposed to any mention of Scripture in a scientific context.

We have not considered the response of Christian Pastors and Teachers through these years. Many would claim that Luther, Calvin and other reformers had no problem with the new science but their views would need greater study than can be indulged at this point. Whilst the idea of the "two books" flourished in the natural theological climate of seventeenth-century England, the two books (Scripture and nature/creation) were not always held in comfortable balance. As a single example, the dissenting theologian Richard Baxter (1615–1691) argued that:

> ... nature was a 'hard book' which few could understand, and that it was therefore safer to rely more heavily on Scripture.[74]

The fall.

Part of the reason for this loss of understanding concerning general revelation as creation and its Biblical basis, must be laid at the poor understanding the early natural philosophers had of the doctrine of the fall. George Hendry points out that the development of modern science occurred in the main because of this dramatic change in understanding "nature":

> Modern science arose out of a revolt against the implicit or explicit imperialism of the theological perspective on nature, or, less violently expressed, by the discovery that there is another way of looking at nature than that of theology.[75]

Hendry suggests that Bacon's whole programme of re-instating a natural philosophy can be attributed to the limit he placed on the doctrine of the fall:

> An important requirement for the rise of modern science was "the rehabilitation of nature," and this . . . was a main achievement of Bacon. Bacon offered a theological reinterpretation of the Fall which limited its effect to the moral order. . . . The most significant difference in this view of nature from that found in the piety of the Middle Ages, in which it was seen as a realm of dark and sinister forces with which it was dangerous to meddle, is that nature has been exempted from the effects of the Fall and reinstated in that pristine perfection in which it issued from the Creator's hand at the beginning.[76]

Although Bacon was not a cleric or theologian he used some theologically sound reasoning to challenge traditional medieval arguments. The forbidden tree in the Garden of Eden, for example,

---

74   Richard Baxter. *The Reasons for the Christian Religion*, 1667.
75   G. S. Hendry, Theology of Nature (Philadelphia: Westminster, 1980). P27.
76   As for footnote 75. P55,56.

had been symbolically viewed by some as the knowledge of nature, and sin had been seen as a man-centred invasion of this realm. Bacon and other scientists denied this view, claiming that the tree was the moral knowledge of good and evil and not necessarily having anything to do with science. Bacon did not, however, address the statements in Biblical passages that support the idea of a curse on the physical world, choosing rather to ignore them in his writing.[77] His reasoning was heavily dependent on a view of nature in its pristine condition. Bacon's view of the fall is shown in his work *"Novum Organum"*:

> For man by the fall fell at the same time from his state of innocency and from his dominion over creation. Both of these losses however can even in this life be in some part repaired; the former by religion and faith, the latter by arts and sciences. For creation was not by the curse made altogether and forever a rebel, but in virtue of that charter "In the sweat of thy face shall thou eat bread," it is now by various labours (not certainly by disputations or idle magical ceremonies, but by various labours) at length and in some measure subdued to the supplying of man with bread, that is, to the uses of human life.[78]

Bacon did not deny the widespread effects of the fall but he believed passionately that it was a reversible change. Consequently, the stage was set for the ultimate rejection of Biblical authority.

[3] General revelation – some key texts.

In order to gain some idea of the importance of general revelation and the role it plays, we shall consider some key texts. The Scriptures to be examined are:

[a] Romans 1v19-21.

[b] Psalm 19.

[c] Acts 14v17.

[d] Ecclesiastes 3v11.

[e] Romans 2v14-16.

[a] Romans 1v19-21.

> **19** *because what may be known of God is manifest in them, for God has shown it to them.* **20** *For since the creation of the world His invisible attributes are clearly seen, being understood by the things that are made, even His eternal power and Godhead, so that they are without excuse,* **21** *because, although they knew God, they did not glorify Him as God, nor were thankful, but became futile in their thoughts, and their foolish hearts were darkened.*

---

77   Genesis 3:17–19; 5:29; Romans 8:20–22.
78   Francis Bacon Novum Organum LVII.

In verse 19 Paul states that the knowledge of God is "manifest" in people because God has displayed this knowledge to them. Behind this, of course, is a Biblical view of the doctrine of creation. Man, of course, is a part of the creation so it is evident that what may be known of God can be seen in man himself. We make no apologies then, for stating as true that man as a component of creation, may come to some knowledge of God because this is the way God has created and ordered things. In verse 20, Paul then works out what it was about the nature of God which may be known. Thus right from the very creation of the world the "invisible attributes" are evident through what God has made and created. The two attributes listed are God's "eternal power" and the "Godhead." These signify the infinite and eternal nature of the Creator, and His being the One and Only God.

However there is a problem, and it is this problem which Bacon and others seem to have missed. Man is not just fallen and in need of special tools and helps to overcome the terrible results of the fall as Bacon originally conjectured. Mankind has rebelled and as a result of this has become "futile" in his thoughts, they have "foolish hearts," and these have become "darkened." Creation clearly displays God and His infinite eternal nature and power, but man suppresses these truths, and chooses alternative follies instead.

[b] Psalm 19v1-4.

> *1 The heavens declare the glory of God; and the firmament shows His handiwork. 2 Day unto day utters speech, and night unto night reveals knowledge. 3 There is no speech nor language where their voice is not heard. 4 Their line has gone out through all the earth, and their words to the end of the world.*

The Psalmist is keen to show that the entire creation (the "heavens" and the "firmament" stand together for all of creation) does indeed display God's glory all the time (day by day). And why shouldn't it? After all God has created it and his masterpiece shows something of the One who made it just as any artwork depicts something of the artist. But note that what is shown is "the glory of God" and "His handiwork." In other words, these are similar in scope to the invisible attributes mentioned by Paul in Romans chapter 1. Now this revelation is not comprehensive for it only shows certain aspects of God's work.

One crucial fact concerning this Scripture, is that it forms one of the main planks of evidence used by the early church fathers to show the priority of general revelation over special revelation. It is to be remembered here, that verses 7 to 11 of Psalm 19 describe special revelation *after* the general revelation of the first four verses. We shall consider these verses elsewhere.

[c] Acts 14v17.

> *Nevertheless He did not leave Himself without witness, in that He did good, gave us rain from heaven and fruitful seasons, filling our hearts with food and gladness.*

The Scriptures constantly make use of the creation as a witness to God's power and being.[79] Here the focus is on the promise originally given to Noah that seasons and times would continue unabated until such a time as judgement will come.[80] Man, in his ridiculous folly, attributes the immutability of the created order, its regularity and dependence, upon scientific law. The Scriptures speak otherwise. These things, (the rain and seasons) come direct from the hand of God. There are only scientific laws because God is the God of order and kindness.

[d] Ecclesiastes 3v11.

> *He has made everything beautiful in its time. Also He has put eternity in their hearts, except that no one can find out the work that God does from beginning to end.*

The book of Ecclesiastes requires particular attention especially concerning its teaching about human inquiry and "discovery," but this verse is important for our consideration here. It is God who has made everything and these things fit the time they are in. But more importantly, God has placed "eternity" in the hearts of man. This is staggering. There is, therefore, some witness inside of our hearts that links and connects to eternity – the abode of God. We have a constitutional connection to the divine. If we deny the Creator, if we deny God, we are doing damage to our own beings, for we would have to ignore this "eternity" which finds a lodging in our souls. However this eternity – sometimes expressed by sinful man as a yearning curiosity – is frustrated. It is not possible for man to discover or find out the work of God through time! And yet herein lies our great problem. We want to know, but we have no means or capability of knowing correctly. It isn't that we don't try, but that in trying we are doomed to failure. God has so engineered things that with eternity set in the heart we cannot satisfy our innately curious minds. Is this harsh and unfair? By no means! It is a mercy, for if it were in our power to scale the heights of eternity and come to a knowledge by dint of human ingenuity, then we would never turn and repent and seek to be reconciled with God. God has frustrated our desire to know because He loves us. It would seem that if God allowed man to find out the work of God, it would cement him in his pride and arrogance and he could never then be saved. It is something akin to the experience of the builders of the tower of Babel in Genesis 11. God frustrated their wayward efforts as an act of mercy to prevent them being cemented into the

---

79   Deuteronomy 4v26 and Isaiah 1v2 are two examples.
80   Genesis 8v22.

wrong course and thence to damnation.

God wants us to receive what He has revealed to ensure that we do not go astray. You see unless we follow the divinely directed plan of salvation we will always be lost. God is holy and pure so cannot look on sin and rebellion. But He has found the way to ensure that wicked sinners can be cleansed and forgiven and brought back into fellowship with Him. It is only through the death and resurrection of the Lord Jesus that reconciliation may be accomplished. This is what is revealed in the Scriptures. It isn't what man discovers because man is always looking in the wrong direction. Left to his own devices man would seek out strange and curious schemes and inventions.[81]

[e] Romans 2v14-16.

> **14** *for when Gentiles, who do not have the law, by nature do the things in the law, these, although not having the law, are a law to themselves,* **15** *who show the work of the law written in their hearts, their conscience also bearing witness, and between themselves their thoughts accusing or else excusing them)* **16** *in the day when God will judge the secrets of men by Jesus Christ, according to my gospel.*

The conscience is a precious thing but sadly many have seared or dulled their conscience to the point of damnation. The teaching here is not identical in idea to that we found in Ecclesiastes 3v11. Conscience and the inner witness to the rightness of the law speaks and points to a Creator God. As one has said, "we know it is wrong to kill because we don't want to be killed and we know it is wrong to steal because we don't want to have our possessions taken from us."[82]

Other ideas.

Apart from creation and conscience we have also the witness of history, or providence. This is extensive as is evidenced by the unveiling and the prophecy of history as recorded in Scripture. We mention in passing the many prophetic words for the surrounding nations to Israel in Scripture which speak of God as sovereign over all things.

[4] Special revelation.

The Bible is God's special revelation to mankind. Whilst creation speaks of some of God's attributes clearly, even though man chooses to ignore such information, the Scriptures give us far more detail about the God of all things and what He has done. We shall consider this theme under the following seven headings:

---

81   Ecclesiastes 7v29.
82   Barry McGuire in a gospel music event.

Mike Viccary

     [a] Revelation is not discoverable by man.

     [b] Revelation is graciously given by the Lord.

     [c] Revelation is about Christ.

     [d] Revelation occurs through the medium of words.

     [e] Revelation is given only to certain people.

     [f] Revelation is given for the benefit of all people.

     [g] Revelation is God revealing Himself to men through His Special Revelation.

[a] Revelation is not discoverable by man.

The content and object of revelation is totally un-discoverable by man and his ingenuity. To show this we shall endeavour to look at a number of Scriptures and then conclude with some further observations of a general nature. The first text we shall consider is one that comes in the last book of Moses, namely Deuteronomy:

> *The secret things belong to the Lord our God, but those things which are revealed belong to us and to our children forever, that we may do all the words of this law. (Deuteronomy 29v29).*

Here we can see that "things" are classified under two headings. First we have "secret" things which are those hidden, and second there are things "revealed" or those things made naked. The first category are those that belong to the Lord, whilst those things made known are for all people. It is eminently clear from this straight forward text that things fall into one of these two general categories, and in whatever category they come, this determines who may know them. If they are secret, then only the Lord knows them. If they have been revealed, then we may known them but only in order that we might obey them and do all that they instruct us to.

The second Scripture which teaches this general idea of revelation being hidden and not discoverable by man, comes in a book which is focused on the problem of knowing what is of true worth and what can be known.

> **16** *When I applied my heart to know wisdom and to see the business that is done on earth, even though one sees no sleep day or night,* **17** *then I saw all the work of God, that a man cannot find out the work that is done under the sun. For though a man labours to discover it, yet he will not find it; moreover, though a wise man attempts to know it, he will not be able to find it. (Ecclesiastes 8v16,17).*

Solomon the king has set his mind and heart to seek out what was true and wise. His concluding statements ought to be standard reading for aspiring scientists! The great problem we have as people "under the sun" is that there is far too much for us to comprehend. It is therefore impossible for mankind to "find out" the work done under the sun. This means there is a limit to our searching and seeking. It also means that any understanding we adopt will always be in need of correction because whatever knowledge we do possess is only a small part of the whole. But there is more to this text because Solomon concludes that even if a very perceptive man attempts to comprehend and discover the work of God, he will never be able to "find it" (this phrase is twice repeated).

For our third Scripture we turn to the prophet Daniel. In the second chapter we have the events which centred around Nebuchadnezzar's dream. The Babylonian king wanted the wise men to not only interpret his dream, but to describe it as well. When Daniel discovers the king's impossible request, he seeks out his friends and calls on the Lord for mercy. The Lord graciously reveals the king's dream to Daniel and its interpretation. Daniel gives thanks to the Lord for this as he speaks to the king. This is what he says:

> *He reveals deep and secret things; He knows what is in the darkness, and light dwells with Him. (Daniel 2v22).*

The implication of these words must be discerned from the context of the story. The king knew the dream, but no one else did. Only God could reveal what was deeply hidden in the kings' heart. There is no other way that people can read another's mind.

For our Fourth Scripture we turn to words the apostle Paul wrote to the Roman Christians:

> *33 Oh, the depth of the riches both of the wisdom and knowledge of God! How unsearchable are His judgements and His ways past finding out! 34 "For who has known the mind of the Lord? Or who has become His counsellor?" (Romans 11v33,34).*

This burst of praise describes something wonderful about the nature of God who is truly infinite. It is, perhaps, far too obvious to note that God is immeasurably deep in knowledge and wisdom, but the implications of such depth is that what He decides and what He thinks simply cannot be measured or discerned. If we cannot describe the thoughts of another man when he dreams, the thought of plumbing the depths of God's wisdom is unspeakably impossible! And yet the Lord our God has indeed revealed much to us! How vital it is to take this in and meditate upon it and honour it by our faithful obedience!

In our fifth Scripture we take a look at another view of this subject. In the book of Isaiah we often find that there are questions posed which ought to raise a laugh or, at least, a cry of astonishment. The purpose of these is to develop deeper thought into what the Lord is doing. In chapter 40 we discover that the plan of salvation is about to be enacted. Comfort is proclaimed, the fore-runner announced, for the Lord is coming![83] But then we read these amazing words:

> *13 Who has directed the Spirit of the Lord, or as His counsellor has taught Him? 14 With whom did He take counsel, and who instructed Him, and taught Him in the path of justice? Who taught Him knowledge, and showed Him the way of understanding? (Isaiah 40v13,14).*

The questions are ridiculous! The answers don't need repeating. None can, because the Lord knows all! In this text we are reminded that any presumptuous or arrogant person who seeks to advise the Lord or give him the benefit of their opinion is walking a very dangerous path. A very similar thought is found in our sixth Scripture which comes from the book of Jeremiah:

> *For who has stood in the counsel of the Lord, and has perceived and heard His word? Who has marked His word and heard it? (Jeremiah 23v18).*

Who was with God in the beginning? Were there any created beings present? Of course not! God alone knows His own mind and will. This is not something we can ever know, *except He reveal it*! Praise God that we have His word revealed to us!

Considering Paul the apostle we must note in our seventh Scripture that his message was not one he dreamed up nor was it one that was taught to him by men:

> *For I neither received it from man, nor was I taught it, but it came through the revelation of Jesus Christ. (Galatians 1v12).*

All that he had and preached was revealed to him by the Lord Jesus Christ. In his first letter to the Corinthians in our eighth Scripture, we note again this concept that spiritual truths are not available to the natural man:

> *13 These things we also speak, not in words which man's wisdom teaches but which the Holy Spirit teaches, comparing spiritual things with spiritual. 14 But the natural man does not receive the things of the Spirit of God, for they are foolishness to him; nor can he know them, because they are spiritually discerned. 15 But he who is spiritual judges all things, yet he himself is rightly judged by no one. 16 For "who has known the mind of the Lord that he may instruct Him?" But we have the mind of Christ. (1Corinthians 2v13-16).*

Note closely what the apostle Paul says. The natural man does not just fail to receive what the Spirit

---

83   Isaiah 40v1,3,10.

brings, he cannot even "know them." The Christian can only know these things because they are "spiritually discerned" and because they "have the mind of Christ."

For our ninth and final Scripture we return to the Old Testament and to the book of Isaiah. These words have often been quoted by Christians. At the most basic level they teach a clear distinction between God and ourselves:

> **8** *"For My thoughts are not your thoughts, nor are your ways My ways," says the Lord.* **9** *"For as the heavens are higher than the earth, so are My ways higher than your ways, and My thoughts than your thoughts. (Isaiah 55v8,9).*

The separation between the thoughts and ways of God and us is immense. How then could we know God and His ways with such a huge gulf between us?

If we viewed the Old Testament and how the prophets received the word of the Lord, we will find again that no one taught them. They did not make up what they preached. Instead the vision of God and the reception of His word was something which compelled them to speak and write as they were moved and carried along by the Spirit.[84] The word they received was given directly by the Lord.[85] The Scriptural evidence we have considered makes a mockery of the liberal idea that the Bible is man's thoughts about God. Each writer claims that what he is giving us is none other than that which God has revealed, and it is thus something we could otherwise never have known about. Thus, unless the Lord had taken the initiative we would forever have remained in the dark. This is evident from a true objective look at our position in this world. We come into it with nothing. We are on a planet in the middle of a universe that we know very little about. As we get older we learn that the world has learnt some things over the last few thousand years, but we still know so little (as witnessed by the fantasy and sci-fi films churned out by the score). All true scientists who are experts in their fields all acknowledge that they know nothing. The journey towards knowing is expressed in some religions as a never-ending quest. This is obvious because to know the truth we would really have to know everything. And so the Lord has revealed exactly what we need to know.

[b] Graciously given by the Lord.

The Lord is known as the God of all grace.[86] He is certainly not unwilling to reveal Himself

---

84   2Peter 1v21.
85   See, for example, Jeremiah 23v30; 2Kings 17v13; Psalm 103v7; Hebrews 1v1,2.
86   1Peter 5v10.

to men for immediately the first human pair sinned we have the revelation of the gospel.[87] There are many Scriptures that testify to the fact that revelation is given and initiated by God alone. We shall consider a few of these. In our first Scripture we consider the response of the Lord Jesus to Peter's confession that He was the Christ, the Son of God:

> *Jesus answered and said to him, "Blessed are you, Simon Bar-Jonah, for flesh and blood has not revealed this to you, but My Father who is in heaven." (Matthew 16v17).*

It was in the Father's gift alone to give such a revelation. In our next Scripture we read about how God can only be known through Jesus Christ:

> *No one has seen God at any time. The only begotten Son, who is in the bosom of the Father, He has declared Him. (John 1v18).*

Christ is the most gracious gift to humanity of all.[88] And in Him we are given the most amazing revelation of all, to know God through Christ, for Christ (alone) made God the Father known. The Lord made known things to His disciples:

> *No longer do I call you servants, for a servant does not know what his master is doing; but I have called you friends, for all things that I heard from My Father I have made known to you. (John 15v15).*

It wasn't just to those who knew Christ whilst He was on the earth, however, for the third person of the Trinity has a part to play too. The Holy Spirit will teach too:

> *But the Helper, the Holy Spirit, whom the Father will send in My name, He will teach you all things, and bring to your remembrance all things that I said to you. (John 14v26).*

The Holy Spirit will bring whatever the Lord Jesus decides:

> *13 However, when He, the Spirit of truth, has come, He will guide you into all truth; for He will not speak on His own authority, but whatever He hears He will speak; and He will tell you things to come. 14 He will glorify Me, for He will take of what is Mine and declare it to you. (John 16v13,14).*

It is the Lord alone who reveals His will to those whom He chose:

---

87 Genesis 3v15.
88 John 3v16.

I have given them Your word; and the world has hated them because they are not of the world, just as I am not of the world. (John 17v14).

And it is God alone who reveals through the Spirit:

But God has revealed them to us through His Spirit. For the Spirit searches all things, yes, the deep things of God. (1Corinthians 2v10).

Contrary to the world's beliefs, God the Father has revealed in an open and public manner.

I have not spoken in secret, in a dark place of the earth; I did not say to the seed of Jacob, 'seek Me in vain'; I, the Lord, speak righteousness, I declare things that are right. (Isaiah 45v19).

His open and public revelation has been from the very beginning:

Come near to Me, hear this: I have not spoken in secret from the beginning; from the time that it was, I was there. and now the Lord God and His Spirit have sent Me. (Isaiah 48v16).

The importance of this Scripture cannot be overstated. Right from the very beginning of all things God has openly and publicly declared His word and will. Those who argue for a long age of the earth have a serious problem here, because there is an inordinately long age between creation and the start of Biblical revelation in such a world view. However if we accept the that the world is just 6,000 years old, as I believe the Scriptures do teach, then we have no problem. Soon after Adam and Eve sinned, we have the promise of the gospel in Genesis 3v15. Thereafter we have the revelation of God's plan and purpose unfolded through the rest of Genesis, the Pentatuech and so on. In fact God's revelation is something we must be so thankful for. The Lord has chosen to reveal through the prophets but especially through **The** Prophet, Christ Jesus our Lord:

Surely the Lord God does nothing, unless He reveals His secret to His servants the prophets. A lion has roared! (Amos 3v7).

[c] Revelation is about Christ.

The main object of revelation is Christ and His work. Paul wanted to know nothing save Christ and His crucifixion.[89] The cross was all his glory and boast.[90] Consider also our Lord's

---

89   1Corinthians 2v2.
90   Galatians 6v14.

teaching after He rose from the dead as recorded by Luke:

> *And beginning at Moses and all the Prophets, He expounded to them in all the Scriptures the things concerning Himself. (Luke 24v27).*

> *Then He said to them, "These are the words which I spoke to you while I was still with you, that all things must be fulfilled which were written in the Law of Moses and the Prophets and the Psalms concerning Me." (Luke 24v44).*

It is to be noted here that all of the Old Testament Scriptures are referenced here. Christ uses the threefold division of the Hebrew Bible. Wherever we look we will encounter the Lord Jesus Christ. Not just in direct prophecy, nor either simply through types and symbols (e.g. the tabernacle, the sacrifices), but in the historical events recorded and in the cries of the Psalmists.

Now in establishing the fact that Scripture is all about Christ, we must remember that other themes are not neglected. We have words about our nature, the direction we should take, our sanctification, and so on. Then also we have teaching for life in general, which means that all we (legitimately) do has impulse from God and thence (by inference) from Scripture.[91] In other words Scripture has greater scope than its main ruling theme and message, but these are always subordinate and secondary to the main focus which is Christ Jesus. These thoughts are, however, not disconnected to the idea that the main theme is Christ and His work. The reason for this is that God's revelation of Christ uses the vehicles of history, (for example the history of Abraham, of Israel, of other nations, of our Saviour), and geography, (for example, Paul's missionary journeys). In fact when you think about revelation it is impossible to consider it without taking account of the means and methods God used to bring it to us. This necessarily implies that the vehicles of revelation (the history, the geography, the science and so on) are all a part of God's revelation. As examples, consider the healing of Naaman, the events of Noah and the flood, the great details of the Passover and the Exodus. The incidental information concerning such things as, creation and its operation, the history of nations, and, peoples and events, must all be employed as the vehicles of God's revelation. This means that these are equally true.

[d] Revelation occurs through the medium of words.

This aspect of revelation is not generally accepted in our day. Many would want to receive revelation by dream and vision, or by other means. Yet even the mechanism of revelation by dream and vision in the Old Testament was (as we shall observe) through the medium of words. When the

---

91   2Peter 1v3f.

Lord spoke and revealed to Abraham we have these words recorded:

> *After these things the word of the Lord came to Abram in a vision, saying, "Do not be afraid, Abram. I am your shield, your exceedingly great reward." (Genesis 15v1).*

It was the "word of the Lord" that came in a vision and this "word of the Lord" utters words ("saying"). After this Abram expresses his doubts and worries about the situation he faced. In response to these we next find the word of the Lord speaking again:

> *And behold, the word of the Lord came to him, saying, "This one shall not be your heir, but one who will come from your own body shall be your heir." (Genesis 15v4).*

In this verse we learn incidentally that the "word of the Lord" is a person, for it is this person who speaks. The concept of the word of the Lord as a person prior to John 1v1f is not confined to Abram and Genesis. In 1Samuel we read about Samuel's early experiences with the Lord. At the beginning we note that he was unaware of the Lord:

> *Now Samuel did not yet know the Lord, nor was the word of the Lord yet revealed to him. (1Samuel 3v7).*

After the events of this chapter in which the Lord reveals Himself to Samuel we then find:

> *Then the Lord appeared again in Shiloh. For the Lord revealed Himself to Samuel in Shiloh by the word of the Lord. (1Samule 3v21).*

The Lord reveals Himself to Samuel by the word of the Lord. We can take this to mean first that "the word of the Lord" is communication from the mouth of God, that is, words. Or we can take this to mean that the pre-incarnate Christ, the word of God, came to Samuel. But either of these clearly indicate that the primary means by which we receive revelation is by words. In Isaiah 21v14 we find that revelation comes by hearing (words):

> *Then it was revealed in my hearing by the Lord of hosts, "surely for this iniquity there will be no atonement for you, even to your death," says the Lord God of hosts. (Isaiah 21v14).*

The phrase "the word of the Lord" is one that we find in other Scriptures besides those we have already considered. The prophets, for example, frequently made use of the phrase "the word of the

Lord came to me, saying ..."[92] This concept of revelation coming by words is not contradicted by the fact that Isaiah (and others) received visions, nor by the fact that Jacob and Daniel received dreams. These visions and dreams were communicated by means of words, otherwise how could such symbols and images be understood? The prophet Isaiah starts by telling us of the "vision" that he "saw," then carries on by telling us of the "word" that he "saw."[93] In the Old Testament we are taught that God revealed Himself to the prophets by means of vision and dream.[94] This would have been by means of words as we have noted above, but would have been a partial, piecemeal type of revelation (various times, various ways), as we are taught in Hebrews 1v1f.[95] This is not to say that it was in error in any way at all, for all revelation is perfect and pure being from God Himself.

In stark contrast to the prophets of old, the Lord spoke directly to Moses face to face. This contrast was set in order to highlight the distinction between Old Testament revelation and New Testament revelation, for the Lord Jesus Christ was "The Prophet" prophesied by Moses:

> *The Lord your God will raise up for you a Prophet like me from your midst, from your brethren. Him you shall hear. (Deuteronomy 18v15).*

Thus whilst the Lord spoke piecemeal and in part (although completely without error) through the prophets in the Old Testament, He spoke with unfettered clarity in the New Testament through His Son the Lord Jesus Christ, (and those commissioned by Him).[96] Being the very Word of God, the Lord Jesus Christ of course reveals the Father perfectly (they are One).[97] The connection between the word of God (words revealed unto men) and the Word of God (the Son of God who became flesh and dwelt among men) is not to be limited to John chapter 1. It is also to be seen (as we have already observed) at the occasion when Abraham met with the Lord recorded in Genesis 15v1f, when Samuel was spoken to by the Lord in 1Samuel 3, and the time when Elijah was met by the word of God in a cave:

> *And there he went into a cave, and spent the night in that place; and behold, the word of the Lord came to him, and He said to him, "What are you doing here, Elijah?" (1Kings 19v9).*

---

92   Isaiah 38v4; Jeremiah 1v2,4,11,13; 2v1; 7v1; 13v3,8; 16v1; 18v5; 24v4; 32v6; Ezekiel 1v3; 12v17,21,26; 22v1,17,23; 29v1,17; 33v1; 34v1; 35v1; Hosea 1v1; Joel 1v1; Jonah 1v1; Micah 1v1; Zechariah 4v8; 6v9; 7v1; 8v1
93   Isaiah 1v1; 2v1.
94   Numbers 12v6,7.
95   Hebrews 1v1f.
96   Hebrews 1v1f.
97   John 1v1,18; 10v30.

[e] Revelation is given only to certain people.

Now revelation has not been given indiscriminately to anyone and all. God has chosen "holy men" through whom He has willed to reveal what He wants us to know.[98] The sovereign Lord chose those whom He wanted to receive His word. Now we must point out here that when revelation is given to a certain person, this person has a duty to make known what they have received. However the initial revelation is given only to certain specific people. We have a number of Scriptures which teach this fact.

> *25 At that time Jesus answered and said, "I thank You, Father, Lord of heaven and earth, that You have hidden these things from the wise and prudent and have revealed them to babes. 26 Even so, Father, for so it seemed good in Your sight. (Matthew 11v25,26).*

The Father has actually hidden what was revealed to Peter from the wise! In the next Scripture we read that God has only revealed the mysteries and wonders of His love to the holy apostles and prophets through the Spirit:

> *... which in other ages was not made known to the sons of men, as it has now been revealed by the Spirit to His holy apostles and prophets. (Ephesians 3v5).*

This idea is also found in Paul's first letter to the Corinthians:

> *9 But as it is written: "eye has not seen, nor ear heard, nor have entered into the heart of man the things which God has prepared for those who love Him." 10 But God has revealed them to us through His Spirit. For the Spirit searches all things, yes, the deep things of God. 11 For what man knows the things of a man except the spirit of the man which is in him? Even so no one knows the things of God except the Spirit of God. (1Corinthians 2v9-11).*

Old Testament prophets were called of God in special ways and were commissioned by the Lord. These spokesmen for God were attested by signs and wonders and by their prophecies coming true. False prophets were in evidence, of course, but they were not sent of God. No matter how much they may have wanted this, they were not the Lord's and this was evident by what they said and did (or did not) do.[99]

One clear demonstration of this principle that God chose only certain men for revelation is shown in the book of Daniel. Here we recall from our earlier discussions that Nebuchadnezzar tried to get the "wise" men to tell him both the content of his dream, and also its interpretation. The wise

---

98   2Peter 1v21.
99   1Corinthians 12v29.

men replied:

> *10 ... There is not a man on earth who can tell the king's matter; therefore no king, lord, or ruler has ever asked such things of any magician, astrologer, or Chaldean. 11 It is a difficult thing that the king requests, and there is no other who can tell it to the king except the gods, whose dwelling is not with flesh. (Daniel 2v10,11).*

Thus here we have a confession that true revelation is not in the gift of men. After it was made known that the king was displeased with his advisers, and that they would all be slain, Daniel and his three friends call to the Lord for help.[100] Next we discover that the Lord revealed the secret to Daniel. He did this not because Daniel was wise or had great learning, but only because God decided to use him and no one else.[101] It could equally have been any of Daniel's friends that God chose, but in the end it was Daniel alone.

Incidentally this passage of Scripture reinforces earlier thoughts we have established. Thus it is God alone who reveals, for no man can reveal or "discover" revelation.[102] Then also, that which is revealed is secret, dark, deep, and therefore unknown and unknowable by men.[103] This passage also teaches that revelation is understandable, a thought we shall consider under the doctrine of illumination.

[f] Revelation is given for the benefit of all people.

Having stated that revelation is given to special men chosen by the Lord, we need to state also that this revelation was not just for these people alone. All revelation is to be open for all. This idea is as a consequence of the nature of God. He is willing to reveal Himself to men, and, furthermore, He is not partial and He is always fair. God is described as the "Judge of all the earth" who always does right, He is a "just God and a Saviour," He shows no favouritism, and is totally impartial.[104] Revelation was to be made available for all generations:

> *10 Of this salvation the prophets have inquired and searched carefully, who prophesied of the grace that would come to you, 11 searching what, or what manner of time, the Spirit of Christ who was in them was indicating when He testified beforehand the sufferings of Christ and the glories that would follow 12 To them it was revealed that, not to themselves, but to us they were ministering the things which now have been reported to you through those who have preached the gospel to you by the Holy Spirit sent from heaven—things which angels desire to look into. (1Peter 1v10-12).*

---

100   Daniel 2v17,18.
101   Daniel 2v19,20.
102   Daniel 2v18,22,28,29,47 and Daniel 2v10-13,27,30.
103   Daniel 2v19,22.
104   Genesis 18v25; Isaiah 45v21; Galatians 2v6; James 3v17.

Note in these words of Peter that the revelation revealed to the prophets was not for them but for "us," or, in other words, those to whom Peter was writing.

There are two further conclusions to be drawn from this fact that revelation whilst given only to specially selected individuals was to be made available for all. First, the revelation given to these special people must have been given free from all error, stain and sin (so that contemporary hearers could also benefit). Second, such a revelation (committed to writing) must also have been preserved in its pure form throughout the ages so that later generations could benefit. The first point teaches us the need for ***divine inspiration***, whilst the second point teaches the need for ***divine preservation***. However these two doctrines can be derived from the Bible itself.

[g] Revelation is God revealing Himself to men through His Special Revelation.

The revelation of God is complete in Scripture and no new revelation is to be given or expected. This is a direct consequence of Hebrews 1v1f. That being said we know that God still chooses to reveal *Himself* to men of all ages and times. We have this thought from the Scriptures! In Isaiah we read that the Lord chooses to dwell with the humble and contrite of heart:

> *For thus says the High and Lofty One who inhabits eternity, whose name is Holy: "I dwell in the high and holy place, with him who has a contrite and humble spirit, to revive the spirit of the humble, and to revive the heart of the contrite ones." (Isaiah 57v15).*

Our Lord and Saviour Himself spoke of this fellowship with God:

> *He who has My commandments and keeps them, it is he who loves Me. And he who loves Me will be loved by My Father, and I will love him and manifest Myself to him. (John 14v21).*

> *Jesus answered and said to him, "If anyone loves Me, he will keep My word; and My Father will love him, and We will come to him and make Our home with him. (John 14v23).*

And so God is willing to reveal Himself to all who keep the Lord's commandments and who are humble and contrite in heart. We can receive this revelation from God every time we read the Scriptures. Listen to these words the Lord Jesus spoke to the Sadducees:

> *31 But concerning the resurrection of the dead, have you not read what was spoken to you by God, saying, 32 'I am the God of Abraham, the God of Isaac, and the God of Jacob'? God is not the God of the dead, but of the living." (Matthew 22v31,32).*

We can read in Scripture what God has spoken, not just to the original readers, but to those who read them today.

We end with these words of further encouragement:

Behold, I stand at the door and knock. If anyone hears My voice and opens the door, I will come in to him and dine with him, and he with Me. (Revelation 3v20).

Chapter 2

Inspiration.

Introduction.

Having dealt with revelation, we come now to the means and process whereby the word of God actually becomes known to mankind. This is the doctrine of divine inspiration. Revelation has to do with the fact that there is knowledge that we need, but which we cannot discover and which God is graciously willing to show us. Inspiration has to do with *how* this revelation enters our world and experience.

In our studies we shall start by considering some key texts which teach this idea of inspiration. Following this we shall gather some thoughts from these texts to define and illustrate what inspiration is and is not. Finally we shall make some further comments on the nature of inspiration and the implications of this doctrine.

Key texts.

Now in modern usage the word "inspiration" has a variety of meanings, but in the Bible it has a very technical sense, and to understand this teaching we shall look first at a selection of key texts. These are:

> [1] 2Timothy 3v16,17.
> [2] 2Peter 1v20,21.
> [3] 1Corinthians 2v10-13.
> [4] 2Samuel 23v2 and Numbers 22v38; 23v5,12,16,26; 24v12,13.

[1] 2Timothy 3v16,17.

Although the word "inspiration" can only be found in 2Timothy 3v16, the *idea* of inspiration is expressed through the use of other terms and phrases which we shall consider shortly.[105] We must first set the context for our passage. How did Paul come to write these words? One break-down of the letter is shown in table 2.1.

In the opening introduction of the letter Paul declares his status as an apostle, "by the will of

---

105   2Timothy 3v16 is the only verse which uses the word "inspiration," but the concept can be found in 2Peter 1v19-21, and also in Scriptures such as Numbers 22v38; 23v5,12,16,26; 24v12,13 and 2Samauel 23v2.

God," but, interestingly, he also states that this is in accord with "the promise of life," so that in this letter the gospel is uppermost in his thinking.[106] In the second section Paul exhorts the young pastor not to be ashamed of the "testimony of our Lord" but to suffer "for the gospel" alongside him.[107] A wonderful statement of the gospel is provided next, and Paul explains his calling and then exhorts Timothy to "hold fast the pattern of sound words" that he had heard from the apostle.[108] In the third part of the letter Timothy is exhorted to carry on in spite of much opposition. He was to pass on what he had heard and learned to faithful men enduring hardship as a soldier of Christ. In the fourth

Table 2.1: Breakdown of 2 Timothy.

[A]	Introductory greeting and Paul's compassion and prayers for the genuine believer Timothy.	1v1-5.
[B]	Five important personal instructions for Timothy concerning the mission of the gospel.	1v6-14.
[C]	Four exhortations to pursue the Great Commission to generations in the face of opposition.	1v15-2v10.
[D]	A faithful saying, idle babblings, and household vessels.	2v11-26.
[E]	Perilous times will come but continue with Scripture alone.	3v1-17.
[F]	Eight final charges for furthering faithful gospel ministry.	4v1-8.
[G]	Closing instructions of a practical nature – God is faithful whilst men may not be.	4v9-22.

section the young pastor is given a series of doctrinal statements designated as "a faithful saying." Timothy is exhorted to ignore the profane, idle, ignorant and foolish nonsense of the false teachers, but rather he is to "be diligent" and unashamed in "rightly dividing the word of truth."[109] The fifth section begins with a warning that "perilous times" were about to come.[110] Paul then details two stark contrasts. First Paul points out that Timothy has followed Paul's example of life and teaching.[111] Then second, in the midst of increasing apostasy, Paul exhorts Timothy to "continue in the things" that he had heard.[112] These things that he had heard, were those he had heard from childhood and were the things which he had known from the Scriptures. At this point the apostle gives us his doctrine regarding the Scriptures – 2 Tiothy 3v16,17. In the penultimate section Paul opens with a charge to Timothy to "preach the word" in all weathers. Then in the final section Paul

---

106   Compare 1 Timothy 1v1 "promise of life" with 1v10 "brought life and immortality to light through the gospel,"
107   2 Timothy 1v8,9.
108   2 Timothy 1v9-13.
109   2 Timothy 2v15,16,23.
110   2 Timothy 3v1-8.
111   2 Timothy 3v10,11.
112   2 Timothy 3v13,14.

shows how God is always faithful even though men are fickle.

And so, having exhorted Timothy to be unashamed and to get back to the Bible, Paul in the central section gives us the main reason for such confidence. Thus it is because:

> **16** *All Scripture*
> *is given by inspiration of God, and*
> *is profitable*
> > *for doctrine,*
> > *for reproof,*
> > *for correction,*
> > *for instruction in righteousness,*
> > > **17** *that the man of God may be*
> > > *complete,*
> > > *thoroughly equipped for every good work.*

So what then do these two verses teach us? In essence what he have here is, the compass or scope of the term "Scripture," how the Scriptures have come to us, how they can be used, and, their essential purpose. We shall consider the text under the following four headings:

All Scripture

Is given by inspiration of God.

Is profitable for ….

That the man of God may be ….

All Scripture.

The subject of our text is, of course, "all Scripture," but we need to ask the question: to what does the apostle refer? The term "Scripture" could easily be translated as "writing," as the Greek word is **_graphe_** which means writing. We shall consider the Bible as a written document later on, but for now it is vital to recognise that the written record which we know as the Bible has a definite form. It comprises the 66 different 'books' of the Old and the New Testaments.[113] There is only one place in the Old Testament where the translators have used the term "Scripture" in the New King James version, namely, Daniel 10v21. However the word "write" and cognates are used throughout. In the New Testament the term "Scripture" is used primarily to refer to the Old Testament. As an example listen to what the Lord Jesus said to the chief priests and Pharisees whilst he was in the temple:

---

113   The Bible is a single book. It is practical, however, to refer to the different sections as 'books' but these are all part of the one book, the Bible.

> *Jesus said to them, "Have you never read in the Scriptures: 'The stone which the builders*
> *rejected Has become the chief cornerstone. This was the Lord's doing, and it is marvellous*
> *in our eyes'? (Matthew 21v42).*

The quote Jesus uses is from Psalm 118v22,23. The Lord Jesus referred to many other Old Testament books and passages during the course of his time on earth, and these were all known by this term "Scripture" or, to be exact, "Writing."

What then, of the New Testament? Well Peter refers to Paul's writings as Scripture in 2Peter 3v15,16. Then also Paul in 1Timothy 5v18 takes a passage from Luke's gospel and combines it with words from Deuteronomy and refers to these both as "Scripture."[114] We could develop this idea from another angle. The Lord Himself taught that the Holy Spirit would lead the disciples into all truth as the Holy Spirit revealed to them. This was fulfilled as the New Testament Scriptures were written and accepted as the word of God. Then further, the writer of Hebrews opens his letter with a kind of summary statement that gives us the superiority of the New Testament revelation over the Old Testament. He tells us that whilst the Old Testament is the word of God, a fuller and more complete revelation was given *in* the "language" of the Son of God, or, in other words, centred in, focused on, and originated from, Christ the Lord.[115] So the term "all Scripture" refers to all the written words which have as authority and author none other than God Himself. All of these written words we find in the Bible are Scripture.

Is given by inspiration of God.

The phrase "is given by" have been supplied by the translator. Literally rendered the words are: "All Scripture [is] God-breathed." We have to put some form of verb in to make sense in English. The choice of "is given by" is not wrong and can be suggested by the very fact that the main emphasis is on the idea of God-breathed. Actually the Greek *theopneustos* (translated as "God-breathed"), can also be rendered as "God-spirited" leading to the idea of God the Holy Spirit as author. The usual translation, however, is "God-breathed" and it homes in on both the idea of revelation, (that the Scriptures are from God), and the idea of God speaking.

So what are we to make of this notion that "all Scripture is God-breathed?" Where does that leave the human authors? Paul's point is that the origin and source of the Scriptures are actually that which was spoken by God. This idea is one which the Saviour held to as can be seen by his words in answer to the conundrum concerning the resurrection posed by the Sadducees we considered earlier. The Lord Jesus stated:

---

114   Luke 10v7; Deuteronomy 25v4.
115   John 16v13; Hebrews 1v1-3.

31 But concerning the resurrection of the dead, have you not read what was spoken to you by God, saying, 32 'I am the God of Abraham, the God of Isaac, and the God of Jacob'? God is not the God of the dead, but of the living. (Matthew 22v31,32).

The key verse for our consideration is the words in verse 31: "have you not read what was spoken to you by God." Note what the Lord says. He states that the people to whom he was speaking could read the Scriptures and in so doing where actively hearing God speaking at the same time. If the reading of the Scriptures equates to the hearing of God speaking, then we have the idea of inspiration reinforced.

Is profitable for ....

The Scriptures, which have come from the very mouth (or breath) of God, are "profitable," that is, they are advantageous, or, in other words, for our very best interests. The main focus is on righteousness, or the way to live in right relationship, which is grounded in truth. The four different ways in which the Scriptures are profitable are highly significant and seem to cover all bases. First we have "doctrine" which amounts to teaching about the truth. We use this word "doctrine" specifically to refer to those truths about God and His works. We talk about the doctrine of God, or of the atonement. These are the truths and realities concerning those subjects. Scripture has doctrine, teaching about truth. Then next we have "reproof" which indicates "conviction" brought about by convincing evidence. The Scriptures, therefore, have within themselves convincing proofs which convict the soul of the importance and rightness of what the Scriptures teach. Thirdly we have "correction" which amounts to bringing about a restoration into a state of uprightness. Finally we have "instruction." This last word is, perhaps, the most significant of all, for it indicates the entire scope and realm of training and education given to children. We shall have course to return to the theme of profitability when we look at the fruitfulness or efficacy of the Bible.

That the man of God may be ....

The Scriptures have a definite purpose in view. It is so that the "man (or woman) of God," (a designation of true believers), may be "complete." This word indicates the idea that the believer may have special aptitude for specific purposes or given uses. Earlier Paul instructed Timothy about being a vessel to honour, fit for the Master's use.[116] The Scriptures enable a person to become complete, that is, the vessel for honour that God intended them to be. This idea is then further emphasised. It is not just that the believer will become what was intended, but rather that they will

---

116   2Timothy 2v20,21.

become "thoroughly equipped." The Scriptures, then, have this perfect, complete and thoroughness about them. And notice it is for all good works. There isn't an area where the Scriptures fail. They are sufficient for every "good work." This thought will be taken up further when we look at the scope and sufficiency of the Bible.

[2] 2Peter 1v20,21.

> **20** *knowing this first, that no prophecy of Scripture is of any private interpretation,* **21** *for prophecy never came by the will of man, but holy men of God spoke as they were moved by the Holy Spirit. (2Peter 1v20,21).*

The passage we are to consider falls in the centre of Peter's letter and it is essential we consider the context before we unpack the details of these important words. There are five sections which may be headed as follows:

[A]   Like precious faith and the knowledge of God.   1v1-4.

[B]   The importance of "these things" for the true knowledge of God.   1v5-11.

[C]   A reminder of the truth through the prophetic word confirmed.   1v12-21.

[D]   The danger of false prophets and teachers and their seven-fold character.   2v1-22.

[E]   A seven-fold set of instructions in the face of scoffing.   3v1- 18.

Peter opens this "general" epistle with some extremely important details which are as well to consider before we move to the matter at hand. Note first how Peter grounds his letter in the gift and righteousness of God. Thus the "like precious faith" that the recipients of this letter have, has come to them by the righteousness of God. Then further, note that it is the "knowledge of God" that is key in possessing such faith. Knowing God is the business of those of us who have faith and have received grace from God. This grace or gift of God has come to us by His divine power. So what does this grace consist of? The divine power has given us two things. First we have received everything necessary to enable us to live a godly life here on earth. Remarkable! Second we have been gifted the "exceedingly great and precious promises," or, in other words, the Scriptures! Tremendous! More wonderful, (is that really possible?), we find that it is through these great and precious promises that we may become partakers of the divine nature (that we may know God).

In the second section Peter details how the faith of those who have true knowledge of God may be unpacked and developed. He encourages the readers of this letter to ensure that the things of which he speaks are worked through with care and diligence. This is an essential teaching on the true nature of faith, a faith that works and grows. Then next comes the section within which our verses are located. Peter is particularly concerned to make sure that the readers of his letter may be enabled to remember the truth, especially as he is soon to depart this world. The apostle then recalls a particular incident (the transfiguration) to show that what he has declared to them was not formed from "cunningly devised fables" because they were eyewitnesses of His glory. The prophetic word received was confirmed by such an amazing incident on the mountain when the voice of God was heard. Peter then exhorts the readers to listen carefully, and to continue to do so until Christ returns, so that they should obey the prophecy, because it is a light shining in the terrible darkness of this doomed world. It is at this point that Peter stops to explain something about the nature of prophecy.

After this we have a chapter which details the nature of false prophecy and teaching. Examples are given from the Old Testament and there is a seven-fold description of the nature of false teaching and teachers. Finally Peter issues seven instructions to his readers on how to continue in the face of scoffing. They should "be mindful" of the words of the apostles and prophets (i.e. Scripture), especially as the scoffers misuse and misquote the word of God which, it is to be remembered, actually gave rise to creation. Then towards the end of this letter Peter points out that Paul's letters have the status "Scripture."

It is in this context of the knowledge of God by faith which is a gift of God and which comes to us through Scripture (the exceedingly great and precious promises), that our text may be found. What then does it teach us?

> **20** *knowing this first, that no prophecy of Scripture is of any private interpretation,* **21** *for prophecy never came by the will of man, but holy men of God spoke as they were moved by the Holy Spirit. (2Peter 1v20,21).*

We learn two things about the nature of prophecy, and we learn about how these prophecies came to us through men of old, or, in other words, something about the process of inspiration. On the nature of prophecy we first read that prophecy cannot be interpreted in a singular or private way. This does not violate the principle whereby everyone knows the Lord individually and can receive of God personally. These things are certain. No one can become a believer vicariously. God does not have grand children. Each person must come to a knowledge of God personally. However what we must say from these words (i.e. "no prophecy of Scripture is of any private interpretation") is that it is not possible that as a person comes to an understanding of Scripture prophecy, they will come to an interpretation differing from other godly believers. Instead what ought to happen, is that as a godly believer reads and seeks in Scripture, their understanding of what God has revealed will accord and agree with what other believers have understood. Looking at this negatively, whenever someone comes up with an interpretation all of their own and which differs markedly from other believers, you can be sure that they are on the wrong track. Joseph Smith who formed the Mormon Church, and the Jehovah's Witnesses are two cases in point but there have been many others before and since that time.

The second thing we discover about the nature of prophecy is that it does not originate with man, or come from their own wills. This is a statement which reinforces the idea of revelation. We can never come to a knowledge of the content and detail of God's revelation by will, human discovery or effort. This point is established clearly by Scripture, but equally by mankind's experience of seeking truth.[117] Now some may object that if the prophecy does not involve the will of the men through whom it comes, then what we are talking about is mere automatic dictation. This is nonsense, of course, for God is sovereign and stands infinitely higher above mere creatures. God has so orchestrated all things so that as a man thinks and wills and acts, his words are entirely his own but equally entirely all that God intended for us to know, in so far as they have become the inspired word we have in Scripture.

This point leads us on to consider the nature of inspiration, for we find first that "holy men of God spoke," which statement teaches us that such an act was free and a matter for the individual. Then, secondly, (and importantly), they spoke "as they were moved by the Holy Spirit" which statement serves to indicate the sovereign superintendence of God. Those who have a small view of God, or who cannot grasp the nature of God as revealed in Scripture, fail to see the wonder of this verse. No personality is obliterated or violated, but the infinitely great and sovereign Lord chooses each man as he speaks, to speak those things that He alone intends.

[3] 1Corinthians 2v10-13.

> **10** *But God has revealed them to us through His Spirit. For the Spirit searches all things, yes, the deep things of God. **11** For what man knows the things of a man except the spirit of the man which is in him? Even so no one knows the things of God except the Spirit of God. **12** Now we have received, not the spirit of the world, but the Spirit who is from God, that we might know the things that have been freely given to us by God. **13** These things we also speak, not in words which man's wisdom teaches but which the Holy Spirit teaches, comparing spiritual things with spiritual. (1Corinthians 2v10-13).*

In chapter one of 1Corinthians, Paul teaches that the essential thing for him was to preach the gospel, because the "message (literally word) of the cross" is what distinguishes between the saved

---

117   Scripture examples include: Ecclesiastes 8v16,17 and Romans 11v33-35. The history of science, objectively considered, shows this truth clearly. Modern science is ever learning but never able to come to a knowledge of the truth.

and the perishing.[118] He then appeals to the Old Testament Scriptures for support where the Lord makes clear that the wisdom of this world is of no account whatsoever, and the only thing to glory in is, knowing the lord.[119] This world's wisdom will not wash. God's "foolishness" (as far as the world views it) is over and above any "wisdom" this world has to offer. Then in chapter two he speaks of his witness by word to the Corinthians. Paul came not in the wisdom of this world with its rhetoric and persuasion, but in "demonstration of the Spirit and of power."[120] But Paul then goes on to make clear that he does bring a wisdom to his hearers which is "the wisdom of God in a mystery" and "the hidden wisdom" that God had before time and which no one knew about.[121] It is this wisdom that has been revealed by the Spirit to the apostle. Paul unfolds the doctrine of revelation here, for we see that no one can know about the things of God except the Spirit of God.[122] But the Spirit is given to the apostles. It is this revelation that Paul speaks of, and it is the Holy Spirit which teaches. Thus we have in Paul's second chapter of the first letter to the Corinthians, a detailed teaching of how revelation is accomplished by the Spirit of God. It is the Holy Spirit that reveals to the inspired writers because the Holy Spirit alone knows the deep things of God. The hidden plan (wisdom) is now made manifest by the Holy Spirit. The things which come via the Holy Spirit do not come with words of worldly wisdom, but rather they come in words which the Holy Spirit teaches.

[4] 2Smuel 23v2 & Numbers 22v38; 23v5,12,16,26; 24v12,13.

The Spirit of the Lord spoke by me, and His word was on my tongue. (2Samuel 23v2).

This verse comes in a passage written by David at the very end of his life. David, "the son of Jesse," was a "man raised up on high." He was the "anointed of the God of Jacob" and "the sweet psalmist of Israel."[123] Reflecting back in time David could say that the Lord God "spoke by me," or, in other words, that David was God's mouthpiece. This idea is then enhanced by the second part of the verse which tells us that God's word was on David's tongue. The two parts of this verse go together. Thus when the Spirit spoke by David, it was because the word of the Lord was placed or put on David's tongue.

This idea of the word of God being given to the very mouth of the prophet is shown in a very detailed and graphic way in the case of Balaam whom we meet in the book of Numbers. It is as

---

118   1Corinthians 1v17,18.
119   Isaiah 29v14; Jeremiah 9v24.
120   1Corinthians 2v4.
121   1Corinthians 2v7,8.
122   1Corinthians 2v11.
123   2Samuel 23v1.

Mike Viccary

well to begin this consideration by noting that the New Testament gives Balaam a poor review. Balaam is described as one who "loved the wages of unrighteousness," whose covetousness and profiteering were "error," and, was one who put a stumbling block before the faithful.[124] Despite this, Balaam was a prophet of God who received revelation and whose words we have in Numbers were inspired. Before we look at the text in Numbers it is worth pausing with these thoughts for a moment. Just because a person has received revelation and whose writing is inspired and a part of Scripture, this is not to be taken as an indication of their right standing before the Lord. Balaam was a false prophet not because the information he received and passed on was in error, but because his life was in error. He did not listen to the revelation he received and lived in opposition to all that God was doing. This is a sobering thought. We may understand all wisdom, be fully versed in orthodox theology, and be the fount of all wisdom, but we may equally be cursed, unsaved and damned.[125]

Turning to the story of Numbers 22 we find that Israel are camped in the plains of Moab across from Jericho and about to enter the promised land. The king of Moab is worried, very worried, and so he sends to Balaam, who dwelt in Pethor of Mesopotamia, to come and to curse Israel as they camp in his land. The very interesting thing in the story is that Balaam tells Balak the king right from the beginning that he cannot do anything against the word of God. Here is Balaam's opening statement to Balak:

> *And Balaam said to Balak, "Look, I have come to you! Now, have I any power at all to say anything? The word that God puts in my mouth, that I must speak." (Numbers 22v38).*

This statement of Balaam gives the same idea as the one we found with David (although later in time). God puts the word into the prophet's mouth. Next, as the story progresses, we read that the Lord instructs Balaam to go to Balak after the king has prepared the sacrifices. Here is what the Lord says:

> *Then the Lord put a word in Balaam's mouth, and said, "Return to Balak, and thus you shall speak." (Numbers 23v5).*

Balaam then proceeds to deliver the word that the Lord had placed on his mouth. It was not what the king expected because Balaam blessed Israel rather than cursed them, and he was, to say the least, rather angry. Balaam responds to Balak's protestations by re-iterating that what the Lord gave

---

124   2Peter 2v15; Jude 1v11; Revelation 2v14.
125   Matthew 7v21-23; 1Corinthians 13v2.

was placed in his mouth, and so could not be altered:

> *So he answered and said, "Must I not take heed to speak what the Lord has put in my mouth?" (Numbers 23v12).*

Balak tries for another go at getting Balaam to curse Israel, and we read again how the Lord places a word on Balaam's mouth:

> *Then the Lord met Balaam, and put a word in his mouth, and said, "Go back to Balak, and thus you shall speak." (Numbers 23v16).*

Once again Balaam blesses Israel as he takes up the word God placed on his mouth. Balak is exasperated but Balaam again remonstrates with the king:

> *So Balaam answered and said to Balak, "Did I not tell you, saying, 'All that the Lord speaks, that I must do'?" (Numbers 23v26).*

It is interesting that Balaam states that whatever God speaks to him, the prophet "must do." It would appear from these words that the prophet did not actually want to do what the Lord commanded him really. He was under duress to comply. Now it is unthinkable that God suppressed the prophet in any way to coerce him into giving the word. The prophet could not speak anything other than what the Lord had given him, not through coercion and manipulation by God, but (presumably) by some dint of conscience. These were the words that the Lord gave Balaam, so these were the words that Balaam would speak for Balak. Balaam does not seem to like these words that God was giving at all. If he had he would perhaps have defied the king and rejoiced with the revelation he had received. But we see nothing at all of this and it seems that Balaam was more than reluctant in giving the word from God. At the end of the story Balaam re-iterates the situation he found himself in:

> *12 So Balaam said to Balak, "Did I not also speak to your messengers whom you sent to me, saying, 13 'If Balak were to give me his house full of silver and gold, I could not go beyond the word of the Lord, to do good or bad of my own will. What the Lord says, that I must speak'? (Numbers 24v12,13).*

Balaam could not go against God's word – he had to speak what God wanted and nothing else. It may seem from this encounter that Balaam was coerced and forced to speak against his own will. As I have already said, I think that such an idea is very far from what the Scriptures teach. Balaam

Mike Viccary

could have spoken against God, and could have tried to alter what God had declared. If he had done this, we can be sure that what God wanted Balak to hear would have come to him unscathed by some other means, for God's intentions (and his very words) are never thwarted. Rather I think that Balaam was very clear about what the Lord had spoken to him, and his conscience would not allow him to tamper with what he had heard. He was not one in spirit with the Lord or his word, but he could not alter the revealed word despite his disdain of it.

One of the objections to the idea of inspiration, which sometimes comes after considering the Balaam story, is that if the words are God's and come solely from him, then this means necessarily that the personality and will of the prophet must have been squashed, subverted or bypassed in some way. Here in Numbers we may have a prophet who was unhappy with what he was receiving, but just because the message he received wasn't what his audience wanted to hear, this in no way serves to indicate that the prophet's personality had been subverted. Furthermore, that the reception of prophecy does not undermine the prophet's personality can be easily demonstrated by looking at the prophet Jeremiah. For in Jeremiah we note that the word of God comes not just as a message independent of the person, but in the very person of the prophet himself. What I mean is that the prophet himself is part of the message that God is bringing to the people.[126]

Definitions.

As a summary of what we have learned from Scripture we must note several important things. First, from 1Corintians 2v10-13 we learn that it is the Holy Spirit who alone knows the very things of God, and it is He alone who brings the words of God in words he chooses, not in words the world may use. Second, from 2Smauel 23v2 and Numbers 22-23 we note that the word of God is placed on the mouth, so that a prophet is the very mouthpiece of God. However, this does no violence to the humanity, personality, or will of the prophet. Third, from 2Timothy 3v16,17 we learnt that all that is considered "Scripture" (the Old and New Testaments) have the quality of being "God-breathed." These written words are straight from the breath and mouth of God. Consequently they are useful and profitable. This theme of the efficacy of Scripture will form a separate study to be considered in a later chapter. Finally, from 2Peter 1v20,21 we noted that prophecy is never simply for personal interpretation. Rather it is something which the whole body of Christ (true believers) will share and understand in common agreement. This is why Paul often exhorts his readers to be of "one mind."[127] Then also we have found that the Scriptures have come to us as men spoke. They were not coerced, for it was God the Holy Spirit who carried them along or moved

---

126   The same ideas can be seen in other prophets but in Jeremiah they are very visible.
127   Romans 12v16; 15v5; 2Corinthians 13v11; Philippians 1v27; 2v2.

them on in this way. What this amounts to is that as a man was of a mind to speak, and as he did so, the Lord ensured that what he spoke was exactly that which the Lord so intended. The origin of the words are to be found in God, but the will and personality of the man were not subverted in the process. Having summarised some of the teaching we have encountered, it would be interesting to consider some definitions that others have provided of this doctrine to see whether each fits with what we have learned. The following are taken from evangelical believers almost at random. I will state them first and append some comments on each.

B. B. Warfield:

Inspiration is, therefore, usually defined as a supernatural influence on the sacred writers by the Spirit of God, by virtue of which their writings are given Divine trustworthiness.[128]

Rene Pache:

Inspiration is the determining influence exercised by the Holy Spirit on the writers of the Old and New Testaments in order that they might proclaim and set down in an exact and authentic way the message as received from God. This influence guided them even to the extent of their use of words, that they might be kept from all error and omission. A like inspiration was granted to the sacred writers in regard to events or facts already known by them without special revelation, that the accounts of them might be that which God willed.[129]

Erich Sauer:

Biblical inspiration ... is that ... activity of the Holy Spirit through which He mysteriously filled the human spirit of the Biblical writers and guided and overruled them, so that there arose an infallible, Spirit-wrought writing, a sacred record, a Book of God, with which the Spirit of God ever more organically unites Himself.[130]

Charles C. Ryrie:

My own definition of inspiration is that it is God's superintendence of the human authors so that, using their own individual personalities, they composed and recorded without error His revelation to man in the words of the original autographs.[131]

No one definition seems to capture all that we mean by inspiration. Warfield's view is rather "thin" in that it does not speak specifically about the fact that the writings are God-breathed. The idea of trustworthiness has a latitude which is unsettling. Something which is trustworthy may not

---

128   B. B. Warfield The Inspiration and Authority of the Bible. Philipsburg NJ. The Presbyterian and Reformed Publishing Company. 1948. P131.
129   Rene Pache "The Inspiration & Authority of Scripture" Moody Press 1969. P45.
130   Erich Sauer. From Eternity to Eternity. Eerdmans 1978. P107.
131   Charles C. Ryrie A Survey of Bible Doctrine. Moody Press. 1972. P38.

necessarily be pure and accurate. Erich Sauer's view takes account of the action of the Holy Spirit infusing the Biblical writers, but I do not think the idea of overruling is helpful. God is, of course, sovereign and rules over all. However he does not make men and women automatons. Overruling has the connotation of altering and changing things which I do not think is implied in the doctrine of inspiration. For example, Caiaphas spoke by inspiration when he demanded the death of Christ. Listen to how John puts It.

> *49 And one of them, Caiaphas, being high priest that year, said to them, "You know nothing at all, 50 nor do you consider that it is expedient for us that one man should die for the people, and not that the whole nation should perish." 51 Now this he did not say on his own authority; but being high priest that year he prophesied that Jesus would die for the nation, 52 and not for that nation only, but also that He would gather together in one the children of God who were scattered abroad. (John 11v49-2).*

It is certain that Caiaphas did not mean that Christ would die for the nation in the sense of true salvation. He mean that the Romans would not start a fuss if they removed Christ. However John describes Caiaphas' statement as prophecy. What Caiaphas willed to say was in fact what God wanted him to say as a piece of prophecy. What Caiaphas meant and what God signified were not the same.

Charles C. Ryrie's definition seems to focus too much on the personalities of men. It seems that what he is saying is that when God revealed to the prophets his message, they in turn using their own words and ideas, set forth the truth without error. I am not sure this takes account of the idea that the words God intended were put on the prophet's mouth.

Rene Pache's definition comes the closest, I think, to the idea of inspiration. He goes further than most by talking not just about the message, but about the words used. In the last sentence he is attempting to cover areas in which the individual writers used their own knowledge which they had apart from special revelation. Thus, for example, Luke records that his work was carried out through research. Moses too would have received documents handed down over generations.

For what it is worth, here is my definition borne out of the Scriptures we have looked at and having the benefit of others' attempts·

> Inspiration is that special divine movement of the Holy Spirit upon the Biblical writers, that whatever words, phrases and sentences these men chose to use in the formation of Scripture, were at one and the same time the exact same words, phrases and sentences that God intended for us to receive.

I do not say that this definition is infallible or inerrant! For that, stick with the Scriptures we have considered. What I want to convey is that the Biblical writers were still human personalities all the while their writings were being inspired. The Biblical writers were not inspired, their Scriptural writing was. All that was inspired, (God-breathed), and thus has the status, "Scripture," has the stamp "spoken by God" on it, for Scripture's origin is to be found in God alone.

The testimony of the church.

I mentioned earlier that interpretation is not a matter for personal choice. We look at Scripture and we interpret it individually but we make sure that we do not go off at a tangent, for God has spoken to the church. If I understand the word of God correctly, then others will share my understanding. We have followed this course by looking a little at what other evangelical writers have said.[132] Now it is worth recalling what other Christian writers of past ages have said on this subject. I am indebted to L. W. Munhall for the following selection from those believers who have written in the early centuries of the Christian church[133]:

Justin Martyr (100 – 165):

We must not suppose that the language proceeds from the men that are inspired, but from the Divine Word himself, who moves them. Their work is to announce that which the Holy Spirit proposes to teach, through them, to those who wish to learn the true religion ... The history Moses wrote was by the Divine Inspiration.

Irenaeus (130 – 202):

The writers spoke as acted on by the Spirit. All who foretold the coming of Christ received their inspiration from the Son, for how else could Scripture 'testify' of him alone? ... The writers are beyond all falsehood.

Clement of Alexandria (150 – 215):

The foundations of our faith rest on no insecure basis. We have received them through God himself through the Scripture, not one jot or tittle of which shall pass away till all is accomplished, for the mouth of the Lord, the Holy Spirit, spoke it. He ceases to be a man who spurns the tradition of the Church, and turns aside to human opinions; for the Scriptures are truly holy, since they make us holy, God-like. Of these Holy Writings or Words, the

---

132   It is pointless quoting liberal or modernist views on this subject for these writers would not share my world view. "Evangelical" is a term which (sadly) is widening in meaning, but generally speaking those who are described by this term have the same basic world view that all **true** believers share. This includes such doctrines as the substitutionary atonement of Christ, the physical bodily resurrection of Christ, the deity of Christ and His sinless humanity, the virgin birth, an acceptance of true miracles, the return of Christ amongst other important teachings.

133   All quotes taken have been from "Inspiration" By L. W. Munhall. Chapter 15 of "The Fundamentals" (P160-162). See also P47f of "The Battle For The Bible" by Harold Lindsell.

Bible is composed. Paul calls them God-breathed (2Timothy 3v15,16). The Sacred Writings consist of these holy letters or syllables, since they are "God-breathed."
Origen (185 – 254):

It is the doctrine acknowledged by all Christians, and evidently preached in the churches that the Holy Spirit, inspired the Saints, Prophets and Apostles, and was present in those he inspired at the Coming of Christ; for Christ, the Word of God, was in Moses when he wrote, and in the Prophets, and by his Spirit he did speak to them all things. The records of the Gospels are the Oracles of the Lord, pure Oracles purified as silver seven times tried. They are without error, since they were accurately written, by the co-operation of the Holy Spirit. ... It is good to adhere to the words of Paul and the Apostles as to God and our Lord Jesus Christ. There are many writings, but only one Book; four Evangelists, but only one Gospel. All the Sacred Writings breathe the same fullness. There is nothing, in the Law, the Prophets, the Gospel, the Apostles, that did not come from the fullness of God.

Augustine (354 – 430):

The Scriptures are the letters of God, the voice of God, the writings of God. ... The writers record the words of God. Christ spoke by Moses, for he was the Spirit of the Creator, and all the prophecies are the voice of the Lord. From the Spirit came the gift of tongues. All Scripture is profitable since it is inspired of God. The Scriptures, whether in History, Prophecy, Psalms or Law are of God. They cannot stand in part and fall in part. They are from God, who spake them all. ... As it was not the Apostles who spoke, but the Spirit of the Father in them, so it is the Spirit that speaks in all Scriptures. ... It avails nothing what I say, what he says but what saith the Lord.

So once again we have a very close consensus throughout time that Scripture has been inspired, or God-breathed.

Further considerations.

The essential idea contained in the word "inspiration" is: "God-breathed." You can see this idea from the root of the English word "inspiration" since it comes from the Latin verb *inspirare* meaning to breathe in. Inspiration, Biblically speaking, is not an indication of human genius. In contrast, inspiration spoken of in the arts and literature may well suggest human ingenuity. Many may lay claim to be inspired in their art, their science or their literature, but the **Scriptures** alone are inspired of God. The difference is twofold. First inspiration relates not to the people but to the writings. Second inspiration is divine and not human – God-breathed. Inspiration relates, therefore, to the written word, not to the people that God used as vehicles. Thus Moses, David, John and so on were not always and everywhere inspired, for then they would be infallible and inerrant men. These prophets and apostles sometimes made mistakes, and erred in thought and conduct. However when under the inspiration of the Holy Spirit, the inspired writings that were produced through them were inerrant and infallible because they had their origin in God Himself. Inspiration is usually limited to the original autographs, that is, the original written documents. However the doctrine of inspiration is closely connected with the doctrine of preservation. Indeed the four doctrines, reservation, inspiration, preservation and illumination are all very close in connection, and form a seamless train of thought.

On some occasions the human agent is totally unaware of this inspiration. Many other instances show that the prophets knew they were in the hands of God as they spoke and wrote the message of God. Whether aware or not, the God who created all things, people included, is capable of arranging things to suit His perfect intentions. Even the use of a godless prophet like Balaam or of a man bent on destroying the Saviour like Caiaphas is no obstacle to the infinite and omnipotent God. The revealed word of God is inspired – God breathed. Consequently it is indeed the word of God.

There have been a number of theories constructed to explain this idea of inspiration. We shall consider four views commonly held by theologians and will make some comments on each.

Four views.

Looking at inspiration from a theoretical point of view four views have been expressed, only one of which is truly Biblical. It will be worthwhile considering the three that have been expressed by unbelieving scholars, as well as the Biblical view, as the refutation of these false views will be of benefit to the believer. The four views are as follows:

[1] It is only a human book with no divine inspiration.
[2] It is partially inspired by God.
[3] It is only divine with no human component.
[4] It is at the same time divine and human, God having fully inspired the writings of the sacred authors who spoke and then wrote in His name.

[1] A human book.

It is almost a given that the vast majority of people in modern times will consider the inspired Scripture as a book of human construction only. The word "inspired" in this view is little more than being of an "extraordinary quality." If, for the sake of argument, we grant that this is so, then we must conclude that the Scriptures are the greatest book ever written. Nothing in the modern (or any other era for that matter) comes anywhere close to it in extent of use, in influence on culture, or in sublimity. What could account for this? It not only outstrips all other published literature, but having been written by a variety of people (40+) of differing cultures over 15 centuries it must thence be the most remarkable book ever to be known on earth. No collaboration, no anthology, and no work of man can surpass its greatness. Given the greatness of the Scriptures how can anyone consider it in an evolutionary way? Such a thought is preposterous. There is no development of thought from primitive to educated as may be the belief of evolutionary anthropology, rather we have the sublimest truths detailed from the very beginning.

Given these facts, how can we explain the contents from an earthly human point of view? Is it true, for example, to say that humans would have developed the concepts of love, forgiveness, mercy, sin, holiness and so on? How about the beauty and perfection of the Lord Jesus Christ? Is that possible from a human origin? Surely an artist who creates a personality could not create one who is so good and so obviously perfect? Then further consider this, would sinful human beings humble themselves to tell their story "like it is"? Wouldn't they dress it up and smooth over the uglier side of their lives? How do modern (or ancient) human biographies fair in comparison to the Bible's examination of the human heart? Do they reveal sin as ugly and offensive to a holy God, or do they cover things up, or put a good spin on character traits that are unwholesome and unsavoury?

The conclusion from all of this is that it really is impossible to consider the Bible as a human book and nothing else.

[2] A part-inspired book.

Since the Bible has had so much influence, and since it is clearly more than a book penned simply by human minds, many opt for a partially inspired view. There are four ways in which this idea is expressed:

> [a] Some say that inspiration pertains only to the author's thoughts not the words.
> [b] Others hold that some parts of the Bible may be divinely inspired, but some are of human origin.
> [c] The Bible "contains" but is "not" the word of God.
> [d] Only Christ is the "Word of God."

[a] Thoughts only inspired.

Some would suggest that whilst God expressed the idea, it was men who supplied the words. Taking a cue from expressions like those of Ezekiel in describing the vision of God, some hold that the mode of expression is a human touch.[134] Now in considering this suggestion we must immediately object because thoughts are always expressed by means of words. At the end of the day all communication is by means of words. At this some may object and ask, what of non-verbal

---

134   Ezekiel uses expressions such as "it was like," "the appearance was like" ...

communication? Well it is true that there is such a thing, but these types of communication are sophisticated shorthand body movements and so forth which were at one time explained in terms of words. And people only really understand them fully when they are explained in terms of words. You only have to consider the different cultural expressions of body movements to see this. The symbolic expressions and body language of a culture that is new to one have to be explained by means of words.

Turning to legal documents such as contracts and in cases where judgements are made, these must be given in precise terms using words which are clearly defined. The whole issue may depend upon a single word, so the correct one must be used. Now the apostle Paul informs us in 1Corinthians 2v13 that the revelation of God is given by means of "words" which the Spirit gives. If the words were the choice of man how then can we understand the concepts that God intends? In Genesis 1, for example, we have the words "let there be" followed by "and it was so." Are we to understand that whilst God enacted creation, it was men who chose these words "let there be" and "it was so"? Where does this leave us? Of course those who do not hold that God can really be known, make much of this for in their estimation the Bible is merely man's efforts art trying to grasp hold of God.

However we are entitled to ask the question, why make such a distinction? What advantage do we gain by this? Does it make it any easier for us to say that God inspired the ideas, or that He inspired the very words? Surely since He is God He could do either? In fact believing that God inspired only the ideas makes it very difficult for us because we then have no way of knowing whether the ideas that God inspired are correctly communicated to us by the words chosen by men. Then also we must enquire as to how we explain, using such a distinction between words and ideas, the following passages:

[i] Genesis 1 where the details of creation are recorded before man was created (e,g, "let there be ...").

[ii] The words of Psalm 22 (e.g. My God, My God why hast thou forsaken me?), and other Messianic prophecies.

[iii] Daniel's prophecy of future kingdoms in detail.

[iv] Speaking in tongues at Pentecost (unknown languages).

Rene Pache's conclusion on this notion that man supplied the words for God's concepts is worth repeating:

Mike Viccary   65 of 319

"Any who say that the thoughts are of God but the words only those of men begin at once to attribute to the words all kinds of contradictions, misunderstandings and mistakes. These supposed errors, therefore, are in the men's thoughts much more than in the words. We cannot separate the two, for a revelation of the thoughts of God always requires the inspiration of the Word of God."[135]

To continue we ought to consider again the story of Balaam in Numbers 22f. It cannot have been that God merely inspired him as to the thoughts, because his thoughts were antagonistic to God's will. Rather Balaam was constrained (by conscience) to speak only the words that God gave to him. Or what also of the instances where the writer passes on the word of God with no understanding of what he has passed on? How can this be explained using the concept that God inspires the thoughts not the words? Examples of this include the following:

[i] Daniel wrote about things that were to be sealed (Daniel 12v8,9).

[ii] Caiaphas prophesied without realising the import of his declaration (John 11v51).

[iii] The old prophet spoke without having either willed or anticipated what he spoke (1Kings 13v21).

In short, the idea that God inspired thoughts and man supplied the words doesn't make any sense. Thoughts can only be expressed by words, and it matters a great deal which words are chosen and how they are put together.

[b] Certain parts (spiritual & moral) only inspired.

Another way in which some limit inspiration is to make a distinction between the science, geography and history of a text, and the theology or matters concerning salvation. Some contend that the geography, science, and history of the Bible is merely what was accepted at the time and is therefore subject to correction and alteration by modern scholarly insights not given to the ancients. This is, of course, the height of pride, and, arises, in part, due to a belief in an evolutionary world view. Now, if we accept this view of the Bible, it would leave it open to the charge of double-mindedness. How can we accept a witness who speaks infallibly on some issues but with recklessness on other issues, (that are, incidentally, considered by modern thinkers to be more important)? Again making such a distinction between the salvation issues and the vehicles through which these are conveyed, (the science, history and geography), is impossible to sustain.

When we come to examine the details of Scripture then holding such a distinction simply

---

135   Rene Pache. "The Inspiration & Authority of Scripture." Moody Press 1969. P59,60.

cannot be maintained. The inspiration of much of the doctrine of the Bible (like the atonement for example), is, in fact locked up in the history of the nation of Israel. If the history is all wrong and uninspired, then what of the doctrine based on it? Furthermore, the Bible itself works on the principle that the details of the history are correct. Thus the Lord Jesus refers to historical events in the Old Testament, (e.g. creation, Adam and Eve (their marriage), Noah and Jonah in the belly of a large fish to name just a few). The Psalmist makes a great use of recounting the history for the purpose of illustrating great truths.[136] Jude speaks of Enoch being the seventh generation from Adam, and Stephen recounts the early history of Israel in his defence of the gospel.[137] Then also we note that Paul stated that the details of the Biblical history were written for our instruction.[138]

[c] The Bible "contains" the word of God.

Of all views of this type, this is the most pernicious. It is held by some that the Bible is a mixture of legend, myth, truth, inspired truth, and other content. We are left in a hopeless state because we would thence have no idea which parts are divinely inspired and which are not. Critics who follow this line have very harsh words to say about those of us who believe in a "book dropped from the sky" as they conceive of it. Apparently, according to Rene Pache, we espouse a "Biblical fetishism which, brushing away difficult problems, is well adapted to a primitive mentality."[139] Rudolf Bultmann attempted to remove all myths from the Bible to leave what he believed was the essential gospel. The following are some of the things Bultmann eliminated as being myth from the gospels:[140]

# The pre-existence of Christ.	# His return in glory.
# His virgin birth.	# The final judgement of the world.
# His deity.	# The existence of spirits, both good and evil.
# His miracles.	# The personality and power of the Holy Spirit.
# His substitutionary death on the cross.	# The doctrine of the Trinity.
# His resurrection and that of believers.	# Death as a result of sin.
# His ascension.	# The doctrine of original sin.

There is not much left!! Apparently Bultmann's knife was more exacting on the Old Testament. One

---

136   Psalm 78 is a classic example.
137   Jude 1v14; Acts 7v1f.
138   1Corinthians 10v4,6,11; Romans 15v4.
139   Rene Pache. "The Inspiration & Authority of Scripture." Moody Press 1969. P62.
140   As for footnote 139. P62,63.

wonders why he didn't go the whole hog and say that the whole Bible was myth? What Bultmann (and others like him) believed was that God spoke to the sacred writers, but then left them to their own devices to write what they received down. In this way embellishments, legend, myth and even downright error crept in. Clearly, as we have said before, there is no way we can discover truth from error. As a result of such ideas, the notion that the Bible *becomes* the word of God to us in our individual experience as God communicates to us has taken root. Consider such phrases: "what does that passage mean to you?" and "is that how you read it?" These and other expressions common today may have their root in Bultmann's theology.

Considering these erroneous views of inspiration, we must ask the question: By what means are we to decide which is the inspired part and which is not? Do we need another infallible standard to do this? We could ask on what basis Bultmann did his surgery? By what authority? If we are all to wield a knife to Scripture the end result will be a very subjective and personal result. Surely sinful men will chose which things to accept and which to cut out. The actor Ian Mackellan chose to cut out Old Testament passages condemning homosexuality. Was he wrong to do this? All of this, of course, means that we can never share our faith either by means of evangelism or in corporate worship. If we all have subjective choice, then we will all have gods made in our separate images. We will not thereby agree and we will not be able to form the church as conceived in Scripture! It also renders preaching useless, for what shall a man preach? If the Bible is infused with myth why should we invest so much time and effort into it? Why engage in mission? What of all those men who gave their lives (and who are giving up their lives now) because of the Bible and its faith?

[d] Christ alone is the "Word of God."

People who chose this line say that the Bible is merely an "echo" and that Christ alone is the word of God. However we may then be entitled to ask: Which Christ? Matthew's, Mark's, Luke's, John's, Paul's? Or is it Bultmann's Christ we believe is the word of God? How are we to establish whom Christ truly is?

In contrast to this vague notion, the Bible itself declares that it is the word of God, and it does so in multitudinous ways. For example in the Old Testament there are 3,808 occasions where we read the words; "the Lord saith," or "the word of God came saying," or "thus saith the Lord."[141] If we are left with the nebulous idea that Christ only is the word of God, we are back to asking the question, what is the standard by which we can judge truth from error, what is legitimate about Christ (the word) and what isn't?

141　Rene Pache. "The Inspiration & Authority of Scripture." Moody Press 1969. P64.

[3] A divine only book.

Otherwise known as "mechanical dictation," or "automatic writing," this idea has never been held by evangelical or reformed theologians. It has, however, been proffered as the view held by Bible believers, by those who do not understand either the Bible or God. It was invented as a caricature by opponents who could not grasp the evangelical view. To these people, either the Bible was mechanically dictated, or men had some part in it, in which case it could not be without error. [142] The question that arises if this mechanical dictation view is true is: why did God bother with human authors at all? People who follow this line say that it is the only way the text can be flawless, for a mechanical dictation by-passes the personality with all its defects and flaws.

Now it is unthinkable that God would obliterate, or by-pass, the personality of the writer. It would be a violation of their being human. The great wonder is that God chose to use humans to bring His word. This is a great comfort to us. He still chooses to use humans to spread His word. In fact we can readily discern the personality of a Jeremiah or of a Jonah. Indeed the Lord actually makes use of their personalities in the revelation/inspiration process. These people and part of their make-up were important in the conveying of the truths that they bought to us. Scholars make much (perhaps too much) of the style of Paul's, John's, and others' writing in the New Testament. But it is these differences which make the word of God so fascinating, for God inspired these differences as well as the words and phrases used.

A mechanical dictation view would probably have yielded a uniform type of revelation. However we have a diverse revelation made up of many different facets. This fact indicates that the Lord made use of the people through whom He chose to reveal. The mechanical dictation view is really a desperate one with a limited understanding of the power of God. He is not limited by our failures. He can so order things that His book, the Bible, was written completely infallibly and inerrantly through different people. The words were chosen by God and have their origin in Him. However the personality of the human author was in no way violated.

It is to be remembered that our Lord and Saviour has a human nature and a divine nature. The word of God also has its human part and its divine part. We would never conclude that our Lord Jesus Christ's humanity rendered Him less than divine. In the same way the human character of the Bible does not render the divine nature of Scripture redundant or substandard. Just as the humanity of Christ is sinless, so also the human element of Scripture – the inspired written words – are without error or fault. Only a high view of God will do. One in which we understand the fact that God is so powerful that He can order things without violating personalities or human wills. The

---

142   Rene Pache. "The Inspiration & Authority of Scripture." Moody Press 1969. P69.

words of Erich Sauer are worth repeating here:

> "Let us not be mistaken. We do not speak of a stiff, mechanical, dictated inspiration of the Word. This would be completely unworthy of a divine revelation. A mechanical inspiration [automatic dictation] is found in occultism, spiritism, and therefore demonism, where the evil inspiring spirit works by setting aside [substitution] and excluding the human individuality. Divine revelation, however, has nothing to do with such suppression of human personality. It will not sanction the annulling of the God-given laws of human consciousness, nor transforming the man into an automaton; it causes rather the intensifying and heightening than the excluding of the human faculties. "Light cannot produce darkness, but rather acuter sight". The divine revelation desires fellowship between the human spirit and the Divine Spirit. It seeks the sanctifying and transfiguring of the personality and setting it to serve. It desires not passive "mediums", but active men of God, not dead tools, but living, sanctified co-workers with God, not slaves, but friends (John 15v15). Therefore its inspiration is not mechanical but organic, not magical but divinely natural, not lifeless dictation but a living word wrought by the Spirit. Only so can God's word be man'd word and man's word God's word."[143]

[4] It is at the same time divine and human.

This is the view we are seeking to establish. The Scriptures have been inspired – God-breathed. God fully inspired the writings of the sacred authors who spoke and then wrote in His name. No personality was violated and all the words we read are the exact ones that God choose and organised. This view of Scripture accords with the doctrine of Christ who at one and the same time is fully human (100% sinless and pure) and wholly divine. The Scriptures are equally unblemished and have a human and divine flavour. In this case whilst each human through whom the Lord worked themselves were not sinless, the words that God inspired were 100% free from error and fault. No other idea of inspiration fits all the evidence and no other idea of inspiration satisfies the soul of man.

Inspiration is "plenary" and "verbal."

To begin this section it will be helpful to start with two statements made by different authors which affirm the ideas we wish to develop. Thus Frank Gaebelein has written about "plenary inspiration":

> The doctrine of plenary inspiration holds that the original documents of the Bible were written by men, who, though permitted the exercise of their own personalities and literary talents, yet wrote under the control and guidance of the Spirit of God, the result being in every word of the original documents a perfect and errorless recording of the exact message

---

143   Erich Sauer – quoted in: Rene Pache. "The Inspiration & Authority of Scripture." Moody Press 1969. P70.

which God desired to give to man.[144]

B. B. Warfield wrote that the church has always believed in "verbal inspiration," so that the very words of Scripture were those inspired of God:

> "The Church has held from the beginning that the Bible is the Word of God in such a sense that its words, though written by men and bearing indelibly impressed upon them the marks of their human origin, were written, nevertheless, under such an influence of the Holy Ghost as to be also the words of God, the adequate expression of His mind and will. It has always recognised that this conception of co-authorship implies that the Spirit's superintendence extends to the choice of the words by the human authors [verbal inspiration, but not a mechanical dictation] and preserves its product from everything inconsistent with a divine authorship - thus securing, among other things, that entire truthfulness which is everywhere presupposed in and asserted for Scripture by the Biblical writers [inerrancy]."[145]

The two terms "verbal inspiration" and "plenary inspiration" are terms which sum up the extent and sweep of the idea of inspiration. The term "plenary" is used to signify that inspiration is entire and without restriction of any kind. Thus the inspiration of the Scriptures includes the whole, and every individual part of it. Furthermore we must add that the written revelation is complete and none can add to it or take from it.[146] By the term "verbal" we mean to refer to the words. Not only does inspiration cover the entire Bible and all its parts, but also it goes so far as to include the individual words themselves, (verbum = word). Words are inseparable from the message. Consider a message passed on by word of mouth ("Chinese whispers"). Confusion results as words are altered. Consider, on the other hand, a royal messenger delivering a message for his monarch. Who would dare to change or alter the message? Surely the messenger would be careful to preserve the message as received? Erich Sauer puts it well:

> "We believe in full inspiration because of the inner connection of thought and word. For the unmistakable expressing of thought there is necessary a careful choice of corresponding words ... The thinking of man arises from indistinct notions, sensations, and conceptions. But this does not contradict the fact that everything spiritual, if it is to attain to clear unfolding of a real thought or "idea" reveals itself in words. A thought only becomes properly a conscious thought if out of the subconscious realm of sensation and the indeterminate impression of will and feeling a word is born ... The word may be regarded as the body of the thought, giving the spirit "visibility" and form. Therefore if the word is blurred, the thought is blurred; and all becomes foggy and indistinct."[147]

---

144   Frank Gaebelein. As quoted by Rene Pache. "The Inspiration & Authority of Scripture." Moody Press 1969. P71.
145   B. B Warfield. As quoted by Rene Pache. "The Inspiration & Authority of Scripture." Moody Press 1969. P71.
146   Revelation 22v18-19.
147   Quoted in Rene Pache. "The Inspiration & Authority of Scripture." Moody Press 1969. P75.

As Luther remarks, "Christ did not say that His thoughts were spirit and life but that His words were."[148] Jeremiah testifies that what was given to him were the *words*.[149] In Ezekiel we find that the Lord would open the prophet's "mouth" not his "mind" or "thought."[150] Paul states that the Holy Spirit taught His spokesmen a spiritual language the words of which transmit the supernatural message, the thought of Christ.[151]

We come now to some examples where New Testament writers use Old Testament quotes and base their arguments on a single word. For example, it is worth considering the occasion when the Lord Jesus refuted the Sadducees on the resurrection. He quotes Exodus 3v6 and the main point He makes is that God is the "I am" or the living God of living people. It is "I *am* the God of ..." and not "I *was* or *will be* the God of ..."[152] In a second example we have the Lord questioning the Pharisees on the nature of the Messiah. The Lord refers to Psalm 110v1 and asks:

If David then calls Him 'Lord,' how is He his Son?" (Matthew 22v45).

The key point is the use of the word "Lord." In John chapter 8 the Lord makes use of the title that God gave to Moses, ("I am"). In doing so the Pharisees took up stones to kill the Lord but failed.[153] Once again we note that our Lord makes use of this phrase "I am" which is definite. Can you imagine if the words were not inspired and were altered somehow? This use of the Old Testament shows the need for a verbal inspiration. Perhaps the most impressive use of an Old Testament reference which indicates the need for a verbal inspiration is found in Paul's reference to Genesis 12v7:

Now to Abraham and his Seed were the promises made. He does not say, "And to seeds," as of many, but as of one, "And to your Seed," who is Christ. (Galatians 3v16).

Paul argues that the Genesis 12v7 use of the word "seed" is vital for our understanding as this indicates not descendants in a general sense but one specific descendant, namely Christ. In Hebrews 1v5 we have a direct quote from Psalm 2v7. If inspiration is not verbal (words inspired) how then can we make sense of such a use? A study of the way the writer of the letter to the Hebrews uses the Old Testament is well worth embarking upon, but we shall content ourselves with looking at a few other examples that show inspiration as verbal. A particularly important example comes in Numbers

---

148   John 6v63.
149   Jeremiah 1v7,9; 15v9; 26v2; 36v2.   -
150   Ezekiel 2v9-3v3; 3v27
151   1Corinthians 2v13,16.
152   Matthew 22v31.
153   John 8v58; Exodus 3v14.

where we read of the prophet Balaam and his testimony. Even though he wanted to alter what God had revealed so that he could reap the financial rewards offered by Balak king of Moab, he simply couldn't do it!

> *And Balaam said to Balak, "Look, I have come to you! Now, have I any power at all to say anything? The word that God puts in my mouth, that I must speak." (Numbers 22v38).*

> *So he answered and said, "Must I not take heed to speak what the Lord has put in my mouth?" (Numbers 23v12).*

> *Then the Lord met Balaam, and put a word in his mouth, and said, "Go back to Balak, and thus you shall speak." (Numbers 23v16).*

We could also look at the commissioning of the prophets Moses and Jeremiah. In both cases the Lord reminds the prophet that it was He who made the mouth and so would be with the prophet as he prophesied:

> *Then Moses said to the Lord, "O my Lord, I am not eloquent, neither before nor since You have spoken to Your servant; but I am slow of speech and slow of tongue." So the Lord said to him, "Who has made man's mouth? Or who makes the mute, the deaf, the seeing, or the blind? Have not I, the Lord? Now therefore, go, and I will be with your mouth and teach you what you shall say." (Exodus 4v10-12).*

> *Then said I: "Ah, Lord God! Behold, I cannot speak, for I am a youth." But the Lord said to me: "Do not say, 'I am a youth,' For you shall go to all to whom I send you, And whatever I command you, you shall speak. Do not be afraid of their faces, For I am with you to deliver you," says the Lord. Then the Lord put forth His hand and touched my mouth, and the Lord said to me: "Behold, I have put My words in your mouth. (Jeremiah 1v6-9).*

In thinking of the importance of the words of inspiration we should record David's words of testimony concerning how the Lord spoke through him:

> *Now these are the last words of David. Thus says David the son of Jesse; thus says the man raised up on high, the anointed of the God of Jacob, and the sweet psalmist of Israel: "The Spirit of the Lord spoke by me, and His word was on my tongue. (2Samuel 23v1,2).*

David tells us that it was God's very word that was on David's tongue.

That a message can only be conveyed accurately if the very words originally inspired are the ones intended can be shown by looking at Scripture and its intent. For example, in John 5v24 and 1John 5v13 we are told specifically about the important parts concerning salvation:

> *Most assuredly, I say to you, he who hears My word and believes in Him who sent Me has everlasting life, and shall not come into judgement, but has passed from death into life. (John 5v24).*

> *These things I have written to you who believe in the name of the Son of God, that you may know that you have eternal life, and that you may continue to believe in the name of the Son of God. (1John 5v13).*

It is only the one who hears Christ's words and believes in Him sent of the Father who will have everlasting life. A true trust in the Son of God alone and which continues is necessary for the assurance of salvation. It is very difficult to imagine what could be changed here (i.e. what words could be altered) without dramatically affecting the meaning. We conclude by stating that thoughts without words are as meaningless as a tune without notes or a sum without numbers.

Proof & demonstration.

The message of the Bible has had its saving effects throughout the generations. People who have been born again through its message in the different centuries can warm to the same thoughts and beliefs as we do today. These thoughts, which are truly wonderful, are clear evidence of the divine inspiration of the Bible. What other book can compare? Furthermore, the actual contents of Scripture attest to its divine origin. Who else would be as honest about the nature of sin? Who else could give us the truth, or could reveal the wonders of Christ? Who, other than God Himself, could give us such a unified consistent testimony to the truth?

Arguments for the Old Testament:

The phrase "thus says the Lord" occurs 2,000 times.[154] If we include other similar phrases such as "the word of the Lord" this would bring the total to 3,808 occurrences.[155] One other thing to take into account is the way in which utterances produced by the Old Testament writers are introduced into the New Testament. For example, Matthew refers to what was written in the Old Testament by saying:

> *So all this was done that it might be fulfilled which was spoken by the Lord through the prophet, saying. (Matthew 1v22).*

Notice that it was not the prophet, but the *Lord* through the prophet who spoke. The same idea is

---

154   James M. Gray. "The Inspiration of the Bible – Definition, Extent and Proof." PP 137-170. Chapter 14 of The Fundamentals. Edited by R. A. Torrey. Kregel Publications. Grand Rapids, USA. 1990
155   Rene Pache. "The Inspiration & Authority of Scripture." Moody Press 1969. P65.

expressed by Peter in Acts 1, and by Paul in Acts 28 where words are quoted from the Psalms and from Isaiah as coming from the Holy Spirit.[156] Then also in Hebrews chapter 3, the writer states that it was the Holy Spirit who uttered the words which are found in Psalm 95.[157]

Its is instructive to consider also how Christ thought about the Old Testament. We read, for example, that our Lord made quite clear that "the Scripture cannot be broken," and further that He came "not to destroy but to fulfil the law and the prophets."[158] On other occasions we note that He fully endorsed the historicity of such characters as Adam, Noah, Jonah and so on, and accepted all Scripture as authoritative.

We have already considered the teaching of the apostles on the subject of Old Testament inspiration when we looked at 2Timothy 3v16 and 2Peter 1v21 and so will not repeat this again. It is enough to know that the apostles were under the impression that it was indeed God the Holy Spirit who was responsible for the Scriptures. In Deuteronomy 31v9 and 2Kings 17v36,37 we read that it was Moses who wrote the law:

> *So Moses wrote this law and delivered it to the priests, the sons of Levi, who bore the ark of the covenant of the Lord, and to all the elders of Israel. (Deuteronomy 31v9).*

> *but the Lord, who brought you up from the land of Egypt with great power and an outstretched arm, Him you shall fear, Him you shall worship, and to Him you shall offer sacrifice. And the statutes, the ordinances, the law, and the commandment which He wrote for you, you shall be careful to observe forever; you shall not fear other gods. (2Kings 17v36,37).*

However in Hosea 8v12 we find that the law was written by the Lord:

> *I have written for him the great things of My law, but they were considered a strange thing. (Hosea 8v12).*

There is no contradiction, of course, because the Lord is the infinite sovereign Lord whose actions cannot be thwarted. When men determine to do anything their wills are always in God's hand.

Arguments for the New Testament:

When it comes to the New Testament we must consider how wonderfully the New Testament connects with the Old Testament. For example, the New Testament sometimes explains

---

156   Acts 1v16,20 & Psalm 69v25; 109v8. Acts 28v25-27 & Isaiah 6v9,10.
157   Hebrews 3v7 & Psalm 95v7.
158   John 10v35; Matthew 5v17.

the Old Testament. Matthew tells us that the events he is recounting concerning Christ's birth make sense of what had been prophesied in the Old Testament.[159] Sometimes the New Testament repeals ordinances that the Old Testament established.[160] This unity of the New Testament with the Old Testament, coupled with the fact that the New Testament explains, expounds and gives meaning to much in the Old Testament, is a good proof of the New Testament's inspiration. In Hebrews 1v1f, we have a declaration that the New Testament is the word spoken in the *language* of the Son which is to be more earnestly heeded than Old Testament truth revealed by mediation of angels.[161] The New Testament is the latter and greater revelation, so since the Old Testament is inspired it follows naturally that the New Testament must be inspired as well. In Hebrews 2v1f we are further taught of the superiority of the New Testament because we ought to give more earnest heed to what we have received.

The New Testament writers were prophets.[162] But it is clear that apostles were above prophets in station and authority due to the fact that they are always mentioned first when mentioned along with prophets.[163] The greater authority of the apostles is further shown by the following thoughts. First they had a greater and higher mission since they were sent forth directly by the Lord Jesus as He had been sent by the Father.[164] Second, they were commissioned to go not just to a single nation (Israel) but to all the world.[165] Third, we read that they received the keys to the kingdom of heaven.[166] Finally they will be greatly rewarded in the regeneration when Christ returns to judge the living and the dead.[167] As a result the authority with which the apostles wrote is higher than that of the Old Testament. Hence the New Testament must also be inspired. In some cases the writers claim divine inspiration. For example James uses these words: "it seemed good to the Holy Spirit, and to us, to lay upon you no greater burden than these necessary things" by which we see that the words James writes were those the Holy Spirit agreed with.[168] In 1Corinthians chapter 2 Paul writes that the words he uses were ones taught by the Holy Spirit.[169] Paul also taught in first Thessalonians that when the people received the word of God from Paul, they accepted his words as the very words of God.[170] Peter writes in such a way as to place his own words on a par

---

159   Matthew 1v22,23. See also Acts 13v19-39 where Paul describes fulfilment of Old Testament prophecies in explanatory detail.
160   Galatians 5v6.
161   Hebrews 2v1f.
162   Romans 16v25-27; Ephesians 3v4,5.
163   1Corinthians 12v28; Ephesians 2v20; 4v11.
164   John 20v21.
165   Matthew 28v19.
166   Matthew 16v19.
167   Matthew 19v28.
168   Acts 15v23-29.
169   1Corinthians 2v13.
170   1Thessalonians 2v13.

with those of the Old Testament prophets:

> ... *that you may be mindful of the words which were spoken before by the holy prophets, and of the commandment of us, the apostles of the Lord and Saviour. (2Peter 3v2).*

How God speaks.

God has spoken through the prophets and apostles of old. Now this speaking most often starts with a decisive meeting with God but not always. Thus, for example, we have the commissioning of Moses, Samuel, Isaiah, Jeremiah, and Ezekiel, as prime examples.[171] These events clearly indicate that it was God who took the initiative and who prepared His instruments for the purpose He had for them.

Inspiration was a sovereign work of God This amounts to saying that these people could not say when they were going to speak God's word. There were intervals of time between prophecies issued. If you look at the life of Abraham, you will find that he received the word of God on rare occasions, with large chunks of time in which he received no word from God. Or consider the dates and times when the word of the Lord was given to Jeremiah:

> In the thirteenth year of Josiah's reign.[172]
>
> On the occasion of the drought during the reign of Josiah.[173]
>
> In the fourth year of Jehoiakim.[174]
>
> At the beginning of the reign of Jehoiakim.[175]
>
> At the beginning of the reign of Zedekiah.[176]
>
> After the attack of Nebuchadnezzar.[177]
>
> In the prison court.[178]

Or take, as another example, the prophet Habakuk who waited to hear what the Lord would say.[179]

As a general rule any prophet receiving revelation retained complete lucidity. This can be demonstrated by the fact that the sacred writers entered into dialogue with the Lord whilst being

---

171   Exodus 4v11-16; 1Samuel 3; Isaiah 6v1-9; Jeremiah 1v4-9; Ezekiel 2v3-3v11.
172   Jeremiah 1v2.
173   Jeremiah 14v1.
174   Jeremiah 25v1.
175   Jeremiah 26v1.
176   Jeremiah 28v11
177   Jeremiah 34v1.
178   Jeremiah 39v15.
179   Habakuk 2v1-2.

inspired.[180] Daniel was terror stricken at his visions but the explanations were given him immediately unless he was given the order to seal the message for the time being.[181]

One of the most compelling reasons to believe in inspiration is that the message received surpassed the comprehension of the prophet. This is illustrated by Daniel being told to seal the message received.[182] He also declared that whilst he heard what was revealed, he did not understand.[183] In the New Testament we find that God's hidden wisdom "entered not into the heart of man."[184] The prophets realised that their messages were to be fulfilled a long while off and that they in fact served future generations. They longed to know more about what was revealed to them.[185] Our Lord taught that what was revealed to the disciples was something far and away above and greater than what had been revealed up to that time, things which the prophets longed to see:

> *Then He turned to His disciples and said privately, "Blessed are the eyes which see the things you see; for I tell you that many prophets and kings have desired to see what you see, and have not seen it, and to hear what you hear, and have not heard it." (Luke 10v23,24).*

Then further we must ask the question: did the Psalmists (David included) understand the messianic character of all their writings? They may have understood some, but certainly not all, and especially not all the detail. Or what also of the types? Were the Old Testament writers aware of the fact that they or their particular actions were intended to typify some aspect of Christ or His work? It may be true of Abraham's offering of Isaac, but it is unlikely that Hagar and Sarah would have known of their significance.[186] All of the above thoughts demonstrate that whilst the human agent plays a part in the transmission of the message, the Lord God has greater plans in view.

Inspiration was given at times in a wholly compulsive way. Jeremiah tried to resist the inspiration imposed on him by the Lord at one time and it became in him a burning fire.[187] Balaam could not prevent God's message getting through him.[188] In Peter we read that it is not by the will of man that prophecy comes.[189] It is to be remembered that the personality of these men were in no way violated by this compulsion. Think also about the apostle Paul's being constrained to preach the gospel.[190]

---

180   Isaiah 6v11; Jeremiah 14v13; 15v15; Ezekiel 9v8; 11v13.
181   Daniel 7v15-16,19,28; 8v15-16,26; 12v4,9.
182   Daniel 8v26; 9v24; 12v9.
183   Daniel 12v8,9.
184   1Corinthians 2v9.
185   1Peter 1v10-12.
186   Galatians 4v22-26.
187   Jeremiah 20v7-9.
188   Numbers 22v35; 24v13.
189   2Peter 1v21.
190   1Corinthians 9v16.

At times the author did not even suspect the divine action brought to bear on him. When Luke gathered together all the documents he had and the eyewitness accounts he had collated to write his books, he was most surely unaware that this was at the hand of the Holy Spirit. We can make this remark also for other historical books such as Chronicles and Genesis. Prophetic inspiration could lay hold on a man:

> Without his anticipation of it – the old prophet.[191]
>
> Without his knowledge of it – Caiaphas.[192]
>
> Without his desire for it – Balaam.[193]
>
> Without his comprehension of it – Daniel.[194]

In essence divine inspiration knows no degrees. It is always perfect and complete:

> "Illumination is susceptible of degrees; inspiration does not admit of them. A prophet is more or less enlightened by God; but what he says is not more or less inspired. It is so, or it is not so; it is from God, or it is not from God; here there is neither measure nor degree, neither increase nor diminution. David was enlightened by God; John the Baptist more than David; a simple Christian possibly more than John the Baptist; an apostle was more enlightened than that Christian, and Jesus Christ more than that apostle. But the inspired word of David, what do I say? the inspired word of Balaam himself is that of God, as was that of John the Baptist, as was that of St. Paul, as was that of Jesus Christ! It is the Word of God."[195]

The prophets fully believed that they were transmitting the very words of God. Moses repeats over 50 times in the book of Leviticus such expressions as "the Lord called unto Moses" or "the Lord spoke unto Moses."[196] David cried out that the Spirit of the Lord spoke by him.[197] Jeremiah constantly used expressions like: "the word of the Lord came unto me."[198] Paul declares that his word, his message, was the word of God which they rightly received as the word of God.[199] John starts his last book by referring to it as the "revelation of Jesus Christ" and he refers to himself as one who bares "witness of the word of God."[200] He also said that what he wrote was what the Spirit

---

191   1Kings 13v20.
192   John 11v51.
193   Numbers 23 & 24.
194   Daniel 12v8,9.
195   Louis Gaussen. as quoted in Rene Pache. "The Inspiration & Authority of Scripture." Moody Press 1969. PP55-56.
196   For example, Leviticus 1v1; 4v1; 5v14; 6v1 etc.
197   2Samuel 23v2.
198   Jeremiah 1v4,11,13; 2v1 etc.
199   1Thessalonians 2v13.
200   Revelation 1v1,2.

declared unto the churches.[201]

Finally we might mention that the Bible is referred to within its own pages in a great variety of ways. Here are some of the following designations of the Scriptures:

> The oracles of God.[202]
> The Word of God.[203]
> The Word of the Lord.[204]
> The Word of life.[205]
> The Word of Christ.[206]
> The Word of truth.[207]
> The Word of faith.[208]

Notice, importantly, that in not one instance do we have a designation such as the "thoughts" of God or the "ideas" of God.

The effects of the word of God.

A final proof that the Bible is inspired is the effects it has. We shall look at this theme elsewhere, but for now we must ask the question: what other book could be so successful? We find that the Scriptures will impart spiritual life and save the soul:

> *Of His own will He brought us forth by the word of truth, that we might be a kind of first fruits of His creatures. (James 1v18).*

> *Therefore lay aside all filthiness and overflow of wickedness, and receive with meekness the implanted word, which is able to save your souls. (James 1v21).*

> *having been born again, not of corruptible seed but incorruptible, through the word of God which lives and abides forever. (1Peter 1v23).*

The Scriptures have cleansing power:

> *How can a young man cleanse his way? By taking heed according to Your word. (Psalm 119v9).*

---

201   Revelation 1v1-2; 2v18,29; 19v9.
202   Romans 3v2.
203   Luke 8v11.
204   Acts 13v48.
205   Philippians 2v16.
206   Colossians 3v16.
207   Ephesians 1v13.
208   Romans 10v8.

You are already clean because of the word which I have spoken to you. (John 15v3).

... that He might sanctify and cleanse her with the washing of water by the word. (Ephesians 5v26).

The Scriptures can keep us from evil:

Concerning the works of men, by the word of Your lips, I have kept away from the paths of the destroyer. (Psalm 17v4).

Your word I have hidden in my heart, that I might not sin against You. (Psalm 119v11).

I have given them Your word; and the world has hated them because they are not of the world, just as I am not of the world. ... Sanctify them by Your truth. Your word is truth. (John 17v14,17).

We shall look more closely at these Scriptures and others in a later chapter.

Inerrancy and infallibility.

The common term for referring to Scripture as being without error is "inerrancy." Some have tried to argue for a limited view of inerrancy and have suggested the term "infallibility" instead, by which they mean that Scripture does not *teach* error although it may *contain* errors. It is the author's belief and contention that Scripture is inerrant and infallible. The God who revealed Himself (and continues to do so) through His word cannot lie. It is unthinkable that the God who created all things would stumble to reveal perfectly all that He intended. Given that God is holy and true, it stands to reason that the words He gives must also be of the same nature, that is, holy and true. How then can there be any errors? We will see in the next chapter that there may be copyist errors amongst the manuscripts, but this does not mean that when the majority of manuscripts are examined the resulting text contains errors. The slips of the pen, spelling mistakes and other minor errors are easily corrected and have no bearing on this doctrine that Scripture is inerrant. Inerrancy depends on inspiration, for the words we have in our hands are those which God breathed-out.

We have already covered a number of Scriptures which teach without doubt that Scripture is without error. We shall not examine these in detail again but must mention a few in passing. Thus we have learnt that God's word is **totally** or completely pure from error, and that the word of God is settled in heaven where nothing impure can reside.[209] We have learnt from Christ's words that not the smallest part of the law will fail or be overlooked, and that Scripture cannot be broken.[210] We

---

209   Psalm 12v6; Proverbs 30v5,6; Psalm 119v89.
210   Matthew 5v18; John 10v35.

have studied the truth that Scripture has come directly from God by means of the inspiration of the Holy Spirit, and we have been warned against adding to, or taking from God's word.[211] Given these, and many other Scriptures, we shall make the assumption that Scripture is indeed wholly error free and consequently cannot teach any false notions. Having stated this I am well aware that the Bible has been used by countless folk to teach error. This is not, of course, the same thing. The apostle Paul went to great lengths to teach both the holiness and perfection of the law even though it was weak and could not bring anyone through to salvation. The law was good, holy and true.[212] Men, on the other hand, were weak and foolish so that even with a good and perfect law, they still could not come to a knowledge of God. Then furthermore, people may often twist Scripture to suit their own ends.[213]

If Scripture has errors what then?

We must begin our thoughts by considering the implications of a Scripture that has errors. The nineteenth century obsession with higher criticism led to the Bible being considered to be a human book rather than divinely inspired. As such the Bible was sliced and diced and examined from every angle just as any other work by men. For example, because it was believed from archaeology and other disciplines that human writing was not supposed to have come about until some time after Moses, it was concluded that Moses could not have written by the Pentateuch. The first five books were then considered to have been written much later during the exile and by different writers. Amongst other developments there was a move to discount the miracles and supernatural elements. Some went as far as demythologising the Bible by removing what were considered to be incredulous parts. Now such departures from an inspired text led rapidly towards a liberal approach.

Now these departures were not without objection and there were many who held to the truth writing in defence of the faith once delivered to the saints. As time progressed the tendency was always towards drifting from the truth towards a human view of things, and so liberalism was born and grew.

There are a variety of what we shall call "liberal" views of Scripture. First there are the true and historical liberals who hold that Scripture is a human book, which contains the attempts of men to grapple with what may be true. At the other end of the spectrum there are those who want to be known as solid Bible believing folk but who struggle with rejection from the academic world. As a

---

211   2Timothy 3v16,17; 2Peter 1v20,21; Deuteronomy 4v2; Revelation 22v18,19.
212   Romans 7v12.
213   2Peter 3v16.

consequence the idea of inerrancy is often rejected. These folk often want to hold all the truths espoused by evangelicals but who suggest that the historical, geographical, and scientific elements may or may not be true.

So what then are the implications and consequences of holding to a liberal view that Scripture contains error, whether they be merely those of science, history or geography, or those errors of doctrine and teaching (as expressed by the true liberals)? Whatever shade of liberalism that is held to, the great problem is how we understand what may be an error. This is the great problem with liberalism. How exactly do we look at Scripture and make judgements about its veracity or otherwise? If we are going to say that certain aspects of Scripture are untrue, by what standard or measure are we making these decisions? Essentially we have to have some standard or measure by which we make our judgements. This is the liberal and new evangelical way. For this present writer these approaches are hopeless. Which values and set of intelligent rules are to be used? Essentially we must use some man-made guides to govern our understanding and appreciation of the Scriptures. A man-made approach suffers from the severe limitations that man has, namely his limited capacity for thought, his limited experience, and, not least, his sinful nature and depravity.

The standard.

A standard is something by which other things are measured. In the world of modern science there are a number of standard measures such as the metre and the kilogram, for example. The standard kilogram by which all others were measured was a platinum-iridium cylinder held at the International Bureau of Weights and Measures laboratory at Sèvres, France. To ensure that weights and measures are accurate these must be calibrated against the standard in France. For mankind the Scriptures speak of another standard which operates not only as that by which all must be measured, but also stands as a conspicuous rallying point.

The first time we come across this concept is in Exodus after the Lord (with the Israelites) defeated the Amalekites. We read:

And Moses built an altar and called its name, The-Lord-Is-My-Banner. (Exodus 17v15).

Since this is the first time we come across the concept it becomes a defining point. The Hebrew word signifies something which is easily seen or conspicuous, and something lifted up which gives warning. But the banner or standard which becomes a focus is not an object, but the Lord Himself! The next occasion where this same Hebrew word is used occurs in a very significant Scripture which is also commented on by the Lord Jesus. I am referring to the incident in which the people were bitten by fiery serpents because of their complaints against the Lord.

> *Then the Lord said to Moses, "Make a fiery serpent, and set it on a pole; and it shall be that everyone who is bitten, when he looks at it, shall live." So Moses made a bronze serpent, and put it on a pole; and so it was, if a serpent had bitten anyone, when he looked at the bronze serpent, he lived. (Numbers 21v8,9).*

The word "pole" is an English translation of the same Hebrew word translated as "standard" or "banner" elsewhere. Our Lord pointed to this incident as a reference to His impending sacrifice on the cross:

> *No one has ascended to heaven but He who came down from heaven, that is, the Son of Man who is in heaven. And as Moses lifted up the serpent in the wilderness, even so must the Son of Man be lifted up, that whoever believes in Him should not perish but have eternal life. (John 3v13-15).*

Thus it is the Lord who is our banner, and it is the Lord lifted on the cross who acts as our Saviour! In Psalm 60 we have another instance where the same Hebrew word can be found:

> *You have given a banner to those who fear You, that it may be displayed because of the truth. (Psalm 60v4).*

This banner is given to those who fear the Lord, and is one that must be displayed declaring the truth.

A different Hebrew word is used to represent the military standard used by each of the different tribes.[214] However this word is used in Song of Solomon and in Psalm 20 where it is rendered "banners" in the NKJV:

> *We will rejoice in your salvation, and in the name of our God we will set up our banners! May the Lord fulfil all your petitions. (Psalm 20v5).*
>
> *He brought me to the banqueting house, and his banner over me was love. (Song of Solomon 2v4).*
> *O my love, you are as beautiful as Tirzah, lovely as Jerusalem, awesome as an army with banners! (Song of Solomon 6v4).*
>
> *Who is she who looks forth as the morning, fair as the moon, clear as the sun, awesome as an army with banners? (Song of Solomon 6v10).*

---

214   Numbers 1v52; 2v2,3,10,17,18,25,31,34; 10v14,18,22,25.

Although the Hebrew word is different, the same idea of conspicuousness, or an easily observable rallying point, is being expressed. In the case of a military banner it also signified the unity and identity of the tribe. In the examples we have referred to (Psalm 20 and Song of Solomon), there seems to be a combination of the concept of a military insignia and the idea of an elevated point of rescue. Consider as just one example of this Song of Solomon 2v4 where we read: "his banner over me was love."

We read a lot about the standard, or banner, in the book of Isaiah. With the exception of Isaiah 59v19, all other instances where the word "standard" or "banner" is found are translations of the Hebrew word *nes* which means "something to be lifted up" or "a token to be seen from afar off," hence a banner or a standard. At Isaiah 59v19 the Hebrew word is *nuws* and means "to flee," "to escape," or "to take flight." Modern translations opt for a rendering which speaks of the Lord's breath or Spirit coming in against the Gentile nations, such as the NASB, for example:

> *So they will fear the name of the Lord from the west and His glory from the rising of the sun, for He will come like a rushing stream which the wind of the Lord drives. (Isaiah 59v19, NASB).*

The old KJAV and the NKJV opt for using the term "standard" to continue this theme found throughout the prophet's work. Thus even though the Hebrew term means "flee" the older translators suggest that the idea of a standard being raised against the enemies to cause them to flee is the proper intention. Perhaps the similar sound of the word triggered this thought in the translators minds? The Spirit of the Lord will cause the coastlands to flee by raising a standard against them.

The other places in Isaiah where this word "standard," or "banner," is found tell a wonderful story. We shall consider just a few of these references. Amazingly we begin with the banner raised to call all nations to rally against the woeful people of God who had departed from Him and His ways. In this first verse we can see the banner as a rallying point to bring justice to bear against the nation of Judah who had failed.

> *He will lift up a banner to the nations from afar, and will whistle to them from the end of the earth; surely they shall come with speed, swiftly. (Isaiah 5v26)*

Then next, we find again the idea of the banner as a person. In this verse we have the promised Messiah referred to as "a Root of Jesse" who will also be for the Gentiles!:

And in that day there shall be a Root of Jesse, who shall stand as a banner to the people; for the Gentiles shall seek Him, and His resting place shall be glorious. (Isaiah 11v10).

This banner is also for all nations as a rallying point which will include the "outcasts" of Israel and Judah:

He will set up a banner for the nations, and will assemble the outcasts of Israel, and gather together the dispersed of Judah from the four corners of the earth. (Isaiah 11v12).

In chapter 13 we have the banner as the standard by which the mighty sanctified ones will come and judge the godless nation of Babylon, which represents the world:

Lift up a banner on the high mountain, raise your voice to them; wave your hand, that they may enter the gates of the nobles. (Isaiah 13v2).

This banner is not one to be seen by a few, but by all the world's inhabitants. It stands both for judgement:

All inhabitants of the world and dwellers on the earth: when he lifts up a banner on the mountains, you see it; and when he blows a trumpet, you hear it. (Isaiah 18v3).

but also for salvation:

Go through, Go through the gates! Prepare the way for the people; build up, build up the highway! Take out the stones, lift up a banner for the peoples! (Isaiah 62v10).

And so we have **the** standard, which is a person (the Root of Jesse), who will be lifted up for all to see. The standard indicates and represents both judgement and salvation. Thus what we are being drawn towards is the gospel, namely, Christ Jesus our Lord, crucified, risen and ascended![215]

---

215   Romans 1v1-3.

Chapter 3.

The doctrine of Preservation.

Introduction.

God has given us His word. He has done this by revealing to us that which we could never discover, particularly those details which help us find our way back to Him. He did this by means of inspiration, that is, through holy men who were moved and carried along by the Spirit of God, so that what these holy men wrote was none other than that which God wanted all to read and hear. Consequently the Scriptures are the revealed will and word inspired, (or breathed out), by God. These thoughts are limited to the first writings of each of the prophets and apostles, commonly called the "autographs." The revelation of God by inspiration occurred over a period of time spanning the first 4,000 years of earth history from the records found in Genesis through to the book of Revelation given to the apostle John. This revelation did not occur continuously through this period but at specific times. The Pentateuch, excluding Genesis, came through Moses at about 1440 BC, whilst other Old Testament writings were given between this date and up to about 400 BC. The New Testament was given in the first century AD. But in all cases, what was given of God was the written word inscribed in the ancient forms and styles. These included tablet, papyrus, parchment and inscriptions on pottery and stone. Such records were kept and treasured by priests and believers as the very word of the living God. However none of the original records (autographs) have survived to our day. Each original was copied and passed down through the ages for successive generations to read and profit by. Now, some 2,000 years after the time of Christ's earthly stay, we have copies of copies of copies of these original writings which were inspired of God. That being said, the original words as revealed by the Lord are still with us today because of God's singular care over what He wanted all people to know and hear. This is the doctrine of preservation. How this has occurred is a remarkable story and in what follows we shall pay particular attention to a consideration of the New Testament.

Before we begin, however, a word of caution must be issued. There are many who have argued for a particular view of the doctrine of preservation but have expressed this with such vitriol and hate that they do serious dishonour to the cause of Christ. Favouring a particular version or stream of thought may have a firm basis in the data and may be theologically sound, but we must not engage in attacks and slanderous name-calling. I am reminded of the apostle Paul's words to Timothy which I always remember from the NASB:

> *But the goal of our instruction is love from a pure heart and a good conscience and a sincere faith. (1Timothy 1v5 NASB).*[216]

We aim at love. That is, love for God supremely and as a consequence of this love, a love for our fellow man. Without the latter the former is suspect at best. This love issues not from the natural man but from a redeemed heart which is born again of the Spirit of God. Paul stresses a threefold identity for the disciple:

a pure heart.

a good conscience.

a sincere faith.

And so we are seeking *truth* that we might love our great, glorious, good and gracious God all the more, and in so doing, we might increasingly reflect His character for a dying world.[217] With these thoughts in mind we shall approach the subject under the following six headings:

[1] A tour through the Biblical evidence on preservation.

[2] The manuscript evidence we have.

[3] Two critical views.

    [a] James White, the critical text and an historical approach.

    [b] The critical view of Kurt and Barbara Aland.

[4] A caution on academia and a plea for Biblical scholarship.

[5] Biblical considerations.

[6] Conclusions.

---

216   Scripture readings will be normally taken from the NKJV unless otherwise stated.
217   Psalm 145.

[1] A tour through the Biblical evidence on preservation.

The doctrine of inspiration is grounded upon two vital Scriptures, namely, 2Timothy 3v16 and 2Peter 1v20,21. However there are numerous passages throughout the Scriptures which can only be understood with a doctrine of inspiration in place as displayed by these verses. For example, all of the places where we read "thus says the Lord," imply the doctrine of inspiration as outlined in Paul and Peter's statements. The doctrine of preservation is also a logical follow on from the doctrine of inspiration. If we had no Biblical data indicating the truth of this teaching, (preservation), we would still hold to it, for a doctrine of inspiration without the necessary follow-on of preservation would result in nonsense. Of what purpose, we must ask, is an inerrant and infallible word revealed by inspiration to the apostles and prophets, if that same word is corrupted by the centuries that separate us from the original writers? Would the Lord God take such care over ensuring that only *His word* (that which He wanted us to know) was given to the prophets and apostles with no additions or deletions supplied by men, only for it all to suffer from the corruption of unscrupulous scribes and copyists? The answer is of course, most certainly not! However we shall discover that the way in which the Scriptures have been preserved is quite different to the way in which the Scriptures were inspired. Our first task will be to examine the Scriptures to find the evidence that it gives for holding to a belief in the doctrine of preservation.

Purity and some warnings.

The Scriptures, by virtue of their origin, (the work of the holy and pure God), must be considered pure in an absolute sense. We have internal testimony to this effect, for three times we read that God's word is pure:

> *The words of the Lord are pure words, like silver tried in a furnace of earth, purified seven times. (Psalm 12v6).*

> *Your word is very pure; Therefore Your servant loves it. (Psalm 119v140).*

> *Every word of God is pure; He is a shield to those who put their trust in Him. (Proverbs 30v5).*

If God's word delivered by the saints of old had this quality of purity, how can it remain "God's word" without remaining pure? An impure word cannot be considered to be God's word.

Now, not only is the word of God pure, it is also wholly perfect:

Mike Viccary   89 of 319

The law of the Lord is perfect, converting the soul; the testimony of the Lord is sure, making wise the simple; the statutes of the Lord are right, rejoicing the heart; the commandment of the Lord is pure, enlightening the eyes; the fear of the Lord is clean, enduring forever; the judgements of the Lord are true and righteous altogether. More to be desired are they than gold, yea, than much fine gold; sweeter also than honey and the honeycomb. Moreover by them Your servant is warned, and in keeping them there is great reward. (Psalm 19v7-11).

Without a pure and perfect word, we cannot hope to have a ministry of the word that is effective. Only a perfect and pure word of God will do those things the Psalmist records. It is the perfect law which turns the erring soul around to repentance. As a consequence of such perfection and purity, any thought of altering it (by removing words, adding words, or changing words), would not only adulterate and corrupt it, but, more importantly, such tampering would surely invoke God's extreme displeasure. Four times we read of warnings for those who would tamper with God's word:

You shall not add to the word which I command you, nor take from it, that you may keep the commandments of the Lord your God which I command you. (Deuteronomy 4v2).

Whatever I command you, be careful to observe it; you shall not add to it nor take away from it. (Deuteronomy 12v32).

Do not add to His words, lest He rebuke you, and you be found a liar. (Proverbs 30v6).

For I testify to everyone who hears the words of the prophecy of this book: if anyone adds to these things, God will add to him the plagues that are written in this book; and if anyone takes away from the words of the book of this prophecy, God shall take away his part from the Book of Life, from the holy city, and from the things which are written in this book. (Revelation 22v18,19).

I am not at all sure that people understand how important it is to take such warnings seriously. The Scriptures are routinely tampered with especially in the way they are taught or published in the world. James warned that not many should be teachers of the word because the judgement faced by such will be much stricter.[218] Those who received the word by revelation were often fearful and trembling.[219] Why is it that modern people have such disregard for the Scriptures? Such a question has a book's worth of answers! But just imagine, for a moment, that you were a messenger for some high up military official and you took it upon yourself to remove the odd word here and there in the message. How do you think your senior officers would view this? Or, what author would be happy if a third party routinely adjusted, added or subtracted words and phrases in the work they had so lovingly produced? Now extend these concepts to the One whose nature and speech is perfect and

---

218   James 3v1.
219   See: Isaiah 6v1 and Daniel 10v8,9 as two examples amongst many others.

pure! Any alteration amounts not just to corruption, but to filthy soiling.

The Old Testament witness to preservation.

With these thoughts concerning the purity of God's word in mind, let us now consider what the Scriptures say on this topic of preservation. First we shall look at Psalm 33. In verse 11 we read these words:

> *The counsel of the Lord stands forever, the plans of His heart to all generations. (Psalm 33v11).*

This verse comes in a section which centres on the "word of the Lord." Verse 4 speaks of the word of the Lord being "right," whilst verse 6 informs us of it being the agent of creation. Verses 7 and 8 continue the theme of creation and in verse 9 we have a wonderful summary statement which speaks about how God's commands are effective:

> *For He spoke, and it was done; He commanded, and it stood fast.(Psalm 33v9).*

Verses 10 and 11 end the section, and form a neat bridge into the next which centres on the nation whom God has chosen to be His heirs. The Psalmist does not use the phrase "word of the Lord" but switches to "counsel." Thus we have:

> *The Lord brings the counsel of the nations to nothing; He makes the plans of the peoples of no effect. The counsel of the Lord stands forever, the plans of His heart to all generations. (Psalm 33v10,11).*

There is a contrast between what the nations plan and purpose following advice, and what the Lord does. His plans and counsel are eternal and what He has purposed is available for all generations. Although we do not have the term "word" here, the use of such a term beforehand would indicate that what God speaks, (i.e. His word), is very much in view. Thus His counsels, which are the plans He has made and which consist of words, sentences and narratives, will stand forever and will be available for all generations. It is to be noted that Psalm 107v11 identifies and defines the term "counsel" with the phrase "word of the Lord":

> *Because they rebelled against the words of God, and despised the counsel of the Most High. (Psalm 107v11).*

Next we have Psalm 100 which is one of the smaller Psalms in the Psalter, and which we shall quote in full:

> *1 Make a joyful shout to the Lord, all you lands! 2 Serve the Lord with gladness; come before His presence with singing. 3 Know that the Lord, He is God; it is He who has made us, and not we ourselves; we are His people and the sheep of His pasture. 4 Enter into His gates with thanksgiving, and into His courts with praise. Be thankful to Him, and bless His name. 5 For the Lord is good; His mercy is everlasting, and His truth endures to all generations.*

After the call to worship and serve the Lord, we have a statement about whom the Lord is ("He is God"), which is worked out with reference to the people's status as created beings, but here put in terms of the Shepherd-sheep image. Following this we read a second injunction to thank, praise and bless the lord (verse 4), and then the Psalm concludes with three reasons for giving God such praise. First, it is because the Lord is "good." This is one of the great themes of the Scriptures demonstrated in countless ways, but supremely in the sending and giving of the Saviour as our substitute.[220] Second, we praise the Lord for His mercy which is everlasting. Finally, we worship the King because:

> *... His truth endures to all generations. (Psalm 100v5).*

It is worth having a look at the Hebrew here;

$$\text{כִּי-טוֹב יְהוָה. לְעוֹלָם חַסְדּוֹ: וְעַד-דֹּר וָדֹר, אֱמוּנָתוֹ}$$

Hebrew phrase	Translation
כִּי-טוֹב יְהוָה	For[221] good [is] the Lord.
לְעוֹלָם חַסְדּוֹ	To for ever [is] His mercy.
וְעַד-דֹּר וָדֹר, אֱמוּנָתוֹ	And until generation and generation [is] His truth (faithfulness).

You will note here that the English verbs are in square brackets. This indicates that there is no Hebrew word equivalent that is being translated. The NKJV translators supplied the word "endureth" for the last phrase. This makes sense in English and gives the force intended. The

---

220   It is well worth holding the thought that **God is always good** in your heart at all times.
221   The Hebrew כִּי has a range of meanings (when, if, but, for …) which must be translated with reference to the context.

emphasis is on the continuation of God's goodness, mercy and truth. In particular the truth or faithfulness of the Lord is from one generation to the next. Again we do not have the term "word" here but it is to be remembered that "truth" is defined elsewhere as God's word.[222] Furthermore we must remember that the descriptions of the Lord, His mercy and His truth are not monolithic. In other words we may also say that the Lord's mercy is good and is available from generation to generation, or that the Lord's truth is good and eternal.

In Psalm 111 we have a Psalm in which the main focus is the works of the Lord, or that which God does:

> *1 Praise the Lord! I will praise the Lord with my whole heart, in the assembly of the upright and in the congregation. 2 The works of the Lord are great, studied by all who have pleasure in them. 3 His work is honourable and glorious, and His righteousness endures forever. 4 He has made His wonderful works to be remembered; the Lord is gracious and full of compassion. 5 He has given food to those who fear Him; He will ever be mindful of His covenant. 6 He has declared to His people the power of His works, in giving them the heritage of the nations. 7 The works of His hands are verity and justice; all His precepts are sure. 8 They stand fast forever and ever, and are done in truth and uprightness. 9 He has sent redemption to His people; He has commanded His covenant forever: holy and awesome is His name. 10 The fear of the Lord is the beginning of wisdom; a good understanding have all those who do His commandments. His praise endures forever.*

This Psalm is particularly concerned with God's especial work of redemption, the subject of verses 5 to 10. In verses 7 and 8 we have a wonderful statement of the preservation of God's word. What God works with His "hands" is always characterised by these two words "verity" and "justice." That is, what God does always has the ring of truth and rightness about it. Every one of His precepts (commandments) is "sure," or, in other words, they are stable and firm. They are firmly established for ever and will not alter. The implication is that God's commandments will not be changed through time.

Psalm 117 is the shortest Psalm consisting of only two verses:

> *1 Praise the Lord, all you Gentiles! Laud Him, all you peoples! 2 For His merciful kindness is great toward us, and the truth of the Lord endures forever. Praise the Lord!*

Once again we have to supply a verb (usually a form of the verb "to be") in English to make sense of the Hebrew. The translators have chosen "endureth" once more, but the literal translation of this last phrase is:

---

222   See, for example, Psalm 33v4; 119v160; John 17v17.

and the truth of the Lord to forever

If God's truth lasts forever, it must certainly be available today. Note that the first phrase of verse 2 must not be disconnected from the second phrase. We have here a couplet of two ideas expressing the reason why the Gentiles should praise God. Since the merciful kindness of the Lord is great towards us, it is this truth which lasts forever. However since God is always good and cannot lie, whatever He does and says has this sure, firm and truthful quality about it.[223] God is for us! His truth, His word, is available to all generations!

Psalm 119 has a number of verses which indicate that God's word is preserved for every generation. Verses 89 and 90 speak about the eternal nature of God's word:

> *89 Forever, O Lord, Your word is settled in heaven. 90 Your faithfulness endures to all generations; You established the earth, and it abides.*

Heaven is where God dwells. It is, therefore, a place of complete and absolute purity. Nothing of a corruptible nature can exist in heaven. Consequently, the word of God must be pure for it to be "settled" in heaven. The word of God is not left in heaven, however, for God's faithfulness extends throughout all generations. Verse 90 is not a disconnected thought which centres only on the enduring earth. The idea is that because God created the world by His word, all things will certainly endure (until He sees fit to say otherwise). That being the case, whatever God *says*, whenever He *speaks*, or whenever His *word* is given, these will be available for all generations because He is faithful and true.

In verses 151 and 152 of Psalm 119 we get a statement about how the commands and testimonies of God have been established to endure:

> *151 You are near, O Lord, and all Your commandments are truth. 152 Concerning Your testimonies, I have known of old that You have founded them forever.*

The statements of these verses are clear. God, who is near at hand to the righteous, has given true commands. His testimonies, (the outworking of His commands), were established long, long ago, and they have been set to endure throughout all time. These testimonies are settled, immovable and certain. The implication of such teaching for the doctrine of preservation is unmistakable. The faithful God whose works and words are true and faithful, whose love and mercy endures, has given

---

223   Although it may be obvious that God cannot lie, we have Scriptural evidence to this effect at: Titus 1v2; Hebrews 6v18.

His word to us for all time. God never has to repeal His laws and He never has to redesign His plans. Psalm 119v160 is another important verse which indicates that God's word is eternal and thus preserved. We will be looking at this verse in detail later on in chapter 8 when we consider the purity of the word of God. For now it will be enough simply to quote it from the KJAV and make some brief comments:

> *Thy word is true from the beginning: and every one of thy righteous judgements endureth for ever. (Psalm 119v160, KJAV).*

In other words, from the beginning of God's word until the end of time all God's just decisions will endure and last. Such a statement is beautifully constructed and clever to boot. The word of God from beginning to end is true. Contained within this "word of God" are God's wonderfully just judgements and decisions, and all of these will last for all time. You can be sure, therefore, that God has seen fit to preserve His word for all generations.

In Psalm 146v6 we have a statement that God is One who "keeps truth forever":

> *1 Praise the Lord! Praise the Lord, O my soul! 2 While I live I will praise the Lord; I will sing praises to my God while I have my being. 3 Do not put your trust in princes, nor in a son of man, in whom there is no help. 4 His spirit departs, he returns to his earth; in that very day his plans perish. 5 Happy is he who has the God of Jacob for his help, whose hope is in the Lord his God, 6 Who made heaven and earth, the sea, and all that is in them; who keeps truth forever, 7 Who executes justice for the oppressed, who gives food to the hungry. The Lord gives freedom to the prisoners. 8 The Lord opens the eyes of the blind; the Lord raises those who are bowed down; the Lord loves the righteous. 9 The Lord watches over the strangers; He relieves the fatherless and widow; but the way of the wicked He turns upside down. 10 The Lord shall reign forever— Your God, O Zion, to all generations.*

It is important to note the context here. We are not to trust mankind even if they are of royal birth. There is a stark contrast given between the mortality and futility of man and the great God who created all things. No man can do the things God does. None but God can open blind eyes and raise the downcast. This One is the only one who "keeps truth forever." God preserves his truth for ever. The Hebrew word translated as "keepeth" means "to hedge about" or "to protect." Bear in mind that we also have been given the duty of keeping and preserving the word of God.[224] As a final thought from this Psalm, consider also the reminder in verse 6 that God created all things. Given this truth (which is repeated so often in the Old Testament) we must ask, cannot the Creator preserve what He has revealed and inspired?

---

224   See, for example: 2Thessalonians 2v15; 1Timothy 6v20; 2Timothy 1v13; 2v2; Jude v3.

Moving now to the book of Isaiah we have the following words which are also quoted by Peter in his first letter:

> *All flesh is grass,and all its loveliness is like the flower of the field. The grass withers, the flower fades, because the breath of the Lord blows upon it; surely the people are grass. The grass withers, the flower fades, but the word of our God stands forever. (Isaiah 40v6-8).*

> *All flesh is as grass, and all the glory of man as the flower of the grass. The grass withers, and its flower falls away, but the word of the Lord endures forever. (1Peter 1v24,25).*

Here we have another stark contrast between the frailty and mortality of man compared to the endurance and eternality of God's word. Clearly the first reference is to what the Lord spoke at the time when Isaiah was prophesying, but we cannot limit the phrase "the word of the Lord" simply to those words in Isaiah. All of what God says and speaks, and particularly, all that God has caused to be written from what He has spoken, must stand forever enduring.

In Isaiah 51v7,8 we read that the Lord's righteousness and His salvation will also endure throughout time:

> *Listen to Me, you who know righteousness, you people in whose heart is My law: do not fear the reproach of men, nor be afraid of their insults. For the moth will eat them up like a garment, and the worm will eat them like wool; but My righteousness will be forever, and My salvation from generation to generation. (Isaiah 51v7,8).*

The Lord's righteousness and His salvation form a key theme in Isaiah 51. In verse 5 it is near and has gone forth. In verse 6 it will be forever and will never be abolished. Then in verse 8 we find that it will be forever and, in particular, "from generation to generation," so that all will be able to turn back to God from the dark paths of sin. If God's salvation is available in every generation, then His pure word must be too, for:

> *faith comes by hearing, and hearing by the word of God. (Romans 10v17).*

If there is no word of God, then consequently there will be no hearing of it, and as an obvious follow-on, the only result will be no faith, which means no salvation. Thus whenever we read that God has provided the way of salvation for all generations we can be sure that His word must be preserved for all generations too, for this is the means whereby people come to true faith.

A particularly strong case for the doctrine of preservation can be found in the last verse of

Isaiah 59:

> *"As for Me," says the Lord, "this is My covenant with them: My Spirit who is upon you, and My words which I have put in your mouth, shall not depart from your mouth, nor from the mouth of your descendants, nor from the mouth of your descendants' descendants," says the Lord, "from this time and for evermore." (Isaiah 59v21).*

It is to be noted that the Lord is speaking here, and He is speaking in the context of His covenant of grace. In this text we find that it is God's "words" which have been placed in the mouths of the true and faithful believers. Please note that it is not just in the mouths of Isaiah and his followers, but also in the mouths of their descendants, and their descendants' descendants. This verse is very reminiscent of Christ's high priestly prayer of John 17 where the Lord prays for the disciples and those who would believe through them.

Turning to the New Testament, we find in Matthew 5v17-20 that we have another very clear teaching concerning the preservation of the word of God:

> *17 Do not think that I came to destroy the Law or the Prophets. I did not come to destroy but to fulfil. 18 For assuredly, I say to you, till heaven and earth pass away, one jot or one tittle will by no means pass from the law till all is fulfilled. 19 Whoever therefore breaks one of the least of these commandments, and teaches men so, shall be called least in the kingdom of heaven; but whoever does and teaches them, he shall be called great in the kingdom of heaven. 20 For I say to you, that unless your righteousness exceeds the righteousness of the scribes and Pharisees, you will by no means enter the kingdom of heaven. (Matthew 5v17-20).*

Contrary to popular belief, the Lord came not to obliterate the Law and the Prophets (the Old Testament), but to fulfil it. In verse 17 the Lord says something quite remarkable about the persistent nature of God's word, for not the smallest letter, nor the smallest stroke of a letter will fall out from the word of God until all has been fulfilled. We must pay particular attention here to the fact that the Lord was speaking about the Law that was penned by Moses some 1,500 years before. In doing this the Lord is upholding the doctrine of preservation.

The whole of Scripture teaches this idea that God's word is pure, perfect, and available in every generation. We can look almost anywhere in Scripture to find this consistent teaching, but a particularly important Scripture we must consider is Psalm 12.

A look at Psalm 12.

The text of Psalm 12 has proved somewhat of a battle ground in the debate about preservation. This is chiefly because of verses 6 and 7 which in the NKJV reads as follows:

> **6** *The words of the Lord are pure words, like silver tried in a furnace of earth, purified seven times.* **7** *You shall keep them, O Lord, You shall preserve them from this generation forever.*

The controversy centres on the reference for "them" in verse 7. Does it refer back to verse 6 ("The words of the Lord") or is it a reference back to verse 5 ("the poor" and "the needy")? In other words, does the Lord promise to keep His **words** from this point on, or does He promise to keep the **needy** and **poor** from this point on? It is worth considering the Psalm as a whole to ensure we get the context correct. The Psalm in its entirety is shown below:

> **1** *Help, Lord, for the godly man ceases! For the faithful disappear from among the sons of men.* **2** *They speak idly everyone with his neighbour; with flattering lips and a double heart they speak.* **3** *May the Lord cut off all flattering lips, and the tongue that speaks proud things,* **4** *who have said, "with our tongue we will prevail; our lips are our own; who is lord over us?"* **5** *"For the oppression of the poor, for the sighing of the needy, now I will arise," says the Lord; "I will set him in the safety for which he yearns."* **6** *The words of the Lord are pure words, like silver tried in a furnace of earth, purified seven times.* **7** *You shall keep them, O Lord, You shall preserve them from this generation forever.* **8** *The wicked prowl on every side, when vileness is exalted among the sons of men.*

Before we go much further we must ask, what is the essential message of this Psalm? What is the prime focus?[225] Some argue that the main feature is the contrast between the "godly man" and the "wicked" (compare verses 1 and 8). Others suggest the main point is the contrast between God's pure words and the false flattering words of frail and wicked men. At this point it is worth doing some exegetical analysis which is shown in table 3.1. In this I have attempted to divide the text according to its main points paying particular attention to themes and ideas. Looking at the exegetical analysis we can see the following points of importance:

[1] The phrase, "the sons of men" (Adam) form book ends in verses 1 and 8. Verse 1 focuses on the godly and faithful, whilst verse 8 centres on wicked and vileness.
[2] Verses 2 – 4 form a unit as can be seen by the red words which centre around the speech and the lips of mankind. We have "speak(s)" (x3), "flattering lips" (x2), "tongue" (x2), "said," and "lips." In this section we have some recorded words of the sons of men: "with our tongue we will prevail; our lips *are* our own; who *is* lord over us?"
[3] Verse 5 seems to stand alone. It records a statement by the Lord in rebuttal to the words of the sons of men: "For the oppression of the poor, for the sighing of the needy, now I will arise," says the Lord; "I will set *him* in the safety for which he yearns."
[4] Verses 6 – 7 form another unit which parallels verses 2 – 4. So in contrast to the flattery,

---

225   This is always a good question to ask, especially if we are those who preach and teach.

falseness and futility of the words and lips of the sons of men, we have the pure words of the Lord. In this analysis it seems natural to interpret verse 7 as relating to verse 6 rather than verse 5. If we make verse 7 refer back to verse 5, the symmetry is lost.

[5] Verse 8 speaks of the ubiquity of the wicked which contrasts with the disappearance and ceasing of the godly.

Taking the Psalm in this way, we have verse 7 closely linked in thought to verse 6. This means that we have a clear statement of the preservation of God's words. Despite the structure we have shown,

Table 3.1: Exegetical analysis of Psalm 12:

1 Help, Lord,
  for the godly man ceases!
  For the faithful disappear from
    among the sons of men.

  2 They speak
      idly everyone with his neighbour;
      with flattering lips *and*
      a double heart they speak.
  3 May the Lord cut off
      all flattering lips, *and*
      the tongue that speaks proud things,
      4 who have said,
          "with our tongue we will prevail;
          our lips *are* our own;
          who *is* lord over us?"

                  5 "For the oppression of the poor, for the sighing of the needy, now I will arise," says the Lord; "I will set *him* in the safety for which he yearns."

  6 The words of the Lord *are*
      pure words,
      like silver tried in a furnace of earth, purified seven times.
  7 You shall
      keep them, O Lord,
  You shall
      preserve them from this generation forever.

8 The wicked prowl on every side,
  when vileness is exalted
    among the sons of men.

however, many commentators argue that verse 7 links to verse 5. Part of the reason is due to the Hebrew. Some claim that because the noun "words" in verse 6 is feminine, whilst the "them" of verse 7 is masculine, we cannot link verse 7 to verse 6. The masculine "them" must go back to the nearest masculine nouns which are to be found in verse 5 (i.e. poor and needy). However there appears to be a strong argument against this usual grammatical rule that the genders must match. It turns out that there often occurs a "gender discord" whereby masculine pronouns are used for feminine antecedent nouns. Examples where this has been found are shown in table 3.2. The idea of such gender discord is fairly common according to Davis, for example, who states:

> Disagreement in gender between a pronoun and its antecedent is common enough in Biblical Hebrew that it has been treated in the field's major reference grammars. Most often, the gender discord consists of a masculine pronoun standing for a feminine noun, and the grammars agree that this replacement is related to "a weakening in the distinction of gender" by which the feminine plural suffix was subsumed under its masculine counterpart.[226]

Waltke and O'Connor in their Introduction to Biblical Hebrew also refer to this gender discord.[227]

Table 3.2: Examples of "gender discord."

Scripture	Details
Psalm 119:111	I have inherited Your testimonies [Fem.] forever, for they [Masc.] are the joy of my heart.
Psalm 119:129	Your testimonies [Fem.] are wonderful; therefore my soul observes them [Masc.].
Psalm 119:152	Of old I have known from Your testimonies [Fem.] that You have founded them [Masc.] forever.
Psalm 119:167	My soul keeps Your testimonies [Fem.], and I love them [Masc] exceedingly.
Joshua 1:7	Only be thou strong and very courageous, that thou mayest observe to do according to all the law [feminine], which Moses my servant commanded thee: turn not from it [masculine] to the right hand or to the left, that thou mayest prosper whithersoever thou goest.
Psalm 78:5	For he established a testimony [feminine] in Jacob, and appointed a law in Israel, which he commanded our fathers, that they should make them [masculine] known to their children.
Leviticus 26:3	If ye walk in my statutes [feminine], and keep my commandments [feminine], and do them [masculine].
1 Kings 6:12	Concerning this house which thou art in building, if thou wilt walk in my statutes [feminine], and execute my judgments [feminine], and keep all my commandments [feminine] to walk in them [masculine].

---

226   The Literary Effect of Gender Discord in the Book of Ruth, Andrew R. Davis. JBL 132, no. 3 (2013): 495–513. P495.
227   Waltke, B.K. & O'Connor, M.P. 1990. An Introduction to Biblical Hebrew Syntax. Eisenbraums. Winona Lake, IN. #16.4b. P302.

More cases of feminine antecedents to masculine *them* can be found at: Isaiah 3v26 *(daughters - feminine)*; Exodus 1v21, *(midwives - feminine),* and; Genesis 26v15 *(wells – feminine).* Consequently the discord of gender between verse 7 and verse 6 is not a bar to making "words" the referent for that which shall be preserved. As a result Psalm 12 is a very strong example in Scripture which teaches that God shall preserve the words He has spoken from that generation forever!

The witness of the word in John.

John's writing was inspired by God the Holy Spirit. Every word was one which finds its origin in the heart and mind of God. However God's sovereign superintendence of Scripture does not obliterate the personality and mind of the human "author." Hence we note that in writing this gospel, John uses particular terms in his gospel to convey particular meanings.[228] Although John was careful in selecting his words, the resultant work is, nonetheless, a work of the Holy Spirit. Now one of these especial terms is the term "word."[229] The gospel of John opens with the idea that Christ Jesus, the second person of the Holy Trinity, is the One who came to make the Father known.[230] He is the Word made flesh who has declared and "explained" God the Father.[231]

> *No one has seen God at any time. The only begotten Son, who is in the bosom of the Father, He has declared Him. (John 1v18).*

This idea of making the Father known is a theme that is not just contained in the first chapter. In John 3v34 the Baptist gives his testimony about Christ:

> *For He whom God has sent speaks the words of God, for God does not give the Spirit by measure.(John 3v34).*

Here are some of the other references in John linking Christ's mission as a faithful messenger giving the world the Father's very words:

> *Then Jesus said to them, "When you lift up the Son of Man, then you will know that I am He, and that I do nothing of Myself; but as My Father taught Me, I speak these things. (John 8v28).*

> *For I have not spoken on My own authority; but the Father who sent Me gave Me a*

---

228   Examples include, "belief," "word," "life," "truth," "light," ....
229   It is found 46 times in John.
230   The concept of Christ as "the Word" has an Old Testament origin. See, for example, Genesis 15v1,4,5; 1Kings 19v9.
231   John 1v1,14,18.

command, what I should say and what I should speak. (John 12v49).

Do you not believe that I am in the Father, and the Father in Me? The words that I speak to you I do not speak on My own authority; but the Father who dwells in Me does the works. (John 14v10).

He who does not love Me does not keep My words; and the word which you hear is not Mine but the Father's who sent Me.(John 14v24).

For I have given to them the words which You have given Me; and they have received them, and have known surely that I came forth from You; and they have believed that You sent Me. (John 17v8).

I have given them Your word; and the world has hated them because they are not of the world, just as I am not of the world. (John 17v14).

A part of Christ's mission, then, was to come and to speak the words of God with *exact* precision. If the Lord Jesus took such pains to give the disciples the word the Father gave to Him, would He not equally see to it that such words were preserved in purity too for future generations? We have in these words a clear statement that when Christ spoke it was as though the Father were speaking directly. This, of course, is a clear fulfilment of the prophecy given by Moses that a prophet will come who will speak directly from the Father:

I will raise up for them a Prophet like you from among their brethren, and will put My words in His mouth, and He shall speak to them all that I command Him. (Deuteronomy 18v18).

Of course the Son of God gives us the words of God in a more sure and complete way than the prophets of old as Hebrews 1v1,2 puts it:

God, who at various times and in various ways spoke in time past to the fathers by the prophets, has in these last days spoken to us by His Son, whom He has appointed heir of all things, through whom also He made the worlds. (Hebrews 1v1,2).

This is not to say that the prophets of old were not giving us God's word in purity. It is just that they gave us God's pure word in pieces, bit-by-bit, whilst Christ who is the very "Word of God" gives us the words of God in their fullness.

In John chapter 2 the Lord rebuked the money changers in the temple alluding to words from Jeremiah 7v11 about His Father's house being a place of merchandise rather than prayer.[232] The disciples, however, are reminded of Psalm 69v9 where the zeal of the Lord is referred to. The

---

232   Compare this with the second time he purged the temple – see Matthew 21v13; Mark 11v17; Luke 19v46.

Jewish authorities demand some explanation in the form of a sign, and the Lord Jesus responded that if they destroyed "this temple" then He would raise it up. The authorities misunderstood the reference and the disciples only understood it after the resurrection. At this point in John's gospel we are told something important about the link between the Lord Jesus' words and Scripture. Here is how John refers to this reckoning of the disciples:

> *Therefore, when He had risen from the dead, His disciples remembered that He had said this to them; and they believed the Scripture and the word which Jesus had said. (John 2v22).*

Notice how John puts this. After the resurrection the disciples recalled the words of Jesus when he rebuked the money changers. In remembering the incident and what the Lord had actually said, they then come to faith by believing both "the Scripture" (i.e. Psalm 69v9) and "the word which Jesus had said." It is clear that the apostle John is linking Christ's words with Scripture. In other words, the Lord's very words that they remembered, were on the same level of authority as the Scripture they were reminded of when the incident occurred.

In John 4 we learn something else about how Christ's words operate. This chapter recounts the story of Christ's meeting with the woman of Samaria. After her conversation with the Lord she rushes back to her town and testifies to what the Lord had spoken to her. As a consequence of her testimony we read that:

> *And many of the Samaritans of that city believed in Him because of the word of the woman who testified, "He told me all that I ever did." (John 4v39).*

This is extremely encouraging. However when the Samaritans urged Christ to remain with them we find that:

> *And many more believed because of His own word. (John 4v41).*

These Samaritans now believe because of Christ's word:

> *Then they said to the woman, "Now we believe, not because of what you said, for we ourselves have heard Him and we know that this is indeed the Christ, the Saviour of the world." (John 4v42).*

It is the word of Christ which matters. First the woman testifies to Christ's words and some believe, then next many hear Christ's words themselves and many more believe. Isn't this encouraging? We find, then, that the word of Christ can bring true faith, and further that the word of Christ through one who testifies (a true believer), can also bring true faith.

The words that Christ spoke and which came directly from the Father are vital and it is imperative that we believe them.[233] Such is exemplified (in part) by the nobleman whose son was sick at Capernaum whilst Jesus was in Galilee. When the Lord told the man that his son would live, the nobleman believed the Lord:

> *Jesus said to him, "Go your way; your son lives." So the man believed the word that Jesus spoke to him, and he went his way. (John 4v50).*

It is faith in Christ's word that brings fruit, and especially eternal life. This idea of a connection between believing and the word is made explicitly clear in the next chapter. If we hear Christ's voice and word, then we have true everlasting life:

> ***24** Most assuredly, I say to you, he who hears My word and believes in Him who sent Me has everlasting life, and shall not come into judgement, but has passed from death into life. **25** Most assuredly, I say to you, the hour is coming, and now is, when the dead will hear the voice of the Son of God; and those who hear will live. **26** For as the Father has life in Himself, so He has granted the Son to have life in Himself, **27** and has given Him authority to execute judgement also, because He is the Son of Man. **28** Do not marvel at this; for the hour is coming in which all who are in the graves will hear His voice **29** and come forth—those who have done good, to the resurrection of life, and those who have done evil, to the resurrection of condemnation. (John 5v24-29).*

Was the voice of the Lord only heard when Christ walked this earth? The above verses seem to indicate that the word and voice of the Lord will continue to be heard right up until judgement day. Since this is true we must ask the question: how will people hear the voice and word of God?

A true faith in Christ and His word implies that the word of God the Father must have a place within us. Without both of these things (faith in Christ and a heart trust in God's word) we cannot say we believe in the Scriptures. The Pharisees of old declared that they trusted the Old Testament, but they rejected Christ. This was tantamount to actually confessing their rejection of the Old Testament because they rejected Christ:

> *But you do not have His word abiding in you, because whom He sent, Him you do not believe. (John 5v38).*

> *Then Jesus said to those Jews who believed Him, "If you abide in My word, you are My*

---

233   John 8v30.

> *disciples indeed." (John 8v31).*

Therefore if we believe in Him and are truly His disciples, we will let His word abide in us.

> *If you abide in Me, and My words abide in you, you will ask what you desire, and it shall be done for you. (John 15v7).*

If we do not have the word of God and the word of Christ, how then can we be disciples? Without God's perfect and pure word none can be true disciples.

That which the Lord Jesus spoke on and brought to the disciples all those years ago, had the same quality in authority as that which Moses wrote about. Both are to be believed wholly.

> *But if you do not believe his writings, how will you believe My words? (John 5v47).*

However Christ's words are spirit and life, and they have this quality of being eternal:

> *It is the Spirit who gives life; the flesh profits nothing. The words that I speak to you are spirit, and they are life. (John 6v63).*

> *But Simon Peter answered Him, "Lord, to whom shall we go? You have the words of eternal life." (John 6v68).*

Not only so, but Christ's words have the ability to cleanse!

> *You are already clean because of the word which I have spoken to you. (John 15v3).*

If Christ's words have this cleansing and eternal quality about them, then surely they will be preserved intact?

In John 8 where we have the Lord identifying clearly as God in the flesh, we also find some further teaching about Christ's word. It is imperative that people believe in Christ's deity, for otherwise they will die in their sins.[234] If they do not believe now, they will when Christ is crucified.[235] With such sayings some believed.[236] At this point the Lord taught about the importance of discipleship:

---

234   John 8v24.
235   John 8v28.
236   John 8v30.

Mike Viccary

> ***31** Then Jesus said to those Jews who believed Him, "If you abide in My word, you are My disciples indeed. **32** And you shall know the truth, and the truth shall make you free." (John 8v31,32).*

A disciple is one who abides in Christ's word. What exactly does this mean for those who cannot now hear His earthly voice speaking? Notice also the connection between Christ's word and "truth." What Christ speaks is from the Father perfectly, and thereby must be absolutely true with no falseness, fickleness or futility fixed to it. Those who believe and heed the voice and word of God have a place within themselves where the word can lodge.[237] This thought reminds us of the parable of the soils. Only the good soil can take the seed and enable proper growth.[238] Because some cannot hear what Christ is saying, they are unable to heed the word of God whether it be Scripture (the Old Testament at that time) or what Christ was saying.[239] Christ spoke from the Father and gave the truth. People who rejected His words were rejecting God because the word of God was not in them and they were not "of God."[240]

Further on in the conversation with the Jews in John 8 the Lord speaks about "keeping" His words:

> ***51** Most assuredly, I say to you, if anyone keeps My word he shall never see death. **52** Then the Jews said to Him, "Now we know that You have a demon! Abraham is dead, and the prophets; and You say, 'If anyone keeps My word he shall never taste death.' (John 8v51,52).*

The word "keep" in John 8v51 means to protect and preserve. Clearly it is not sufficient just to keep the word of God in a box or left in a book that is never read or believed. We must honour Christ's word and keep it by believing and following it in our lives. We are to be living epistles.[241] We could limit this word "keep" to the idea of obedience. That sense is shown later on in the gospel:

> ***47** And if anyone hears My words and does not believe, I do not judge him; for I did not come to judge the world but to save the world. **48** He who rejects Me, and does not receive My words, has that which judges him—the word that I have spoken will judge him in the last day. (John 12v47,48).*

However I think, in view of what we have already seen in John's gospel, the idea of preservation must be in view. When the Lord speaks of "keeping" His words, it cannot merely be a question of

---

237　　John 8v37.
238　　Matthew 13v3f.
239　　John 8v43.
240　　John 8v45-47.
241　　2Corthians 3v3.

simply obeying them. There must be an element of holding onto, and preserving the very words that Christ actually spoke. However, since we do not have Christ here on earth, how then can we hear and obey (or, keep) His word? The only answer to this is through what is written in Scripture. In this sense then, we are being taught that the disciples were to keep or preserve Christ's word. In fact this idea of preservation is also seen in the last Scripture quoted. At the end of what the Lord says in John 12v48 we find that what will ultimately judge us if we do not believe is "the word that I have spoken." How can the word that Christ spoke judge us if it is not preserved? In the academic literature much is made of the beginning of Christian witness being solely a matter of the disciples remembering Christ's words, and not being that bothered to write anything down. Academics like to point out that writing was not a common thing in those days and people simply committed things to memory. However in these words of Christ exhorting the keeping of His word, I cannot but think that efforts were made by the disciples to remember the word, not just in memory but in writing. Consider these words from the apostle Peter:

> *12 For this reason I will not be negligent to remind you always of these things, though you know and are established in the present truth. 13 Yes, I think it is right, as long as I am in this tent, to stir you up by reminding you, 14 knowing that shortly I must put off my tent, just as our Lord Jesus Christ showed me. 15 Moreover I will be careful to ensure that you always have a reminder of these things after my decease. (2Peter 1v12-15).*

> *1 Beloved, I now write to you this second epistle (in both of which I stir up your pure minds by way of reminder), 2 that you may be mindful of the words which were spoken before by the holy prophets, and of the commandment of us, the apostles of the Lord and Saviour, (2Peter 3v1,2).*

How could Peter (whilst he was alive) stir up their minds to remember such important things? Well, of course, he could preach and teach them, but that would not be possible all the time. So how can he ensure that they would always have a reminder of such things when he had died? The only answer, of course, is through his inspired letters. Since it is known that Mark's gospel was informed by Peter, it may also be that Peter was indicating that the gospel of Mark was a part of the way the people would be reminded.

The idea of keeping Christ's words gets a second airing in the upper room teaching, the night before the Saviour was betrayed and died. Again, the notion of keeping includes more than obedience. Doing what the Lord required was, of course, central, but the one who sought to obey the Lord and what He commanded would surely have ensured that what He commanded would be remembered? What better way to remember than to write it down? Are we to believe that the disciples stood around and gawped at the Lord in wonder without taking up a tablet and marker, or a pen and parchment to scribble His words of eternal life down? If we love Christ then we would also keep His commandments.[242] Again we can only keep His commandments if we have them to hand. This means they must be written down for us in Scripture. It will not be enough that we preserve the written record of them, of course. Christ meant that we heed the commands and do them. But that the commands were preserved must be the first essential thing, and it is imperative as Christians that we keep and preserve these commands for future generations. We do this by ensuring the commands are kept intact – word-for-word – and, more importantly, we do this by following them and doing them. A little while later in this discourse the Lord says the following:

> *He who has My commandments and keeps them, it is he who loves Me. And he who loves Me will be loved by My Father, and I will love him and manifest Myself to him. (John 14v21).*

It is the one who "has" the commandments of Christ who truly loves Christ. How do we have these? We may have them in our minds and hearts – and this is essential – but this cannot have been the case unless we have them in the written word first. Then we have another injunction to keep the words of Christ:

> **23** *Jesus answered and said to him, "If anyone loves Me, he will keep My word; and My Father will love him, and We will come to him and make Our home with him.* **24** *He who does not love Me does not keep My words; and the word which you hear is not Mine but the Father's who sent Me. (John 14v23,24).*

The disciples would not be left to remember the things they had heard on their own, for the Holy Spirit would remind them of these too:

> **25** *These things I have spoken to you while being present with you.* **26** *But the Helper, the Holy Spirit, whom the Father will send in My name, He will teach you all things, and bring to your remembrance all things that I said to you. (John 14v25,26).*

Similar teaching is given later on in John 15 where the Holy Spirit is referred to as "the Spirit of truth":

> **26** *But when the Helper comes, whom I shall send to you from the Father, the Spirit of truth who proceeds from the Father, He will testify of Me.* **27** *And you also will bear witness, because you have been with Me from the beginning. (John 15v26,27).*

---

242   John 14v15.

The importance of abiding in Christ is shown in the teaching of John 15 on the vine. For our present purposes the important thing is that we have the Lord's words abiding in us.[243] Again this clearly means that our lives are to be governed by His word in such a way that we follow His commands. But that the words must first be written for us, so that we can then allow them to abide in us, is a truth we must equally affirm. The Lord then exhorts us to keep his commandments in the same way that He kept the Father's commands.[244]

John 17, Christ's high priestly prayer, has much to teach us about the abiding word of God. The Lord Jesus speaks of the disciples "keeping" the Father's word:

> *I have manifested Your name to the men whom You have given Me out of the world. They were Yours, You gave them to Me, and they have kept Your word. (John 17v6).*

Were they obedient? Well not perfectly. How then did they "keep" the Father's word? Listen to Christ's confession:

> *For I have given to them the words which You have given Me; and they have received them, and have known surely that I came forth from You; and they have believed that You sent Me. (John 17v8).*

> *I have given them Your word; and the world has hated them because they are not of the world, just as I am not of the world. (John 17v14).*

The disciples were "given" the Father's words, and they "received" them. We could, again, limit this to a simple mental/heart operation, but what if in hearing these words they copied them down on parchment? We are not told that they did, but given the instructions by God to Moses to write down what he had received, are we not compelled to state that some at least of the disciples wrote Christ's words down as they heard them?[245] Remember these disciples were Jews who knew the Law of Moses in which we get clear indication of the importance of writing what God has said down.[246]

Later on we find that our Saviour prays for the disciples' sanctification. This was to be effected by the Father's truth which is defined by our Lord as "Your word."

> *Sanctify them by Your truth. Your word is truth. (John 17v17).*

---

243   John 15v7.
244   John 15v10.
245   See, for example: Exodus 17v14; 34v1 etc.
246   Exodus 17v14; 34v27.

Mike Viccary   109 of 319

Again are we to imagine that the Lord simply meant by this term "Your word," that which they had retained in their memory? I hardly think so! In the next verse we read of Christ's commissioning:

> *As You sent Me into the world, I also have sent them into the world. (John 17v18).*

The disciples must therefore take the words they had received from Christ and pass them on to new disciples. How then are they to do this? Clearly It Is by having these words in their very beings, by obeying these words so that the life of Christ is evident, and, importantly, it is by keeping and preserving these very words in a form that others may access them – i.e. by writing.[247] We can assert this with some degree of confidence because of what the Lord continues to pray for. He does not stop at praying for the disciples He had trained, but goes on to pray for those who would believe after He had risen and ascended. Here is what He prays:

> *I do not pray for these alone, but also for those who will believe in Me through their word. (John 17v20).*

Note carefully how He puts this. He is praying for those who would believe in Him "through their word." This word which He had from the Father and which He faithfully passed on to the disciples, and which they had received, was to be passed on to others that they may believe too. If the word was transmitted unfaithfully accumulating errors as it progressed, what sort of belief would these future disciples have? The word that is described as "their word" must, of necessity, be the same word that we can describe as "the word of Christ" which was the same word that Christ received from the Father.

The synoptic gospels and other New Testament writings.

When we consider the synoptic gospels we have some interesting statements in connection with Christ's words. In His temptation the Lord rebuffed the enemy with the word of God quoting Deuteronomy 8v3 and declared that man's life depended upon "every word that proceeds from the mouth of God" or "every word of God."[248] Christ's mission was to preach the word of God to the

---

247   It cannot be objected here that because the Lord Jesus did not write anything down, (apart from some writing in the ground – John 8v8), this means that the disciples may then not have written anything down. In the first place we do not know that Christ never wrote anything at all. It is eminently possible that He did write some material that we have no evidence of. In the second place we know that Christ was to leave the world after only three and half years in the public's view. It was thus more likely that in preparing the disciples He knew they would be attending to the writing of the New Testament.

248   Matthew 4v4; Luke 4v4.

people.[249] As He preached the word the people bore witness to His preaching. His word was like nothing the people had heard before, for it was full of grace, and authority.[250] He exhorted the people to not only hear what He was preaching, but to "keep it" as well.[251] In the parable of the soils the Lord made clear that the word of God could only settle and grow in good soil.[252] In all three synoptic gospels we have these important words of the Saviour:

> *Heaven and earth will pass away, but My words will by no means pass away. (Matthew 24v35; Mark 13v31; Luke 21v33).*

Both Mark and Luke record Christ's words of warning not to be ashamed of Christ's words.

> *For whoever is ashamed of Me and My words in this adulterous and sinful generation, of him the Son of Man also will be ashamed when He comes in the glory of His Father with the holy angels." (Mark 8v38).*

> *For whoever is ashamed of Me and My words, of him the Son of Man will be ashamed when He comes in His own glory, and in His Father's, and of the holy angels. (Luke 9v26).*

The reference in Mark highlights the people of Christ's day, but the words in Luke's account indicate that whomever is ashamed of Christ's words in *whatever generation*, then the Lord will be ashamed of them when He returns. How can people be ashamed of Christ's words if they have not been preserved intact?

In Luke's opening introduction to the gospel, we find a witness to early writing. Here is the introduction:

> *1 Inasmuch as many have taken in hand to set in order a narrative of those things which have been fulfilled among us, 2 just as those who from the beginning were eyewitnesses and ministers of the word delivered them to us, 3 it seemed good to me also, having had perfect understanding of all things from the very first, to write to you an orderly account, most excellent Theophilus, 4 that you may know the certainty of those things in which you were instructed. (Luke 1v1-4).*

Many, it seems had tried to write the narrative of Christ's life. Furthermore, Luke tells us about "those who from the beginning were eyewitnesses and ministers of the word," which statement indicates the apostles. In Luke's second volume (the Acts of the apostles), we find that the apostles were concerned to continue in the "ministry of the word":

---

249   Mark 2v2; Luke 5v1.
250   Luke 4v22,23.
251   Luke 11v28.
252   Matthew 13v3f; Mark 4v3f; Luke 8v5f.

> *2 Then the twelve summoned the multitude of the disciples and said, "It is not desirable that we should leave the word of God and serve tables. 3 Therefore, brethren, seek out from among you seven men of good reputation, full of the Holy Spirit and wisdom, whom we may appoint over this business; 4 but we will give ourselves continually to prayer and to the ministry of the word." (Acts 6v2-4).*

The apostles were "ministers of the word" which phrase means that they spent time in the Old Testament Scriptures, but probably also indicates that they were busy writing about what they had heard and seen when Christ walked the earth. Most take the reference to the apostles as "ministers of the word" as an indication that they were preachers only. However consider the fact that the apostle John mentions writing throughout his letters and in the apocalypse, that Jude also speaks of writing, as does the apostle Peter:[253]

> *1 Beloved, I now write to you this second epistle (in both of which I stir up your pure minds by way of reminder), 2 that you may be mindful of the words which were spoken before by the holy prophets, and of the commandment of us, the apostles of the Lord and Saviour, (2Peter 3v1,2).*

Paul, who was the last apostle, also mentions writing extensively throughout his epistles. These men were certainly not averse to making the word of God permanent by committing it to the written form.

Some conclusions.

We have seen that the Scriptures indicate throughout that the Lord God has preserved His word faithfully and truthfully in every generation. Of course some may object that the Scriptures were not completed until the first century AD. What then of the times before the New Testament was written down? Or what of the time between Abraham and Moses? Well of course parts and portions of God's word were available in these (and all times). The wonderful thing about Scripture is that it is repetitive although not in any monotonous way. What I mean to emphasise here is that the essential truths and doctrines concerning God, man, sin and salvation are found from beginning to end. For us in these days the important thing, of course, is that we believe that God has kept pure the word He originally revealed so that any may read clearly what God has spoken. Given these sure and certain truths it is time now to consider the evidence in the original languages we have available today. What exactly is the evidence for our Scriptures? Now much of the debate has centred around the New Testament and so we shall limit further discussion in the main to that part

---

253   1John 1v4; 2v1,7,8,12,13; 2John 1v12; 3John 1v13; Jude 1v3; Revelation 1v11,19; 2v1,8,12,18; 3v1,7,12,14; 10v4; 14v13; 19v9; 21v5.

of Scripture. We will have occasion to mention the Old Testament at points throughout our discussions, but we shall not consider the Old Testament manuscript evidence in this study.

[2] The manuscript evidence we have.

One of the great problems of all intellectual enquiry or scholarly pursuit is the great difficulty of presenting "facts" without any adorning ideas or theory. We simply cannot present information without some presuppositions. In fact our very presuppositions will guide us in the selection of those facts we choose to recount. Consequently, so that the reader is under no illusion, I will make it clear here that my presuppositions include, the notion that God has revealed Himself inerrantly and infallibly to certain men by inspiration, and, that He has divinely preserved these revealed words in the Greek manuscripts. In this section I want to give some generally accepted facts, but I will not avoid making some concluding comments as we progress.

The manuscript evidence.

As an ancient text the New Testament stands alone amongst ancient writings by virtue of the incredible number of manuscripts available. Taking the Greek manuscripts on their own there are more than 5,600, but if we include translations into Latin and other ancient languages this number rises to in excess of 24,000.[254] Other ancient texts have far less in terms of number of manuscripts.[255] The Greek manuscripts are of four types and have been further classified by scholars according to date and location of influence. Some of the details of these gathered in 1994 are shown in the table 3.3 below.

One of the interesting facts about the Greek manuscript evidence is that it is always on the increase (see table 3.4). In fact from the days when a Greek edition of the New Testament was first published by Erasmus in 1516 until today the number of manuscripts has increased dramatically. This situation cannot continue indefinitely, of course, as there will come a time when no new discoveries can possibly be unearthed. In view of the ever expanding manuscript witness to the New Testament we must ask what significance such new discoveries have, and how these affect the the New testament we are reading today? This and other questions will form the essence of our discussions concerning the evidence we have at our disposal.

---

254   https://carm.org/manuscript-evidence.
255   There are no more than 10 copies of Caesar's Gallic War (58-50 BC) the earliest of which date 1,000 years after the events. We have only 10 copies of the work of the Roman historian Cornelius Tacitus (born circa AD 52) which gives us knowledge of Roman emperors from Augustus to Nero and the earliest dates 900 years after the original. We have 643 copies of Homer's Illiad none of which are early in date. Details taken from: John Blanchard "Does God Believe in Atheists?" p390f.

Table 3.3: Manuscript evidence.

DETAILS	Major examples
85 Papyri.	Papyrus was an ancient type of writing material made from the fibrous pith of the papyrus plant which (in ancient times) grew plentifully along the Nile. These manuscripts are mainly fragments and have, for the most part, been discovered in Egypt where the climate and conditions have helped to preserve them. These are the earliest witnesses to the New Testament. About 80 are mere fragments of papyrus. The oldest known is the John Rylands fragment dated 123 - 135 AD. It measures only 2.5 inches by 3.5 inches and contains a few verses from the Gospel of John (18v31-33,37-38). Two of the most important groups of papyri are the Chester Beatty Papyri, and the Bodmer Papyri: **(a) Chester Beatty Papyri:** - published in 1933 -1937 These include, amongst others: - Papyrus 45 (Gospels and Acts) dated circa 225 AD - Papyrus 46 (Pauline epistles) dated circa 225 AD - Papyrus 47 (Revelation) dated circa 275 AD **(b) Bodmer Papyri:** - published in 1956 - 1962 The most important of these are: - Papyrus 66 (John) dated circa 200 AD - Papyrus 72 (1 & 2 Peter, Jude) circa $3^{rd}/4^{th}$ century - Papyrus 75 (Luke and John 1v15) dated circa 200 AD
268 Uncial codices	Upper-case, capital letter leather manuscripts with no punctuation. Written on parchment or vellum. The word majuscule, meaning large or capital letter, is a synonym for uncial. The three oldest uncials are complete or nearly complete New Testaments. These are as follows: - **Codex Vaticanus B:** - dated: the middle of the fourth century AD. Located in the Vatican library Rome. Not studied until 1866 by Tischendorf for 42 hours. Copy published in 1867. - **Codex Sinaiticus Aleph:** - dated: second half of the fourth century AD. Discovered by Tischendorf in 1844 in a waste-paper basket in the monastery of St. Catherine on Mount Sinai. Seen properly by Tischendorf in 1859. Copy of it produced in 1862. - **Codex Alexandrinus A:** - dated: first half of the fifth century AD. Presented to the king of England in 1627. Three other important uncial manuscripts are: - **W:** - dated: fourth or fifth century AD. Contains the Gospels. - **Codex Bezae D:** - dated: fifth or sixth century AD. Contains the Gospels and Acts. - **D2:** - dated: sixth century AD. Contains the Pauline epistles.
2,792 Minuscule codices	Also called "cursives." These were lower-case, handwritten leather manuscripts. This style of writing had been used for centuries in private documents but it was not until the ninth century that it was used for literary purposes. With the demand for New Testament books ever increasing, this Script had the advantages of taking less time to write and of occupying less space on the parchment. The two earliest known miniscules are: **Minuscule 33:** - dated: ninth century AD. Contains all but the book of Revelation. **Minuscule 1424:** - dated tenth century AD. Contains the entire new testament.
2,193 Lectionaries	The lectionaries were Greek service books that contained Scripture readings arranged in order for use in worship services. These service books, (found in both minuscule and uncial form), date from the eighth century AD.

A significant and critical point with regard to manuscripts for the textual critic is the date each manuscript was written. It turns out, according to scholars, that whilst the papyri are the oldest, the uncials come a close second, with the miniscules being much later in date. Aland and Aland, suggest a broad range for dates for the different manuscripts as shown in table 3.5.[256]

---

256   Kurt Aland and Barbara Aland. "The Text of the New Testament: An Introduction to the Critical Editions and to the Theory and Practice of Modern Textual Criticism." Eerdmans. Grand Rapids, USA. 1981. P81.

Table 3.4: Newer discoveries since the nineteenth century.

Type	Data known in 1956[257]	Data reported in 1994[258]	Data reported in 1998[259]
PAPYRI	81	85	96
UNCIALS	267	268	299
MINISCULES	2,764	2,792	2,812
LECTIONARIES	2,143	2,193	2,281
TOTAL	**5,255**	**5,338**	**5,488**

Table 3.5: Manuscript types and dates.

Type	Earliest	Majority	Latest
PAPYRI	125AD	Pre 4th century AD	8th century AD
UNCIALS	3rd century AD	5th to 9th century AD	11th/12th century AD
MINISCULES	9th/10th century AD	10th to 15th century AD	16th century AD
LECTIONARIES Uncials	4th century AD	8th to 12th century AD	13th century AD
LECTIONARIES Miniscules	9th century AD	10th to 16th century AD	16th century AD

Apart from the manuscript evidence, there is also early evidence for the New Testament in the early translations of the Bible and in quotations made by the Church Fathers (see table 3.6). In short, the wealth of material available as witness to the New Testament is astounding. So much material is available that a large part of this is still un-researched.

Text types or collation by mistakes.

It may come as a surprise to the reader that no two manuscripts we have are exactly identical in their wording. Each manuscript bears some errors in the text. However these errors are not the same in all manuscripts. Scholars have grouped the manuscripts we have into families of texts taking account of these textual errors or "variants" as they are known. Many of these variants amount to mere spelling mistakes, whilst others include the omission or addition of words. In recent years the idea of text types has been questioned, but since most still use these categories it will be necessary to describe these next.

---

257   E F Hills. "The King James Version Defended." P115,116.
258   M H Watts address at School of Theology. 1994. "The Authentic New Testament Text".
259   M H Watts booklet "The Lord gave the word" published by TBS. 1998. In 2001 the number reached 5,686 according to Norman Geisler & Peter Bocchino *Unshakeable Foundations*, (Minneapolis, MN: Bethany House Publishers, 2001) p. 256.   https://carm.org/manuscript-evidence.

Table 3.6: Ancient translations.

Type	Details
LATIN VERSIONS:	[] First version of the Gospels made in North Africa. Late second century AD. 50 manuscripts extant. [] As well as this early version there is also Jerome's Latin Vulgate promoted by the church of Rome - 382 AD - of which 8,000 manuscripts are still extant.
SYRIAC VERSIONS:	[] The Peshitta(o) - the historic Bible of the whole Syrian church. Dated: second century AD. 350 manuscripts extant. [] There are also some later Syriac versions.
COPTIC (NT) VERSION:	[] Exists in two dialects: Sahidic (Southern Egypt), and Boharic (Northern Egypt). [] Sahidic dates from the third century AD. The earliest Sahidic manuscript dates from the mid-fourth to the sixth century AD. [] Boharic extant in many later manuscripts.
GOTHIC VERSION:	[] Translated from the Greek in the middle of the fourth century AD by the missionary Ulfilas. 6 manuscripts of this version are still extant.
ARMENIAN VERSION:	[] Made in the fifth century AD. 1,244 manuscripts of this version are still extant.
GEORGIAN VERSION:	[] Produced by Christians from the mountains situated between the Black Sea and the Caspian Sea. Several manuscript copies are still extant.

The majority, Byzantine text.

Of the more than 5,600 manuscripts we have today more than 90% of them fall into one group or "text type" known as the Byzantine or majority text type.[260] A text type is a form of wording with particular variants and readings. The manuscripts of this "majority" have a very close agreement amongst them. This text type originated in Antioch in Syria but is found across a wide region of the ancient world. It was kept and followed by the Greek speaking peoples of the Byzantine empire which is why it is known as the "Byzantine" text type.[261] Many of the manuscripts of the Byzantine text type are miniscules, but there are also representatives amongst the uncials too, the oldest of which are, A (Codex Alexandrinus, 5th century) and C (Codex Ephraemi, 5th century). None of these manuscripts are earlier than the fourth century AD and many are dated as late as the 9th to 15th centuries AD. The Byzantine text type is also found in the many lectionaries, which were Greek "service" books in which readings have been arranged in a particular order for

---

260   The idea of "text types" has a long history. It is not always clear how these are defined by scholars, and in recent years textual critics have argued against using this notion. See: James R. White. The King James Only Controversy. Can you trust modern translations? Bethany House: Minneapolis, Minnesota, 2009.
261   It is sometimes called the "majority" text because it has 90+% of all manuscripts in its favour. It is also called the "Syrian" or "Antiochan" text.

worship. Now it ought to be an obvious truism that a majority of manuscripts would be much more likely to be representative of the original than any smaller grouping of texts, assuming that the transmission of the text follows a normal course.[262] However the academic world has generally rejected this group as a late *edited* collection that has accumulated many scribal alterations. These views have been repeated in the literature numerous times, but they are without any real or substantiated evidence, and depend heavily upon the history of the manuscripts which has been *manufactured* by textual critics.[263] But surely, it is just as easy to see a history of the text in which the great uniformity and smoothness of the Byzantine text type may instead be taken as proof that they were copied using a *high degree of accuracy* and care by scribes for a period of 1,000 years (AD 400 – 1400)? More recently some scholars have been arguing for them to be reconsidered in light of the hopeless situation that textual criticism has found itself in as a result of the last 130 years fruitless study.

The Alexandrian text.

About 10% of all manuscripts fall into what has been called the "Alexandrian" text type. This text type originated in Egypt.[264] The papyri discovered in the twentieth century are amongst this grouping as are some important uncial texts, two of which are Codex Vaticanus and Codex Sinaiticus, which we shall consider in more detail shortly. It turns out that the earliest manuscripts we have (the papyri) and some of these uncial texts are very rough, or impure. The wording varies between manuscripts and there is evidence of later corrections and additions to the text. Not only does the wording of these manuscripts differ from the Byzantine text type, but also (unlike the Byzantine) they show a considerable number of differences amongst themselves. The smoothness and agreement within the Byzantine text type was taken as indicating some form of standardisation and editing, for which there is no historical proof. However the variation between manuscripts of the Alexandrian text type, especially in the manuscripts before the fourth century AD is certainly indicative of poor copying which is surely not befitting of true Christian belief. According to one writer:

> ...some of the early copies show more liberties being taken by some early copyists. They often felt free to paraphrase, change words, or add or omit words in the early years of the copying of the NT.[265]

262   Clive E. Govier. The Majority Text Debate: A Study in New testament Text-Critical Method. MA Thesis. Edith Cowan University, Perth WA. 1996. P86.
263   As for footnote 262. P92,93.
264   Alexandria in northern Egypt boasted an impressive library where many Church Fathers were located.
265   http://www.nttext.com/newcms/index.php/nt-textual-criticism/majority-text.

This is certainly the case for these early papyri manuscripts found in the desert sands of Egypt. Such a fact is highly significant. It is to be remembered that in the earliest days of the Christian faith persecution, which included the destruction of the Scriptures in possession by Christians, was widespread. It is probable, therefore, that the number of manuscripts we have remaining today, represent a small proportion of the total number that existed in the early centuries after Christ. The fact that the earliest witnesses (papyri) came from the same region, the remote areas of Upper Egypt, is simply due to conditions. This is the region where the papyri may be preserved best. These thoughts suggest that there must have been large numbers of manuscripts in many other locations across the Roman Empire which we do not now posses, and which were probably burned in the fires of many persecutions. Of the many manuscripts that we do posses, we find that there are very few that can be linked in any way by relationship. In other words, there are extremely few manuscripts in our possession which can be shown to be copies of other manuscripts that are also extant.[266] This fact lends support to the idea that our current evidence in manuscripts is a small representative of the total that have been written and used.

Before we consider the two manuscripts held to be the most important by critical text followers in some detail (Vaticanus and Sinaiticus), we must note that there are two other text types. Thus there is the Western text type which was used by the church in the West and in North Africa, and the Caesarean text type which seems to have been a mixture of the Alexandrian and Western texts. The Western text is represented by the Old Latin translations, the Syriac versions, many of the Church Fathers and by D (Codex Bezae) for the book of Acts. The Caesarean text has W (Washington Codex, fifth century), P45, and two groups of minuscules and lectionaries as witness.[267] However most consider that these two text types are not the best representatives of the New Testament.

Codex Vaticanus.

A codex was a type of book made up of stitched vellum leaves. Vellum was an expensive type of parchment which was made from calf skins. Vaticanus (also named, B or uncial 03) is a fourth century uncial codex containing the Old and New Testaments and the apocrypha, but is missing most of Genesis, a part of 2Kings, some Psalms, and ends in the New Testament at Hebrews 9v15.[268] The text is Alexandrian in type. This codex was written using brown ink. Each leaf of the codex was around 27 to 28 centimetres square. There were three columns on each page

---

266   This is particularly true of the Byzantine text type. See: Clive E. Govier. The Majority Text Debate: A Study in New testament Text-Critical Method. MA Thesis. Edith Cowan University, Perth WA. 1996. P51.
267   Information gleaned from: http://www.theopedia.com/new-testament-textual-criticism.
268   http://www.catholicapologetics.info/Scripture/vulgate/codex.htm#Vaticanus.

and each column had about 40 to 44 lines. The text was written in a continuous form with uncial (capital) letters which are closely joined to one another. Codex Vaticanus was first noted in the Vatican library in the fifteenth century (1475) and is still kept at the Vatican to this day, although a number of facsimiles have been produced for study purposes.[269] Scholars believe that the codex was written by two different scribes and has had at least two correctors. One scribe wrote the Old Testament and the other wrote the New. As to the corrections it is believed that one corrected the manuscript in about 350 AD some time after it was originally written. A second corrector of the tenth or eleventh century retraced over the original Script which was fading. Although there are a few places where the original Script can still be seen, the work was of very poor quality and the original Script was spoilt.[270] Accents, breathing marks, and punctuation, have been added by a later hand. The manuscript has its own peculiar system of division rather than that followed by later scribes into chapters and sections, and all of the uncial capital letters are of the same size throughout. There are a large number of itacistic faults where vowel combinations are altered, and there are 795 places where the manuscript shows small horizontally aligned double dots known as "umlauts" or "distigmai." It is not known when these double dots were added, but Payne was the first to identify their significance. Based on a study of 1Corinthians 14v34,35 of the codex, Payne suggested that they were indications of another textual variant.[271] Thus someone who read through the manuscript shortly after it was written added these umlauts to indicate places where another textual variant was known.[272] One final point to note concerning Vaticanus is that at Hebrews 1v3 there is a very interesting marginal note which reads as follows:

"ἀμαθέστατε καὶ κακέ, ἄφες τὸν παλαιόν, μὴ μεταποίει."

"Fool and knave, leave the old reading and do not change it!"

Codex Sinaiticus.

Sinaiticus (also referred to as Aleph or uncial 01), is a fourth century uncial codex containing an Alexandrian text.[273] It contains some parts of the Old Testament (about half), the apocrypha, and all of the New Testament except John 7v53-8v11, Mark 16v9-20 and Romans

---

269   John C. Miney, Preservation of the Copies PP123-162. In God's Word in our Hands. Edited by James B. Williams & |Randolph Shaylor. Ambassador Emerald International, South Carolina USA. 2003. P140.
270   As for footnote 269. P139
271   Philip B. Payne and Paul Canart, *The Text-Critical Function of the Umlauts in Vaticanus, with Special Attention to 1 Corinthians 14.34 35: A Response to J. Edward Miller*, JSNT27 (2004). PP105–112.
272   As for footnote 271.
273   http://www.catholicapologetics.info/Scripture/vulgate/codex.htm#Sinaiticus.

16v24.[274] It probably originally had about 730 leaves but today we have only 390 leaves plus fragments of 3 more leaves. Each page has four columns of text and each column has 48 lines. Like Vaticanus the uncial form is continuous with no spaces and no punctuation and it is written on expensive vellum parchment. The codex is to be found in four separate places. It was originally discovered in St. Catherine's monastery in the middle of the nineteenth century. The British Library in London has the largest surviving portion (347 leaves) comprising all of the New Testament. Other parts of this codex can be found at St. Catherine's Monastery, Leipzig University Library in Germany, and the National Library of Russia in St. Petersburg. The codex is thought to have been written by four different scribes of very differing ability, although some suggest that as many as ten scribes have had their hand in the work. Metzger has this to say on the corrections in Sinaiticus;

> In the light of such carelessness in transcription, it is not surprising that a good many correctors (as many as nine) have been at work on the manuscript . . . Tischendorf's edition of the manuscript enumerates some 14,800 places where some alteration has been made to the text . . . [with] more recent detailed scrutiny of the manuscript . . . by the use of ultra-violet lamp, Milne and Skeat discovered that the original reading in the manuscript was erased . . .[275]

The scribe who copied the prophets was apparently a terrible speller, whilst the scribe responsible for the historical and poetic books and much of the New Testament is thought to be slightly better. The best scribe copied some of the apocrypha and a few Psalms. There is also evidence of corrections possibly done by the original scribes, although there is evidence to suggest other correctors added their penmanship too. The British Library website editor comments that the corrections:

> contain many significant alterations and, together with further extensive corrections undertaken probably in the seventh century, are some of the most interesting features of the manuscript.[276]

In the nineteenth century Dr. Scrivener made a study of Codex Sinaiticus and found that there were numerous alterations and corruptions on every page in the text, added by as many as ten different hands.[277] One of the scribes who copied the text does not appear to have known Greek, for he

---

274   The first two of these are now, as a result, seriously disputed as being original by many commentators.
275   Bruce Metzger, ManuScripts of the Greek Bible (Oxford: Oxford University Press, 1991), 77.
276   http://www.bl.uk/onlinegallery/sacredtexts/codexsinai.html.
277   Dr. Scrivenenr, *A Full Collation of the Codex Sinaiticus.* 1864. PP xix,xxv. See also Philip Mauro. *Which Version?* P45.

habitually split words at the end of lines, even two letter words, even though there was plenty of room on the one line.[278] This is what Scrivener had to say about the codex:

> It must be confessed, indeed, that the Codex Sinaiticus abounds with similar errors of the eye and pen, to an extent not unparalleled, but happily rather unusual in documents of first-rate importance; so that Tregelles has freely pronounced that "the state of the text, as proceeding from the first scribe, may be regarded as *very rough*" (N. T. Part ii. p. 2). Letters, words, even whole sentences, are frequently written twice over, or begun and immediately cancelled: whilst that gross blunder technically known as Homoeoteleuton ..., whereby a clause is omitted because it happens to end in the same words as the clause preceding, occurs no less than 115 times in the N. T., though the defect is often supplied by a more recent hand.[279]

Sinaiticus and Vaticanus compared.

Both Vaticanus and Sinaiticus have a blank space at the end of Mark's gospel and so the scribes who copied the text were well aware of the longer ending of Mark.[280] Theses two codices seem to show evidence of a text which was poor and which needed correction. Dean Burgon, the textual critic who opposed Westcott and Hort, made the following comments on these two manuscripts:

> It is in fact easier to find two consecutive verses in which these two MSS differ the one from the other, than two consecutive verses in which they entirely agree.[281]

According to textual critic H. C. Hoskier there are 3,036 textual variations between Vaticanus and Sinaiticus in the gospels alone (Matthew: 656; Mark: 567; Luke: 791; John: 1022).[282] Such facts do not lend themselves to a favourable view of these fourth century witnesses to the New Testament. We must rememenr also that these witnesses were unknown to the world until the middle and end of the nineteenth century.

Attitudes to these two codices vary wildly. Those in the KJV Only camp believe it was a work of Satan! Critical text advocates from Westcott and Hort onwards esteem these manuscripts as the best of all. White has suggested that whilst Byzantine text advocates' view that the many

---

278   Dr. Scrivenenr, *A Full Collation of the Codex Sinaiticus*. 1864. P xiv. See also Philip Mauro. *Which Version?* P46.
279   As for footnote 278.
280   http://www.catholicapologetics.info/Scripture/vulgate/codex.htm#Sinaiticus.
          http://www.thetextofthegospels.com/2016/04/codex-vaticanus-and-ending-of-mark.html.
          http://www.thetextofthegospels.com/2015/09/codex-sinaiticus-and-ending-of-mark.html.
281   Dean John W. Burgon, *Revision Revised* (1883). P12.
282   Herman C. Hoskier, *Codex B and its Allies*, Bernard Quaritch, London 1914.

correctors of Codex Sinaiticus render it useless and corrupt, a better judgement is to take precisely the opposite view! He states:

> We have already noted that what this really demonstrates is that the manuscript was so highly esteemed as to be used so often and for so long as to collect so many corrections.[283]

White goes on to say that the correctors were attempting to bring the text into line with the Byzantine text type.[284] This is quite interesting. Why would they do this? Critical text followers believe it to be an attempt to edit and standardise the text. However it is equally probable that the believers of the day were concerned to correct the text *from* its corruptions rather than *away* from a pure beginning. We can say this on the basis that the **original** shows clear evidence of error and corruption. Chiefly, we note the blank space at the end of Mark's gospel, and the many umlauts or double dots. White tries to chart a balanced course between the curious and wild opinions on Codex Sinaiticus:

> Codex Sinaiticus is not nearly as bad as its enemies would say, nor as good as Tischendorf or others wished. It is neither demonic nor infallible. It is instead a great treasure, for a while the oldest manuscript known, and for all time a tremendously valuable asset to our knowledge of the New Testament text. ... Others accuse it of being so full of errors as to be almost useless, but while there are indeed many corrections in the text of א , such is hardly surprising. A handwritten text used for fifteen hundred years is going to collect a few corrections along the way.[285]

Such a series of statements is quite difficult to accept once they have been processed. The problem is that White has bought into the academic view that texts are always corrupt and in need of correction. Academia cannot accept the much purer Byzantine text and constantly assume corruption and error to be the norm. Byzantine text followers and KJV Only folk have argued repeatedly that this manuscript (along with Vaticanus) was, in fact, ignored by the church in general as evidenced by the pristine condition of the leaves (hardly thumbed or worn) and by the fact that they had to be re-discovered in the nineteenth century. Although the corrections and additions have occurred over the centuries, showing that isolated scholars may have worked on the manuscripts, this is not evidence that they were actually *used* by believers. These texts seem to have been discarded by the church, or, at best, an attempt (or attempts) were made to correct them.

---

283   James R. White. The King James Only Controversy. Can you trust modern translations? Bethany House: Minneapolis, Minnesota, 2009. P230.
284   As for footnote 283.
285   As for footnote 283. P58

Greek New Testament editions.

Currently there are three competing Greek editions of the New Testament.[286] These are: the Textus Receptus, the Majority Text, and the 27th edition of the Nestle-Aland Text. There are 138,019 words in the Nestle-Aland text, 140,259 words in the Majority text, and 140,744 words in the Textus Receptus.[287] The difference in word count between the extremes is 2,755 which amounts to about 2% of the total, so that all three texts are at least 98% identical in words. Considered from the point of view of the texts overall, it turns out that the agreement in text between that produced by Westcott and Hort (which is very close to the Nestle-Aland text), and the Textus Receptus amounts to 98.33%.[288] Such an assessment is universally acknowledged by scholars of all types. Of the remaining 1.67% of textual differences about 90% of these are so trivial they have no material affect on translation. In other words they would not even appear as a result of translation. Of the difficulties that are left, only about 50 or so would affect the meaning of a text but none alter any Christian doctrine. The end result is summed up by White:

> The reality is that the amount of variation between the two most extremely different New Testament manuscripts would not fundamentally alter the message of the Scriptures! ... The simple fact of the matter is that no textual variants in either the Old or New Testament in any way, shape, or form materially disrupt or destroy any essential doctrine of the Christian faith.[289]

Thus, at the outset we must establish the unassailable fact that even though there are differences, and we must not ignore these in view of such Scriptures as, Deuteronomy 4v2; Proverbs 30v6 and Revelation 22v18, nevertheless no differences amount to an alteration in doctrine or teaching. The same message can be preached regardless of the Greek text used. Having said this we have a duty as Christians to examine the evidence from a Biblical perspective and come to a reasoned conclusion based on Scriptural grounds. When we have established exactly which is the New Testament text, we must endeavour to preach and teach from this in a spirit of peace and love and not with rancour or bitterness.

---

286   I am well aware that each of these has had several "editions" throughout the years since they were first published, (with the exception of the Majority text as it is quite recent), but my point is that we have three *different* Greek editions or, more properly, selections from amongst the manuscript evidence.

287   Mark Minnick, How Much Difference Do The Differences Make? PP229-277. In God's Word in our Hands. Edited by James B. Williams & Randolph Shaylor. Ambassador Emerald International, South Carolina USA. 2003. P233,234. NA – Nestle-Aland; M – Majority; TR – Textus Receptus. The 4th UBS text is identical to the 27th NA text except in regard to the critical apparatus. Note that the difference between the Majority text and the TR amounts to 0.34-0.35%.

288   James R. White. The King James Only Controversy. Can you trust modern translations? Bethany House: Minneapolis, Minnesota, 2009. P66.

289   As for footnote 288. P67.

The story of how each Greek edition of the New Testament came into existence is quite revealing. With regard to the Textus Receptus its origins can be traced back to the work of Erasmus, a Roman Catholic scholar of high distinction, who is credited with the honour of producing the first Greek New Testament published in 1516. Much has been written in discrediting the worth and value of Erasmus' 1516 edition, especially by those who want to rebut the "KJV Only" groups who invest it with the status of being inspired. Erasmus' text was constructed from somewhere between 4 and 7 Greek manuscripts, all from the Byzantine text type, and the last few verses of Revelation were translated from the Latin![290] He was propelled into producing the edition far too quickly for fear that a rival would gain the honour of having the first Greek New Testament published. Consequently there were numerous mistakes and errors in the printed editions. This is understandable given the haste and the fact that the typeface had to be set manually. In fact it is difficult to establish which of the extant 1516 versions is the real one because two sites were used to print the work and different mistakes were found in these different printed editions. Consequently in the first edition there were in fact at least two different versions! There were several revisions of this work, and other textual critics built on the work of Erasmus. The reader can trace the details of the story elsewhere as it is not my intention to reproduce the events suffice to say that although Erasmus was the first to produce a Greek text, the Greek text we have as the "Textus Receptus" today (printed by the Trinitarian Bible Society), is far from identical to the one produced by Erasmus. We must be generous to Erasmus and the times he lived in. Not only was it a dangerous time to be producing a Greek New Testament, but Erasmus laboured at a time when Greek manuscripts were quite hard to come by. It must be noted that Erasmus' work is always reported as being of the highest quality. One fact not often realised, is that the number of Greek manuscripts he was aware of and which he ignored, has not been taken into account. Merle D'Aubigne the French historian made this comment on Erasmus' work:

> Nothing was more important at the dawn of the Reformation than the publication of the Testament of Jesus Christ in the original language. Never had Erasmus worked so carefully. 'If I told what sweat it cost me, no one would believe me.' He had collated many Greek MSS. of the New Testament, and was surrounded by all the commentaries and translations, by the writings of Origen, Cyprian, Ambrose, Basil, Chrysostom, Cyril, Jerome, and Augustine. ... He had investigated the texts according to principles of sacred criticism. When a knowledge of Hebrew was necessary, he had consulted Capito, and more particularly Ecolampadius. Nothing without Theseus, said he of the latter, making use of a Greek proverb.[291]

---

290   James R. White. The King James Only Controversy. Can you trust modern translations? Bethany House: Minneapolis, Minnesota, 2009. PAGE ??????
291   J.H. Merle D'Aubigne, History of the Reformation of the Sixteenth Century, New York: Hurst & Company,

E. F. Hills, who wrote in defence of the KJV, noted that Erasmus was aware of most of the variant readings scholars know of today:

> Through his study of the writings of Jerome and other Church Fathers Erasmus became very well informed concerning the variant readings of the New Testament text. Indeed almost all the important variant readings known to scholars today were already known to Erasmus more than 460 years ago and discussed in the notes (previously prepared) which he placed after the text in his editions of the Greek New Testament. Here, for example, Erasmus dealt with such problem passages as the conclusion of the Lord's Prayer (Matt. 6:13), the interview of the rich young man with Jesus (Matt. 19:17-22), the ending of Mark (Mark 16:9-20), the angelic song (Luke 2:14), the angel, agony, and bloody seat omitted (Luke 22:43-44), the woman taken in adultery (John 7:53-8:11), and the mystery of godliness (1 Tim. 3:16)".[292]

It would seem, then, that the Textus Receptus, which was formed through the revisions of Erasmus work and others who followed, was not that much different from a text derived from the majority witness to the New Testament.

It would not be until the latter part of the nineteenth century that a very different Greek edition would be produced. There is no doubt that the edition produced by Westcott and Hort was born out of a dislike of the Textus Receptus, and followed in the wake of the startling new discoveries of Vaticanus and Sinaiticus.[293] Westcott and Hort's working hypothesis was that the later Byzantine text was one which had been edited and thus constructed by an ecclesiastical leader or council some time around or just after the fourth century AD. As such it was then considered to be an inferior text which was distant to the original New Testament, and the two academics preferred the newly discovered Alexandrian uncials (Sinaiticus and Vaticanus) which were the earliest witnesses available at that time, referring to these as the "neutral" text. Their new edition, published in 1881, was based, in large part, on these new discoveries. It did not escape some scrutiny, especially by Dean John Burgon who argued for the priority of the majority text. However academia was generally persuaded by the new Greek edition of Westcott and Hort. This was a critical text and its close descendants, the Nestle-Aland and UBS editions, whilst by no means identical to their father, nevertheless all follow in similar fashion. Modern critical texts such as the 27th edition of Nestle-Aland and the 4th edition of the UBS are so close to the Westcott Hort text as to make very little difference.

1835, Vol. 5. P157.
292   E. F. Hills. The King James Version Defended, 1956, 1979. P198-199.
293   Other acadmics such as Tischendorf hated the TR too.

The theory propounded by Westcott and Hort to explain the manuscript evidence suffered some fatal blows in the twentieth century, but this has not changed academia's preference for the oldest manuscripts. As the twentieth century dawned and then progressed, Egyptian papyri were discovered which were earlier still than Vaticanus and Sinaiticus. These papyri have changed much, but the critical text built upon the latest discoveries still owes a great deal to Westcott and Hort's Greek edition and thinking. Unsurprisingly, the Byzantine majority text is still largely ignored by academia.

A few scholars have broken the mould in recent years and have argued within academia for the Byzantine majority text as the basis for a Greek edition of the New Testament. Thus Hodges and Farstad produced a Greek text based on the majority of manuscript evidence in 1982, whilst Robinson and Pierpont published another in 2005.[294] There has been no translation based on these Greek texts, but that they have been produced indicates some movement away from the reliance on the ideas of Westcott and Hort.

[3] Two critical views.

We could have selected any number of examples from amongst those who follow a critical text view, beginning with the originators, Westcott and Hort who propelled a critical theory in 1881. However we have selected two proponents of the critical view who figure quit prominently in discussions about the New Testament text. Our first example comes from one who argues as an evangelical scholar and who attempts to counter the "KJV Only" camp.[295] The second comes from two scholars (a married couple) who have been instrumental in establishing the main critical Greek text used by scholars and commentators.

[a] James White, the critical text and an historical approach.

James White has done a masterful job of presenting the modern case for accepting the critical scholarly view of New Testament textual criticism. His work is well written and his aim is to defend the Christian faith and to warn unsuspecting believers of the unscrupulous claims of some KJV Only proponents who make unsubstantiated claims. White's basic starting point is to consider the whole topic from the point of view of history rather than theology. This is a characteristic of many who accept the critical text, and it is in stark contrast to those who opt for the KJV alone, who

---

294   The New Testament in the Original Greek (Greek edition). Maurice A. Robinson and William G. Pierpoint editors. Chilton Book Publishing. 2005. The Greek New Testament According to the Majority Text. Zane C. Hodges and Arthur L. Farstad editors. Thomas Nelson. 1982.
295   The "KJV Only" camp are those who believe either that the KJV is inspired, or that the Textus Receptus is inspired.

attempt to approach the subject from a theological beginning. Now I must state here that many who advocate the KJV alone position are clearly guilty of hyperbole and sensationalism, and White demonstrates this clearly by looking at the worst proponents. One of the main criticisms against the KJV Only position is that these folk take as their starting point the Textus Receptus or the KJV Bible. This is usually a point of sheer belief, although it sometimes has an historical component. White shows that the Textus Receptus has a long and developed history, and the KJV translation is not without its faults, facts which KJV only folk seem to ignore. White's rebuttal and criticism against the KJV only group is important. However his position, following the critical text, is equally problematic. The main criticism I want to bring against the critical text position is that it starts from the point of view of history. That is, it is essential for critical text advocates to have a knowledge of the history of the manuscripts we have available today. Thus only by understanding the history of the manuscripts, the way the scribes copied manuscripts, and how the texts may have developed over time, will we be able to *recover* the New Testament text. These two approaches, an historical one followed by critical text followers, and a theological one followed by KJV Only advocates are the only two approaches we can make. If you read any works from either camp it is very easy to see the differences. KJV Only advocates start with Scripture and quote Biblical texts in support of their views. Critical text followers argue almost exclusively in an historical manner, and apart from using Scripture examples to debate the weight and value of texts, they do not make appeals to the essence of the Scriptures (and what they affirm) to argue their case. Critical text advocates hold that taking a theological stance is not the way to approach the problem.

So what are we to say in response to these two positions? First of all we must contend with the critical text group concerning the insistence of an historical only approach to the text. It seems wholly erroneous from all points of view as a Christian, to approach any subject without starting from a Biblical and theological perspective. The Scriptures alone are our authority and this is true no matter what subject we care to mention, including the text and canon of Scripture. Now some may argue that this amounts to circular reasoning. We want to look at the manuscript evidence and point directly to the true Scriptures, and we are going to use those same Scriptures to do this job. How can anyone suggest such a scheme and be taken seriously? I think such an objection is one which will be presented often and must be considered. The problem is that this argument of circular reasoning actually applies to *any* arguments we care to make from any starting point and is not just applicable to Scripture's use to understand Scripture and its origins. Taking a critical text view requires us to have some opinions and beliefs concerning history and the pursuit of historical enquiry. In fact this problem is at the heart of all epistemological thinking. When Betrand Russell and Alfred North Whitehead tried to produce mathematics from scratch they realised that you must start from some "assumed" axioms.[296] It is impossible to begin any enquiry without first stating the grounds upon which you start out. Kurt Gödel, (a mathematician), framed a theorem which showed that for any system there must be at least two reference points. It is known as the "incompleteness theorem." No statement can ever prove its own truth. There must be another independent reference point. Critical text advocates believe they have the upper hand by dint of numbers. So many scholars agree about the underlying assumptions in their system that no one calls them into question. In conclusion, for the Christian, it is essential and necessary that in approaching this subject we take a Biblical and theologically informed stance and starting point. Sadly the approach by many who profess faith amongst the KJV Only camp leaves much to be desired with poor exegesis and scant acceptance that the historical data, whilst not being determinative, must be interacted with

Looking at White's work we begin with a reminder that he insists on an historical approach to the problem:

> One will note that to this point I have referred to the facts of history. I have not injected theology into this discussion.[297]

We must pause here and ask the difficult question: exactly what are the "facts of history?" The same types of problem are encountered when we examine the fossil record in our debates with evolution. It is vital that we accept the "facts," but it is equally vital that we question the theoretical accretions that infuse many stated "facts." White also cannot help but indicate that certain matters are not a matter of historical fact but must be believed. Of course this is couched in highly academic terms as though the layers of scholastic achievements and writings could somehow turn "belief" into "evidence." For example, when talking about the majority of manuscripts (the Byzantine text type) White states:

> Most scholars today (in opposition to KJV Onlyism) would see the Alexandrian as representing an earlier, and hence more accurate, form of text than the Byzantine text-type.
> Most also believe the Byzantine represents a later period in which readings from other text-types were put together (conflated) into the Byzantine reading.[298]

---

296   http://www.storyofmathematics.com/20th_russell.html.
297   James R. White. The King James Only Controversy. Can you trust modern translations? Bethany House: Minneapolis, Minnesota, 2009. P87.
298   As for footnote 297. P71.

This quote showing the faith stance of scholars is by no means a one-off as White himself uses this phrase to demonstrate the scholarly views he holds to.[299] It is imperative that we read the words of the above quote carefully. There is no objective evidence for the statements made. It is true that manuscripts can be dated, provided the assumptions used to assign dates are cogent.[300] But the link between the earliest manuscripts and the degree of accuracy is not a necessity. For example, let us suppose that we have a fourth century uncial codex containing the gospels and a tenth century miniscule which also reproduces the gospels. Let us further suppose that the fourth century codex was a tenth generation copy, whilst the tenth century miniscule was a copy of a second century document which, in turn, was a copy of the autographs. The later manuscript will surely be more reliable than the earlier one. Such a scenario is not outside the realms of possibility for we do not have knowledge of the provenance of the manuscripts. Consider the genealogical relationships described in Scripture. Thus covering approximately 215 years from the descent into Egypt by Jacob and his sons to the Exodus, there were but four generations from Levi to Moses, whilst from Joseph via Ephraim to Joshua there were eleven generations.[301] In the same way manuscripts can have numerous ancestors or through longevity have much fewer. The great problem is that no one actually knows what the genealogy of any manuscripts are, as we have very few manuscripts which are related (i.e. where we know that one is derived from another). In the second part of White's statement he continues to base ideas on the belief of scholars. To try and explain why the Byzantine text is "fuller" (i.e. longer) than the critical text he suggests that the explanation is that when the Greek scribes were copying manuscripts they took readings from different sources and joined them together or "conflated" them. There is no evidence for this. It is simply stated as a belief. This is a deeply entrenched belief in the academic world, but there isn't any objective evidence provided for it. It is just as easy to believe that the Alexandrian text is "shorter" or "less full" because the scribes who copied the manuscripts in this way omitted words and phrases.

In order to "explain" the Byzantine text type and its being the majority, White resorts again to an appeal to history.[302] The story he constructs reads a lot like any secular inquiry and gives us no theological or Biblical impetus. It is worth spending some time outlining White's argument in some

---

299   James R. White. The King James Only Controversy. Can you trust modern translations? Bethany House: Minneapolis, Minnesota, 2009. P82.
300   We do not have the time to discuss the dating of manuscripts. Many are not dated at all. Some have dates on them because they were used for other purposes (e.g. a manuscript which was first used to copy some portion of the New Testament could then later have some other document written on the opposite side which is dated or a document which was written and dated may have then be used later to copy some part of the New Testament). Uncials (upper case letters) are thought to have been written earlier, whilst cursives (miniscules) are thought to be later. We shall assume that the dating of manuscripts is accurate but note that there are reasons for debate still.
301   Genesis 15v16 ; Exodus 6v16-19; Numbers 26v58,59; 1Chronicles 7v20-27.
302   As for footnote 299. P72,194.

detail, for it is only then that we can examine it to see if it is worth holding on to. Thus White begins with what he considers to be obvious:

> It is plainly evident that most textual variations arose quite early in the history of the New Testament, during that period of time when the Christian faith was still illegal, persecution was common, and most of those engaged in copying the Scriptures were not professional scribes but simple laypeople who hungered to have a copy of any portion of the inspired writings themselves.[202]

This statement conceals a variety of assertions which are based on further speculation. Thus, for example, White asserts that the earliest copyists were poor and slapdash in their work. White contends that the early Christians did not posses copies of the Scriptures as we do in our day, and the reason for this is partly because of persecution, but mainly because writing was a tedious and extremely tricky procedure.[304] How does he know this? There is no doubt that White overstates the case here because a little later he contradicts this pessimistic picture with these words:

> Since the gospel went to "all people," all sorts of different people had direct access to the New Testament and therefore were able to make copies of the documents in a language they understood. Christians were open about spreading their message far and wide, and as a result, the New Testament text went far and wide as well. Rather than being limited to trained scribes, we discover that business,en, soldiers, and even literate slaves often made personal copies of one of the Gospels so ad to be able to read about their Lord Jesus. Less trained individuals might make more transcription errors than the experienced scribes, but this was unavoidable given the Christian belief that the message of Christ was to go to everyone.[305]

Apart from the obvious fact that early Christians must have been scrupulous about the content of the text because it was all about their wonderful Saviour Jesus Christ, White suggests that we have a situation where copies were not made much because of the difficulty of copying, and yet he then contends that Christians of all types copied the text at any opportunity!

We cannot deny that the manuscripts do show differences and variations. This is something which none can deny. However White is also trying to explain the evidence we posses. That is, that the earliest manuscripts in our possession (the papyri found in Egypt) are the ones that contain the most variations and defects. To explain this White resorts to assuming that early Christians under persecution copied the Scriptures very carelessly. We cannot let such an assertion pass. It may be

---

303   James R. White. The King James Only Controversy. Can you trust modern translations? Bethany House: Minneapolis, Minnesota, 2009. P195.
304   As for footnote 303. P52,53,55.
305   As for footnote 303. P70.

true that those who copied the Scriptures in Egypt in the early centuries were careless, but does that mean that Christians everywhere were so careless? Arguing on the basis of the evidence in Egypt (which was unknown until the twentieth century) to explain the way things occurred throughout the ancient world is poor history to start with, and to cap it all it ignores the supreme witness of the Scriptures themselves. These give witness to writing being a normal activity, and are replete with warnings about twisting or peddling the word of God amongst other things.[306] Thus whilst we recognise that our earliest witnesses to the New Testament are, perhaps, the poorest copies, we do not allow such information to determine the rest of our understanding. These are an extremely small percentage of all the Greek texts we have, and come from just one area of the world (Egypt). The Scriptures teach us otherwise than White asserts. If the Scriptures are truly the inspired writings, then Christians would undoubtedly have taken much more care than White is allowing for. White continues his historical explanations with these words:

> After the faith became legal at the beginning of the fourth century, more accurate methods of copying and more professional copyists helped to "freeze" the readings of the text, keeping variations due to unprofessional scribal work down to a minimum in the centuries that followed. The Alexandrian, Western, and Caesarean text-types described in chapter 3 were already in existence at this time, having arisen in those first few generations of the Christian church.[307]

So, according to critical text followers, in the early centuries the copying of the Scriptures was poor and loose. When Christianity became the state religion the professional scribes began taking control and the text-types we know of became evident and settled. All of this is mere speculation. Why suddenly are there "more accurate methods"? Where is the evidence for this? Once again, given the importance of the New Testament revelation in connection with the Old Testament, isn't it patently obvious that the copying of Scripture would have been a sacred and careful task undertaken by the early evangelists and apostles?

Now White continues with reference to the Byzantine text-type which he believes (along with all other critical text advocates) arose late on the scene:

> The Byzantine text-type, however, arose later, and here is the great area of conflict. The question we must ask proponents of this type is: Upon what basis should we believe that the Byzantine text, simply because it ended up being the majority text later in history, was the best representative of the original writings during those vital first few centuries? If we were

---

306   Luke 1v63; 2Corinthians 2v17; Philemon 1v19; 2Timothy 4v13; 2peter 3v16.
307   James R. White. The King James Only Controversy. Can you trust modern translations? Bethany House: Minneapolis, Minnesota, 2009. P195.

to transport ourselves to AD 200 and look at the New Testament text at that time, ignoring for the moment what was to come later, what would we find?

The evidence right now indicates that this text looked most like the Alexandrian text-type. How do we know this? Every papyrus manuscript we have discovered has been a representative of the Alexandrian text-type. ... the Byzantine is not found in full form until the fourth century and does not become the majority until the ninth century.[308]

Aside from the contradiction made here about which text-types were in evidence in the early centuries, White is certain that the Byzantine text-type did not exist in this time. It only arose in the fourth century![309] Interestingly though, the Byzantine text-type was well known from this time onwards in the Greek speaking world and we must therefore ask: Where did it come from? There must have been a source. What White and other critical text followers want to assert is that the evidence we have is all the evidence that is needed. The papyri came first (these are quite corrupt), the uncials come next (these are Alexandrian), and the Byzantine comes last (this is an edited smoothed conflated text). What, however, if the Byzantine text-type had a long history within the region from Syria through Asia Minor up through Greece, and owes nothing whatsoever to the papyri? Why is this "history" any less legitimate than the one White favours? In fact such a history is far more likely given that Antioch and Syria were the regions with the greatest number of apostolic writings. It is more likely, surely, to suggest that the Byzantine text type is a direct descendant of the autographs copied within this mainly Greek speaking area. White's assertion about the papyri and uncials witnessing to the Alexandrian text-type alone is actually not quite true. There is evidence of Byzantine readings in papyri, uncials and amongst the Church Fathers.[310]

However, I do not want to labour such a contest. What I am really concerned about is showing up the arguments based on history as not just weak, but theologically dangerous. If we base our understanding of the New Testament text on history we will be woefully prepared. We need to grasp the fact that our Scriptures have not arisen in some haphazard and bizarre way. The evidence of history is scant and does not tell the whole story. This is so obvious as to not need working out, but that we only have a very small proportion of the manuscripts that have been copied must be accepted by all. It is inconceivable that the early disciples did not write and copy the manuscripts from day one after the resurrection! Given the rise and spread of the Christian faith we can assert from a Biblical perspective, that the "Great Commission" must have included copying the

---

308   James R. White. The King James Only Controversy. Can you trust modern translations? Bethany House: Minneapolis, Minnesota, 2009. P195,196.

309   Other scholars argue that there is abundant evidence for the Byzantine text type in the papyri, uncials and in the writings of the Church Fathers. See, for example, Wilbur N. Pickering, The Identity of the New Testament text. Thomas Nelson, 1977. P68,152.

310   http://www.logosresourcepages.org/Versions/received.htm.

Scriptures to enable proper discipleship to take place.[311] Given further that persecution resulted in the destruction of not just many Christians but their Scriptures as well, we have lost much of the evidence that would be needed to construct any fair reading of history. The problem of all history is that is bedevilled by a hopeless lack of evidence. So much for constructing our view of the text on an historical footing!

The real pain in the neck for critical text followers is the smoothness and limited variants found in the Byzantine text-type. The only way that this is routinely explained by the academic world which favours the critical text, is to say that someone edited the text and forced it into a smoothed out form. Why not believe, instead, that the Christians who copied these manuscripts were *extremely careful* because of their love for Christ? Why isn't this explanation an option? From a Biblical point of view, the fact that the majority Byzantine text type is so smooth and does not have the wild variations evident in the Alexandrian text type must be seen as a wonderful indication of the providence of preservation. Some may respond that the Alexandrian text type has been preserved too. However its use throughout the last two thousand years has been limited, unlike the use made by the church of the Byzantine text type.

Having outlined the problem of a critical text approach because of its reliance on history rather than theology, it will be instructive to look a little more at some of the examples White offers that show (in his opinion) the scribal errors that result in the longer Byzantine text type. One type of example he suggests is referred to as of "expansion of piety," whereby a scribe adds a divine title that was not present in the original (according to White). Another type of error apparently arises from the insertion from a "parallel passage," whereby a scribe inadvertently adds text from his own remembered knowledge of similar wording elsewhere. These suggestions really only amount to speculative flights of fancy which owe more to the assumptions made than any clear proof. We shall consider some of the many White lists. For example, Ephesians 1v2 compared to Colossians 1v2 shows the following in the NKJV and the NIV:

Table 3.7: Comparison of two texts following White.

	Ephesians 1v2	Colossians 1v2b
NKJV	Grace to you and peace from God our Father and the Lord Jesus Christ.	Grace to you and peace from God our Father and the Lord Jesus Christ.
NIV	Grace and peace to you from God our Father and the Lord Jesus Christ.	Grace and peace to you from God our Father.

---

311   Matthew 28v18f.

In Ephesians 1v2 both translations agree (except in English word order, which is irrelevant here). However there is a discrepancy between the NIV and the NKJV for Colossians 1v2b. So in Colossians 1v2b either the NIV omits the words: "and the Lord Jesus Christ," or, the NKJV adds these words. Textual data shows that whilst the uncials B, D, K, L, and Ψ support the shorter reading, uncials א, A, C, F, G and I support the longer reading with the words "and the Lord Jesus Christ" as being original.[312] How do the experts come to the conclusion that these words are not original in Colossians 1v2b? White uses this example to suggest that a scribe was guilty of harmonizing the text as he copied out the letter to the Colossians. As he was writing out the letter he comes across the shorter reading, but because he was aware of the longer phrase (apparently used in liturgical services), he adjusts the text before him to harmonise with the longer reading. Apart from the textual evidence we have given (and this is not exhaustive because the cursives have not been consulted), the "explanation" is pure fantasy! We can just as easily invent a story to explain why uncials B, D, K, L, and Ψ omit the phrase as a careless slip of the mind. How do we know which is correct?

White also suggests in another example that the NKJV/AV translation of Colossians 1v14 includes a phrase borrowed from Ephesians 1v7. However the manuscript evidence in favour of the NKJV/AV translation which includes the phrase is strong. The assumption that the phrase has been "borrowed" from Ephesians 1v7 is sheer conjecture.

Next we should look at the case of Mark 9v44f where White suggests that the repetition of a phrase is an obvious insertion by scribes. Here is White's statement:

> In both Mark 9:44 and 46 the phrase "where their worm dieth not, and the fire is not quenched" has been inserted in later manuscripts in both places, repeating the very same phrase found in verse 48. The manuscripts that do not contain the phrase, while in the minority, make up a wide range of witnesses against these verses. There is no reason for them to have been accidentally omitted, and obviously they were not purposefully omitted because all the manuscripts contain the very same words at verse 48. Hence, both verses are rightly removed from the text as not being part of what Mark originally wrote.[313]

It is to be noted that the textual evidence for these verses being present is much greater than the evidence which omits them. The rejection of these verses by White and many others comes only through a set of beliefs based on the priority of the Alexandrian text form.[314]

---

312   https://www.stepbible.org/?q=version=VarApp|reference=Col.1&options=GNHVU.
313   James R. White. The King James Only Controversy. Can you trust modern translations? Bethany House: Minneapolis, Minnesota, 2009. P199.
314   Clive E. Govier. The majority text debate : a study in New Testament text-critical method. MA thesis. 1996. Edith Cowan University. P134f.

White suggests that John 5v4, which describes the angel troubling the waters for the sick to be healed in, is a clear case of a marginal note being inserted into the text. Here is how White explains this verse:

> This verse is a classic instance of how a marginal note explaining something in the text can end up as part of the text somewhere down the line.[315]

As evidence, White suggests that the many variants found at this place is sufficient to "prove" the case! In fact the textual data is much greater for the inclusion of the words as original than omission. For the words:

> *those who were sick, blind, crippled, withered. And a certain man*

the evidence is: two papyri and four uncials.[316] For the words:

> *those who were sick, blind, crippled, withered, waiting for the moving of the water, for an angel of the Lord went down at certain seasons into the pool, and troubled the water; then the one who got in first after the troubling of the water became healthy, [regardless] of whatever disease he was being held by. And a certain man*

the evidence is: a host of uncials, and many other witnesses including all the Byzantine manuscripts.[317] Once again the assumption of Alexandrian priority based on the "oldest is best" mantra is in force here against the majority of Greek witnesses. Later, White suggests that the word "firstborn" in Matthew 1v25 has been inserted by a scribe who was remembering or looking at Luke 2v7, despite the fact that the vast majority of Greek manuscripts favour the inclusion of the word![318] There are many other examples of this conjectural game, such as a scribe borrowing the name "Jesus" from the similar passage of Mark 1v24 to add to the title "Son of God" in Matthew 8v29! I forbear to consider any more of these for it is just as likely that many manuscripts have omitted the words rather than borrowed them from elsewhere. The great problem with these assertions is that they are just speculative, and so the whole thing becomes just a game. He who shouts the loudest and has the most favour amongst the people (of the academic world) is he whose ideas will become

---

315   James R. White. The King James Only Controversy. Can you trust modern translations? Bethany House: Minneapolis, Minnesota, 2009. P200.

316   P66, P75 S, B, C*, 0125, one lat, syr(c), most cop. The papyri P66 and P75 date from the third century.

317   {A*}, A^2, C^3, K, {L}, X(commentary), Delta, Theta, Pi, Psi, 078, f1, f13, 28, 565, 700, 892, 1010, 1241, Byz Lect, most lat, later vg, syr(p,h,pal), some cop(north). 078 dates from the sixth century but the earliest Latin manuscripts to include the verse is ita from the fourth century. Tertullian (third century), Ambrose (fourth century) and Chrysostom (late fourth century) all quote the account.

318   As for footnote 315. P202.

the accepted norm. This is not Biblical scholarship. It may be the approach of modern academia but I believe it is simply sheer hogwash.

Explaining why the NIV omits the words "take up the cross" in Mark 10v21, White suggests:

> ... the NIV and other modern translations do not include "take up the cross" because the Greek texts they used do not contain those words. The text utilized by the NIV translation committee was virtually identical with the *Nestle-Aland* text, and it is the judgement of the scholars who compiled it that the phrase was not a part of Mark's original gospel.[319]

Once again the majority of Greek texts favour the inclusion of these words, but then the modern critical text approach is the one favoured by the scholars of today.[320] It is worth highlighting White's words in the above quote. We cannot pass over the assertion by White that it was "the judgement of the scholars" who came to the conclusion that the words were not original! This is the very crux of the problem with the critical text view of the New Testament. It all comes down to what the *scholars* say. Is the Christian to be beholden to the scholars and their whims? Is the text of the New Testament a decision to be arrived at by scholarship? I think not. White continues with this particular verse and accepts that the KJV has the words because of the witness of the majority of Greek manuscripts:

> Why, then, does the KJV contain the phrase at Mark 10:21? Because the TR contains the phrase in the Greek. In point of fact, the majority of Greek texts contain the phrase.[321]

White then argues on the basis that the oldest manuscripts do not have the phrase! He also suggests that the phrase has been "borrowed" from elsewhere but again we must hang our hands up in despair at the speculative and conjectural nature being employed here. It simply seems that these "reasons" are adduced because of a prior commitment to the "oldest is best" mantra. A similar type of explanation surfaces at John 7v8. In the newer translations the Lord Jesus is quoted as saying that he would "not" go up to the feast whilst in the NKJV (and in the KJV) the words are "not yet." White says:

---

319   James R. White. The King James Only Controversy. Can you trust modern translations? Bethany House: Minneapolis, Minnesota, 2009. P205.
320   https://www.stepbible.org/?q=version=VarApp|reference=Mark.10.21&options=GNHVU
321   As for footnote 319. P206.

Many modern scholars feel that early on in the transmission of this section of John the same concern that motivates Dr. Waite to object to the reading "not" ... prompted them to change it to "not yet" ... In this case, though, the external evidence is greatly in their favour. The UBS 4th edition gives the reading "not" a C rating, and for good reason. The reading "not yet" is supported by an awesome array of witnesses.[322]

Note that the vast majority of witnesses favour the majority text view as reflected in the NKJV and KJV. White does not attempt to explain why in the face of all the evidence for the phrase "not yet" the critical text insists on the word "not"!

[b] The critical view of Kurt and Barbara Aland.

Two noted textual scholars, Kurt and Barbara Aland, have provided us with their view of the history of the New Testament. In essence it appears to be the same in general outline to that provided by others of the critical text following. Thus according to the Alands, the New Testament was written by the original penmen between AD 50 and AD 100. From this time and then into the second century only single copies of the originals were made by private individuals in the areas where the texts were located (e.g. Ephesus, Rome, Colossae etc.). The Alands believe that the text of the New Testament at this time was very free and somewhat loose:

> To understand the textual history of the New Testament it is necessary to begin with the early manuscripts. By this we mean manuscripts no later than the third/fourth century, for in the fourth century a new era begins. Every manuscript, of the earlier period, whether on papyrus or on parchment, has an inherent significance for New Testament textual criticism: they witness to a period when the text of the New Testament was still developing freely.[323]

During this time the Christians who copied the text were not as scrupulous as the Old Testament scribes, for Christians did not consider the text to be as holy as their forefathers viewed the Old Testament Scriptures.[324] This early "free" text is represented by the papyri and some early uncials. Apart from these factors, another reason for this looseness, according to the Alands, was that there was no institutional organisation capable of standardising the text:

> The text of the early period prior to the third/fourth century was, then, in effect, a text not yet channelled into types, because until the beginning of the fourth century the churches still lacked the institutional organization required to produce one. ... Until the third/fourth

---

322   James R. White. The King James Only Controversy. Can you trust modern translations? Bethany House: Minneapolis, Minnesota, 2009. P221.
323   Kurt Aland and Barbara Aland. "The Text of the New Testament: An Introduction to the Critical Editions and to the Theory and Practice of Modern Textual Criticism." Eerdmans. Grand Rapids, USA. 1981. P56.
324   Such a view seems preposterous to a true Christian.

century, then, there were many different forms of the New Testament text ... but not until the fourth century, following the decades of peace prior to the Diocletianic persecutions, did the formation of text types begin.[325]

From about 200 AD, translations were made as the number of Greek speakers decreased and the gospel spread throughout the ancient world. Persecutions during these early years decimated the manuscripts and copies, but then in the third and fourth centuries when more peaceful times ensued, manuscripts were copied in "Scriptoria" and a more professional approach was applied. During these centuries there was rampant editing:

> The form of text or the particular manuscripts which were used as exemplars and undoubtedly mass produced in these Scriptoria now became a determinative influence. And so Egypt, where the most varied texts had been in circulation, saw the development of what we know as the Alexandrian text, which was to develop further (under the influence of the Koine text) and in the course of centuries become the Egyptian text. And in the different parts of the empire what is called the Koine text (later to become the Byzantine Imperial text) spread rapidly as students from the exegetical school at Antioch, who occupied many of the important sees of the time, either adopted the text of Antioch for their newly established diocesan Scriptoria, or used it to replace the earlier standard exemplar where a Scriptorium already existed.[326]

Editing was not of the philological form (attending to grammar) but for theological purposes.[327] Exactly how the Alands came to such an assertion is not made clear. In fact the whole historical scheme outlined thus far is manufactured. Thus, in the opinion of these textual critics, text copying developed from an Egyptian beginning (represented by the papyri), and this was to develop through the Alexandrian form in the third century, and finally becomes the Byzantine text much later on. Here is a final quote from the Alands in which we can see the essential stance of their position with regard to the Christian faith:

> Until the beginning of the fourth century the text of the New Testament developed freely. It was a "living text" in the Greek literary tradition, unlike the text of the Hebrew Old Testament, which was subject to strict controls because (in the oriental tradition) the consonantal text was holy. And the New Testament continued to be a "living text" as long as it remained a manuscript tradition, even when the Byzantine church moulded it to the procrustean bed of the standard and officially prescribed text. Even for later scribes, for example, the parallel passages of the Gospels were so familiar that they would adapt the text of one Gospel to that of another. They also felt themselves free to make corrections in the text, improving it by their own standards of correctness, whether grammatically, stylistically,

---

325   Kurt Aland and Barbara Aland. "The Text of the New Testament: An Introduction to the Critical Editions and to the Theory and Practice of Modern Textual Criticism." Eerdmans. Grand Rapids, USA. 1981. P64.
326   As for footnote 325. P70,71.
327   As for footnote 325. P50,51.

or more substantively. This is all the more true of the early period, when the text had not yet attained canonical status, especially in the earliest period when Christians considered themselves filled with the Spirit.[328]

I want to highlight just two points from this last quote. First the assumption that Westcott and Hort originally made about the Byzantine (majority) text is here repeated. It was not one carefully copied and faithfully preserved, but one constructed, edited and "moulded" by the Byzantine church into a "standard and officially prescribed text." This mantra is one repeated ad nauseam by critical text advocates, but it is wholly fallacious and without evidence. This historical construction is a manufactured lie. Secondly, the Alands contend that because the early Christians claimed to be "filled with the Spirit" they were therefore at liberty to "make corrections in the text, improving it by their own standards of correctness, whether grammatically, stylistically, or more substantively." But such a view is wholly anti-Christian! The Holy Spirit was to guide the early disciples into all **truth!**[329] To imagine that Christians who loved the Lord Jesus and were indwelt by the Holy Spirit would stoop to altering and amending the Scriptures does not bear consideration.

As a result of such a history, the Byzantine text type becomes essentially redundant. It is believed to be not only late, but edited and standardised by the Greek speaking church, and therefore cannot be used to construct a New Testament text. A mere fragment of an uncial with a "valuable text" is "far more significant" than any complete manuscript with a Byzantine text.[330] The Alands show their contempt not just for the Byzantine text, but for the "hated" Textus Receptus as well:[331]

> We can appreciate better the struggle for freedom from the dominance of the Textus Receptus when we remember that in this period it was regarded as preserving even to the last detail the inspired and infallible word of God himself. ... The initial campaign in the battle against the Textus Receptus and for a return to an earlier form of the text was launched in the nineteenth century by a professor of classical philology at Berlin, Karl Lachmann (1793-1851). His program was first announced in 1830: "Down with the late text of the Textus Receptus, and back to the text of the early fourth-century church!" This slogan set the goal for the generations following.[332]

---

328   Kurt Aland and Barbara Aland. "The Text of the New Testament: An Introduction to the Critical Editions and to the Theory and Practice of Modern Textual Criticism." Eerdmans. Grand Rapids, USA. 1981. P69.
329   John 16v13.
330   As for footnote 328. P103.
331   Hort in a private letter of 1851 makes this comment on the Textus Receptus: *I had no idea until the last few weeks of the importance of texts having read so little Greek Testament and dragged on with the villainous Textus Receptus. Think of that vile Textus Receptus leaning entirely on late manuscripts.* . Hort, Life and Letters of Fenton John Anthony Hort (2 Vols.; London: Macmillan and Co. Ltd., 1896), I, 211.
332   As for footnote 328. P11.

In the opinion of these two critical text scholars, the Byzantine uncials are of no importance at all. These are:

> ... quite irrelevant for textual criticism. In terms of age, only uncial manuscripts which derive from the third/fourth century or earlier have an inherent significance, i.e., those of the period before the development of the great text types. Unfortunately, these amount to no more than five.[333]

Amongst the five accepted uncials are Codex Vaticanus and Codex Sinaiticus, of course! The Alands repeat the idea that the Byzantine texts are irrelevant for textual criticism, whatever form they are found in (miniscule, uncial), despite admitting the fact that "no adequate history has yet been written of the Byzantine text."[334] This reduces the "relevant" witnesses considerably. Such a wholesale sweeping aside of manuscripts is carried even further by the Alands because they consider the lectionaries to be of little significance too:

> Actually, the text we find in the Greek lectionaries is almost identical with the Byzantine Imperial text. ... Summarizing these considerations we can only conclude that for New Testament textual criticism, so far as the original text and its early history is concerned, nearly all the approximately 2,300 lectionary manuscripts can be of significance only in exceptional instances.[335]

Given that the history they recount is built largely on speculation and a lack of complete evidence, and given that their view of the Byzantine texts is biased and not built on any **real** history, one wonders how much respect these folk ought to command. The critical view of the history of the New Testament Greek text according to Kurt and Barbara Aland has been shown in schematic diagram form on the next page. The essential point is that, according to these scholars, we do not have the original copies either in and of themselves or in terms of their text. The development of a "free" text was not standardised until the 4th century in the different centres. The Alexandrian text type is preferred by these critics because it has earlier attestation than the Byzantine.

It is necessary to point out here that Kurt and Barbara Aland suggest an alternative view of considering the manuscripts rather than simply relying on the text-types. In their scheme they have suggested "categories" of texts which are more or less important or significant for constructing a New Testament. Although they do not discount the text-types, they advocate this new scheme for textual criticism:

---

333   Kurt Aland and Barbara Aland. "The Text of the New Testament: An Introduction to the Critical Editions and to the Theory and Practice of Modern Textual Criticism." Eerdmans. Grand Rapids, USA. 1981. P104.
334   As for footnote 333. P142.
335   As for footnote 333. P169.

Category I: Manuscripts of a very special quality which should always be considered in establishing the original text (e.g., the Alexandrian text belongs here). The papyri and uncials through the third/fourth century also belong here automatically, one may say, because they represent the text of the early period.

Category II: Manuscripts of a special quality, but distinguished from manuscripts of category I by the presence of alien influences (particularly of the Byzantine text), and yet of importance for establishing the original text (e.g. the Egyptian text belongs here).

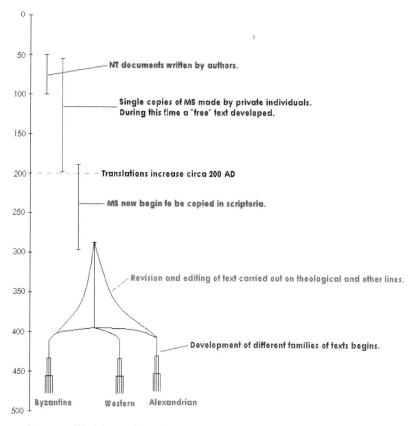

Category III: Manuscripts of a distinctive character with an independent text, usually important for establishing the original text, but particularly important for the history of the text.

Category IV: Manuscripts of the D text.

Category V: Manuscripts with a purely or predominantly Byzantine text.[336]

---

336   Kurt Aland and Barbara Aland. "The Text of the New Testament: An Introduction to the Critical Editions and to the Theory and Practice of Modern Textual Criticism." Eerdmans. Grand Rapids, USA. 1981. P106 (cf. P159).

Part of the reason for suggesting this new idea is that, in their opinion, apart from the Byzantine and Western text-types, the other text types are not all clearly or easily defined:

> The new concept of categories introduced in this book has need of some further explanation with regard to the distinction it draws and its relationship to recognized text types, groups, and families. Text types and their subgroups are the traditional means of New Testament textual criticism for describing the history of the New Testament text. ... These traditional procedures of textual criticism are in no way supplanted or challenged by the introduction of categories. ... New Testament text types have always suffered from two weaknesses. Their definitions have been inadequate: that is, with two exceptions there has been no clear identification of what readings constitute a text type for all the New Testament writings. Only the Byzantine text and the D-text (formerly called the "Western text") have been defined precisely enough (i.e. with a sufficient number of characteristic readings) to be useful for classifying manuscripts. All the other text types used by textual critics need to be defined more precisely. ...[337]

Their scheme is quite clearly one constructed on the basis of accepting the scholarly view of the history of the text. The Byzantine text is relegated to category V because it is late and considered to be an edited text. This viewpoint continues the ideas developed in the nineteenth century by Westcott and Hort and others who detested the Textus Receptus and had a mind to "improve" the Greek New Testament. Nowadays such a motivation is lacking as few believe it possible to reconstruct the original New Testament text. Such unbelieving scholarship is monstrous. It has no place for the true believer. Surely believers are entitled to ask the scholar, where is your Biblical, Scriptural proof or ground for your scholarly opinions?

[4] A caution on academia and a plea for Biblical scholarship.

It will be apparent from what has been written so far, that one of the major problems in this great debate is the problem of academia. What do I mean by this? Well in short it is the same problem we also find in the scientific world. There is an acceptable set of truths or rules which operate in academia and if you disagree or offer an approach not acceptable to the academic world you simply will not get a hearing. In short, in order to be heard amongst the academic elite you have to play the game. You have to have read and interact with all the literature, much of which comes from the position of unbelief. To rebut these positions on the basis of Scripture is not acceptable to these folk. The only basis upon which you are allowed to engage with the published literature is to take it seriously and employ the tools of academia. This means that there is a mass of literature which is hopeless nonsense because it does not come from a position of faith. It is like a house of

---

337   Kurt Aland and Barbara Aland. "The Text of the New Testament: An Introduction to the Critical Editions and to the Theory and Practice of Modern Textual Criticism." Eerdmans. Grand Rapids, USA. 1981. P332.

cards. Of course we must engage at some level to challenge the unbelieving academic world. What is so galling, however, is to find evangelical believers sold into the idea that to advance you need to be a part of the academic set. Inevitably this requires either an incredibly strong heart and mind which continues despite the opposition to the gospel, or a degree of compromise. In my limited experience I have always wondered how some modern day scientists who are believers managed to continue in their discipline actively as a Christian. One well respected scientist Christian I know once said that he could only rise to the position of influence he now has by "keeping his head down" in the early years as a lecturer and research scientist. I respect this man greatly and he does a lot of good work as a scientist and Christian and faces great opposition despite his credentials. However I question the wisdom of "keeping one's head down" as a young professional. I don't think Daniel did this! To be fair there are always going to be Daniels who are within the thick of this world's systems (be they government, university life, academia or any other professional situation), and there will always be Ezekiels who operate on the fringes outside the mainstream and considered outsiders and outlaws by the world. I appreciate these two positions but surely we must challenge the world and its ways at all opportunities? When it comes to simply following the academic way without challenging the assumptions and operations of this world we are on slippery ground.

One of the surprising things about the subject of the Bible's history is that those who write on it seem to be blinded by academia. What I mean is that godly folk who love the Lord Jesus seem to have abandoned the first principle of all study. That is, whatever we do, whatever we study, we must start with God. We must proceed not with a blank slate, nor with the false notion of having a neutral stance.[338] In short, we cannot start to examine this subject by approaching it historically, as though history is the means by which we ought to consider the subject on its proper grounds. We must start from a theological ground. In fact those who believe that we must not approach the subject theologically, but from an historical perspective are deluding themselves. Who can hide or set aside their theological beliefs? Whatever may be claimed, all of us proceed on the basis of some theological principles. If we assume that history is the proper starting point then what we have done is to abandon our true theological grounding. I make this claim on the basis that we are created by God and we owe allegiance and reverence to Him first. Consequently all that we do must, of necessity, have a theological component. Surely as Christians it is our task to ensure that this theological aspect takes priority and is correct? By taking the academic or historical approach (in the case of New Testament textual studies), it is as though we have suspended belief for one moment and proceeded along a secular footing. The secular footing is not neutral. Its theological

---

338   This is what the current secular world believes – that it starts from a neutral ground and objectively, dispassionately makes judgements – but this is nonsense because all start with a set of basic principles and beliefs.

stance is practical atheism. It is for this reason that a Biblical and theological approach is essential.

The problem of an academic approach.

One of the modern academic rules with regard to assessing manuscripts is found in the adage that manuscripts need to be "weighed and not counted." Early textual criticism followed the majority rule. If more manuscripts agreed on a particular reading this was taken to be the true one. With Westcott and Hort's new ideas that the majority of manuscripts were merely late copies of a single edited copy, the new mantra of weighing manuscripts became the fashion. The trouble with this new mantra is that it is not really possible to "weigh" a manuscript objectively, if what is meant by this is a fair and impartial assessment of its worth. Dean Burgon who opposed Westcott and Hort and their theory of the New Testament text, pointed out in response to this new development, that:

> It assumes that the 'witnesses' we possess, meaning thereby every single Codex, Version, Father, (1) are capable of being weighed: and (2) that every individual Critic is competent to weigh them: neither of which propositions is true. . . . The undeniable fact is overlooked that 'number' is the most ordinary ingredient of weight and . . . is an element which even [sic] cannot be cast away. (p. 43) [339]

Weighing a text requires the scholar to apply standardised principles of enquiry as he or she studies the evidence. But who is to "set" the standards, and how can these always be applied in an objective manner? When it comes to "weighing" the uncial texts which come from the Alexandrian stable, the textual scholar Burgon made this assessment for his readers:

> We venture to assure him, without a particle of hesitation, that **א B D** are *three of the most scandalously corrupt copies extant*:—exhibit *the most shamefully mutilated* texts which are anywhere to be met with:—have become, by whatever process (for their history is wholly unknown), the depositories of the largest amount of *fabricated readings*, ancient *blunders*, and *intentional perversions of Truth*,—which are discoverable in any known copies of the Word of God. [340]

We have already considered the details of corruption within the Vaticanus and Sinaiticus manuscripts. We remind ourselves that there is evidence of correction by numerous later scribes, poor grammar indicating that the copyist may not have known the Greek language, as well as other serious problems and deficiencies within the texts. Now naturally others have "weighed" the evidence and have come to vastly different conclusions. But this is the point, because "weighing"

---

339   Burgon, J. W. B. (1896a). The traditional text of the holy Gospels vindicated and established (E. Miller, Ed.). London: George Bell. P43.
340   Burgon J. W. B. 1883. The Revision Revised. P42.

the evidence depends upon prior presuppositions and especially the world view held by the one doing the weighing. It is obvious that the weight of academic influence has weighed in heavily on this topic and has concluded that the oldest manuscripts being closer in time must be the best, and so the Vaticanus and Sinaiticus manuscripts are held in high esteem. Modern academic scholarship treats the Bible as any other book and refuses to listen to any theological presuppositions which need to be heeded. That such corrupt manuscripts (that is considered within themselves let alone in comparison with other manuscript evidence) are used as the basis for translation in opposition to a far purer set of witnesses (the Byzantine text type) because these are later and therefore considered by the scholars to be a fabricated edited edition (without any proof of this save conjecture and speculation) is clearly evidence of reckless bias and a secular mind set. For the Christian, it must be self-evident, that such corrupt copies as Vaticanus and Sinaiticus cannot be reliable witnesses to the pure and true New Testament text, except that they indicate the existence of the New Testament when they were composed. The more pure Byzantine manuscripts will in contradistinction show that they are the witnesses to the New Testament because they are purer and smoother in form. The unbelieving scholars will not accept such statements because the evidence of purity amongst the Byzantine manuscripts must be explained *away* as fabricated or as a result of an editing process. For the believer the greater purity amongst the Byzantine texts indicates God's sovereign care. Of course we are not suggesting a divine miracle of preservation, but the evident care taken by the copyists of the Greek speaking world overshadows whoever it was who "scandalously" copied the earlier uncials. The open corruption of the earlier uncials (Vaticanus and Sinaiticus) are taken as more representative because of their date by the critical text elite, despite the evident nature of alterations and corruption.

A plea for Biblical scholarship.

In what has been said thus far I hope that the reader is not under the misconception that I am advocating a "blind faith" approach or a laxity in effort. Far from it. My particular concern is to warn the reader against getting sucked into a world where the emphasis is on the pursuit of an intellectualism which is governed not only by a secular set of rules and an assumption of neutrality, but also is devoid of any devotional or spiritual element or, better still, grounding. We are talking about *knowing God*. All that we are thinking about, studying, researching, writing on, and speaking on, ought to have the single ground and aim of a true and living knowledge of Christ Jesus our Lord.

An equally pernicious situation that many find themselves in, is the reactionary one. I mean by this the attitude that rejects the academic and intellectual approach and which then clings simply to beliefs with no grounding. We have all seen a dry and dusty presentation which lacks life. The technical details and the mountains of error that is waded through by some intellectuals in order to get to the main point is painful to say the least. But the reaction to this dryness, this intellectual academic approach, is to jettison biblical scholarship and simply present a "thin" easy-believism. Some speakers and writers have great characters. They are charismatic and bubbly people. These folk may see the academic world and shrug in horror and present a Christ who is simple, straight forward and (unfortunately) vacuous. By this I mean such folk simply parrot truths with no substance, and denounce the unbelieving and academic dross, but do not present something *substantial* which not only answers the nonsense of the intellectual academic set, but that also brings life. True biblical scholarship is not afraid of the world's questions, nor of the evidence of reality, and it is certainly not afraid of a depth of study and investigation, but there must be a good grounding and some settled principles established first, and these must be Biblical.

The Christian scholar must engage with the world and its questions, with the reality we all live in. However we are not to engage with the minutiae of every intellectual pursuit. I need to qualify this last statement somewhat. It may be that some have been given the task of pointing out the errors of a particular discipline at its frontiers, and this is necessary. What I mean to say is that the average Christian does not need to examine every subject in every detail. This would be impossible, of course. However the average Christian must have within their armoury sufficient weaponry and armour to deal with any eventuality, including from the different aspects of the academic world. How is this possible? Well the starting point is always the ground, the basis, or the presuppositions held dear. We can challenge the world's academic pursuits and conclusions by examining the assumptions and starting points used at the outset. We can do this if we have at our fingertips the essential truthful basis by which we were made to operate under. Thus, if we know whom it is really that we love and worship, then we have the armour and weaponry to bring down all arguments of falsehood, whatever they may be.[341] The thing is that we cannot merely repeat the Lord's prayer, or the creed, or a modern statement of faith when we face a difficult question or part of reality. We need to know Christ and His work in detail. This means that we must engage in some very serious and deep Biblical study, and, we must be ready to learn the lessons Christ is teaching us in our life experiences. I do not mean that these two things (Scripture and life) are separate. Not at all. I mean that in our studying of whom the Lord is and how He acts and has acted, we take on board and learn from the Master in the situation and life we are currently living.

---

341   2Corinthians 10v4.

What then are the tools of the Biblical Scholar? Well we shall have occasion to examine these in detail when we consider the topic of hermeneutics – how we are to understand the Scriptures. For now I want to establish a few basic principles. First, in order to be a true Biblical scholar (as opposed to one who is accepted in the academic world) we must be truly born again and saved. This is so important that I want to emphasise it again. Unless we really know the Lord, and unless we have been translated from the kingdom of this world to the kingdom of the Son of His love, we simply cannot begin to start.[342] We state this in full knowledge of the fact that countless folk have embarked on Biblical studies (both academic and pastoral) in an ungodly and unbelieving way. There is so much Biblical data and information provided by such unbelieving folk "out there" that we need to be ready and prepared to face this. Thus a second important tool is to be fully alert to this danger. The number of times the Scriptures warn us to be ready and alert is immense.[343] Now, of course, that does not mean we reject it out of hand. We must be aware that what the world offers is not necessarily right and must be carefully examined. How do we do this? Well this brings us to a third principle. We must always **start**, and then continue, in the word of God, no matter what we are studying or faced with, for it is this alone which is the revealed will and purpose of God and in Christ alone are hid all the treasures of wisdom and knowledge.[344] This means being systematic in our study. We need to gather the doctrines and learn them. I do not merely mean think on them and have them in our minds in an intellectual way. What I mean is that as we study each doctrine we must combine it with prayer and devotion to the One whom we are reading and meditating on. The Bible is, effectively, a love letter from the Lord to us. Let me hasten to add that our relationship to the Lord has many levels and aspects. He is God and we are His created beings, but He is also our Father and we are His sons (and so on). By studying theology (systematically) we begin to see the aspects of the Lord and His work which never change. We must not stop there for two important reasons. First, because it is easy to forget things, so we must always endeavour to remember and remind others as well. Second, because we need to look at the Lord and His work from other aspects. Thus Biblical theology and Historical theology are important aspects we need to take on board, along with church history. These aspects of considering the Lord and His dealings with man will help us immensely as we come to realise that we are not alone (there are believers throughout history), and the Lord is Lord of history (as demonstrated through the history revealed in Scripture). There are other ways we could extend our studies and meditation to get to know the Lord Jesus, but enough has been said here to illustrate that this is no mere ten-minute read of a passage and a short

---

342   Colossians 1v13.
343   For example: 1Peter 1v13.
344   Colossians 2v2,3.

Mike Viccary

prayer! Consider these verses:[345]

> *Be diligent to present yourself approved to God, a worker who does not need to be ashamed, rightly dividing the word of truth. (2Timothy 2v15)*
>
> *He who earnestly seeks good finds favour, But trouble will come to him who seeks evil. (Proverbs 11v27).*
>
> *Therefore we must give the more earnest heed to the things we have heard, lest we drift away. (Hebrews 2v1).*

In the first Scripture, which we have taken from 2Timothy, I urge the reader not to rest content that this is spoken to a pastor. The exhortation in this verse is for us all. Diligence in our looking at the Scriptures indicates hard work. The second Scripture from the book of Proverbs brings our attention to the Biblical theme of seeking. The exhortations to seek the Lord and His word in Scripture are numerous. In our verse there is a contrast between seeking "good" and "evil," but note that to seek good requires an earnestness which seeking evil does not! In our last verse from the book of Hebrews, the quality of earnestness is again to the fore. This time we must pay particular attention to what we hear. The context is the word of God. Consequently our hearing must be acute and tuned to hear the word. The parable of the soils emphasises this point. There are many more principles of Biblical scholarship including rejecting the world's futile ideas, and being obedient to what we receive but we shall save these for our discussion of hermeneutics.

[5] Biblical considerations.

Having looked at the modern critical view, it is now time to consider the text of the New Testament from a Biblical perspective. To start with we must address the concept of Scripture as a rule or authority, that is, the "canon" of Scripture. The Scriptures are the rule and standard by which all things must be measured. But how do we know what is "Scripture" and what is not? The answer is that only those writings which have the stamp of **inspiration** can be called "Scripture." Since the initiative of revealing by inspiration was God's alone, it follows that the publication and distribution of God's word would also be owned by the Author of Scripture too. In the case of preservation, however, the church as a whole – the priesthood of all believers – as moved and indwelt by the Holy Spirit had a hand in establishing the canon or rule of Scripture. It was not by means of a church council or by some ecclesiastical authority that Scripture was established, but rather by the work of the Holy Spirit within the life of the church as believers accepted and made use of those

---

345   See also: Psalm 119v162; Colossians 2v2,3.

writings which were inspired. Such general acceptance by believers ensured that manuscripts of the New Testament, for example, were copied copiously for use by different groups of believers. Pache sums this point up quite nicely:

> Because the writings of the apostles and prophets were canonical by virtue of their intrinsic quality the canon, in principle, existed from the time their books were written; and it was added to with successive appearances of new inspired books. It happened that the church was a long time in expressing its unanimous acknowledgement of certain of the writings; but when it finally came to it, all it did was bow in recognition of that which already existed.[346]

E. F. Hills made a similar point:

> Why did the Christian Church receive the twenty seven New Testament books and these only as her canonical New Testament Scripture? ... this question can be satisfactorily answered only on the basis of Christian faith. And when we look with the eye of faith upon the history of the New Testament canon, then we see in that history a mighty conflict between God and Satan, between the Holy Spirit on the one hand and the spirit of darkness on the other.
> First, God gave to His Church the twenty seven New Testament books through the inspiration of the Holy Spirit, and then through the Spirit also He began to lead the Church into a recognition of these books as her canonical New Testament Scripture. During the second century, however, Satan endeavoured to confuse the Church by raising up deceitful men who wrote pseudonymous works, falsely claiming to be apostolic. These satanic devices hindered and delayed the Church's recognition of the true New Testament canon but could not prevent it. Soon after the beginning of the fifth century the opposition of the devil was completely overcome. Under the leading of the Holy Spirit the Church was guided to receive only the twenty seven New Testament books as canonical and to reject all others.[347]

The point that Hills makes is vital. We must look at the history with the eye of faith and we must remember that there is an opponent who is keen to destroy.

Scribes and their work.

There has been much debate and discussion about how the New Testament manuscripts were copied through the centuries, and a great deal of this focuses on scribes and how they operated. New Testament textual critics when faced with the manuscript evidence have resorted to a series of rules which they refer to as "canons" to help in reconstructing the New Testament from all available witnesses. There are four "canons" or rules that textual critics use when having to decide amongst variant readings produced by the scribes. These are as follows:

---

346   Rene Pache "The Inspiration & Authority of Scripture" Moody Press 1969. P161.
347   E F Hills. "The magnificent Burgon." PP86 – 105. In Which Bible? Edited by David Otis Fuller. Institute For Biblical Textual Studies. Grand Rapids, USA. P98,99.

[1] Prefer the shorter reading.

This is based on the assumption that scribes tended to add to text rather than omit words.

[2] Prefer the harder reading.

This is based on the assumption that scribes tended to improve the sense of a text or try to sort out supposed difficulties.

[3] Prefer the non-harmonised reading.

This is based on the assumption that scribes tended to conform a passage to its parallel elsewhere or to the immediate context.

[4] Prefer the harsher reading.

This is based on the assumption that scribes wanted to make the text more familiar or smoother in form.

It turns out that none of these rules are proven or demonstrated in the text-critical literature, and nowhere can a student find reasons given for their validity, other than the provision of a few examples. However in some recent studies it has been found that at least some of these rules must be called into question. Andrew Wilson, for example, has made a study of what are described as "singular readings" in the manuscripts, that is, those readings found in one manuscript alone. Wilson describes why such an approach may be taken as a *measure* of scribal habits:

> The logic of this approach is simple and sound: if external evidence counts for anything, a reading found in only one manuscript is extremely unlikely to be the genuine reading of the NT text. Instead, it is more likely to be an individualism of its scribe. While it is possible that any given singular reading might theoretically be the authentic reading, it would be extremely unlikely that large numbers of singular readings were original. Singular readings studied in sufficient numbers thus provide us with our best guide to typical scribal errors. To use James Royse's words, in singular readings, we attempt "to discover the actual habits of scribes on empirical grounds, in a manner as free as possible from any presuppositions about scribal behaviour". Juan Hernandez Jr. writes that singular readings are "the safest place to speak confidently about scribal tendencies."[348]

Wilson's work (which looked at about 10% of the New Testament) indicated that far from having a tendency to add words, scribes more often omitted words. The rule "prefer the shorter reading" has thus tended to reduce the New Testament in size. Wilson's findings seems to be true in all types of manuscripts and is supported by the work of others:

---

[348]   http://www.nttext.com/newcms/index.php/nt-textual-criticism/13-scribal-habits-in-greek-new-testament-manuscripts. See also: "Digging for the Truth." Edited by Mark Billington and Peter Streitenberger.Published 2014.

When singular additions and omissions were analysed according to the type of manuscript in which they were found, the results showed that papyri, majuscules, minuscules and lectionaries all tend to omit rather than add. These results align with earlier studies such as Royse's, Head's and Hernandez's which called Lectio Brevior Potior[349] into question. Contrary to Royse's confident expectation, later manuscripts tend to omit rather than add just like earlier manuscripts, although not as frequently.[350]

Wilson also discovered that the rule, "prefer the harder reading" is also highly unlikely to be true. He looked at one third of the 33 chapters in the New Testament that he had used previously for the "prefer the shorter reading" study. In these chapters 2,279 singular readings showed that in 62% of the cases the singular reading (which is assumed to be non original and probably introduced by the scribe), produced either nonsense, a harder sense or a harder style. Wilson comments:

> By far the most significant result here is that of easier sense readings, readings that removed difficulties or improved the text semantically. Only 8 readings out of over 2000 fell into this category (0.4%). By contrast, there were 30 times as many readings where the scribe made the text more difficult, yet without producing nonsense (244 cases). Set against the expectation that scribes tended to improve the sense of the text or remove difficulties, a result of less than 1% fails to inspire confidence in the canon.[351]

Wilson's work is based on a testable method. The assumption that the singular readings are always incorrect and caused by a scribe may be incorrect, but the methodology, at least, can be reproduced. This work is not isolated as Wilson makes reference to the work of Colwell, Royse and Hernandez who have reported similar results.[352]

Given that the canons or rules for textual criticism are not founded on any reasonable grounds and that Wilson's work (and the work of others) casts serious doubt over two of these rules, we can see that a scholarly approach to establishing the original text simply will not do. Making up "rules" to decide what is and what isn't Scripture seems, to this writer at least, to be the height of presumption. So what are we to do?

The vast majority of New Testament textual criticism is based on historical speculation rather than any Biblically grounded approach. If we consider the subject of manuscript copying from a Biblical point of view by looking within Scripture for evidence of scribal behaviour we are surely on safer grounds. Let it be first stated that we have no Biblical warrant for assuming that the scribes who copied the New Testament were infallible, or that inspiration applied to their work.

---

349   That is, prefer the shorter reading.
350   http://www.nttext.com/newcms/index.php/nt-textual-criticism/13-scribal-habits-in-greek-new-testament-manuscripts.
351   As for footnote 350.
352   http://www.nttext.com/newcms/index.php/scribal-habits/sbl-2011-paper.

Inspiration is limited to the "Scriptures" or writings as originally given as 1Timothy 3v16 and 2Peter 1v20,21 would imply. However we cannot immediately jump to the conclusion that many New Testament textual critics do and say that the scribes were hopeless and careless in their efforts based on the poor quality of papyri or the repeated correcting of fourth century uncials like Vaticanus and Sinaiticus.

We need to begin our thoughts concerning scribes and their work by looking at the Old Testament, for it is there we can view how they operated. The scribe of the Old Testament was one learned not just in the art of writing but also in the law. It is highly probable that the first scribes were Levites:

> *And the scribe, Shemaiah the son of Nethanel, one of the Levites, wrote them down before the king, the leaders, Zadok the priest, Ahimelech the son of Abiathar, and the heads of the fathers' houses of the priests and Levites, one father's house taken for Eleazar and one for Ithamar. (1Chronicles 24v6).*

A detailed discussion of the way in which the Lord revealed His will and purposes prophetically through the Patriarchs, Moses and later prophets is a subject for another book. Suffice it to say at this point, that a prophet claiming to bring God's word was to be carefully tested.[353] Those writings deemed as canonical, or part of the rule, were to be laid up in, or by, the ark of the covenant in the holy of holies.[354] However it cannot be that these inspired works simply remained in the ark, for their purpose was that the people would heed the Lord and obey His voice. Consequently it is evident that the inspired texts were copied for general use.

The law was delivered by Moses to the Levites whose responsibility it was to keep the tabernacle, and, in particular, the ark of the covenant where the law was held:

> *So Moses wrote this law and delivered it to the priests, the sons of Levi, who bore the ark of the covenant of the Lord, and to all the elders of Israel. (Deuteronomy 31v9).*

We note in this last verse that the law was also delivered to "all the elders of Israel" so that the law was not just preserved in the ark out of sight to all Israel (in the holy of holies), but was spread openly throughout the camp. Perhaps the situation is akin to that which we read of in Jeremiah concerning the prophet's purchase of some land in Anathoth:

> *Take these deeds, both this purchase deed which is sealed and this deed which is open, and*

353   Deuteronomy 13v1f; 18v15f.
354   Exodus 25v21; Deuteronomy 31v26.

put them in an earthen vessel, that they may last many days. (Jeremiah 32v14).

Thus there were two copies of the deeds. One was sealed and one was open for all to examine. In the same way the Scriptures were sealed in the ark in the holy of holies as a witness, and open copies were available for the priests and Levites to work from. The Levites were also responsible for teaching the law to the people. The charge given to Aaron was thus:

> *... and that you may teach the children of Israel all the statutes which the Lord has spoken to them by the hand of Moses. (Leviticus 10v11).*

The priest had to teach specific rules governing things such as an outbreak of leprosy:

> *Take heed in an outbreak of leprosy, that you carefully observe and do according to all that the priests, the Levites, shall teach you; just as I commanded them, so you shall be careful to do. (Deuteronomy 24v8).*

However teaching was not just in regard to the rules concerning leprosy, but all matters of the law:

> *8 And of Levi he said ...   10 they shall teach Jacob Your judgments, and Israel Your law. They shall put incense before You, and a whole burnt sacrifice on Your altar. (Deuteronomy 33v8,10).*

> *And Hezekiah gave encouragement to all the Levites who taught the good knowledge of the Lord; and they ate throughout the feast seven days, offering peace offerings and making confession to the Lord God of their fathers. (2Chronicles 30v22).*

> *Then he said to the Levites who taught all Israel, who were holy to the Lord: "Put the holy ark in the house which Solomon the son of David, king of Israel, built. It shall no longer be a burden on your shoulders. Now serve the Lord your God and His people Israel. (2Chronicles 35v3).*

> *And Nehemiah, who was the governor, Ezra the priest and scribe, and the Levites who taught the people said to all the people, "This day is holy to the Lord your God; do not mourn nor weep." For all the people wept, when they heard the words of the Law. (Nehemiah 8v9).*

Given such a responsibility it is inconceivable that they did this without making copies of the law available for people to read and study.

Mike Viccary   153 of 319

Evidence for copying.

Copying revealed writings is first mentioned in connection with the ten commandments. You may recall that Moses broke the originals and these had then to be re-written:

And He wrote on the tablets according to the first writing, the Ten Commandments ... (Deuteronomy 10v4)

Then, importantly, we find that the king himself had to make a copy of the law as instructed by the Lord:[355]

Also it shall be, when he sits on the throne of his kingdom, that he shall write for himself a copy of this law in a book, from the one before the priests, the Levites. (Deuteronomy 17v18).

Some think that the king actually got others to do this for him.[356] Apart from the priests, magistrates and judges must also certainly have had copies of the law to enable them to carry out their respective functions.[357]

In Isaiah we find the prophet making an appeal to the law and the testimony for a guide.[358] Such an appeal is meaningless if there were no accurate copies of the law to hand. In Jeremiah we find also that when the scroll written by Baruch at the dictation of Jeremiah was destroyed by king Jehoiakim, a second copy was made which had all the words on the former scroll with new additions:

Take yet another scroll, and write on it all the former words that were in the first scroll which Jehoiakim the king of Judah has burned. (Jeremiah 36v28)

Then Jeremiah took another scroll and gave it to Baruch the scribe, the son of Neriah, who wrote on it at the instruction of Jeremiah all the words of the book which Jehoiakim king of Judah had burned in the fire. And besides, there were added to them many similar words. (Jeremiah 36v32)

In Jehoshaphat's reign we read that the king enacted many reforms, amongst which was the teaching of the law throughout Judah. Here we read that they actually had a copy of the law with them for this task:

---

355 See also 2Chronicles 23v11.
356 Compare: 1Samuel 1v3; 13v9; 1Kings 8v62; John 19v19 - where certain men are said to do what, in the event, was almost certainly done by others.
357 1Chronicles 19v10.
358 Isaiah 8v20.

> *7 Also in the third year of his reign he sent his leaders, Ben-Hail, Obadiah, Zechariah, Nethanel, and Michaiah, to teach in the cities of Judah. 8 And with them he sent Levites: Shemaiah, Nethaniah, Zebadiah, Asahel, Shemiramoth, Jehonathan, Adonijah, Tobijah, and Tobadonijah—the Levites; and with them Elishama and Jehoram, the priests. 9 So they taught in Judah, and had the Book of the Law of the Lord with them; they went throughout all the cities of Judah and taught the people. (2Chronicles 17v7-9).*

A particularly important example of the preservation of the Old Testament comes from a study of the Israelites after the exile. When Jerusalem fell in 586 BC to Nebuchadnezzar and the Babylonians it is probable that the original autographs of much of the Old Testament would have been destroyed with the destruction of the temple.[359] However copies would have been available. The exiled prophets Ezekiel and Daniel show that they were cognizant of the details of the law in their inspired works. Of course, Ezra, Nehemiah, Esther, the books of Chronicles and the last three minor prophets were yet to be written. On return from Exile in 537 BC Ezra the scribe was largely responsible for re-establishing worship "as it is written in the book of Moses."[360] In Nehemiah 8v1 we are told that Ezra was asked to bring the book of the law of Moses. Ezra seems to have been a leader of the learned and wise scribes of that time.[361] We read that Ezra was:

> *... a scribe of the words of the commandments of the Lord, and of his statutes to Israel. (Ezra 7v11)*

Given his circumstances, this must have meant that he made copies of the law which were then taught and explained to the returnees.[362]

Then also, the words of Psalm 1 and Psalm 119 (for example) lead us to believe that true believers had access to the law and the testimony, otherwise how could they delight in the law or look into all the commandments?[363] Finally we have a witness to accurate copying in the New Testament in an incidental comment made by the Lord when in discussion with the Sadducees. We have already considered this particular incident in which the Sadducees, who did not believe in resurrection or spirits, had posed a conundrum they felt that the Lord could not answer. However the Lord was more than equal to the task and informs them that they were mistaken because they did not know the Scriptures. He makes the point forcefully as follows:

> *31 But concerning the resurrection of the dead, have you not read what was spoken to you*

---

359   2Chronicles 36v17-19.
360   Ezra 6v18.
361   Nehemiah 8v4,7,13; cf. Ezra 7v6,11,22.
362   Nehemiah 8v3,8,18; 9v3.
363   Psalm 1v2; 119v6.

by God, saying, **32** *'I am the God of Abraham, the God of Isaac, and the God of Jacob'? God is not the God of the dead, but of the living." (Matthew 22v31,32).*

We noted earlier the significant fact that in Christ's questioning of the Sadducees about their view of Scripture we have some vital teaching on the very nature of Scripture. Thus by asking them, "have you not read what was spoken to you by God," the Lord was making plain that what the Sadducees could actually read in the first century AD was in fact what God was still speaking! This meant that the copies the Sadducees (and others) worked from must have been accurate for the Lord Jesus to make such a claim.

The Massoretes.

The work of the scribes was clearly meticulous and exacting. That they succeeded in producing accurate copies can be demonstrated by reference to 1 Kings 2v3. Here we read that David commanded Solomon to keep all the commandments and statutes of the Lord "as it is written in the law of Moses." Now the law of Moses that he would be referring to would be a copy made by a scribe for the king, not the original autograph. Yet he does not hesitate to say that this copy is also the word of God from the hand of Moses, (i.e. written by Moses' hand). We have even more evidence when we consider how the Old Testament was preserved through the centuries following the beginning of the Christian church. This task was carried out by the Massoretes. The name means "tradition" and these Massoretes were families of Jewish scholars and textual critics who eventually opened academies (one at Tiberius on the coast of the Sea of Galilee, and one in Babylon). No one knows when the Massoretes first appeared. Some trace them to the first century AD others suggest a date around 500 AD. Whatever the case may be, these lovers of Scripture were meticulous and precise in their work of maintaining faithful copies of the inspired Old Testament writings. Their greatest contribution was in the methods used to preserve the text. Their work was extensive. They made the Hebrew consonantal language readable by adding vowel points and accents. They explained the meaning of Hebrew terms and added pause points to aid in reading and comprehending the text. They actually counted verses, words and letters of the Scriptures to aid in their copying. So, for example, the letter "aleph" occurs 42,377 times, "beth" is found 38,218 times and "gimel" is written 29,537 times. They identified the middle letters of books and had other signals and pointers to ensure accurate copying. They followed the Talmud's method of strict rules for copying manuscripts. Of these we should note the following. Only the skins of clean animals were to be used to write on, and each leaf produced from the clean animal skin should have the same number of columns. There should be no less than 48 and no more than 60 lines per column.

The ink should be black and was to be made following a particular recipe. No word or letter was to be written from memory. If so much as a letter was omitted, or wrongly inserted, or even if one letter touched another, the sheet had to be destroyed. If there were three mistakes on a page the whole manuscript was condemned. Revision of a copy had to take place within 30 days otherwise it was rejected. Copyists were watched carefully and held accountable by what was known as the "Massorah" or the "fence of the law" which was a collection of detailed notes and requirements the copyists were to stick to. Such exacting requirements ensured that the Old Testament was preserved intact with considerable accuracy. The work of the Massoretes was so precise that the discovery of the Dead Sea Scrolls which contained many Old Testament Scriptures posed no problem and no necessity to alter the text.

The story of the Massoretes makes us understand that those who had a mind to preserve and copy the Scriptures were extremely careful in their work. This is understandable given the awesome way in which God first revealed Himself to the people of Israel, starting with the great prophet Moses. We could look almost anywhere in the Pentateuch from Exodus onward to show the great reverence the people of God would have had for the word of God, but perhaps the giving of the law in Exodus 20 will be sufficient. The people were terrified of the appearance of God and rather than hear Him speaking they asked that Moses would be their intermediary.[364] Later we find that the care with which the words of God were recorded and passed on was meticulous.[365] Now given these attitudes to the copying of God's word, it would seem extremely strange that the early Christians would have adopted a free and careless approach to the copying of New Testament texts. We can say this with confidence because of a Scripture like Hebrews 1v1-4:

> *1 God, who at various times and in various ways spoke in time past to the fathers by the prophets, 2 has in these last days spoken to us by His Son, whom He has appointed heir of all things, through whom also He made the worlds; 3 who being the brightness of His glory and the express image of His person, and upholding all things by the word of His power, when He had by Himself purged our sins, sat down at the right hand of the Majesty on high, 4 having become so much better than the angels, as He has by inheritance obtained a more excellent name than they. (Hebrews 1v1-4).*

The Old Testament was the revelation of God both pure and perfect throughout, but it was piecemeal: "at various times and in various ways." All Scripture is God-breathed but the New Testament, in contrast, was given to us "by His Son" whom is of far superior status and nature to

---

364   Exodus 20v18,19.
365   Exodus 25v9,30; 26v30; 35v29; Leviticus 8v36; 10v11; 26v46.

the prophets, to the angels, to Moses and so on.[366] The revelation of God's word through His Son is to be considered far more superior, surely, than the fore-running revelation given through the prophets? Since this is true, would the Lord have left the copyists of the New Testament to their own devices without some oversight? Surely the apostles and early Christians would have been more careful in publishing the inspired writings?

New Testament views.

By New Testament times we have the witness of the New Testament writers and the witness of the Lord Jesus to the canon of the Old Testament. Christ, for example, refers to the threefold division of the Old Testament:

> *Then He said to them, "These are the words which I spoke to you while I was still with you, that all things must be fulfilled which were written in the Law of Moses and the Prophets and the Psalms concerning Me." (Luke 24v44).*

The Lord quoted from at least 24 Old Testament books and referred to the Old Testament with the authoritative words "it is written."[367] Christ read from the Scriptures in the synagogue.[368] He spoke of the Scripture as the "commandment of God," and as the "word of God," and He stated that Scripture could never "be broken."[369] He quoted the Scriptures in His public ministry, and exhorted His hearers to read them for themselves.[370] He would often correct misunderstandings of Scripture, but He never once corrected them. For the Lord, Scripture was indestructible![371] The Lord Jesus confirmed many of the Old Testament accounts as being true. Thus He referred to creation, to the destruction of Sodom, the death of Abel, the events of Noah and the flood, the calling of Moses, the giving of manna in the wilderness to name but a few.[372] Given such extensive use and reverence for God's word, the Lord Jesus Christ was incidentally giving assent to the idea that God's word had been preserved.

In considering the writing, copying and preservation of the New Testament, it is obvious both from the nature of our Saviour and His intention to reveal, and further from what He actually said, that the Lord Jesus Christ clearly intended all believers to have access to the word of God.[373]

---

366   2Timothy 3v16; Hebrews 1v1f.
367   Matthew 4v4,6,7,10.
368   Luke 4v16.
369   Matthew 15v3; Mark 7v13; John 10v35.
370   Matthew 19v3-5; 21v16,42; John 5v39.
371   Matthew 5v13.
372   Matthew 19v4-6; 24v37f; Mark 12v26; Luke 11v51; 17v29,32; John 6v31-51.
373   John 1v18; 17v6.8, (compare also Isaiah 48v3,5,7,16); John 14v6,17; 15v26; 16v7,13.

Heaven and earth will pass away, but My words will by no means pass away. (Matthew 24v35).

18 And Jesus came and spoke to them, saying, "All authority has been given to Me in heaven and on earth. 19 Go therefore and make disciples of all the nations, baptizing them in the name of the Father and of the Son and of the Holy Spirit, 20 teaching them to observe all things that I have commanded you; and lo, I am with you always, even to the end of the age." Amen. (Matthew 28v18-20).

For whoever is ashamed of Me and My words, of him the Son of Man will be ashamed when He comes in His own glory, and in His Father's, and of the holy angels. (Luke 9v26).

To this end we find that He made provision for believers after His departure from earth. Thus on the night He was betrayed the Lord Jesus declared that the Holy Spirit's task was to teach the disciples and to remind them of everything the Lord spoke to them.

But the Helper, the Holy Spirit, whom the Father will send in My name, He will teach you all things, and bring to your remembrance all things that I said to you. (John 14v26)

Furthermore the Holy spirit would guide the apostles into all truth:

However, when He, the Spirit of truth, has come, He will guide you into all truth; for He will not speak on His own authority, but whatever He hears He will speak; and He will tell you things to come. (John 16v13).

Importantly we note further that the Lord promised that there would be those skilled in writing as well as prophets being spread throughout the world:

Therefore, indeed, I send you prophets, wise men, and scribes: some of them you will kill and crucify, and some of them you will scourge in your synagogues and persecute from city to city (Matthew 23v34)

Scribes would be important in the kingdom of heaven. After speaking a series of parables concerning the kingdom of heaven the Lord then asks:

... "Have you understood all these things?" They said to Him, "Yes, Lord." Then He said to them, "Therefore every scribe instructed concerning the kingdom of heaven is like a householder who brings out of his treasure things new and old." (Matthew 13v51)

Why would the Lord mention scribes except that they have an especial purpose? Scribes would be needed to copy and write the Scriptures for the faithful to read and hear being read.

Although the theme of Scripture as writing forms the content for another chapter, it is important to highlight here that as an incidental aside, the New Testament makes copious reference to writing and writing materials. A few pertinent references will serve to indicate that far from the Biblical culture being pre-eminently oral, as many contend, the art of writing was prevalent. Paul requested from Timothy that he bring some books and especially the parchments.[374] We do not know what these books and parchments contained. They could have been Old Testament Scripture, or they could have been gospels or other New Testament writings. It is useless to speculate of course but that writing was part of normal life is clear from such an incidental reference. In other books of the New Testament we note further clear references to writing. For example, Zacharias asked for a writing tablet on which he could write John's name.[375] Paul notes in the letter to Philemon that he was writing in his own hand.[376] In Luke 16 the Lord Jesus tells of the parable of the unrighteous steward. In this he has the steward telling his master's debtors to write out false bills.[377] Pilate had a note written in three languages which was fixed to the head of Christ's cross.[378] The first letter written to the church was recorded in Acts 15v23, and then of course we have the abundant witness of writing in all the letters of the New Testament. It was natural for the apostles to write to the churches as they were being formed. The idea that several decades passed before anything was committed to paper seems to be nonsense given the clear fact that writing was a normal part of New Testament life and times. Levi (Matthew) was a tax collector and so was probably skilled with pen and ink.

In the early days of the new Christian church we find an amazing response to the gospel message preached. On the day of Pentecost three thousand were added to the small band of disciples.[379] We have to understand that although there were many from different regions as Acts 2v8-11 tells us, the vast majority of these converts would have been Jews. These folk would have been steeped in the Old Testament truths and ways. As the gospel spread, and before the time of Paul and persecution, we find that amongst the new converts many had been Old Testament priests:

> *Then the word of God spread, and the number of the disciples multiplied greatly in Jerusalem, and a great many of the priests were obedient to the faith. (Acts 6v7)*

---

374   2Timothy 4v13.
375   Luke 1v63.
376   Philemon 1v19.
377   Luke 16v6,7.
378   Luke 23v38; John 19v20.
379   Acts 2v41.

These priests would have lost all of their Old Testament responsibilities and functions. However their Old Testament training, especially in scribal and teaching duties, would have been very useful in the transmission of the revealed texts.

The 27 New Testament texts we have today were all apostolic in origin. By this we mean that the entire New Testament was written by apostles or by those guided by them. Thus Mark was under the tutelage of Peter, and Luke under the guide and instruction of Paul. Paul was a Pharisee taught under Gamaliel and all the New Testament writers were Jews. It is inconceivable that these Jewish men would have allowed anything less than the Jewish reverence for the word of God to be evident amongst Christians. Given this reverent basis for the inspired writings of the New Testament, we must point out that the epistles were often copied and circulated to various disparate churches:

> *I charge you by the Lord that this epistle be read to all the holy brethren. (1Thessalonioans 5v27.*

The reference to "all the holy brethren" is not clear. Does this mean all in the church at Thessalonica, or all who named the name of Christ wherever they may be? Then also, the letter to the Colossians was to be read by the church at Laodicea. It is inconceivable that the Colossians would let the original go to Laodicea and more likely that it was copied.

> *Now when this epistle is read among you, see that it is read also in the church of the Laodiceans, and that you likewise read the epistle from Laodicea. (Colossians 4v16).*

The apostle Peter speaks about Paul's letters and thereby indicates that copies were obviously available:

> *15 ... as also our beloved brother Paul, according to the wisdom given to him, has written to you, 16 as also in all his epistles, speaking in them of these things, in which are some things hard to understand, which untaught and unstable people twist to their own destruction, as they do also the rest of the Scriptures. (2Peter 3v15,16).*

The book of Revelation with its seven letters to the churches was probably copied and distributed to each church. Furthermore, we read at the start of the book that it was actually intended to be read widely:

> *Blessed is he who reads and those who hear the words of this prophecy, and keep those*

things which are written in it; for the time is near. (Revelation 1v3).

Turning to the Acts of the apostles we read there of the wonderful spread of the word of God.

> *Then the word of God spread, and the number of the disciples multiplied greatly in Jerusalem, and a great many of the priests were obedient to the faith. (Acts 6v7).*
>
> *But the word of God grew and multiplied. (Acts 12v24).*
>
> *And the word of the Lord was being spread throughout all the region. (Acts 13v49).*
>
> *So the word of the Lord grew mightily and prevailed. (Acts 19v20).*

These texts are often taken merely to mean that people who trusted in the word of God were moving about, but this is a forced understanding. The word of God being spread is what is referred to here not people. It is true, of course, that the word of God is within the people of God as the parable of the soils indicates, but the word of God is also written down and this too was multiplying. We reaffirm the indisputable fact that the Biblical cultures were not simply oral in nature, passing things down only by word of mouth, but were steeped in a history of revelation that was written down when it was received. The early emphasis on writing in the Pentateuch surely indicates this?

As the church continued to grow, early on in the church's life there came a point when the apostles had to make a determined effort to focus solely on the word of God:

> *2 Then the twelve summoned the multitude of the disciples and said, "It is not desirable that we should leave the word of God and serve tables. 3 Therefore, brethren, seek out from among you seven men of good reputation, full of the Holy Spirit and wisdom, whom we may appoint over this business; 4 but we will give ourselves continually to prayer and to the ministry of the word." (Acts 6v2-4)*

But what exactly do the apostles mean here by concentrating on the "ministry of the word"? Clearly it would involve preaching and teaching, but would it not also involve writing and overseeing the copying of the written inspired texts? It would simply make no sense to suggest that the inspired writings were merely written and not copied copiously. Coupled with the fact that these new Christians were from the Jewish Israelite traditions, it is not fanciful to suggest that they reverently, carefully and faithfully provided copies of the originals.

Turning attention to the most prolific New Testament writer, Paul, we see that his ministry to deliver the gospel must have included the copying of inspired texts. Paul was clearly concerned for all the churches, and this meant that he was eager to ensure correct leadership so that these churches could flourish.[380] These leaders were to teach their congregations in the gospel, but from what were they to teach? In the pastoral epistles we note how often the word "doctrine" and "commandment" occurs, and the repeated warning to avoid "fables" and other "myths." If Paul was concerned for all the churches then surely he would have wanted to ensure that good copies of the Scriptures (the inspired writings) were readily available? He instructs Timothy in Ephesus to give attention to the public reading of Scripture.[381] How could he instruct this if there were no Scriptures available? Paul also considered himself to be a steward of the gospel. He exhorts Timothy to "hold fast the pattern of sound words" and to pass on the things he had heard from Paul "to faithful men who will be able to teach others also."[382] Given these exhortations are we to believe that this did not include the accurate copying of the Scriptures?

It is not without significance that many of the writings of the apostles and New Testament writers include severe warnings against tampering with what had been revealed and written. Such warnings do not just speak to those who would preach and teach. It certainly includes the operation of copying the text for many to read. Paul wrote that the inspired writings were "spiritual" in nature, and were not formed out of the wisdom of men.[383] There were many unscrupulous folk who thought they could make great (financial) gain by hoodwinking unsuspecting and weak people. Paul protested that he was not a "peddler" of the word:

> For we are not, as so many, peddling the word of God; but as of sincerity, but as from God, we speak in the sight of God in Christ. (2Corinthians 2v17).

The KJV translates the Greek rendered "peddling" as "corrupt" in this verse. The thought behind the Greek word is of one who is seeking to sell something for financial gain. How many do this in our day! Paul spoke openly in the clear view of the Lord. Part of his speech included the writing of this letter. He is not "peddling" the word of God but publishing it. An explicit warning against tampering comes in the last book of the New Testament, or, in other words, right at the end of God's revelation:

> **18** For I testify to everyone who hears the words of the prophecy of this book: If anyone adds to these things, God will add to him the plagues that are written in this book; **19** and if anyone takes away from the words of the book of this prophecy, God shall take away his part from the Book of Life, from the holy city, and from the things which are written in this book. (Revelation 22v18,19).

---

380   2Corinthians 11v28.
381   1Timothy 4v13.
382   2Timothy 1v13; 2v2.
383   1Corinthians 2v13.

Mike Viccary

There are two ways that a person may fall foul of this warning. First, a person may add or take from the words by changing the meaning in some way. They may listen to someone reading the text and interpret it to suit themselves. Then second they may add or subtract by actually altering the words of copied text. There have been many who want to scratch out sections of Scripture and many who have attempted to do so such as the actor who played Gandalf in the Lord of the Rings films.

It might be objected that the New Testament has no **direct** instructions on how the manuscripts were preserved and copied. The response to this is that the Bible does not have precise instructions on a great many things. If it did it would not only be unwieldy, but most of these added parts would be redundant. Nevertheless, given instructions such as, holding fast the pattern of sound words, passing the message on faithfully, and being good stewards of the gospel, coupled with the many necessary requirements for the preservation of the text, it is certain that the inspired writings were faithful copied and spread from the earliest of times following Pentecost.

A Biblical view of the New Testament and its preservation.

The original text of the New Testament documents were written somewhere between AD 30 and AD 90. Most scholars suggest much later dates but there seems to be no real reason to believe that the first apostles and disciples did not commit their newly found revealed faith to writing as soon as they could after the resurrection.[384] The original documents would have been penned in the common Greek language "koine" which was used throughout the Mediterranean world. Since these were all handwritten documents we no longer have these original "autographs."

Given the spread of the Christian faith northwards into Syria (Damascus, Antioch) and throughout the Greek speaking world (Greece, Greek Asia Minor and the Greek Mediterranean islands) it is highly probable that many of the original autographs were in the possession of the churches in this region. Thus, for example, Luke's works (the gospel of Luke and Acts), Paul's letters, John's gospel, letters and apocalypse, Peter's letters, James' letter and possibly the letter of Jude were all to be located in this broad region. This accounts for 23 of the 27 New Testament books so that only Matthew's gospel, Mark's gospel, Hebrews, and Romans were sent outside this part of the world.

It is certain that the original autographs were copied extensively by the early Christians. However since we have no assurance that the copying of the originals was perfect, it is clear that no two copies of any manuscript were identical. The differences between manuscripts arose due to

---

384   Wilbur N. Pickering, The Identity of the New Testament text. Thomas Nelson, 1977. P92. Pickering suggests that there is evidence in the manuscript title pages that Matthew was written eight years after Christ's ascension in AD 38, Mark came two years later (AD 40), Luke another five years after Mark (AD 45) and John in AD 62.

simple copying mistakes such as missing the place you were copying from, and going back to another place, or misspellings and so on. Whilst the autographs were inspired and error free, the copies did not have this status. Thus, inspiration is limited to the autographs and does not extend to the manuscript copies we have in our possession. At first sight such a statement seems terribly wrong. If God inspired the writings of the apostles and prophets so that they were error free, why then did He leave the transmission of the text throughout the ages to the vagaries of men's abilities? Let it be stated at once that the Lord could easily have extended His miraculous intervention to include the copies, but it is clear from the extant evidence we have (the manuscripts we have in our possession) that there are errors and differences. But, we must not stop at this point, for we have the witness of Scripture as a whole that the Lord has promised us His word and truth for all generations. Whilst we cannot say that any **one** manuscript is perfect and pure, what we can say is that the inspired text is to be found in the whole manuscript evidence. Given this we must then look carefully at the manuscript evidence to construct the infallible and inerrant New Testament text. We will find that whilst a particular manuscript has a mistake at one point, many others will be pure and perfect at such a place whilst having mistakes in other places. By comparing manuscripts together we can be sure of the New Testament as a whole.

We have stated that preservation of the word occurred through providence rather than by direct miracle (inspiration) but this does not mean that the Lord's work of preservation is undone. I feel that far too many scholars have resorted to assuming that accurate copying is virtually impossible and will always leave a trail of destruction and ruination of any text that is copied. We can see such reasoning in the academic ignoring of the Byzantine text. Such a smooth and largely error-free text is considered by academics to be a fabrication (an editing job done by ecclesiastical authority) rather than as a result of the careful work of Christian scribes. However when it comes to the sacred word of God, those who would bother to copy such would surely have been of a mind to be careful in what they were doing? This does not mean that they would be perfect, of course. It merely means that they would have been as careful as they possibly could.

At this point we must point out that the entire manuscript evidence is remarkably pure overall. We can be confident that the New Testament we posses in our Bibles is accurate and faithful. First we must note that we have manuscripts that date from before the middle of the second century. Second we have such an enormous number of copies of the New Testament (whole, portions, or fragments) that no other ancient text comes anywhere near the New Testament for strength of witness. Thirdly, and finally, the numerous copies of the New Testament say virtually exactly the same thing as our present-day Bibles. The discrepancies are minor. The vast majority of differences due to text copying mistakes do not appear when we translate the New Testament because they consist of such things as spelling mistakes or obvious slips of the pen. Of the remaining differences none affect any doctrines. In short we can be confident that the correct reading is available within the extensive range of manuscripts we have available to us. We need to add something here in respect of history since the number of manuscripts has been increasing over the years. What we can be sure of is that the whole New Testament has been available throughout the ages. This will inevitably mean that newer manuscript discoveries cannot correct the New Testament today.

Given the above thoughts we must be extremely careful about devising a history to account for the Greek manuscript evidence we have in our possession. It has been the norm for textual critics to devise a history to explain the evidence, and to use this historical "data" to inform them on how to select the best manuscripts as containing the true New Testament. As the prime example, we have Westcott and Hort's theory of 1881, which held that the two uncial texts with the Alexandrian text type (Codex Vaticanus and Codex Sinaiticus) were the best representatives of the New Testament, and that the majority of manuscripts (the Byzantine text type) were formed through a recension (a form of standardised editing) carried out in Antioch in the fourth century. In constructing this historical situation, these two textual critics effectively reduced the 90% of manuscripts (the Byzantine text type) to being a single witness, and because they were much later than the uncials they favoured, they ignored them. Westcott and Hort's ideas are not now followed. However their view of the Byzantine text as late and edited, rendering them of no use in textual studies, is still adhered to by many as we have already noted earlier. In recent years the newly discovered papyri (which Westcott and Hort knew nothing of), have changed textual critics thinking.[385] Since these manuscripts show evidence of sloppy copying and many errors, some have abandoned the idea of ever recovering a pure New Testament text. It is often stated that the worst of scribal errors and mistakes occurred in the first two hundred years since the autographs were penned. This statement is made on the basis of the evidence from the papyri. Consequently those who look for an historical picture of the manuscripts fall into despair. If all we have are corrupt and poorly copied papyri in the earliest centuries followed by uncials of the fourth centuries which show signs of scribal correction and repair, and then followed by a very coherently smoothed out collection of Byzantine manuscripts that have been standardised somehow, whatever are we to do?

As a result many have chosen an "eclectic" method for locating the New Testament text.[386]

---

385   Clive E. Govier. The Majority Text Debate: A Study in New testament Text-Critical Method. MA Thesis. Edith Cowan University, Perth WA. 1996. P22.
386   As for footnote 385, P25.

This amounts to a matter of subjective choice based on a favoured set of rules or assumptions. Such a sorry state of affairs is due simply to a reliance on an historical method for identifying the New Testament text within the manuscripts rather than a theological and Biblical one. Of course the problem with the historical scenario painted in the paragraph above, is that it is a history devised (imagined) with the poorest of source material. No one knows the true history of the Byzantine text. The textual critic Birdsall makes the following confession:

> ... one of the major problems of the historian of the New Testament text. ... The origin of the Byzantine text is [not] known .... [It] is frequently ascribed to Lucian of Antioch, and the aScription is turned to fact by frequent repetition ... but ... there is no direct evidence of any philological work by him upon the New Testament text.[387]

To make the assumption that these manuscripts owe their origin to uncials like Vaticanus and Sinaiticus, which in turn must have derived from the papyri that have been unearthed in the twentieth century, is rank stupidity at best, and certainly naivete at least. We should add here, that given that many of the autographs were located in the Greek world, and given that the Greek copyists were in the habit of destroying the originals from which copies were made, it is far more likely that a true history of the Byzantine text owes nothing whatsoever to the Egyptian papyri.[388]

A more likely reconstruction of the historical antecedence for the Byzantine text type has been suggested by Van Bruggen who asked the following important question:

> How can this text ... suddenly be known, for example, in the writings of Eustathius of Antioch (beginning fourth century), and in the writings of the Syrian Aphrahat? How can this text then be found in a section of Chrysostom's works as the known text? [If one says,] this now proves that this Byzantine text was made at the time of Nicaea [then] ... how did it manage to spread so quickly? Through what influence? And why are there no indications, in the writings of the fourth century, that the writers were aware that they were introducing a newer text?[389]

Thus if the writers of the fourth century were using the Byzantine text as their normal one, they cannot have regarded it as new. It must have been the one handed down from previous generations which stands to reason given the locale, since Antioch has more claim to autographic and apostolic

---

387   Birdsall. J. N. (1970). The New Testament text. In P.R. Ackroyd and C. F. Evans (Eds.), The Cambridge history of the Bible: Vol. I. From the beginnings to .Ierome (pp. 308-377). Cambridge: Cambridge University Press. P320.

388   Clive E. Govier. The Majority Text Debate: A Study in New testament Text-Critical Method. MA Thesis. Edith Cowan University, Perth WA. 1996. P94. Wallace disagrees with the idea that the lack of evidence for the Byzantine text has arisen due to the originals being destroyed by copyists or by overuse of manuscripts resulting in them wearing out. Daniel B. Wallace, The Majority Text Theory: History, Methods and Critique. JETS 37/2 (June 1994) 185-215. P206.

389   Van Bruggen, J. (1976). The ancient text of the New Testament. Winnipeg: Premier. P24.

influence than either Alexandria or Rome. There must have been many copies of the gospels and epistles derived from apostolic origin here from which copies were constantly made. The many copies made of the Byzantine text type are surely an indication of its preferment by the believing population. This truth was one which Hort considered possible even though he charted a course against the Byzantine witnesses.[390]

[6] Conclusions.

We have been at pains to detail the manuscript evidence and how it is viewed by many scholars. It is now time to make some conclusions from what we have discussed.

First of all we come to the belief that whatever the many scholars of the last one hundred and more years have said and written, much of their work does not seem to be in accord with a truly *Biblical* view of the subject of the preservation of Scripture. Second we must assert that whilst there are differences between the two extremes in text type (Byzantine vs Alexandrian), the differences do not lead to a different gospel or a different expression of the Christian faith. We believe that the vast majority of differences are minor and easily resolved, and the few cases where there are significant differences none affect Christian doctrine. Consequently it is not in the best interests of the church when any group of believers denounce another set and pour vitriol on them for holding a different view. We must argue the case, of course, but with faith, patience and love. Given these thoughts, a third conclusion is that the Alexandrian text type does not seem to have any claim to being the authentic New Testament. This is because it was late on the scene in the Western world (arriving in 1881), and further because its chief exemplars (Vaticanus and Sinaiticus) seem to be corrupted and impure at the very least. A fourth conclusion must therefore be that the Byzantine majority text type is the one which does indeed preserve the true New Testament. Many in the KJV only camp take the next step and assert that because the Lord promised us a pure and perfect word of God, this necessarily means that the Textus Receptus must be the true representative of the Greek New Testament. Some go even further and claim that the KJV is the only true Bible. Many others do not go this far believing that the majority of manuscripts (i.e. the Byzantine text type) contain the New Testament. The difference between the Textus Receptus and the Majority text is minimal, and yet there are differences. Chiefly these have to do with certain Scriptures such as 1John 5v7,8 and it is therefore important to consider these carefully as we study the Scriptures. As a fifth conclusion we must assert that, despite the differences we have just noted, God has indeed provided us with His word pure in all ages. This does not mean we can simply leave the issue and move on, for we

---

390   Clive E. Govier. The Majority Text Debate: A Study in New testament Text-Critical Method. MA Thesis. Edith Cowan University, Perth WA. 1996. P86.

are exhorted to be diligent in our efforts. The differences between the Textus Recptus (borne out of the Majority of manuscripts) and the two Majority texts recently produced need to be examined. We have not yet engaged in this work and so more does need to be done, but for all practical purposes, the use of the Textus Receptus or one of the Majority Greek editions will not make much difference at all to the believer.

Chapter 4.

The Doctrine of Illumination.

Introduction.

Thus far we have discussed the initiative that the Lord God has taken in revealing truth, and supremely His Son, to a dying world. We have considered the revelation of God by inspiration and God's continual keeping and preserving His revealed will and purpose (the word of God) – the preservation of Scripture – in some detail, and we have concluded that not only has God spoken, but that He has spoken so that all may hear. We can sum up this idea from a particularly interesting Scripture we noted earlier. The Lord points the Sadducees back to the Exodus story and says these wonderful words:

> *have you not read what was spoken to you by God, saying ... (Matthew 22v31).*

The Sadducees could still read in the Scriptures they had in their possession, that which "was spoken" to them by God! The same is true for us as well. Thus God's word revealed is available to one and all throughout the ages. This is all well and good, but it is not the end of the basic doctrine of Scripture that we need to elaborate on. It is not enough that God has spoken so that all could hear what He has to say, for we need also to *understand* what He has said. This is why we have the doctrine of illumination. Or, in other words, the doctrine of the understanding of Scripture revealed by the Lord. In what follows we shall first consider the Scriptural evidence that teaches God's intention that people would understand what He has revealed. Then we shall consider the method of how we can come to an understanding of God's word. This latter topic is referred to as "hermeneutics" in the literature.

Scriptures showing that revelation can be understood.

The doctrine of illumination is the inevitable follow on from revelation, inspiration and preservation. God in all ages wants all people to have access to His word. If He reveals, surely He wants His pure message to be imparted and preserved, and if this is so, surely He wants it to be understood.

We know, of course, that an understanding of Scripture is not a right of any man, woman or child. Yet the general principle that Scripture is meant to be understood by ordinary folk is here being stated plainly. Many (for example, Roman Catholics) have in the past stopped ordinary folk from approaching Scripture. We might be in danger of doing this by suggesting that academic scholarship is required to understand it, or by elevating science as a pre-requisite, or through demanding that a priesthood act as mediator. We must not do this, but what we must do is establish that Christ alone is Mediator, and His chief tool for our lives is the Scriptures.

One of the great stumbling blocks that is often placed in believers' paths is the idea that their Biblical views are a matter of personal interpretation. When I was a young Christian I was shocked to find a Christian pastor who responded to my plea that creation be taken seriously with these horrible words: "that is your interpretation." This response effectively added a barrier between me and the Lord. Many would have us believe that the creation speaks to the scientist in unmistakable terms, whilst the Scriptures are dark, difficult and obscure. How absurd is man that he would reverse the truth! The fact of the matter is that God's word is full of statements that indicate that we can indeed understand what God has revealed. The first Scripture we shall consider, concerns the occasion when David called upon his son, Solomon, to build the temple:

> *Only the Lord give thee wisdom and understanding, and give thee charge concerning Israel, that thou mayest keep the law of the Lord thy God. (1Chronicles 22v12, KJAV).*

David prays for his son Solomon and asks for "wisdom and understanding" so that he may "keep the law" of the Lord. Such a prayer indicates not only that the Lord God is the source of such wisdom and understanding (forgive my pointing out such an obvious fact) but also that the Lord is indeed willing to impart such understanding. Later on we find that David confessed that God had in fact given him understanding when He revealed the details of the temple that would be built by his son:

> *All this, said David, the Lord made me understand in writing by his hand upon me, all the works of these plans. (1Chronicles 28v19).*

It was the Lord who made David understand. Not only that, but we have the added truth that God revealed to the king "in writing" all that was necessary. How important it is for us to reaffirm that our faith in God is no mere fanciful set of ideas dreamed by men and passed through the generations

Mike Viccary

by word of mouth. Not a bit of this! The Lord wanted David to understand very carefully the revealed plan which had been written down under the Lord's direct guidance.

In the next Scripture we find the purpose and aim of preaching explained. A group of men along with the Levites were there with Ezra and (possibly) Nehemiah helping the people understand God's law:

> 7 *Also Jeshua, Bani, Sherebiah, Jamin, Akkub, Shabbethai, Hodijah, Maaseiah, Kelita, Azariah, Jozabad, Hanan, Pelaiah, and the Levites, helped the people to understand the Law; and the people stood in their place.* **8** *So they read distinctly from the book, in the Law of God; and they gave the sense, and helped them to understand the reading. (Nehemiah 8v7,8).*

Here we are taught clearly that it is possible to hear "distinctly" the word of God, so that the "sense" is understood. A bit later on the same occasion we read these words:

> *Now on the second day the heads of the fathers' houses of all the people, with the priests and Levites, were gathered to Ezra the scribe, in order to understand the words of the Law. (Nehemiah 8v13).*

The words of God's revealed law are, therefore, clearly to be understood. In the Psalms we have a series of texts which reinforce this idea that what God has given in His word is to be comprehended and understood. In our first offering we are taught that the Lord Himself is our teacher:

> *Who is the man that fears the Lord? Him shall He teach in the way He chooses. (Psalm 25v12).*

The Lord God is the one alone who can teach us the way! We are reminded that the Lord Jesus taught His disciples the night before He died that He was: "the way, the truth, and the life" indicating a similar teaching.[391] When we come to Him we are not given a formula or a set of truths dispassionately. Instead we come to Him who is "the truth" and He guides us not just along but into eternal life! In the same Psalm we read these wonderful words:

> *The secret of the Lord is with those who fear Him, and He will show them His covenant. (Psalm 25v14).*

The Lord God is not a distant austere and unknowable figure. He is willing to make Himself known. In the words of this Psalm we find that those who respond to the Lord have privileges they never

---

391   John 14v6.

dreamed of. Such folk are brought in to experience the "secret of the Lord" suggesting an intimate and deep relationship, and are those whom God will share His purpose and will ("show them His covenant"). Are these not wonderful words which lead us to accept that God wants us to understand what He has revealed?

In David's penitential Psalm we are brought to a truth which is central to the gospel. Even though David (and all of us) were born in a state of sin, the Lord's aim and purpose is that we will know the truth. Listen carefully to these words:

> *Behold, You desire truth in the inward parts, and in the hidden part You will make me to know wisdom. (Psalm 51v6).*

If the Lord desires truth in our innermost being, then surely we can take it that understanding is a part of this? In other Psalms we find that God has made known certain things to various peoples. Thus in Psalm 103 we read that:

> *He made known His ways to Moses, His acts to the children of Israel. (Psalm 103v7).*

Although Moses was the one who was close to God and received directly from the Lord as His prophet, this Psalm makes it clear that what the Lord made known to Moses was not just for His consumption. The Lord makes things known not just to the prophet through whom revelation comes, but to all who own the name of the Lord. The Lord is a great God. This may sound like a weak statement but that is because our culture has overused terms such as "great." There is nothing that compares with the Lord for He is also good, gracious and glorious. His purpose is not to harm or be hidden. It was God alone who sought to resolve the problem we have ignored and suppressed by sending His Son to die in our place. Surely this heart of the Lord includes the desire for our understanding? In this next Psalm we find the heart of the Lord expressed towards us:

> *For He satisfies the longing soul, and fills the hungry soul with goodness. (Psalm 107v9).*

A more direct statement that the Lord wants us to understand comes in this next Psalm:

> *The entrance of Your words gives light; it gives understanding to the simple. (Psalm 119v130).*

Mike Viccary

In this Psalm we find that when the words of God are brought into view of the "simple," it results in their understanding.

> *Blessed be the Lord my Rock, who trains my hands for war, and my fingers for battle—*
> *(Psalm 144v1).*

The Lord is our stability and security. He is our Father. If earthly fathers train their children to do many different things, surely the Lord God who is the source of all life would want the same for His children? Here David rejoices that the Lord had trained him to deal with the battles and wars he was facing. The picture is of a man being trained to use his arms to wield a sword and his fingers to use a bow. What has this to do with us, you may ask? Well we too face battles. Spiritual battles. The Lord will train us to fight these. But since the battles are spiritual we do not fight with carnal or worldly weapons. Instead, as Paul, writes:

> *4 For the weapons of our warfare are not carnal but mighty in God for pulling down*
> *strongholds, 5 casting down arguments and every high thing that exalts itself against the*
> *knowledge of God, bringing every thought into captivity to the obedience of Christ.*
> *(2Corinthians 10v4,5).*

The intricacies of spiritual warfare demand that those who engage in such have understanding. How otherwise can they succeed? Of course without the Lord's help and work within us we have no hope. But that the Lord expects us to engage and put our shoulders to the task is undeniable, as the following verse teaches:

> *12 Therefore, my beloved, as you have always obeyed, not as in my presence only, but now*
> *much more in my absence, work out your own salvation with fear and trembling; 13 for it is*
> *God who works in you both to will and to do for His good pleasure. (Philippians 2v12,13).*

Having delved into the Psalms, we have three verses from the book of Proverbs to consider. In the first we have the image of wisdom as a woman, (a theme which features throughout the book of Proverbs), who calls in the streets:

> *20 Wisdom calls aloud outside; she raises her voice in the open squares. 21 She cries out in*
> *the chief concourses, at the openings of the gates in the city she speaks her words: 22 "how*
> *long, you simple ones, will you love simplicity? For scorners delight in their scorning, and*
> *fools hate knowledge. 23 Turn at my rebuke; surely I will pour out my spirit on you; I will*
> *make my words known to you. (Proverbs 1v20-23).*

Mike Viccary   174 of 319

Note here that wisdom will pour out her spirit upon the simple ones and will make known her words. Once again the point is clear. The words are not merely to be received but *known*, that is understood. In the next passage we have repeated reference to people coming to an understanding:

> *1 My son, if you receive my words, and treasure my commands within you, 2 so that you incline your ear to wisdom, and apply your heart to understanding; 3 yes, if you cry out for discernment, and lift up your voice for understanding, 4 if you seek her as silver, and search for her as for hidden treasures; 5 then you will understand the fear of the Lord, and find the knowledge of God. 6 For the Lord gives wisdom; from His mouth come knowledge and understanding; 7 He stores up sound wisdom for the upright; He is a shield to those who walk uprightly; 8 He guards the paths of justice, and preserves the way of His saints. 9 Then you will understand righteousness and justice, equity and every good path. 10 When wisdom enters your heart, and knowledge is pleasant to your soul, 11 discretion will preserve you; understanding will keep you. (Proverbs 2v1-11).*

Here we are taught that understanding is not given without some effort. The one who would understand must "apply" their heart to the task and must "lift up" their voice to request it. This is no mere asking or simple enquiry. If a person searches as one seeks for precious metal and treasure then they will come to a knowledge of the Lord. This reference to mining and refining indicates not just effort but process. We shall consider these a bit later when we look at the rules for understanding Scripture. For now we simply note that an understanding is the end result. The Lord is no mean and tyrannical Lord for He gives willingly. However the need for effort and diligence on our part is necessary so that we take what the Lord has given more seriously. Note that we are not talking about salvation here. Salvation is by grace through faith alone, and not by means of works. However once a person has come into the kingdom, the receipt of wisdom and understanding is only given to those who diligently seek it. Our last offering from Proverbs gives us a simple contrast between the wicked and the righteous with regard to understanding.

> *Evil men do not understand justice, but those who seek the Lord understand all. (Proverbs 28v5).*

The contrast is stark. Those who seek the Lord understand not just the justice that evil men do not understand, but everything!

Our next book to consider is Daniel. In the second chapter of this book we have a wonderful event which serves to show us the nature of God's revelation. The king has a dream which disturbs him and to ensure that its interpretation is sound, he asks his advisors not only to tell him the interpretation, but they must reveal the dream as well. After some time we find that Daniel and his friends beseech the Lord for help in this matter, for no one can know what the king dreams except the Lord. Daniel is given the dream and its interpretation by the Lord, and when he is with the king he reveals to the king this truth that none can know such things except the Lord revealed them:

> *But there is a God in heaven who reveals secrets, and He has made known to King Nebuchadnezzar what will be in the latter days. Your dream, and the visions of your head upon your bed, were these ... (Daniel 2v28).*

At the end of Daniel's prophecy we have a statement which echoes Proverbs 28v5:

> *9 And he said, "Go your way, Daniel, for the words are closed up and sealed till the time of the end. 10 Many shall be purified, made white, and refined, but the wicked shall do wickedly; and none of the wicked shall understand, but the wise shall understand. (Daniel 12v9,10).*

No wicked will understand but the wise will!

Having briefly considered the Old Testament we shall look now at what the New Testament has to say. The Lord Jesus taught the same diligence in seeking understanding as we noted in the book of Proverbs:

> *7 Ask, and it will be given to you; seek, and you will find; knock, and it will be opened to you. 8 For everyone who asks receives, and he who seeks finds, and to him who knocks it will be opened. (Matthew 7v7,8).*

There is a progression here. We must ask, we must seek, and we must knock, suggesting progression and persistence. The Lord tells us that those who do these things will succeed. In which case, if we seek an understanding, then we will come to such. After the Lord speaks the parable of the soils to His diciples, He then tells them the following:

> *He answered and said to them, "because it has been given to you to know the mysteries of the kingdom of heaven, but to them it has not been given." (Matthew 13v11).*

The disciples had come to Him asking for an explanation of the parable. Others were not so bothered. Consequently the disciples were those who would "know the mysteries of the kingdom," whilst others are excluded.

After the Lord rose from the dead on one occasion when He was amongst the disciples we find Him doing something quite remarkable. We read:

And He opened their understanding, that they might comprehend the Scriptures. (Luke 24v45).

Here we have a clear teaching that the Lord enables those who truly follow Him to not just read and understand the grammar of Scripture, but He enables them to comprehend them fully. In John we read of the Lord quoting the Old Testament to point out that believing disciples would come to Him because they have heard from the Father:

> *It is written in the prophets, 'And they shall all be taught by God.' Therefore everyone who has heard and learned from the Father comes to Me. (John 6v45).*

You will note here that the Lord states that believing disciples are "taught by God" and have "learned from the Father." Understanding is certainly a part of what is meant by these statements. The Lord quoted from the book of Isaiah:

> *All your children shall be taught by the Lord, and great shall be the peace of your children. (Isaiah 54v13).*

The Lord is our teacher! Once again, this must include understanding. Then in John chapter 8 we find that the Lord makes another wonderful statement:

> **31** *Then Jesus said to those Jews who believed Him, "If you abide in My word, you are My disciples indeed.* **32** *And you shall know the truth, and the truth shall make you free." (John 8v31,32).*

By abiding in the word of the Lord a person will not only be a true disciple, but will also know the truth and will become free. Next we have the following statement from the Lord about the Holy Spirit:

> *However, when He, the Spirit of truth, has come, He will guide you into all truth; for He will not speak on His own authority, but whatever He hears He will speak; and He will tell you things to come. (John 16v13).*

The Holy Spirit is the One who continues the Lord Jesus' mission of declaring the truth from the Father. He will guide into **all** truth and will speak of "things to come." Further teaching about the Spirit's working comes in Paul's first letter to the Corinthians.

> *Now we have received, not the spirit of the world, but the Spirit who is from God, that we might know the things that have been freely given to us by God. (1Corinthians 2v12).*

The Spirit is the One who will bring the things that the Father freely wills to give us. The concept of understanding is expressed later on as Paul points out that the natural man does not accept these spiritual truths because he considers them foolish. It is only the spiritual man who can judge and discern, for we have the mind of Christ. In Paul's second letter to the Corinthians we find a remarkable truth about how the Lord works within us to bring about His purposes:

> *For it is the God who commanded light to shine out of darkness, who has shone in our hearts to give the light of the knowledge of the glory of God in the face of Jesus Christ. (2Corinthians 4v6).*

It is noteworthy that the apostle refers to an aspect of creation to make his point here. Thus just as He made light to shine out of the darkness (nothingness), so He has worked in the new creation to shine in our hearts the "knowledge" of God's glory! This means surely that the ones through whom the Lord shines have some understanding. In the letter to the Colossians we read of Paul's prayers for the Christians there:

> *For this reason we also, since the day we heard it, do not cease to pray for you, and to ask that you may be filled with the knowledge of His will in all wisdom and spiritual understanding. (Colossians 1v9).*

If Paul can pray that the Colossians will be full of the knowledge of God's will with understanding, then surely such a state is something a believer may attain to. James writes that it is possible to ask the Lord for wisdom if anyone lacks:

> *If any of you lacks wisdom, let him ask of God, who gives to all liberally and without reproach, and it will be given to him. (James 1v5).*

Finally we have the following statement from John's first letter:

> *And we know that the Son of God has come and has given us an understanding, that we may know Him who is true; and we are in Him who is true, in His Son Jesus Christ. This is the true God and eternal life. (1John 5v20).*

What could be more clear than this? The Son of God has come to give us an understanding in order that we may know the Lord! These Scriptures make it very clear that an understanding which goes deep and which leads to fruit is the purpose of the revelation given of God.

We could also conclude that the Scriptures can be understood from a knowledge of the Bible as being *efficacious*, or, in other words, it does what God intends for it to do, (save souls, heal the mind, convert and so on). It is also worth mentioning that Scripture is written in a great variety of styles and forms. We have poetry, song, didactic, narrative, edict, letter, commandment, and so on. This great variety has two important uses. First the variety means that different people with different abilities and maturities can access the word of God. A young child may not fully grasp the significance and nuances of the symbolic texts like those found in Revelation or Daniel, but will clearly understand the life and sayings of Christ. Second we note that this variety in styles appeals to each of us at different times in our lives. We may be going through a difficult time and a Psalm read is comprehended readily whilst a series of commands may be difficult to grasp.

Now within some of the above texts you can make out certain prerequisites for an understanding. We shall turn now to consider the rules that Scripture informs us of so that we can understand God's word.

Rules for interpreting Scripture.

There are two types of rules or guides contained within Scripture. First there are the personal requirements, and second there are Scriptural necessities. [392]

Things required of us as persons.

We have already pointed out that unbelievers have no understanding and cannot receive the word of God. However there are a number of other attitudes a believer needs before understanding comes. Our lives as believers must be consistent. Repentance and faith are not actions we do merely at the start of our Christian lives. They are a way of life. It stands to reason, therefore, that heart attitude, an utter dependence on the Lord, and distrust of worldly ways are essential qualities to maintain. We shall consider five dispositions that are needed.

The person has the capacity to receive the truth.

Here we are rehearsing the need for a person to be born again. The Lord Jesus Christ often said: "he who has ears to hear let him hear."[393] Thus only those who have spiritual ears, or, in other

---

392   Sources considered include: A W Pink on hermeneutics and an article by Peter Masters entitled: Interpreting the Bible". Sword & Trowel. 1997. No.3. p18f.
393   Matthew 11v15; 13v9.

words, are of the new creation will be those who can receive the truth. There are countless Scriptures teaching a similar idea. For example the parable of the soils points us to only one type of soil which will result in the growth of the word of God. Then also we have considered briefly the fact that the natural man is unable to receive spiritual things because they are devoid of any spiritual capacity. Or consider Paul's argument in his letter to the Ephesians where he states unequivocally that as unbelievers we are dead in trespasses and sins [394] What can a dead man do? Hence for a person to come to an understanding of Scripture, they must be a regenerate born-again believer. It is simply impossible for anyone to receive the word of God unless they have had their eyes opened, and their ears unplugged, and have been made alive in Christ.

A new born "babe" in Christ will not be able to receive as much as one who has grown in grace and so, as a consequence, there are degrees of illumination. Some believers by virtue of growth will have received more than others. What then should a new believer do to learn more of Christ?

A total dependence upon the Lord God for instruction.

Even though a person may have been born again, it is necessary for them to be trained in learning from the Lord. This training is something which comes (in the main) directly from the Lord, because in the new covenant, believers will all be "taught of the Lord." [395] It is important to come back to this thought because in our natural state we rely on ourselves and place confidence in the flesh. These confidences must be broken and replaced with a complete and total dependence upon the Lord. Thus we bring to mind a very popular passage from Proverbs:

> **5** *Trust in the Lord with all your heart, and lean not on your own understanding;* **6** *in all your ways acknowledge Him, and He shall direct your paths. (Proverbs 3v5,6).*

This attitude is one we need every time we come to the Lord and His word to seek understanding and wisdom. We must remember that the Holy Spirit is the Author of the Scriptures. Since we have the Holy Spirit in our hearts (if we are true believers), we would do well to put our trust completely in the Author. [396] It is so sad to see many putting their trust in academic scholars and the writings of men. I do not say that we ignore what our fellow believers have written. We are not to be isolated believers working things out all alone, but we must recognise the fellowship of the saints through the ages. Others have travelled the path before us and we cannot ignore the advice they may bring.

---

394   Matthew 13v8; 1Corinthians 2v14; Ephesians 2v1,5.
395   Isaiah 54v13; John 6v45. Cf. Jeremiah 31v31-34.
396   John 14v26; 16v13.

Their witness is not perfect, of course, but we recognise the work of the Spirit in our fellow believers. However, here we assert the need to depend solely on the Lord for understanding.

Thus we must turn to the Lord in total and full dependence. This requires also that we turn from the world as we approach our studies in an attitude of reverence and prayer. In what follows, we shall look at a selection of verses from Psalm 119 which teach this dependence.

> *Open my eyes, that I may see wondrous things from Your law. (Psalm 119v18).*

The Psalmist's plea is one we must adopt. Yes we have been converted and had our eyes opened. However whenever we come to the Scriptures we need the Lord to remove the dirt and filth around our eyes that we may have gathered as we walk this earth, or which we have yet to remove.

> *Make me understand the way of Your precepts; so shall I meditate on Your wonderful works. (Psalm 119v27).*

In this verse we note that the Psalmist suffers from a heart and mind which needs help to understand. This ought to be our prayer. It may be that we have a wrong attitude or thought process, and as we come to Scripture we need to have this altered. In which case we must ask the Lord to make us understand. The same type of thinking is shown in the next verse:

> *Give me understanding, and I shall keep Your law; indeed, I shall observe it with my whole heart. (Psalm 119v34).*

Here the Psalmist requests understanding in order to be able to keep the Lord's ways. In the next verse the Psalmist actually makes a request that he is in need of the Lord's teaching:

> *Teach me good judgement and knowledge, for I believe Your commandments. (Psalm 119v66).*

In this instance the Psalmist believes the commandments of the Lord and does not set out to understand them on his own or by other means. Rather he seeks to be taught by the Lord. In the next verse the Psalmist reminds himself that he has been made by created by God:

> *Your hands have made me and fashioned me; give me understanding, that I may learn Your commandments. (Psalm 119v73).*

Once again the Psalmist relies on the Lord for understanding, not himself or others. The same thought is expressed in our next verse:

> *I am Your servant; give me understanding, that I may know Your testimonies. (Psalm 119v125).*

The Psalmist claims to be the Lord's possession and again asks the Master for understanding. Here are two final verses in which the Psalmist asks for understanding:

> *The righteousness of Your testimonies is everlasting; give me understanding, and I shall live. (Psalm 119v144).*

> *Let my cry come before You, O Lord; give me understanding according to Your word. (Psalm 119v169).*

Such dependence upon the Lord is a necessary attitude if we are to come to any understanding. We may conclude this piece by referring to Paul's statements in 1Corinthians chapter 2:

> *9 But as it is written: "eye has not seen, nor ear heard, nor have entered into the heart of man the things which God has prepared for those who love Him." 10 But God has revealed them to us through His Spirit. For the Spirit searches all things, yes, the deep things of God. 11 For what man knows the things of a man except the spirit of the man which is in him? Even so no one knows the things of God except the Spirit of God. 12 Now we have received, not the spirit of the world, but the Spirit who is from God, that we might know the things that have been freely given to us by God. 13 These things we also speak, not in words which man's wisdom teaches but which the Holy Spirit teaches, comparing spiritual things with spiritual. 14 But the natural man does not receive the things of the Spirit of God, for they are foolishness to him; nor can he know them, because they are spiritually discerned. 15 But he who is spiritual judges all things, yet he himself is rightly judged by no one. 16 For "who has known the mind of the Lord that he may instruct Him?" But we have the mind of Christ. (1Corinthians 2v9-13).*

What love! God has wondrous things for us to know. He has revealed them in the Scriptures and has made them known by the Spirit. The natural man is ignorant of these things freely given to us by the Lord. They must be discerned spiritually. Thus it is essential that we lean heavily upon the Lord and turn from any dependence upon man or his ways and wisdom.

A prepared heart (avoidance of wrong attitudes).

We have often had reason to recall the parable of the soils (sower).[397] Usually this is taken to

---

397   See, for example, Matthew 13v1f.

refer to those in whom the word of God would take root and flourish. So we may liken the application to our first point, the need to have a regenerate heart (i.e. to be born again). However, we find that the accretions of the world and the tug of the old nature can clog things up so that we need to do some serious gardening! We need to break up the fallow ground, remove the weeds (the cares and worries of this world) and so on.[398] For our second point, then, we are considering the need to come to the Lord and His word with a heart that is ready and prepared to hear what the Lord has to say. Unless we come with a willing heart, well then we ought never to bother to come at all.

It is a repeated truth in Scripture that God opposes the proud but He gives grace to the humble.[399] We read further that He teaches the humble (meek) only:

The humble He guides in justice, and the humble He teaches His way. (Psalm 25v9).

A proud heart is one that is unteachable. The humble, on the other hand, are those who are ready and willing to hear for they have no "angle" to pursue or "side" to them. We are also taught in the letter that James wrote to:

Therefore lay aside all filthiness and overflow of wickedness, and receive with meekness the implanted word, which is able to save your souls. (James 1v21).

This is a tremendously important verse. In the first part James speaks of us putting off the old ways and the sin we naturally follow. The same teaching is found in Paul's writings.[400] The second part teaches two essential things. First we must receive the word with meekness or humility. That is the main point we are stressing at this juncture, because proud hearts are immovable. But we also have a very important second point to note. And that is that the word we should receive is one *implanted* within us! It would seem that the word of God is something which resides within us. This harmonizes with what the Lord Jesus said in his discussion with the Jews:

But you do not have His word abiding in you, because whom He sent, Him you do not believe. (John 5v38).

For the believer, then, the word of God is something which has a locus within. It would seem that this is given when a person is born again, but in seed form and it must be unpacked by faith as the

---

398   See also Jeremiah 4v3; Hosea 10v12.
399   James 4v6; 1Peter 5v5.
400   Ephesians 4v22-24; Colossians 3v9.

believer grows.

We read elsewhere that the Father is willing to reveal Himself through the Scriptures to those of low and humble estate.[401] This is the sentiment also of such a vital verse as Micah 6v8, which is one watchword of all true believers:

> *He has shown you, O man, what is good; and what does the Lord require of you but to do justly, to love mercy, and to walk humbly with your God? (Micah 6v8).*

We must remember that the Lord Jesus Christ humbled Himself to come to this earth in order to die on the cross. This is the way of Christ. So when we come to the Scriptures we must come as a little child, humbly, waiting to receive that which God has already implanted within in seed form. Humility is the quality of life expressed by the apostle Paul in his letter to the Romans. In chapter 12 we are exhorted to present ourselves as living sacrifices ready to have renewed and transformed minds.[402] This means, of course, that we ought to be ready to obey whatever we receive from the Lord in His word.

The preparations of the heart can take a number of different forms. Negatively we must be careful to avoid wrong attitudes.[403] For example, an over-confident attitude is dangerous. We are, of course, enabled to come boldly to the throne of grace, but an over-confident spirit tends to destroy those things necessary to receive from God.[404] Humility breeds care, patience and openness to teaching, but over-confidence destroys these things. Another negative attitude is the desire to justify an existing opinion. It is, of course, possible to prove almost anything from Scripture given a twisted attitude.[405] It is necessary then to come in such a way to Scripture that our opinions and judgements can be challenged and corrected if necessary. Another wrong attitude is the need some have to always win the argument. If such a disposition is displayed it indicates that the mind is closed. As apologists we often need to follow through with wrong ideas and arguments in order that we can make a good and considered reply, and, so that we can understand where our opponents are coming from. Yet another wrong attitude is the spirit which focuses on the technical in the main. An unduly technical spirit tends towards a devotion-less outcome. We are in the business of seeking and studying Scripture *that we may know the Lord.* Whilst technical issues are important, they must never be allowed to be the main point. The main point is knowledge of our Saviour and worship to Him. One last attitude to avoid is the superficial spirit. Often the message in the passage requires

---

401   Isaiah 66v2; Matthew 11v25; James 4v6.
402   Romans 12v1,2.
403   See the article by Peter Masters in Sword & Trowel. 1997. No. 3. p18f)
404   Hebrews 4v16.
405   We only have to consider Satan's twisted use of the word of God to show this.

some deep digging to get to. Sometimes the superficial sense of the passage under consideration is a starting point, but it is not the only message. We must beware the quick "daily reading" approach.

Expectancy.

When we come to Scripture we must remind ourselves about what it is exactly that we are reading. This is the word of God. It is what the sovereign Lord wants His people to hear. It is the believer's "love letter" from the Lord. Consequently we must come expectantly and eagerly. Included here is a boldness and earnestness.[406] This is not an over-confident heart but one which runs to the Father, with whom we have to deal, as a little child. If we aim at nothing we will get nothing. We must, therefore, come with expectant hearts. We may not get what we thought we would get, but we will receive for God is an abundant giver and has promised those who seek Him a ready response. God cannot lie. If we came to the tea table and found nothing to eat would we not be thoroughly disappointed? Surely God is not a miserly provider?[407]

Diligence and hard work required.

Thus far we have noted the need for dependence on the Lord, for humility, and an expectant heart. Our fourth heart attitude is one of diligence. The diligent get the Lord's approval.[408] The Scriptures are not like some trivial or superficial magazine that may be casually read on a sun-drenched beach.[409] Paul instructs Timothy to be diligent in his work of studying Scripture:

> *Be diligent to present yourself approved to God, a worker who does not need to be ashamed, rightly dividing the word of truth. (2Timothy 2v15).*

The Scriptures are likened to treasure:

> *I rejoice at Your word as one who finds great treasure. (Psalm 119v162).*

Furthermore seeking the Lord and His will is described as a mining operation or as a treasure hunt. Solomon in Proverbs wrote these astute words:

> *1 My son, if you receive my words, and treasure my commands within you, 2 so that you incline your ear to wisdom, and apply your heart to understanding; 3 yes, if you cry out for*

---

406   Hebrews 4v16; Psalm 63v1.
407   Psalm 23v5.
408   Proverbs 8v17.
409   That being said, it is possible to receive blessings on many levels depending where you read!

discernment, and lift up your voice for understanding, 4 if you seek her as silver, and search
for her as for hidden treasures; 5 then you will understand the fear of the Lord, and find the
knowledge of God. (Proverbs 2v1-5).

We have already come across these verses earlier when we considered the idea that God wants us to understand His word. They are well worth re-considering for diligence and hard work are not favourable in the modern church. Seek as you would seek silver, and search as you would search for hidden treasure. Such work is hard. Mining and refining are processes that have several stages. Seeking the Lord requires determination and desire. We are exhorted not just to ask, but to seek and knock.[410] A good student, like the great Solomon, takes care and diligence in his efforts.

9 And moreover, because the Preacher was wise, he still taught the people knowledge; yes,
he pondered and sought out and set in order many proverbs. 10 The Preacher sought to find
acceptable words; and what was written was upright—words of truth. 11 The words of the
wise are like goads, and the words of scholars are like well-driven nails, given by one
Shepherd. 12 And further, my son, be admonished by these. Of making many books there is
no end, and much study is wearisome to the flesh. (Ecclesiastes 12v9-12).

Thus a hard working, diligent and systematic approach to the study of Scriptures is one the Scriptures not only encourage but demand.

Having considered the personal requirements for studying Scripture we must now turn our attention to particular tools the Scriptures provide.

Aids within Scripture for successful study of God's word.

There are a range of different approaches that are contained within Scripture designed to help us come to a knowledge of God and His ways. Below we consider how the Scriptures themselves can help us under eleven different ideas and themes, but there may well be other themes which the reader can discover with further study and worship of the Lord.

Reject worldly wisdom.

We must reject the use and aid of worldly philosophy and wisdom in seeking to understand God's word. It is here that many right-hearted believers have gone wrong. Once saved some believers naturally fall back on worldly methods of studying Scripture, such as the use of science or archaeology as independent witnesses, for example. And yet the Scriptures gives repeated warning not to use these methods.

---

410   Matthew 7v7,8.

19 For it is written, "I will destroy the wisdom of the wise, and will bring to nothing the understanding of the prudent." 20 Where is the wise? Where is the scribe? Where is the disputer of this age? Has not God made foolish the wisdom of this world? 21 For since, in the wisdom of God, the world through wisdom did not know God, it pleased God through the foolishness of the message preached to save those who believe. 22 For Jews request a sign, and Greeks seek after wisdom; 23 but we preach Christ crucified, to the Jews a stumbling block and to the Greeks foolishness.(1Corinthians 1v19-23)

The main essence of these words of Paul's is that for all the ingenuity and cooperative effort of man, even in today's modern world, the intelligentsia of our time come up with nothing in comparison to that which God freely gives. In fact we are entitled to expect the elite and grand of our day to come up with what is right and good and true. So why do they reject what the Lord would bring? Why, in fact, do they not come up with the great gospel? It is because their hearts and minds are desperately wicked and deceitful and their aim is anything but godly.

The warnings against looking to the world and its philosophy and wisdom do not come infrequently. Paul seems to want to drive the point home it would seem, perhaps on account of his intellectual grounding. In fact Paul argues for those who may be considered wise in their age to turn around and choose what the world considers to be the foolish path:

18 Let no one deceive himself. If anyone among you seems to be wise in this age, let him become a fool that he may become wise. 19 For the wisdom of this world is foolishness with God. For it is written, "He catches the wise in their own craftiness"; 20 and again, "The Lord knows the thoughts of the wise, that they are futile." 21 Therefore let no one boast in men. For all things are yours. (1Corinthians 3v18-21).

This text is a challenge to today's Christian academic world. So many of these folk have capitulated to wrong-headed thinking. Many have abandoned a good doctrine of Scripture, especially with regard to inerrancy and infallibility. Many, for example, do not believe that the creation accounts of Genesis are historically true.[411] Such compromise leads to further departures and all of this has been done to appease the academic bent which considers anyone who disbelieves the scientists as foolish and naïve.[412]

---

411   In a recent address I noted that many of the current respected leaders and teachers all reject a 6-day creation. These include such people as Tim Keller, Don, Carson, John Piper and many others. These folk hold a variety of differing views on origins but all believe the earth to be millions of years old and many believe in theistic evolution.
412   Peter Enns claimed at one time to be an evangelical believer. In his books he has taken the next logical step that holding to theistic evolution leads. He suggests that Paul was mistaken in his doctrine of Christ as the second Adam because there never was a first Adam. His work is painful reading but has the virtue of being somewhat consistent if you believe in evolution. Many leaders want to claim orthodox and Biblical views about Christ but because the world ridicules creation, they compromise at this point. Their position is utterly inconsistent and Peter Enns' books point this out. See Peter Enns. The Evolution of Adam. Brazos Press. 2012. Peter EnnsPeter Enns. The Evolution of Adam. Brazos Press. 2012.. Inspiration and Incarnation. Baker Academic. 2005.

Paul is not content to contend this point merely in his writing to the Corinthians, for we see similar warnings to the Colossians and to Timothy at Ephesus:

Beware lest anyone cheat you through philosophy and empty deceit, according to the tradition of men, according to the basic principles of the world, and not according to Christ. (Colossians 2v8)

20 *O Timothy! Guard what was committed to your trust, avoiding the profane and idle babblings and contradictions of what is falsely called knowledge—* **21** *by professing it some have strayed concerning the faith. Grace be with you. Amen. (1Timothy 6v20,21)*

This teaching is not confined to the New Testament only, for the warnings are a feature of the Old as well. In fact the book of Ecclesiastes is a thesis against the trust of worldly thinking "under the sun" which takes no account of God and His rightful demands.[413]

There is a current tendency amongst some evangelicals to treat much (or at least some) worldly scholarship (e.g. science especially) as neutral and therefore acceptable to be used when studying Scripture. Bernard Ramm, and many others who have followed a similar train of thinking, argued that to understand Scripture we need all the worldly advice we can garner!

No interpretation of Genesis 1 is more mature than the science which guides it. To attempt to interpret the scientific elements of Genesis 1 **without** science is to attempt the impossible for the concepts and objects of the chapter have meaning only as they are referred to nature, and the subject matter of science may be called simply "nature."[414]

But Ramm's suggestions are quite contrary to the few texts we have briefly considered. We could extend these thoughts by looking at the many texts on the nature and disposition of man's mind and thinking. It is dark, devoid of truth, and desperately askew! Perhaps a quick look at some words revealed through Jeremiah may serve to end this point. Jeremiah served at a time when Judah was finally about to be taken captive for all their repeated sins. They had rejected God and followed the godless ways of the nations round about them. They had followed the dictates of their own evil hearts and copied the pagan rituals of the Canaanites. In Jeremiah chapter 2 we read these words that summarise the situation beautifully:

For My people have committed two evils: they have forsaken Me, the fountain of living waters, and hewn themselves cisterns—broken cisterns that can hold no water. (Jeremiah

---

413   Compare also: Psalm 146v3; Isaiah 2v22; Jeremiah 17v5.
414   Bernard Ramm. Protestant Biblical Hermeneutics. Baker Book House. Grand Rapids, USA. 1970. P213.

2v13).

The people had not only rejected the Lord who is the fountain source of life, but had turned from Him and had built and dug out their own cisterns which were leaky and stagnant. Such is the way with all modern systems of philosophy. In turning from God and His revealed ways, we turn to make our own ideas and theories. These are fruitless. In the passage from 1 Corinthians chapter 3 we referred to earlier, the apostle Paul quotes from an Old Testament Psalm:

> *The Lord knows the thoughts of man, that they are futile. (Psalm 94v11).*

Notice that there are no exceptions here. We could point the reader to the words we can read in Genesis 6 which inform us of God's view of the situation at that time:

> *Then the Lord saw that the wickedness of man was great in the earth, and that every intent of the thoughts of his heart was only evil continually. (Genesis 6v5).*

Every intent of man's thoughts are only evil continually! I am afraid that if we haven't come to this conclusion first about our own heart and mind, then there really is no hope for us. But to trust in the Lord and believe that He is true, and then to turn and rely on this world's philosophy seems to be the height of folly.

This brings us to consider that we must not just reject the philosophy of the world, but we cannot even rely on our own understanding:

> **5** *Trust in the Lord with all your heart, and lean not on your own understanding;* **6** *in all your ways acknowledge Him, and He shall direct your paths. (Proverbs 3v5,6).*

This is quite important as we often have our own wayward views derived from our parents, our tradition, and the environment we inhabit and grow up in. Scripture is our **sole** authority not just our **supreme** authority.

Rightly divide the word.

Having begun our study by trusting the Lord to direct us and having actively decided to put away this world's philosophy and even our own thinking, we come to the next important task, namely, to rightly divide the word of God.[415] In saying this we recognise some salient *human*

---

415   2Timothy 2v5.

features about God's word. We must pause here and comment that whilst the Bible does have a human component (which is necessary for we need to be able to access what God has revealed), we emphasise the fact that we must not treat the Bible simply as a human book. Thus whilst we must study the words, phrases, context and structure of what we have before us, we must always bear in mind that the Bible has its origin in God. He alone is the Author.

The Bible is divided into 2 Testaments and 66 'books.' These 66 *books* are really sections or chapters of the one book the Lord has given to us, but for ease of reference we refer to each section as a book because each is a complete unit of text as it stands. We shall consider the way to approach the text in terms of the sentences and words used later on. For now we are simply examining the way the Bible is structured as a whole. The Old Testament and the New Testament must be held in their right relationship. There are clear indications within Scripture that show that we have the two main divisions, but we ought always to bear in mind the fact that John the Baptist, for example, effectively had one foot in the Old Testament as well as being the fore-runner announcing the coming Messiah.[416] Augustine, Bishop of Hippo in the fourth century AD came up with the following couplet to show the relationships between the two testaments:

> The New is in the Old concealed;
> The Old is in the New revealed.

There is much truth in this statement. The Old Testament is always pointing forward to the coming of the Messiah and gives us many prophetic pointers showing exactly whom the Messiah is and what He will do. The New Testament writers make extensive use of the Old Testament and quote it copiously in defence of the position that Jesus was indeed the Christ promised of old. In the New Testament the writers unveil the Christ, showing us His nature and work in greater detail. Such information can be found in the Old Testament, but it is veiled amongst the types, historical accounts and prophecies that form the main content of the first part of Scripture. Thus whereas the New Testament unfolds and explains, the Old Testament has these truths somewhat hidden or veiled. Having established this relationship we must add at once the clear fact that throughout both Testaments there is but one main message. God in Christ comes to save the repentant in heart and judge the wicked rebellious. There is one faith throughout, so that Abraham, Moses and all the saints of the Old Testament are to be found in the kingdom of God and have been qualified to be there in the same way that we have, through God's grace and by faith in Christ.

A right understanding of the main division of Scripture is the starting point, but we need to

---

416   Job 33v14-16; Psalm 62v11,12; John 1v17.

consider further some details about the various smaller sections and books we find present. The table below shows books, and collections of books from each Testament with a little information about each. The reader should note that these descriptions are merely a starting point and should be tested carefully.

Table 4.1: Themes of each section ("book") of Scripture.

Old Testament		Main theme
SECTION:	**BOOK:**	
The Pentateuch, (the Law or the Torah)	Genesis	Beginnings. The Creator enacts His plan of redemption through the line of promise.
	Exodus	Rescue. Redemption through sacrifice. God, the mighty deliverer amongst His people.
	Leviticus	Worship. Sanctification and holiness through sacrifice and mediation.
	Numbers	Journeys. Once rescued we need to walk in the obedience of faith, for God will guide us.
	Deuteronomy	Sermons. Trust and obey the covenant-keeping God even though the surrounding peoples reject Him.
Historical books, (former prophets).	Joshua	Conquest. The fulfilment of God's promise for the land of Israel, taken in obedience and faith by the people of God.
	Judges	Sin & salvation. Despite man's repeated tendency to sin, the Lord will provide redemption in every age.
	Ruth	Kinsman redeemer. Even the Gentiles will be saved through the promised King.
	1Samuel	A king? The people want a king for the wrong reasons. God gives them His kings to usher in His King.
	2Samuel	The King will come. God will build us a house to dwell in, for the earth cannot contain Him.
	1Kings	Separation. The united kingdom splits into two (Judah and Israel). Kings need to copy the law in life and those who don't will fail (spiritually).
	2Kings	Dispersion. The failings of earthly kings will never stop the King from coming and ruling righteously.
	1Chronicles	Spiritual history. The retelling of the history to show God's dealings amongst His people.
	2Chronicles	Spiritual heritage.
	Ezra	Restoration. The word of God will restore where man's efforts fail.

Old Testament		Main theme
SECTION:	**BOOK:**	
Historical books, (former prophets).	Nehemiah	Reconstruction. The story of how together God's people accomplish God's work of building.
	Esther	Preservation. Even in the midst of persecution God will keep His people providentially.
Poetry or Wisdom books.	Job	Blessing through suffering. To know that your redeemer lives, the One who suffered eternally.
	Psalms	Praise. Prayer, praise and worship in all life's varied experiences.
	Proverbs	Wisdom. How to live amongst the wicked unbelievers. A tale of two women ("wisdom" and "the adulteress").
	Ecclesiastes	Vanity. Death and judgement are the only certainties in life "under the sun." All else is pointless.
	Song of Solomon	Marriage. Love the Lord with all your heart, soul and mind and bring words of true repentance.
Major Prophets.	Isaiah	Gospel. Despite not knowing the Maker, the Lord will redeem His people through the suffering of His Servant.
	Jeremiah	Repent. In order to redeem, the Lord casts down all, in order that He may raise again.
	Lamentations	Judgement. In your righteous wrath O Lord remember mercy.
	Ezekiel	The watchman warns. A promise of the new creation.
	Daniel	Pressures. God always remains God so stay faithful and resist the temptation to compromise.
Minor Prophets.	Hosea	Love. God has loved us even though we act like an adulterous wife!
	Joel	Watch! Judgement approaches so repent and call on the name of the Lord who will bless.
	Amos	Justice. The sovereign Lord will never accept pride or complacency. He judges all perfectly.
	Obadiah	Divine sovereignty.
	Jonah	Salvation. God's salvation will come (even to Nineveh) despite the reluctance of the messenger.
	Micah	Humility. He has shown man what is necessary: to do what is right, to love mercy and to walk in humility.
	Nahum	The Lord will punish evil and this is good news.
	Habakkuk	Be secure in God despite the unjustness of the world around. God's plans never fail but they are mysterious.

Old Testament		Main theme
SECTION:	**BOOK:**	
Minor Prophets	Zephaniah	Judgement is certain but there is hope for those who turn and repent.
	Haggai	The rebuilding of the temple will result in an ever greater glory.
	Zechariah	Don't just sit and watch! The Lord's plans for future blessing require our obedience.
	Malachi	The Lord loves His people. He is coming soon.

New Testament		Main theme.
SECTION:	**BOOK:**	
The gospels.	Matthew	The good news of the Messiah, the King, who is coming to reign in His kingdom.
	Mark	Jesus, God's Son, King and Servant has come, died and risen so that we may know, confess and serve Him.
	Luke	Christ Jesus was a sinless man amongst men and women. You can be certain that He is true.
	John	Jesus is God's Son who came and did all the Father wanted, and we can fellowship with the Lord.
Historical	Acts	The ascended Lord continues His mission through the Holy Spirit to all nations.
Pauline epistles.	Romans	The gospel is Christ known and shared amongst the people of God that others might see and believe.
	1Corinthians	Believers in Christ are (individually and collectively) God's temple. They should continue in holiness.
	2Corinthians	Gospel proclamation and ministry may be thought of as weak, but it ought to be our confidence.
	Galatians	The grace of God in the gospel and the Spirit are sufficient for salvation and life.
	Ephesians	Believers are one in Christ and so united we must stand firm in Him and the blessings He brought.
	Philippians	Believers should rejoice as citizens of heaven, have the mind of Christ and live worthy of the gospel.
	Colossians	In the same way that you received Christ Jesus as the Lord, so continue to walk in Him in love.
	1Thessalonians	The gospel is true, so continue in living it out despite opposition until Christ Jesus returns.

New Testament		Main theme.
SECTION:	**BOOK:**	
Pauline epistles.	2Thessalonians	Whilst waiting eagerly for the Lord's return be obedient and patient servants.
Pastoral epistles.	1Timothy	The local church needs gospel centred leaders to show and keep the sheep in the truth and love of Christ.
	2Timothy	Ensure that the precious gospel is guarded and passed on for future generations, despite opposition.
	Titus	Changed lives comes by the powerful gospel by the regenerating Spirit.
General epistles	Philemon	The gospel can bring reconciliation between estranged folk.
	Hebrews	Christ is better than all else. There is none that can compare so stay close to Him.
	James	Faith works. Don't stop with thought for as a man thinks so is he, so focus on what God wants.
	1Peter	Faith is precious and should lead to godliness despite persecution.
	2Peter	In the face of godless teachers the faithful will remain with the true gospel.
	1John	You can be assured of your faith if you love Christ Jesus, hate your sin and love the brethren.
	2John	The one who knows the truth and obeys God's commands loves God and will reject false teacher.
	3John	We should walk in truth and partner with other Christians who do the same.
	Jude	Contend for the faith despite godlessness and immorality all around.
Apocalypse	Revelation	A panoramic and symbolic view of the plan of salvation and a call to live out the testimony of Christ.

The main principle we are considering under this heading is the idea of *context*. It is good to begin with at least some understanding of each book of the Bible and its connection to other books close by to it, as well as its place within its testament and Scripture as a whole. Of course for new believers this might be seen as a problem. If we know nothing of Scripture how can we come to it with a knowledge of its main divisions and their relations? However this is not really a problem at all. What the new believer should do is develop a twofold approach. First do some general and systematic reading that will enable a comprehensive covering of the Scripture as a whole. Plan to read through the Bible in a short space of time (say one year). Then, secondly, begin to read and study in depth one smaller portion or book of Scripture. In this way the comprehensive reading will compliment and aid the detailed study. There are, of course, numerous Bible helps such as dictionaries, concordances and word studies which are useful, but the central and most vital thing to do is read and study Scripture continually.

The Scriptures are wonderfully inter-connected so that whatever we read in one book is never contradicted by any other. In fact on the contrary rather than contradict, the books compliment one another. Although we shall consider the importance of grammatical structure later on, we must note how the words, phrases, sentences, paragraphs and so on, fit into the book, the Testament and the whole of Scripture. Often we shall find that a book favours one word or phrase. We will need to consider the significance of this and other peculiarities. The whole point of our studying Scripture is to meet with the Lord and to receive from Him. But it does not stop at this, for we will need to respond to what we hear and receive. This means we will need to heed the specific applications each book brings in the context it delivers it. One final point: we will need to pay attention to how the New Testament writers used or quoted the Old Testament (bearing in mind the fact that the New Testament writers were inspired by the Holy Spirit).

All about Christ and His work.

Before we consider the details of studying Scripture we must attend to the main purpose of the whole Bible. In many cases the human writer gives us the purpose of the book they have penned. For example the apostle John states the purpose of his book:

> *30 And truly Jesus did many other signs in the presence of His disciples, which are not written in this book; 31 but these are written that you may believe that Jesus is the Christ, the Son of God, and that believing you may have life in His name. (John 20v30,31).*

When it comes to the gospels it is clear that the main theme is Christ and His work, but what of the other books of the Bible? Now the main point in what we are doing, surely, is to seek for the Lord. In fact we find that the Lord Himself taught the disciples that we ought to see Him and His work on every page:

> *25 Then He said to them, "O foolish ones, and slow of heart to believe in all that the prophets have spoken! 26 Ought not the Christ to have suffered these things and to enter into His glory?" 27 And beginning at Moses and all the Prophets, He expounded to them in all the Scriptures the things concerning Himself. ......*
> *44 Then He said to them, "These are the words which I spoke to you while I was still with you, that all things must be fulfilled which were written in the Law of Moses and the*

Mike Viccary

Prophets and the Psalms concerning Me." 45 And He opened their understanding, that they might comprehend the Scriptures. 46 Then He said to them, "Thus it is written, and thus it was necessary for the Christ to suffer and to rise from the dead the third day, 47 and that repentance and remission of sins should be preached in His name to all nations, beginning at Jerusalem. (Luke 24v25-27; 44-47).

The aim of Scripture, then, is to speak about Christ and His work. The Scriptures speak of Christ. This is not just in the types or from direct teaching we find throughout (such as prophecies), but also in the details of the history recorded too.

This idea that Scripture speaks of Christ is reflected in Paul's statements concerning what he was doing. Thus we remind ourselves that Paul told the Ephesian elders that he had declared unto them "the whole counsel of God."[417] In two of his letters Paul declared that he was determined to know nothing except Christ and Him crucified, and was determined not to boast in anything except the cross of Christ.[418] Taking these two thoughts together means that the whole counsel of God (i.e. all that Scripture teaches), centres on the Lord Jesus Christ and His death and resurrection. It is to be remembered that the work of Christ includes all the elements of salvation (e.g. the nature of sin, redemption, atonement and so on).[419]

There are no errors or contradictions in Scripture.

We have stated that it is essential to consider Scripture as a single book whose origin is God. Paul in Romans, for example, doesn't hesitate to refer to the gospel as "the gospel of God" highlighting the originator and source.[420] It is unfortunate that we live in a day and age when the human side of Scripture is over emphasised to the point of obscuring the fact that God is the true Author. Taking this thought further, we must state that whenever there *appear* to be contradictions in Scripture, these will always turn out to be a misunderstanding in us and not an error in Scripture. Therefore when we have arrived at a right understanding, all contradictions will disappear. A corollary of this truth is that there is can only be one body of doctrine in Scripture, which the Scriptures sometimes refer to as "The faith."[421] There are not, therefore, a variety of theologies or "bodies of truth" in Scripture as is sometimes claimed by many. It has become fashionable amongst the commentators and theologians of this modern age to consider the different theologies of each

---

417   Acts 20v27.
418   1Corinthians 2v2; Galatians 6v14.
419   2Timothy 3v16.
420   Romans 1v1.
421   Acts 3v16; 6v7; 13v8; 14v22; 16v5; 24v24; Romans 1v5; 3v3; 4v11,16; 14v1; 1Corinthians 16v13; 2Corinthians 13v5; Galatians 1v23; 2v16,20; 3v23; Ephesians 3v12; 4v5,13; Philippians 1v27; 3v9; Colossians 1v23; 2v7,12; 1Timothy 1v2; 3v9,13; 4v1; 5v8; 6v10,21; 2Timothy 2v18; 3v8; 4v7; Titus 1v1,4,13; 3v15; James 2v1; 1Peter 5v9; Jude v3; Revelation 13v10; 14v12.

book as though there are differences in degree. Now it may be true that a particular book emphasises a particular aspect of the one theology that Scripture contains, but there is only one unified body of truth. If there were more than one theology in Scripture, then contradictions and errors would be found in Scripture. The result of this would be catastrophe, for we would always be in doubt about what was true and what was not. This concept is one which is so important I want to dwell on it for a moment. Liberal theologians do not worry about this because their delight is an emphasis on man and his abilities. People of this persuasion do not believe in the supernatural and consider the Bible to be the work of men seeking and groping after God in some indistinct and human way. However believers own that God is the sole Author of Scripture and since this is true, we cannot accept any error whatsoever in what the Lord has written. God cannot lie. Consequently there can only be a single set of unified beliefs or statements of truth. The more we study (reverently) the more we will pick up the one body of truth. As we proceed our conception of this may have to be modified slightly, but it also ought to grow steadily. This will then aid in our further understanding of the Bible

The need for systematic study and reading.

We have already pointed out the merits of reading not just a single book for study, but the whole of Scripture in a comprehensive way, in order that we get not just the detail but the overall view as well. Under this heading we must note that a systematic approach is one that Paul intimated to Timothy:

Till I come, give attention to reading, to exhortation, to doctrine. (1 Timothy 4v13).

We are exhorted to "give attention to" our reading and the teaching we hear. In other words, we are to turn our minds to these things. Beware of reading only your favourite parts of Scripture. This will give you a skewed view. For although all of the various parts of Scripture teach the same truths and doctrines, some books give greater emphasis on some aspects of truth than others. What is more, some parts of Scripture require deeper attention and study than do others. We are all perhaps familiar with dipping into the Psalms for comfort perhaps when this is needed, but a comprehensive and consistent approach is required for a healthy spiritual life. Remember that the Lord took care to give us all Scripture, and all of Scripture is profitable, even those parts we may personally find difficult to comprehend.[422] One final point, if you are in a position of ministry, be careful that you

---

422   2 Timothy 3v15,16.

do not fall into the trap of reading only for the purpose of preaching or ministry. You must read and study first to know the Saviour. Thereafter you may give out what you have received.

There are degrees of understanding.

Having discussed the importance of studying all of Scripture we must next point out that there are different depths to Scripture and we may reach different degrees of understanding of a passage at different times. We shall consider two points in a little more detail. First the idea that some Scriptures are harder to understand than others. Second we shall note that as believers we have different abilities and capacities and different experiences which all influence how we understand.

Some Scriptures are harder than others.

Peter pointed out that some of Paul's writing was not that easy to understand.[423] This does not mean that we may never understand them. What it does mean, however, is that we need patience and perseverance. Deep mining and seeking are required. Scripture is referred to both as "milk" but also as "strong meat," so a degree of maturity is required before digestion of the meatier parts of Scripture is possible.[424]

There are two important truths we must hold in tension as believers concerning the understanding of these harder portions of Scripture. The Lord has seen fit to appoint some men as teachers but these require certain qualities.[425] The second important point to remember is that every believer has direct access to the Lord and is thus taught by the Lord directly.[426] Teachers may be both useful and necessary, but they do not act as mediators, nor do they interject a barrier or gateway to the access of truth. There is, therefore, a balance between knowing that we have the Lord as our tutor, and requiring teachers to help us.[427] However whatever is presented to us, whether in print, online or that which we hear, we must always weigh it carefully and compare this ourselves with what we read in the Scriptures.[428]

Some people require more time than others.

It might be obvious but we must recognise that people are different both in terms of mental

---

423   2Peter 3v16.
424   1Corinthians 3v2; 10v3; Hebrews 5v12-14; 1Peter 2v2.
425   Ephesians 4v11; James 3v1.
426   Isaiah 54v13.
427   Isaiah 54v13; Jeremiah 31v34; John 6v45; Romans 12v7; Corinthians 12v28,29; Ephesians 4v11; 2Timothy 2v2; Hebrews 5v12; 8v11; 1John 2v27.
428   Acts 17v11.

capacity, and in background. Thus a Roman Catholic converted late in life may require some patience and particular applications of specific doctrines (justification by faith alone, for example), as the doctrines or practices he has learned from youth will need to be undone. Youngsters can all understand the gospel, but they will not necessarily learn the finer points of theology straight away.

This is God's sole book.

Again it may be obvious that God has Authored only one book, but the implications of this point are far-reaching. It means, for example, that whatever we need is contained within its pages. It also means that we do not need to go looking elsewhere to help in trying to understand a passage. We can let the Bible interpret itself.[429] Thus hard to be understood passages will often be broken open or illuminated by other passages of Scripture which are easier to understand. It is a great sadness to find that this truth is often overlooked or ignored so that in the academic world we find that many use science, or other "handmaidens" to reach meanings.[430] This approach has reaped great harm. As an example, many interpret the first chapters of Genesis by viewing them through the lens of other Ancient Near Eastern mythologies. As a consequence the truths contained in these early chapters of Scripture have been destroyed. Let me emphasize that Scripture, and thus the Holy Spirit who Authored Scripture, needs no help. What we need is to use Scripture as the tool to understand Scripture, all the while resting totally on the Lord's help and guide.

In general, a matter of faith or a doctrine should be established by more than one Scripture. This is because the Scriptures teach that the testimony of two or more witnesses is required to establish evidence.[431] One thing to consider is that there may well be some *directing* or *controlling* Scripture for the passage under consideration. One example of a directive passage is 1Corinthians 10v1-11. Here we are instructed to look for Christ and His church in the Old Testament.[432] We can easily make mistakes if we do not heed this rule. Some have stated, for example, that the Judges were simply automatons who were manipulated by the Holy Spirit for great exploits that God wanted done. However, a glance through Hebrews chapter 11 will correct this misguided view. These were people of faith and so were believers not just those manipulated by the Holy Spirit.[433]

---

429   1Corinthians 2v13f.
430   The idea that secular disciplines are "handmaidens" to theology has a long history. It is essentially a false notion borne of a misunderstanding of the doctrine of man. God created us in His image with certain faculties and abilities. However the secular world has usurped and ruined these to the detriment of mankind. Mistaken people think we may "baptise" these secular disciplines for use in the Christian enterprise. As Christian believers we have faculties and abilities which God has created for His use, but we need to learn with patience under the guide and direction of God's word first.
431   Deuteronomy 19v15; John 8v17.
432   See, for example, Luke 24 & John 20v30-31.
433   Hebrews 11v32.

Examine the details of the passage.

Start by examining the meaning of the words in the passage under consideration. However we must be careful to consider the context. Matthew 7v1 tells us to "judge not." Are we never to make any judgements? Clearly this is not true, for we must discern the spirits, beware of false prophets, and we must not give what is holy to dogs.[434] What is the context here? We must not judge others for things when we are also guilty of the same ("speck" and "beam" in the eye). Another temptation to be wary of is that of making generalisations before the donkey work is done. It is all too easy to cast a glance over a book and conclude that because it mentions visions of God on every page, this necessarily means they were happening all the time. For example, Abraham's story covers several chapters in Genesis spanning some 100 years. He certainly received visions of God but even though these loom large in the narrative, they were rare and did not occur every day.

When we look at specific words we must be careful to consider their meanings, along with that of phrases and sentences, within the context of the book. Sometimes a book makes use of words in a special sense. The gospel according to John does this frequently. Remember also that when examining a passage there are different literary styles. We would not read Revelation in exactly the same way as Genesis. Revelation is symbolic, Genesis is history.

The *sensible* and obvious (or plain) meaning of the passage is the first step to interpretation. Never overlook this. Ask what did the writer intend to convey to his hearers? Obviously we cannot go back in time and be with the original readers. However we must consider the intention of the writer to his original hearers as far as we are able to do so. Sadly many commentators make the mistake of pressing this to an extreme. When the passage does not inform us of the original culture and situation some have sought to elucidate this from external sources. This is not a good path to follow because the external information is often governed by a secular mindset. Once the sensible sense is gathered we must not stop at this point, because the Bible has a greater depth to it. One obvious example is the types. We have recorded for us the detailed instructions as to the make-up of the tabernacle, for example. We gather the sensible sense first that the tabernacle was made with various materials and in such a way and so on, but then we ask: Is that all the Holy Spirit intended for us to understand? Surely not? This example of the tabernacle has controlling Scriptures (from the book of Hebrews) which tell us that these were patterns of heaven.

Once the plain sense of an historical Old Testament passage is found it needs to be further studied to discover the reason why it was chosen in Scripture. Take, for example, the journeys in the wilderness. Do we not glean much from this passage by considering all the "walk" and "road"

---

434   1Corinthians 2v14; 12v10; Matthew 7v6,15.

passages throughout the Bible? Does it not have something to say about how we are to be guided by the Lord, and about how we should conduct our lives as pilgrims? In essence we are pointing out that we must get to the spiritual meaning of the text. Never be content with mere facts, history and data, even though we believe it important to uphold that the Bible is true and trustworthy. Ask: What does the Lord intend to teach through this historical account? What are the lessons taught here?

Exegetical analysis.

Sometimes also known as "syntactic analysis" this is a tool which is useful for understanding Scripture at the word, phrase and sentence level. We have already made use of this technique when we examined Psalm 12. But to help the reader we shall provide an exegetical analysis of 2Peter. For this exercise we have made use of the New King James Version. The technique involves using a combination of highlighting common words and titles, and indenting phrases of sentences to show relations through the text. It would be helpful to show the analysis as a whole first and then to examine a few details afterwards. Thus below we have my attempt of an analysis of the whole of Peter's second letter. It is important to realise that decisions about how to indent text can take different routes and so this example is not definitive.

Table 4.2: An example of exegetical analysis – 2Peter.

[A] Like precious faith and the knowledge of God. (1v1-4).

```
#1 1 Simon Peter,
        a bond-servant and
        apostle of Jesus Christ,
   to those who
        have obtained like precious faith with us
            by the righteousness of our God and Saviour Jesus Christ:
   2 Grace and peace be multiplied to you
        in the knowledge of God and of Jesus our Lord,
            3 as His divine power has given to us
                all things that pertain to life and godliness,
                    through the knowledge of Him who called us by glory and virtue,
            4 by which have been given to us
                exceedingly great and precious promises,
                that through these you may be partakers of the divine nature,
                having escaped the corruption that is in the world through lust.
```

[B] The importance of "these things" for the true knowledge of God. (1v5-11).

```
5 But also for this very reason,
        giving all diligence,
            [1] add to your faith virtue,
            [2] to virtue knowledge,
            [3] 6 to knowledge self-control,
```

[4] to self-control perseverance,

[5] to perseverance godliness,

[6] **7** to godliness brotherly kindness, and

[7] to brotherly kindness love.

8 For if these things are yours and abound,

you will be neither barren nor unfruitful in the knowledge of our Lord Jesus Christ.

9 For he who lacks these things

is short-sighted, even to blindness, and

has forgotten that he was cleansed from his old sins.

10 Therefore, brethren,

be even more diligent to make your call and election sure,

for if you do these things you will never stumble;

11 for so an entrance will be supplied to you abundantly into the everlasting kingdom of our Lord and Saviour Jesus Christ.

[C] A reminder of the truth through the prophetic word confirmed. (1v12-21).

12 For this reason I will not be negligent to remind you always of these things, though you know and are established in the present truth.

13 Yes, I think it is right, as long as I am in this tent, to stir you up by reminding you, **14** knowing that shortly I *must* put off my tent, just as our Lord Jesus Christ showed me.

15 Moreover I will be careful to ensure that you always have a reminder of these things after my decease.

16 For we

did not follow cunningly devised fables when we made known to you the power and coming of our Lord Jesus Christ, but

were eyewitnesses of His majesty.

17 For He

received from God the Father honour and glory when such a voice came to Him from the Excellent Glory: "This is My beloved Son, in whom I am well pleased."

18 And we

heard this voice which came from heaven when we were with Him on the holy mountain.

19 And so we

have the prophetic word confirmed, which you do well to heed as a light that shines in a dark place, until the day dawns and the morning star rises in your hearts; **20** knowing this first, that no prophecy of Scripture is of any private interpretation, **21** for prophecy never came by the will of man, but holy men of God spoke *as they were* moved by the Holy Spirit.

[D] The danger of false prophets and teachers and their seven-fold character. (2v1-22).

#2 1 But there were also false prophets among the people,

even as there will be false teachers among you,

who will secretly bring in

destructive heresies, even denying the Lord who bought them,

and bring on themselves

swift destruction.

2 And many will follow their destructive ways,

because of whom the way of truth will be blasphemed.

3 By covetousness they will exploit you with deceptive words; for a long time their judgement has not been idle, and their destruction does not slumber.

4 For if God

did not spare

the angels who sinned, but cast *them* down to hell and delivered *them* into chains of darkness, to be reserved for judgement;

5 and did not spare

the ancient world,

but saved Noah,

one of eight *people*, a preacher of righteousness,

bringing in the flood on the world of the ungodly;

6 and turning

the cities of Sodom and Gomorrah into ashes, condemned *them* to destruction, making *them* an example to those who after-ward would live ungodly;

7 and delivered

righteous Lot, *who was* oppressed by the filthy conduct of the wicked **8** (for that righteous man, dwelling among them, tormented *his* righteous soul from day to day by seeing and hearing *their* lawless deeds)—

9 *then* the Lord knows how

to deliver the godly out of temptations and

to reserve the unjust under punishment for the day of judgement,

10 and especially those who walk according to the flesh in the lust of uncleanness and despise authority.

[1] *They are* presumptuous, self-willed.

[2] They are not afraid to speak evil of dignitaries, **11** whereas angels, who are greater in power and might, do not bring a reviling accusation against them before the Lord.

12 But these,

[3] like natural brute beasts made to be caught and destroyed, speak evil of the things they do not understand, and

will utterly perish in their own corruption, **13** *and*

will receive the wages of unrighteousness, as those who count it pleasure to carouse in the daytime.

[4] *They are* spots and blemishes, carousing in their own deceptions while they feast with you, **14** having eyes full of adultery and that cannot cease from sin, enticing unstable souls.

[5] They have a heart trained in covetous practices, *and are* accursed children.

[6] **15** They have forsaken the right way and gone astray, following the way of Balaam the *son* of Beor, who loved the wages of unrighteousness; **16** but he was rebuked for his iniquity: a dumb donkey speaking with a man's voice restrained the madness of the prophet.

[7] **17** These are wells without water, clouds carried by a tempest, for whom is reserved the blackness of darkness forever. **18** For when they speak great swelling *words* of emptiness, they allure through the lusts of the flesh, through lewdness, the ones who have actually escaped from those who live in error. **19** While they promise them liberty, they themselves are slaves of corruption; for by whom a person is overcome, by him also he is brought into bondage.

20 For if, after they have escaped the pollutions of the world through the knowledge of the Lord and Saviour Jesus Christ, they are again entangled in them and overcome, the latter end is worse for them than the beginning.

21 For it would have been better for them not to have known the way of righteousness, than having known *it,* to turn from the holy commandment delivered to them.

22 But it has happened to them according to the true proverb: "A dog returns to his own vomit," and, "a sow, having washed, to her wallowing in the mire."

[E] A seven-fold set of instructions to the beloved in the face of scoffing. (3v1- 18).

#3 1 Beloved, I now write to you this second epistle (in *both of* which I stir up your pure minds by way of reminder), **2** that you may

[1] be mindful

of the words which were spoken before by the holy prophets, and

of the commandment of us, the apostles of the Lord and Saviour,

3 knowing this first:

that scoffers will come in the last days, walking according to their own lusts, **4** and saying,

"Where is the promise of His coming? For since the fathers fell asleep, all things continue as *they were* from the beginning of creation."

5 For this they wilfully forget:

that by the word of God the heavens were of old, and the earth standing out of water and in the water, 6 by which the world *that* then existed perished, being flooded with water. 7 But the heavens and the earth *which* are now preserved by the same word, are reserved for fire until the day of judgement and perdition of ungodly men.

8 But, beloved,

[2] do not forget this one thing, that with the Lord one day *is* as a thousand years, and a thousand years as one day. 9 The Lord is not slack concerning *His* promise, as some count slackness, but is long suffering toward us, not willing that any should perish but that all should come to repentance. 10 But the day of the Lord will come as a thief in the night, in which the heavens will pass away with a great noise, and the elements will melt with fervent heat; both the earth and the works that are in it will be burned up.

11 Therefore, since all these things will be dissolved, what manner *of persons* ought you to be in holy conduct and godliness, 12 looking for and hastening the coming of the day of God, because of which the heavens will be dissolved, being on fire, and the elements will melt with fervent heat?

13 Nevertheless we, according to His promise,

[3] look for new heavens and a new earth in which righteousness dwells.

14 Therefore, beloved, looking forward to these things,

[4] be diligent to be found by Him in peace, without spot and blameless; 15 and

[5] consider *that* the long-suffering of our Lord *is* salvation—as also our beloved brother Paul, according to the wisdom given to him, has written to you, 16 as also in all his epistles, speaking in them of these things, in which are some things hard to understand, which untaught and unstable *people* twist to their own destruction, as *they do* also the rest of the Scriptures.

17 You therefore, beloved, since you know *this* beforehand,

[6] beware lest you also fall from your own steadfastness, being led away with the error of the wicked;

[7] 18 but grow in the grace and knowledge of our Lord and Saviour Jesus Christ. To Him *be* the glory both now and forever. Amen.

The letter is split into five separate sections on the basis of this analysis. It will be seen that there is an overall symmetry and connection from beginning to end as illustrated by the words "knowledge of God/Lord."[435]

In the first section we read of those who have received "like precious faith" and we are told how they have come by this and what such faith entails. Notice how Peter's greeting in verse 2 is expanded. Those who have this precious faith are wished grace and peace through the knowledge of God and of Jesus Christ, and such knowledge is described as a work of grace ("given to us") which comes through His divine power and through His precious promises.

In the second section Peter works out what having faith in God's power and promises leads on to. There are certain items ("these things") listed in verses 5 to 7 which demonstrate the evidence of a true and precious faith. We must be diligent to not only have these things, but in working them out thereby indicate the certainty of our calling and election.

The third section is delineated by the repeated use of the word "remind" (and cognates). Peter is concerned that what he is teaching will not only be remembered and brought to mind frequently, but also that his readers will recognise the source of the truth he is imparting. It is

---

435   2Peter 1v2; 3v18. See also 2Peter 1v8; 2v20.

necessary, therefore, that these things are written down and received as a sure and certain word of prophecy.

The fourth section is all about false teachers and prophets. Although we have not highlighted many words or phrases in this section, the subject matter is clearly seen by how Peter deals with these folk. First he points out that whilst once there were false prophets – and this is evident throughout the Old Testament Scriptures – now there will be a similar set of false leaders (teachers) in the age which Peter is addressing. The symmetry of this passage can be seen in how Peter describes in 2Peter 2v4-7 first how "God" dealt with such false prophets and leaders in old times (angels who sinned, Noah, Sodom), and then details in 2Peter 2v9f how the "Lord" will deliver the ungodly and reserve the unjust for the day of punishment. Peter gives seven detailed character descriptions of such false teachers, concluding with a description of their ultimate end which serves as a potent warning for any who might be tempted to follow in their footsteps.

The final section is easily identified by the repeated use of the designation of those who have the same precious faith as Peter, namely, "beloved."[436] Here Peter gives seven important instructions for the beloved, ending with the whole purpose of such exhortation, namely, to "grow in the grace and knowledge of our Lord and Saviour Jesus Christ."

This example taken from 2Peter is not comprehensive nor is it exhaustive. There are other connections and links that I have not highlighted. But by identifying the structure of sentences, repeated phrases and ideas, the Scriptures can be made easily accessible to the seeking soul.

Use prior **Biblical** learning.

Under this heading we want to point out that we should bring to bear all the truth we have gathered from Scripture when looking at new passages. The Lord of Scripture is the same throughout Scripture. When we have gathered that He is holy from a consideration of one passage, we can keep this truth in mind when we examine a new passage, for God never changes. There is only one "faith" or body of truth in Scripture so that every interpretation which is correct will agree with the body of faith. This rule is actually a corollary of the fact that there are no errors in the Bible. Under this heading, we stipulate five rules:

[1] The interpretation must be checked against fundamental doctrine.

There are many incontrovertible doctrines which are plain in Scripture and on which there is general consensus. God is almighty, good, holy and infinite – these are just a few easily discerned

---

436   2Peter 3v1,8,14,15,17.

truths. If our interpretation clashes with these then we know we have gone wrong.[437]

[2] The interpretation must be checked with other Scriptures on the same subject.

For example, some charismatics teach that Paul modified his methods when he failed to get a successful hearing in Athens. When he went to Corinth, they tell us, he reverted to a signs and wonders ministry and was successful. This type of interpretation is based on 1Corinthians 2v4 ("my speech and my preaching was not with enticing words of man's wisdom, but in demonstration of the Spirit and of power"). However Luke's record of Paul's method in Acts 17-18 shows no deviation at all, so this interpretation is flawed.

[3] We must ask whether other passages are needed to supplement what is taught in the passage under consideration to avoid distortion.

Some in the past have built their doctrine of the church on selected passages of Scripture. For example those who hold to a community-based "all things in common" approach derived from Acts 2 neglect the teaching in the pastoral epistles where leaders and order are part and parcel of the mix as well.[438] Remember that the Holy Spirit has organised the Scriptures perfectly. Information on doctrines is to be found throughout. It is therefore necessary to consult all the passages dealing with the topic and subject under consideration. If we look at a select few we may miss key passages which have a distinct bearing on the truths we are considering.

[4] The interpretation and doctrine to be derived must be taught in more than one place.

One modern teaching which seems to be in vogue today is the private speaking in tongues. Some have taught from 1Corinthians 14 that it is a spiritual gift to pray or sing to the Lord in private (or in corporate settings quietly). Often it is taught that such an act is *spiritual* and does not engage the mind or understanding. However such teaching is contradicted by other Scriptures. We must pray and praise with understanding.[439] The whole purpose of speaking in tongues has an Old Testament origin and so these Scriptures exercise some control.[440]

[5] The interpretation must not depend on non-Biblical information.

Does this mean we should never use outside help? Yes! It is true that Bible aids and helps

---

437   Consider, for example, Hebrews 6v4-6 - can a believer fall away?
438   The Brethren are a prime example here. Rejecting worldly presentations of church leadership has lead them to neglect having pastoral oversight thus ignoring the teaching of the pastoral epistles.
439   Psalm 47v7.
440   See, for example, Genesis 11; Isaiah 28v11; Acts 2v1f.

may confirm our doctrine, but we must never base doctrine on things outside the Bible. Actually good Bible helps use the Bible exclusively. This is more true for older Bible aids. So concordances or word studies which are based on a Biblical only framework are invaluable. Someone who has gathered all the Scriptures bearing on a particular topic will obviously save us some time. But those Bible helps which bring in academic points and theological thoughts derived from secular sources will lead to confusion.

Submit to the instruction received.

We have been considering the details of looking into Scripture to gather meaning, but the main point of all this is to know Christ and to follow Him. Thus this is all a matter of the heart primarily and not of the head only. We should be keen to do as the Lord has instructed us.

Now some instructions may have a cultural element so we must ask whether a passage is normative for today. Clearly the Old Testament sacrifices are all fulfilled in the Lord Jesus Christ's once-for-all sacrifice, so we need not offer sacrifices today. What then of other practices? It is very helpful to remind ourselves, at this point, that God is the same always – He is our Rock. This means that essentially God's character is always the same. Thus His essence of Being is the same. Whilst He has surely used a different method of working in the Old Testament to that of the New Testament (the two covenants) the basic principles that lay behind these two "administrations" are identical. God cannot lie. He is merciful. He is holy. Thence our response should be one of obedience to the will of God and utter delight in our Maker.

However there are many other things which are debated with regards to whether they should be obeyed or not. Some of these things come under the heading of "culture." It is safe to say, however, that this approach has been badly abused where practices that are clearly banned by the Lord are said by some to be merely a question of the culture of the times. Thus sexual practice and orientation is not a matter of culture or choice, for the constitution of man is a created thing. Man was made male and female only. Notwithstanding the abuse of the cultural plea, some things are indeed a matter of culture. For example, greeting with a holy kiss.[441] We would not be disobeying this command if we greeted one another with a hug, a handshake or some other culturally acceptable form. Thus if the practice can be seen to be cultural and the essence of what is expressed can be carried out in a different way, then clearly there is no problem. Problems do arise when the command given cannot be expressed in any other way. Thus, for example, women are prohibited from preaching. Was this the custom of those times? Yes it was, although it is no longer a modern

---

441   Romans 16v16; 1Corinthians 16v20; 2Corinthians 13v12; 1Thessalonians 5v26.

custom. Can this principle of Scripture be expressed some other way? No it cannot. Women are prohibited from preaching for reasons based in creation. Therefore we must continue to uphold the teaching of Paul in the way Paul expresses it.

It is not possible to legislate for all eventualities. In fact doing so amounts to a legalistic spirit. We should aim at love above all else in honouring what the Lord is teaching. In the case of women being prohibited from preaching this must never be taken to indicate that women are inferior to men in any way. It is just that men and women are different. Women have capacities that men are prohibited from too. We conclude this piece by reminding ourselves that we should not strive and argue, but live peaceably with all men giving due respect to weaker brethren.[442]

A spiritual approach is needed.

It is vital that the literal or straight reading of the text be taken first in any exegetical work. This is not to say that all Scripture must be taken *literalistically*, for sometimes Scripture is symbolic or metaphoric. What I mean is that the Scriptures must be taken at face value and expounded in the style they have been written in. But this is by no means the end of our task. Very often there are other layers of meaning – particularly the spiritual meanings – which subject we have already briefly discussed.

As an example consider the first chapters of Genesis. A great deal of harm has been done in these chapters by Christians by not attending to the style of writing. These are historical accounts. Consequently they give us a history of how God made the world and His dealings with the first human pair. When we read Genesis chapter one we must interpret what we find there as six literal 24 hour days within which God first formed and and then filled creation. However a question arises as to why the infinite and omnipotent God took so long to create all things? Why take six days? The creative acts within each day seem to indicate instantaneous creation. It is these acts which Christ Jesus' miracles served to demonstrate clearly and unambiguously that He was indeed the Creator God. Well we are given a comment on creation in six days in the ten commandments. Exodus 20v11 is a controlling Scripture. There we find that the Lord God tells us within the commandments that the reason He took six days was to show us the pattern of work and rest. Just as God worked six days and then rested on the seventh, so also are we to do the same.[443] However the means by which God created has much besides these historical details to teach us. We might use as proof the following words from Paul:

---

442   Romans 12v18; 14v1f; Hebrews 12v14.
443   Exodus 20v8-11.

For it is the God who commanded light to shine out of darkness, who has shone in our hearts to give the light of the knowledge of the glory of God in the face of Jesus Christ. (2Corinthians 4v6).

Here Paul is using the original creation of light as an indication of His intention to bring the knowledge of God to our hearts.

Such a two layered approach, an analysis of the text and its style, and a consideration of other controlling Scriptures is not the end of the matter. When we look deeper into the text of Genesis chapter one we find elements there which are repeated throughout Scripture. For example the idea of separating light and dark, and the idea of abundance and diversity. We must remember that God has created not in any arbitrary way. His creation reflects something of the character of God. Furthermore we must remember that even before creation the Holy Trinity made a pact to not only create but save a number of human beings from the clutches of sin and rebellion. The Second Person of the Trinity agreed to come and offer His life in place of wicked sinners. Given these amazing truths we must begin to see that God's creation of the world was no arbitrary feat but contained within it aspects and themes of our salvation. Perhaps an obvious starting point is the creation of Eve. The historical details are found at the end of Genesis chapter two. There we read exactly how God created Eve. But why did God create her in such a way? The apostle Paul adds some information in the book of Ephesians relating to marriage. Marriage was not something created in the first place for man's benefit. It was rather something which reflected the love that exists within the Trinity. In creating Eve the way He did, God was demonstrating some wonderful truths about the coming Saviour who would also go through a sleep (symbolic for death) and would suffer an invasion in His side (the spear piercing) and from whom the beautiful bride (the church) would be formed. In Genesis chapter one we find that God's creation of the world involved the formation of solid land which is symbolic of the rock of safety, and then made a clear separation between light and darkness. Now it is important to separate these two streams of teaching. Many have rushed to the conclusion that because darkness always means evil in Scripture then it must also mean that in Genesis chapter one. Such a conclusion is wrong, however, because throughout the first chapter of the Bible we are repeatedly told that what God had made was "good" and had no taint or stain of evil whatsoever. Furthermore we note that darkness was named "night" and this signifies that this darkness was a good and necessary thing. Thus the straightforward and historical interpretation must be held as a matter of priority. But this does not exhaust the meanings in the text. The separation between light and dark is a good thing. We tend to think immediately of light revealing and bringing things into view for a right judgement. These themes are absent in Genesis chapter one but the concept of distinction and separation is clearly present. God made a separation and placed a boundary between the two. Then also, God made an abundance of life come into existence in the sea, air and on the land. God is the God of life. This is His character and we should understand that since He is a good and creative God, His salvation will necessarily include these aspects of abundance and diversity. Christ said that He came to bring life and life in abundance.[444]

This spiritual approach is one that is not often followed. Perhaps this is because it is not easy. Perhaps also some have taken aspects of the spiritual to destroy the first and prior meaning (an historical approach). But any consideration of the Scriptures must take account of the fact that God is the same throughout and He does nothing without meaning and intention. Creation is not an arbitrary affair, for God is not just a God of order, but of meaning and communication. If you spend time on this governed closely by how the Scriptures reveal God and His character and work, you will begin to see this spiritual meaning more and more.

---

[444]   John 10v10.

Part 2: The doctrine of Scripture considered under eight headings gleaned from Scripture.

The Scriptures display teaching about its nature under a series of different headings. One of the most prominent is as the "word of God" (or word of the Lord). Everywhere you choose to look in Scripture you will find that there is but one main theme. Furthermore you will find that the same doctrines are repeated throughout so that Scripture displays a wonderful unity that many attempted unified works of mankind would be jealous of. The Scriptures partake of the attributes of the One who is the Author. Thus the Scriptures are pure and right. They are holy and true and nothing can stand above them. Furthermore since God is infinite, we find that Scripture covers all areas that any human may chance upon, and there is nothing else that is required. After all, since God has spoken, what else can be said? These thoughts are wonderful, but in truth all we are doing is to declare the great character of the omnipotent, omniscient and omnipresent God. The Scriptures work. Nothing man offers or does can meet the needs of the human soul, but what God has said, and is saying, through His word is powerful and efficacious. Since what we are discussing is God's word we end our work with a consideration of authority. Only God's word is authoritative.

Chapter 5.

The word of the Lord God.

Introduction.

In seeking to understand the doctrine of Scripture it is imperative to begin by gaining a knowledge of this phrase "word of the Lord" and the parallel phrase "word of God".

The word of the Lord.

The first time we come across this phrase is in connection with the Lord's encouragement of Abram when he was feeling low as recorded in Genesis 15:

> *1 After these things the word of the Lord came to Abram in a vision, saying, "Do not be afraid, Abram. I am your shield, your exceedingly great reward." 2 But Abram said, "Lord God, what will You give me, seeing I go childless, and the heir of my house is Eliezer of Damascus?" 3 Then Abram said, "Look, You have given me no offspring; indeed one born in my house is my heir!" 4 And behold, the word of the Lord came to him, saying, "This one shall not be your heir, but one who will come from your own body shall be your heir." 5 Then He brought him outside and said, "Look now toward heaven, and count the stars if you are able to number them." And He said to him, "So shall your descendants be." 6 And he believed in the Lord, and He accounted it to him for righteousness. (Genesis15v1-6).*

The phrase "word of the Lord" appears twice at verses 1 and 4 and seems to be ambiguous. At first glance it seems to be indicating the *message* that God wanted Abram to receive. But then taking a closer look it seems more to indicate a title of the One who has come to give the message, namely, the Lord in theophany (or Christophany). This is indicated by the statement of verse 5 where we read that "He" (i.e. the word of the Lord) brought Abram outside (presumably of the tent where they were meeting). Thus we have the clear connection which John the Apostle homes in on between the Word of God, the second person of the Trinity who became flesh and dwelt amongst us, and the word of God, the message that he came to bring.

The next time we read the phrase we are in the midst of the plagues of God against Egypt. It is used to represent the message that came from God via Moses to Pharaoh.[445] Those who heeded the word of the Lord took note of it and made preparations, whilst those who did not regard the message they had heard ignored and took the consequences. The message or word from the Lord

---

445   Exodus 9v20,21.

was a warning that soon the terrible hail would descend and kill livestock and any people who were caught outside as it fell. Here, then the phrase is brought in terms of a warning.

The next occasion we read about the word of the Lord is perhaps the most significant yet for it sits amongst the giving of the law at Sinai:

> *3 And Moses went up to God, and the Lord called to him from the mountain, saying, "Thus you shall say to the house of Jacob, and tell the children of Israel: 4 'You have seen what I did to the Egyptians, and how I bore you on eagles' wings and brought you to Myself. 5 Now therefore, if you will indeed obey My voice and keep My covenant, then you shall be a special treasure to Me above all people; for all the earth is Mine. 6 And you shall be to Me a kingdom of priests and a holy nation.' These are the words which you shall speak to the children of Israel." 7 So Moses came and called for the elders of the people, and laid before them all these words which the Lord commanded him. (Exodus 19v3-7).*

Moses was charged with bringing all the words which the Lord had commanded him (verse 7). What follows in the next chapter, of course, is the ten commandments written by the very finger of God.[446] Then some time later, we read again that Moses told the people all the words the Lord had given him and then he wrote down all these words:

> *3 So Moses came and told the people all the words of the Lord and all the judgements. And all the people answered with one voice and said, "All the words which the Lord has said we will do." 4 And Moses wrote all the words of the Lord. And he rose early in the morning, and built an altar at the foot of the mountain, and twelve pillars according to the twelve tribes of Israel. (Exodus 24v3,4).*

Now for the first time we find that the word of the Lord becomes a written word.[447] This is not, of course, to say that the revealed will and word of God had not yet been written down, for patently Genesis pre-dates Exodus and we have warrant from the New Testament use of this first book that it too is the word of the Lord. Rather we are being taught that the word of the Lord is not just a spoken word but a written one too.

In Numbers we find that a command of the Lord to number the people is acted upon "according to the word of the Lord."[448] In Numbers 15v31 the word of the Lord is synonymous with the commandment of the Lord. In Numbers 22v18 we read of Balaam the wicked prophet declaring that he "could not go beyond the word of the Lord" indicating that an exactness is needed when considering the message. Whether Balaam was actually constrained in some way, or made a

---

446   See also Exodus 34v1,28; Deuteronomy 9v10.
447   See Exodus 34v27.
448   Numbers 3v16,51; 4v45.

conscious effort to stick to the message he received is not entirely clear. The teaching is, however, that to go beyond the word by adding or subtracting detail is something which is unthinkable. The story of Balaam is quite instructive because we find that Balaam testified that it was God who put the very words in his mouth. Listen to how he puts it:

> *And Balaam said to Balak, "Look, I have come to you! Now, have I any power at all to say anything? The word that God puts in my mouth, that I must speak." (Numbers 22v38).*

At the end of the saga Balaam reiterates this thought:

> **12** *So Balaam said to Balak, "Did I not also speak to your messengers whom you sent to me, saying, 13'If Balak were to give me his house full of silver and gold, I could not go beyond the word of the Lord, to do good or bad of my own will. What the Lord says, that I must speak'? (Numbers 24v12,13).*

The word of God, then is one that finds its origin in the Lord and it would seem that the Lord is very anxious to ensure that what he instructs is communicated precisely as well as with clarity.[449] In Numbers 36v5 Moses commands according to the word of the Lord, which indicates the idea of being framed and energized by what God requires exclusively.

In Deuteronomy, the sermons that Moses issued to the people prior to their crossing the Jordan, we find the warning given of not adding to or taking from what God commands:

> *You shall not add to the word which I command you, nor take from it, that you may keep the commandments of the Lord your God which I command you. (Deuteronomy 4v2).*

Moses goes on to recall the way in which the words of the Lord were delivered to the people. The Lord spoke and Moses acted as the intermediary.[450] Then we read those wonderful words that teach our desperate need for all the things that God speaks as Moses recounted to the people their experiences of the manna in the wilderness:

> *So He humbled you, allowed you to hunger, and fed you with manna which you did not know nor did your fathers know, that He might make you know that man shall not live by bread alone; but man lives by every word that proceeds from the mouth of the Lord. (Deuteronomy 8v3).*

---

449   See also Numbers 23v5,16.
450   Deuteronomy 4v10,12; 5v5,22,28

In Deuteronomy there are instructions on testing whether a prophet is giving the words of the Lord or words from his own heart.[451]

Our next significant encounter with the word of the Lord comes in the story about Samuel the last judge who was also a prophet. When Hannah his mother gave him into the care of the Lord under the high priest Eli, we are told that the word of the Lord was rare in those days for there was no widespread revelation.[452] This amounts to informing us that the word of the Lord is revelation. Although it may seem obvious, it is in fact reinforcing the idea that the message comes directly from the Lord and could never be found or discovered by men. The story of Samuel unfolds in the rest of the chapter and it ends by confirming this connection between the word of the Lord and revelation:

> **19** *So Samuel grew, and the Lord was with him and let none of his words fall to the ground.* **20** *And all Israel from Dan to Beersheba knew that Samuel had been established as a prophet of the Lord.* **21** *Then the Lord appeared again in Shiloh. For the Lord revealed Himself to Samuel in Shiloh by the word of the Lord. (1Samuel 3v19-21).*

In this text we find that the Lord revealed not just commands, nor even instructions, but he reveals himself "by the word of the Lord." Once again there is a slight ambiguity here. Is this merely the message of the Lord? Or is it the second person of the Trinity, a Christophany? Later we find that Samuel was a faithful prophet because he told the people "all the words of the Lord" when they were wanting a king.[453] Saul the chosen king was finally rejected because he rejected "the word of the Lord" in the matter of the Amalekites.[454]

Moving on to David we find the word of the Lord comes to the prophet Nathan when David wanted to build a temple. David receives a wonderful word and then we read that David declared that all of the Lord's words were true.[455] When David was delivered from the hand of his enemies he wrote a Psalm in praise of the Lord. In it he declares that: "the word of the Lord is proven" by which we can infer that it stands the test of time and is always true.[456]

Numerous times throughout the books of Kings and especially in the prophets we read the phrase "and the word of the Lord came" by which we may infer that not only the message but the second person of the Trinity in dream, vision or Christophanic appearance was brought to those whose job it was to declare the truth as revealed to them.

---

451   Deuteronomy 13v3; 18v21.
452   1Samuel 3v1.
453   1Samuel 8v10.
454   1Samuel 15v23,26.
455   1Samuel 7v4,25,28.
456   2Samuel 22v3. See also Psalm 18v30.

In Psalm 12 we read that the words of the Lord are pure words which can be likened to silver which has been through a perfect refining process.[157] Psalm 33 tells us that the word of the Lord is right, and this thought is extended by stating that what God does, his work, is always done in truth.[458] Psalm 33 also reminds us that the entire universe was brought into being by the word of the Lord.[459] The Genesis account focuses on God's speaking creation into being. The New Testament speaks of Christ Jesus as the agent of creation so we are back to this idea of the word of the Lord being at once the message and equally the Lord Himself.[460]

The phrase is particularly used in the Acts to represent the spread of the gospel. The apostles preached "the word of the Lord," and, the word of the Lord spread all around.[461] From first Thessalonians we discover that the apostle Paul and his band spoke only from the word of the Lord, and this word of the Lord was that which must sound forth from the new church.[462] In Peter we read that the word of the Lord is eternal.[463]

The word of God.

What next of the parallel phrase "word of God"? Well in many cases it is synonymous with the phrase we have briefly studied. Thus, for example, the word of God came to various prophets.[464] Then we read in Proverbs a similar thought to that expressed in Psalm 12, that every word of God is pure.[465] In the New Testament we find that Jesus states that man does not live by bread alone but by every word of God (referring to Deuteronomy 8) in combat with the devil in his temptation.[466] Luke records that the multitudes flocked to hear Jesus as he spoke the word of God.[467] John tells us that Christ was sent of the Father to speak the words of God.[468] The phrase occurs in the Acts of the apostles. For example, after much prayer the ones filled with the Holy Spirit spoke the word of God with boldness.[469] Then further we read that the word of God spread and grew as people moved through the region.[470] Turning in repentance and faith is spoken of as "receiving the word of

---

457   Psalm 1v6.
458   Psalm 33v4.
459   Psalm 33v6.
460   John 1v1f; Colossians 1v16
461   Acts 8v25; 13v49; 15v35,36; 16v32; 19v10,20;
462   1Thesssalonians 1v8; 4v15.
463   1Peter 1v25.
464   1Kings 12v22; 1Chronicles 17v3.
465   Proverbs 30v5.
466   Luke 4v4.
467   Luke 5v1.
468   John 3v34.
469   Acts 4v31.
470   Acts 6v7; 12v24.

God."[471] The word of God was to be preached and heard.[472] It was also to be taught to the disciples.[473]

Then in the epistles we read more about the meaning and use of this phrase the word of God. For example we learn in Romans that faith comes by hearing the word of God.[474] Paul describes the word of God as the sword of the Spirit.[475] Writing to the Thessalonians Paul speaks of the process of preaching, witness and faith. The word of God was spoken to the Thessalonians and they received it not as mere words from men, but words from God. Then we find that this word of God is effectual working out its purpose in the believer.[476] In Hebrews we read of the word of God being living and active and able to judge the thoughts and intents of the heart.[477] We learn that it is possible to taste the word of God and that the world was formed by the word of God.[478] New birth comes through the agency of the word of God which is eternal.[479] The word of God is to abide in us.[480] The Saviour is termed the word of God.[481]

The word of God/the Lord is.....

Looking at the phrases "the word of the Lord is" and "the word of God is" we find ten verses and these have been arranged in a specific order as follows:

As for God, His way is perfect; The word of the Lord is proven; He is a shield to all who trust in Him. (2Samuel 22v31 & Psalm 18v30).

Every word of God is pure; He is a shield to those who put their trust in Him. (Proverbs 30v5).

For the word of the Lord is right, And all His work is done in truth. (Psalm 33v4).

And Jehoshaphat said, "The word of the Lord is with him [Elisha]." So the king of Israel and Jehoshaphat and the king of Edom went down to him. (2Kings 3v12).

To whom shall I speak and give warning, that they may hear? Indeed their ear is uncircumcised, and they cannot give heed. Behold, the word of the Lord is a reproach to them; they have no delight in it. (Jeremiah 6v10).

---

471   Acts 8v14; 11v1.
472   Acts 13v5,7,44,46; 17v13.
473   Acts 18v11.
474   Romans 10v17.
475   Ephesians 6v17.
476   1Thessalonians 2v13.
477   Hebrews 4v12.
478   Hebrews 6v5; 11v3; 2Peter 3v5.
479   1Peter 1v23.
480   1John2v14.
481   Revelation 19v13.

Mike Viccary

But if they are prophets, and if the word of the Lord is with them, let them now make intercession to the Lord of hosts, that the vessels which are left in the house of the Lord, in the house of the king of Judah, and at Jerusalem, do not go to Babylon.' (Jeremiah 27v18).

Woe to the inhabitants of the seacoast, The nation of the Cherethites! The word of the Lord is against you, O Canaan, land of the Philistines: "I will destroy you; So there shall be no inhabitant." (Zephaniah 2v5).

for which I suffer trouble as an evildoer, even to the point of chains; but the word of God is not chained. (2Timothy 2v9).

For the word of God is living and powerful, and sharper than any two-edged sword, piercing even to the division of soul and spirit, and of joints and marrow, and is a discerner of the thoughts and intents of the heart. (Hebrews 4v12).

What can we learn from these verses? First of all we learn from 2Samuel 22v31 & Psalm 18v30, that the word of the Lord is "proven." That is, it has been tested or refined. It has passed through the fire and come out unscathed. Whether we think of the attempts by Satan and the world to destroy it literally, or of those attempts by the world to ridicule it and count it as of no value, the word of the Lord has come through victorious. I am reminded of the story of the enlightenment skeptic Voltaire who wanted to obliterate the Bible from use, and whose house in Geneva was used to distribute Bibles after his demise. How many have sought to ridicule and denounce the Scriptures! They are all of them confounded as the word of the Lord continues and comes out of the fire of testing unharmed whilst all who lay sword or poison to it are found no more.

Our next designation comes in psalm 12. Here we read that every word of God is "pure." That is, it is unalloyed, unmixed or unadulterated. The Psalm goes on to liken it to silver tried in a furnace seven times indicating a perfect purity. Of course in this world perfect purity is impossible, but with regard to God's word we have no hesitation of affirming that it is 100% pure. How can this be? Well a moment's thought will settle the matter. God is pure and holy, so it stands to reason that his very word would equally be pure and holy too.

In Psalm 33v4 we are taught that the word of the Lord is "right." This is emphasised with a comment about truth further on in the verse. By stating that it is right we are brought to consider it as absolute truth and, importantly, as righteous. What God says has this utter truth and rightness about it. You cannot wriggle out from under it or around it. It stands tall and true. It is upright and solid and nothing can tilt it or twist its course.

Next we have a selection of four verses which teach us about who the word of the Lord is with, or how different people respond to it. First we find in 2Kings 3v12 that the prophet Elisha is described as one who has "the word of the Lord with him." As a consequence Jehoshaphat went to inquire of him. All true prophets, and, in fact, all true believers will be described as those who have the word of the Lord with them. Whether it be said that they have Christ (the Word) or the Scriptures, the word of the Lord is within them. And to those who thirst or who are truly seeking life, they will be the ones to seek out. To those who claim to be prophets but are not, there are consequences to such a claim. Thus in Jeremiah 27v18 we learn that Jeremiah admonishes false prophets to recognise that if the word of the Lord was with them, then they had a duty to seek the Lord to see their word fulfilled. Of course they would be found wanting in this exercise, but the key point is that if we claim to have the word of the Lord within, there are consequences. We have not time to consider this for now, but at the very least one who claims to have the word of the Lord within will honour what that word says and will own the truths it states and contains. Then we note that to the unbeliever the word of the Lord is a reproach to them because they are uncircumcised of heart and their ears are dull and stopped up. Such is the import of Jeremiah 6v10. Is this not the case? The unsaved when confronted with the truths of Scripture and the Truth of Christ, consider it all a reproach and have no delight in it. They would rather follow inventions and fantasies their own minds have constructed. But finally, for this selection of four verses, we conclude that this word of the Lord stands against the unbeliever. This is the teaching of Zephaniah 2v5. Those who consider the word of the Lord of no value, will stumble and fall as the word of the Lord comes against them in judgement.

In the New Testament we have two verses where we read about the word of God. The first teaches us something wonderful about God's word. We often feel constrained and hampered by all sorts of difficulties and opponents. Paul was no stranger to these difficulties. Writing as a prisoner in chains, the apostle declared that the word of God was "not chained." It cannot be bridled and tamed! How the academics and the compromisers seek to beat the word of God into submission! How they have sought to limit, pervert and adulterate it to the whims and desires of modern man and his ways! But it cannot be tamed! It cannot be chained! It is free! Our last verse is perhaps the most wonderful, although I confess that all these thoughts make my heart rejoice that God has seen fit to give great confidence in what he has spoken, both in sending His one and only Son, the Word of God, and in revealing the word of the Lord to us. Nevertheless in Hebrews 4v12 we have a threefold description of the word of God. First it is described as "living." This makes wonderful sense when we recall that the Bible, and Christ are so closely connected. The word of God partakes of the very nature of God. It breathes life because it is a living thing. Such wonder! Paul could write to the Corinthians that the believers there were an epistle of Christ written by the Spirit.[482] We have

---

482   2Corinhians 3v3.

the word of God within and this brings life because the word of God is living! Then next we read that the word of God is "powerful." How we have fallen! How weak and inept we are today! We seek all sorts of ways to promote the kingdom of God but we do not seem to trust that the word of God is powerful! How few churches spend more than a few minutes in expounding the Scriptures! We are more concerned with singing streams of repetitive choruses or of engaging in social affairs, or of doing good works! None of these things are wrong and indeed they all have their place, but the word of God alone is described as powerful. The third description shows us this power and goes some way to explaining why unbelievers recoil at it. The word of God is penetrative. It goes deep into the heart like an arrow.[483] It measures, sieves, sifts and sorts us out. How we fail here! Do any have deep mental or emotional problems? The word of God is deep and can fathom the depths of the heart and makes things open and revealed. Forget the psychiatrists and psychologists for they are blind beggars. The word of God will show you up, will reveal the heart, and will do more as it points to the remedy and salve or ointment too.

The word of God, the word of the Lord, has stood the test of time and all-comers. It is absolutely pure and has no admixture of error or evil in it. It is true and right standing tall and upright. It is unchained and runs free and none can hold it back or stay its course. It is a living, powerful penetrative word for the seeking soul. The believer has it within. The unbeliever hates it and considers it a reproach, but it will judge him in the end.

---

483   The image of an arrow is used extensively for God's word in the Old Testament.

Chapter 6.

A single message.

Introduction.

The Bible is a book written by God using (generally speaking) eyewitnesses as His instruments or tools. If the Bible was simply a collection of documents from a variety of human sources, it would be beyond all hope to expect a unity of thought and teaching in the final product. Surely such a collection of writings, if they were truly only authored by a variety of human beings, would be but a hopeless collection of junk and confusion! We need only look at other collections of human writings to establish this fact. To make life simple, let us take, for example, any of the numerous scientific journals that are published. These journals contain articles written in the same style of writing, and, (generally speaking), limit themselves to a narrow field of inquiry. Now let us consider this journal and its papers over a period of several years. You will find, without any difficulty I believe, that there will be expressed within these pages a great deal of diversity of opinion and judgement, of theory and speculation. One man considers that the reaction mechanism operates in one way, another scientist suggests some other way. One researcher suspects that the relations between two variables can be mirrored by a particular mathematical expression, another in some more complex fashion, and so on. The history of science shows clearly that each generation's view of ideas about existence are very different from those of its predecessors. Scientific textbooks very soon become out of date, as new ideas and changing views gain popularity. The writings of men, however clever and scholarly, are always characterised by great diversity, and not by any real unity. The Bible is not like this, for it is a whole, a unit. Scripture must never be considered as a library of 66 books, for this leads to the erroneous conclusion that 66 different authors with differing points of view have expressed themselves. There is but One Author who has written just One Book – "The Book."[484] This is the essential next step, for the God who speaks, speaks clearly. The human penmen were not automatons, and the writings that bear their names all form part of the unit known as "Scripture."

---

484   Job 33v14; Psalm 62v11.

Mike Viccary

One message.

The unity of Scripture can be demonstrated in a variety of ways, but perhaps the most impressive is to consider it from the aspect of its message, or main theme. Throughout the entire Bible, the message is exactly the same. Where in the collected writings of humans do we get such unanimity? Collected human writings are to be characterised by diversity, as we have already noted, yet Scripture continually declares the same message throughout. We do not need great brains or great learning to discern the message. We may turn to any part of Scripture and find it before us. The Lord Jesus Christ taught His disciples that Scripture speaks of Him.[485] The Bible, therefore, is the book that reveals God and His wonderful works. It is, if you like, the Lord God's autobiography, adapted to the minds of men. This, of course, is obvious if we think of the New Testament writings, which clearly focus upon the Lord Jesus Christ as God and Saviour of men. Yet we may also demonstrate this fact by tracing the many prophecies of the Old Testament that point to the Saviour and King. Some of the many that could be noted are listed below in tables 6.1 and 6.2[486]. One other way we can demonstrate the unity of Scripture is to look at the beginning and ending of the Bible. Since every book has a beginning and an ending, we could also demonstrate the unity of Scripture by a comparison between the first and last books, (Genesis and Revelation), as shown in table 6.3. The New Testament writers also continually affirm the fact that Christ is the sum and substance of the Bible.[487] That being said, the Bible must be considered as one complete unit. Throughout the whole Book, the story is the same – Christ the Prophet, Priest, and King, coming to reveal, redeem and reign.

One body, one faith.

We can illustrate this idea of the unity in Scripture further by considering one of the metaphors that is used to represent the church. Paul, writing to the Ephesians, declared that there was only "one body."[488] It may be objected to by some that the Old Testament theocratic nation of Israel constituted a "church" that is now superseded by the New Testament church of Jesus Christ. Yet when we remember that Paul also said that there was only "one faith," this objection breaks down.[489] The same gospel preached by Paul and all the New Testament writers, was also proclaimed to the Old Testament hearers as well.[490] There is only one way of salvation, according to Scripture,

---

485   Luke 24v27; John 5v39,46.
486   These tables are by no means exhaustive!
487   See, for example, Luke 24v25-27,44-46; John 1v45; 5v39,46; Acts 10v43; 26v22,23; Romans 3v21; 1Peter 1v11; Revelation 19v10.
488   Ephesians 4v4.
489   Ephesians 4v5.
490   Hebrews 4v2.

since there is only one Mediator between God and men.[491] Since that is the case, the Old Testament
saints must have had the same faith as that possessed by all New Testament saints. Indeed Paul

Table 6.1: Prophecies of Christ in the Old testament.

Scripture	Key theme
Genesis 3v15	The seed of the woman shall bruise the serpent's head.
Genesis 12v1-7	In Abraham's seed all the families of the earth shall be blessed.
Genesis 22v8	God will provide for Himself the lamb.
Genesis 49v8-12	Out of Judah 'Shiloh' will come.
Numbers 24v17-19	A ruler will come forth from Jacob.
Deuteronomy 18v15-18	A Prophet will arise from amongst the people of God.
2Samuel 7v12-19	The promised seed (a long time off) will establish God's house and an eternal kingdom.
Job 19v25	I know that my Redeemer lives.
Psalm 2v6-12	The Son will be set as King on Zion's holy hill.
Psalm 16v10	The Holy One will not be left in the grave to decay.
Psalm 22	A graphic prophecy of the torments suffered on Calvary.
Psalm 110	The Lord as King and Priest after the order of Melchizedek.
Isaiah 7v14	A virgin shall conceive and bear a son.
Isaiah 9v6,7	Unto us a child is born – expressing the deity of the coming Christ.
Isaiah 11v1-5	The Branch of the Lord will minister in righteousness (cf. Isaiah 4v2).
Isaiah 42v1-4	The Lord's `servant ministers to the Gentiles.
Isaiah 52v13 – 53v12	The Suffering Servant.
Jeremiah 23v5-8	The Branch of the Lord will be "The Lord our Righteousness" (cf. Jeremiah 33v15 & Ezekiel 17v22-24).
Ezekiel 34v23-31	One Shepherd for the Lord's people, (David) (cf. Ezekiel 37v24).
Daniel 9v24-27	The coming Messiah dated.
Micah 5v2	The place of the Messiah's birth.
Zechariah 6v12	The Branch shall build the temple of the Lord.
Zechariah 9v9	Triumphal entry predicted.
Zechariah 11v13	Thirty pieces of silver – Judas' payment for betrayal.
Zechariah 13v7	The sword against the Lord's chosen Shepherd.
Malachi 3v1	The messenger who prepares the way for the Lord to suddenly come (cf. Malachi 4v5,6).

---

491   John 14v6; Acts 4v12; 1Timothy 2v5; Revelation 13v8.

Table 6.2: Prophecies fulfilled by Christ in His rejection, death & burial

	Prophecy detail	OT prophecy	NT fulfilment
1	He was to be sold for thirty pieces of silver	Zechariah 11v12	Matthew 26v14,15
2	He was to be betrayed by a friend	Psalm 55v12-14; 41v9	Matthew 26v47-50; John 13v18
3	The money obtained was to be cast to the potter: (a) silver, (b) 30 pieces, (c) thrown down, (d) in the house of the Lord, (e) used to purchase a field	Zechariah 11v13	Matthew 27v3-10
4	His disciples were to forsake Him	Zechariah 13v7	Matthew 26v56; Mark 14v27
5	He was to be accused by false witnesses	Psalm 35v11; 109v2	Matthew 26v59,60
6	He was to be smitten and spat upon: (a) smitten, (b) on the face, (c) spit upon, (d) upon the face	Isaiah 50v4-6	Luke 22v64; Matthew 26v67,68
7	He was to be dumb before His accusers	Isaiah 53v7	Matthew 27v12-14; 1Peter 2v23
8	He was to be wounded and bruised	Isaiah 53v5	Matthew 27v26,29
9	He was to fall under the cross	Psalm 109v24	John 19v17; Luke 23v26
10	His hands and feet were to be pierced	Psalm 22v16	Luke 23v33; John 20v25-27
11	He was to be crucified with thieves	Isaiah 53v12	Mark 15v27,28
12	He was to pray for His persecutors	Isaiah 53v12; Psalm 109v4	Luke 23v34
13	The people were to shake their heads	Psalm 109v25; 22v7	Matthew 27v39
14	The people were to ridicule Him	Psalm 22v8	Matthew 27v41,43
15	The people were to be astonished	Psalm 22v17; Isaiah 52v14	Luke 23v35
16	His garments were to be parted and lots cast for them	Psalm 22v18	John 19v23,24
17	He was to cry "My God My God, why hast thou forsaken me?"	Psalm 22v1	Matthew 27v46
18	They were to give Him gall and vinegar	Psalm 69v21	Matthew 27v34; John 19v28,29
19	He was to commit Himself to God	Psalm 31v5	Luke 23v46
20	His friends were to stand afar off	Psalm 38v11	Luke 23v49
21	His bones were not to be broken yet they were to be 'out of joint' - "I may tell all my bones"	Psalm 34v20; Exodus 12v46; Psalm 22v14,17	John 19v31-36
22	His side was to be pierced	Zechariah 12v10	John 19v34-37
23	His heart was to be broken	Psalm 22v14	John 19v34
24	Darkness was to cover the land	Amos 8v9	Matthew 27v45
25	He was to be buried in a rich man's tomb	Isaiah 53v9	Matthew 27v57-60

demonstrated that Abraham's faith in God is precisely what we need today for the salvation of our souls.[492] Thus, just as we look back to the great event of Calvary as recorded in the gospels, the Old Testament saints looked forward to that same event which they could see through the types and shadows of the temple and tabernacle, and through the many prophecies (see table 6.1).

Table 6.3: Correspondences between Genesis and Revelation.

	In Genesis:	In Revelation:
[1]	We are told of the creation of the heavens and the earth (1v1)	We are told about the creation of the new heavens and the new earth (21v1)
[2]	We are told about an earthly paradise (Eden) in which the first man Adam and his wife were placed, and of their call to rule over the earth (1v27,28)	We are told about Christ (the second and last Adam), who reigns forever with His bride (the church) in the paradise of heaven (3v21; 21v9)
[3]	We are told of a tree of life and a river in the midst of the garden of Eden (2v9-10)	We find the tree of life and the river of water of life (2v7; 22v1,2)
[4]	We meet the enemy, satan, the tempter (3v1f)	We find that this one will be finally judged (12v9; 20v10)
[5]	We hear of the beginning of sin, the fall of man, the ejection from paradise, and man's subjection to the first death (2v17; 3v1f; 5v5,8)	We hear of the end of sin, the restoration of man into paradise, and the second death for the impenitent (14v10,11; 20v14,15)
[6]	We hear of the first universal judgment by water (6v1f)	We hear of the last judgment by fire (20v11)
[7]	We read of the destruction of the unity of man at the tower of Babel (11v1f)	We find the unity of men restored by the blood of the Lamb gathering together a people from all families of the earth (5v9)

We must also remember that Christ has only one kingdom which has been prepared from the foundation of the world.[493] Many shall come from the east and from the west to this kingdom, within which the Old Testament saints are already to be found.[494] The Scriptures, therefore, comprise just one book with one main theme. It is for this reason that we find so often the phrase "The Faith" spoken of in Scripture.[495] There is only one faith, one body of truth to which we must adhere. This only makes perfect sense, of course, if we conceive of the Bible as a unit. How sad it is then when so-called evangelicals deny this unity of Scripture by forging a "strange" union with those who deny "The Faith" in the ecumenical movement. The Bible as a "unit" with a unified

---

492   Romans 4v1f; Galatians 3v7f; Hebrews 11v8f; 2Peter 1v1.
493   Matthew 25v34; John 18v36.
494   Matthew 8v11.
495   Acts 6v7; 14v22; 16v5; 1Corinthians 16v13; 2Corinthians 13v5; Ephesians 4v13; Philippians 1v27; Colossians 1v23; 2v7; 1Timothy 3v9; 4v1; 5v8; 6v10,21; 2Timothy 4v7; Titus 1v4,13; 1Peter 5v9; Jude v3.

message cries out against all forms of ecumenism. We must not be sectarian, but we must be of the same, common and "like precious faith."[496]

It is quite startling how often the New Testament Scriptures exhort believers to have the same mind, to be of the same thought and heart concerning the gospel.[497] Very little attention is paid to such unity today! Yet this unity of mind, thought, and heart can only arise when we consider that the Scriptures are a unit that declare One Faith, One body of doctrines that centre upon the Lord Jesus Christ and His marvellous work of Redemption. The unity of the Bible as illustrated by its consistency and its single main theme is also a great witness to its truthfulness. Lies and deceit tend to yield a web of confusion whilst truth as Blanchard says, is cohesive:

> By its very nature, error is conflicting, whereas truth is cohesive. The amazing cohesion of the Bible's teaching is a powerful pointer to its integrity.[498]

---

496   Amos 3v3; 2Peter 1v1.
497   Acts 1v14; 2v1,46; 4v24,32; 5v12; 15v25; Romans 15v6; 1Corinthians 1v10; 2Corinthians 13v11; Philippians 1v27; 2v2; 3v16; 2Timothy 1v7; 1Peter 3v8.
498   John Blanchard - Does God Believe in Atheists. Evangelical Press. 2000. P406.

Chapter 7.

It is written.

Introduction.

When I was studying for my degree my final year project supervisor was rather surprised at my Christian faith. He challenged me about the way the Bible came to be. He brought out the old myth that the Scriptures were written down centuries after the event and that the details were passed down from father to son through many generations in verbal form first. His point was that before the Scriptures came to be written, they must have gone through many changes and alterations as each father related the stories to their sons. It was all like the game "Chinese whispers" where a message is whispered from person to person down a line of people, and the original compared to the final whispered one. Now this challenge worried me for a little while until I realised that the origin of such an idea (verbal transmission preceded by written form) was energised and fuelled by an evolutionary world view. You see if we have an evolutionary idea about man, it stands to reason that the earlier peoples may not have had the ability to write or construct written records. In the evolutionary scenario writing came late on the scene. But, of course, the Bible presents a radically different picture. God created man perfect and gave him the same faculties and abilities which we posses today. In fact when you analyse the Genesis record, you find that Adam not only gave names to all the animals – a task which implies far more than simply designating a symbol for each but indicates a kind of classification system – he also seems to have written a book![499]

Further investigation in Genesis and the rest of the Torah showed that writing was something engaged in by the ancient Biblical peoples. Moses, in particular, was commanded by the Lord to write down what he saw and observed with meticulous precision.[500] In fact it becomes clear that whenever God revealed himself to people, the information was very soon afterwards committed to written form. There was, in fact, no delay in time between the revelation and the writing. In several instances God commanded the writing, and so the old idea of a verbal phase where stories were recounted around the fire from generation to generation before being written do not stand up to the scrutiny of the evidence contained within the Bible.[501] A consideration of Scripture as written

---

499   Genesis 5v1.
500   See, for example, Exodus 17v14; 24v4; 34v1,27,28; Numbers 33v2. The expression "by the hand of Moses" can be found at the following places in the pentateuch: Exodus 35v29; Leviticus 8v36; 10v11; 16v21; 26v46; Numbers 4v37,45,49; 9v23; 10v13; 15v23;
501   Compare Exodus 17v14 with 24v4.

material is a subject which presents itself clearly to us in the very word "Scripture," which we will come to see a little later on means "writing." To begin our discussion we will first consider the many types of writing presented to us in the Scriptures. Then next we will look at the materials and techniques used when those of Bible times came to write anything down. Finally we will consider the importance of establishing the idea that Scripture is written material from the point of view of authority.

Writing styles.

The Scriptures are not a text written to any particular formula or a book that follows just one style. Technical and academic works are often presented in this manner, and if you have ever sought to get a piece accepted for publication you will know the constraining feeling of the editors! The editors of newspapers and magazines often require a similar strong emphasis on one particular way of doing things, but the Scriptures are quite remarkable because they cover every type of writing style imaginable. Genesis, for example is written in an historical narrative style whilst the Psalms are written as Hebrew poems and songs. The prophets are written in a combination of historical narrative and poetry but the difference between, for example, the majesty and stateliness of Isaiah and the more gritty earth style of Ezekiel, or the passionate and very human feel from Jeremiah is marked. In the New Testament we have recorded many letters of instruction to various churches and specific people, alongside the gospels each with their distinctive approaches. Nestled between is Luke's second work the "Acts of the Apostles" which records the major events showing the development of the church. Luke was a physician (doctor) and uses many technical words and phrases in his writing. Then also we have the book of Revelation written at the end of the first century AD. This book contains highly symbolic material following seven key letters. The Old Testament has, law, edicts, ordinances, chronicle, registry (the genealogies in Genesis, Chronicles), prophecy, formal letters (Ezra and Nehemiah), riddles, songs, and proverbs or parables (Proverbs). Finally there are biographical sections in both testaments (Ecclesiastes and in Paul's letters).

The great variety of styles displayed in Scripture certainly shows a human flavour but this does not mean that there are a variety of authors, for there can only be One Author for Scripture, namely the Holy Spirit. He so used the human penmen that even though they wrote from their personal human experience, yet in guiding their hands the Holy Spirit superintended them to write precisely that alone which God desired. If we hold the view that the Bible is merely a human production, this rich variety in form and style may lead to the conclusion that there are many authors, but since there is but One Author, who is all-powerful, we conclude rather that such variety is for the benefit of men who will read His great work. If the Scripture was written entirely in a poetic cast, there would be many for whom Scripture would hold no appeal. Likewise if the Bible was all didactic or entirely historical, the result would have few readers or beneficiaries.

It is really quite contrary to the facts enumerated throughout the Bible to assert that, for example, Isaiah really <u>authored</u> the book that bears his name, or to state that the gospel according to Luke was Luke's gospel. All the words of these writings (along with all of Scripture) find their origin in God alone. Yet we have to insist also that the men employed in penning Scripture were not mere passive automatons or robots. Luke tells us that he made enquiry into the things that he intended to write about, whilst of Solomon it was said that he "sought to find out acceptable words."[502] I am sure that God used, not necessarily the most clever in the world's sense of that word (although some undoubtedly were very intelligent), yet the most diligent and conscientious men for the compilation of His word.[503] They sought out the right words and phrases, and used the best type of forms and literary devices to drive home the message they were conveying. Yet none of this mitigates against the fact that *every* word of the Bible was exactly the one that God Himself personally chose for us to read.

The fact that a variety of forms and types of writing were used should give us great heart, for we are not all scholars, neither are we all poets or historians. Many need the entrance of truth via stories or parables. Some require other means. At particular times in our lives certain forms are more readily digested than others. The variety of styles used by the Lord in giving us Scripture was thus for three main or key reasons. First, the Lord knows full well that people are different and sometimes their access to the things of the Lord may need a different approach. Sometimes this is all to do with the depth of a person's willingness to know. Thus whilst the disciples got to know the mysteries of God explained, those who were amongst the crowds and outside the close band heard truth in parables.[504] Then also, Paul admonished the Corinthian Christians for being carnal and for needing to be fed milk and not solid food.[505] Taking a slightly different thought track we may surmise that the more poetically inclined among us would find Scripture written in such a style easier to comprehend, whilst the legally minded may prefer commands and letters and so on. A second reason for the different styles follows on from the first because each person may require different styles at different times. Perhaps we have not really accepted some behaviour we have engaged in as being sinful. In this instance, maybe a parable would be the means for us to come to

---

502   Ecclesiastes 12v3. See also Luke 1v1-4.
503   Acts 4v13; 1Corinthians 1v19f,27.
504   Mark 4v11.
505   1Corinthians 3v1f.

repentance, just as it did for David in the case of his sin with Bathsheba.[506] Or at another time we may be thoroughly downcast and perplexed by enemies. In this case a word from the Psalms may help. Other occasions and times may be suited to other Scripture styles. The Bible is compared to food and like food there is variety according to need.[507] Sometimes a hearty meal may be needed but at other times only the sweet truths need to be administered to the sorrowful soul! A third reason for the variety of styles is that different truths may be conveyed better through one style than in another. A clear and straightforward command or statement is required for many simple acts and behaviours, but to understand or comprehend the true nature of the godhead requires deeper techniques of writing. For example, revelation of the true nature of our Lord and Saviour comes from a variety of passages with widely differing styles. We have, for example, the description of the beloved in the Song of Solomon 5v10-16, the visions given to Ezekiel in chapters 1, 9 & 10, and the visual images in Daniel and Revelation.[508] A fourth reason for difference in style of writing comes when we remember that often the Scriptures are required for different tasks. By this I mean that a Christian worker in the heat of battle may need a quick word of encouragement from the Psalms, or he may need a word "in season" for the people he is working with or ministering to. In more general terms he will need the plain practical instruction that comes from the New Testament epistles. Some parts of the Scriptures are particularly suited to evangelistic work,[509] whilst others have clearly been included for especial teaching on particular themes,[510] and still others are suited to special cases.[511]

Human writing styles vary not only according to the purpose of the writing but also due to the writer's mood. This fact can be shown to some extent in a work like the book of Isaiah. The whole book is undoubtedly the work of the prophet Isaiah under inspiration of God as shown by the almost exclusive use of the phrase "the Holy One of Israel" used as a title for God throughout the book. Yet chapters 40 to 66 are very different in style to chapters 1 to 39. Such is the difference that liberal scholars suggest a different author for each section. Liberal scholars make far too much of such differences.[512] A much better explanation would be that whilst chapters 1 to 39 were written during the reigns of the kings mentioned in Isaiah 1v1 (Uzziah, Jotham, Ahaz and Hezekiah), the latter chapters were probably written whilst Manasseh was king. Manasseh was such a wicked king

---

506   2Samuel 12v1f.
507   Deuteronomy 8v3; Job 23v12.
508   Daniel 7v9-14 & Revelation 1v9-20.
509   There are many, many examples but 2Kings 5 recording the story of Naaman is one of my favourites!
510   A clear example would be the duty of church leaders in 1Timothy, 2Timothy and Titus.
511   This point is amply proved by the fact that many published copies of Bibles have sections within them pointing the reader to Scriptures which may help at different times of life – e.g. Gideon's Bibles.
512   The classic use of literary styles indicating difference in authors is found in the liberal view of Genesis. According to modern scholarship the book was written by different scribes of the exilic period. These are termed 'Jehovist' 'Eloist' 'Deuteronomist' and 'Priestly,' as each supposedly followed a different view of God. This documentary hypothesis has been refuted times without number but is still held to by many liberals today.

that it is probable that Isaiah had to work under cover, or at least not as openly as he had at the start of his ministry.

We must not make too much of writing style as sometimes the work we are reading is actually a compilation, or the work of someone who has researched other's works and used them as source material. Thus, Luke tells us that he made use of many sources in writing his gospel, the chronicler clearly used a variety of works to compile his book, Solomon was a keen researcher, and Moses probably used original writings from Adam, Noah and the other patriarchs in compiling Genesis.[513] Whether the work was original or a compilation, all are inspired and, as such, are the very words that God intended. It may be helpful to us to see that the human writer has used other sources, but the focus on this human element must be kept under the clear teaching that all Scripture is inspired and has God as its ultimate source.

Writing materials.

We must begin our discussion of this point by affirming that the Scriptures give us the correct chronology, or history of the world, for our study. We also assert that the evolutionary world view is **not** the correct one. The correct view is: Creation, Fall, Redemption. The inference from these two principles is that we do not need to look for development in writing but rather we can assume that writing was a natural ability of man from his creation, whilst the form of that writing merely reflects man's environment and the materials that were readily available. There were five basic types of writing used in the ancient times as follows:

[] Inscriptions carved into stone monuments, (e.g. Egyptian hieroglyphs).

[] Cuneiform (wedge-shaped) inscriptions made in wet clay tablets which were then baked hard.

[] Wax writing tablets inscribed with 'iron pens'.

[] Ink written Script on papyrus (reed based paper) or parchment (made from animal skins).

[] Inscriptions or marks made on pottery shards, (ostraca).

We do not have the earliest writing made by man, but the earliest writings must have been Scripture![514] Modern scholarship takes a man-centred view and looks backward using archaeology and suggests that the Sumerian language was the first to be written down. However given that the history of creation tells us that after man was made we find him "naming" the animals, and that in

---

513   Luke 1v1f; Ecclesiastes 12v10.
514   Genesis 5v1.

Genesis 5v1 we have a reference to "the book of Adam" we take the diametrically opposed view that writing is as old as man.

The first writing material the Bible mentions is stone. The Lord wrote the ten commandments on stone tablets, Joshua wrote a copy on stones after the fall of Ai when the covenant was renewed, Job declared his desire that his complaint was "engraved on a rock," and Paul referred to the law "engraved on stones" in his teaching concerning the work of the Holy Spirit in the heart to the Corinthians.[515] We get some insight into the type of method used for these engraved stones from way Job speaks about them:

> **23** *Oh, that my words were written! Oh, that they were inscribed in a book!* **24** *That they were engraved on a rock with an iron pen and lead, forever! (Job 19v23,24).*

It appears from this text that the engravings were carved with an iron tool, and that the grooves cut were then filled with molten lead metal which would harden and form a silver-grey colour against that of the rock. Other techniques included the use of sticks, clay tablets and wax writing tablets.[516] Writing on sticks, bones and antlers is well known amongst cave cultures. Clay tablets were inscribed with a sharp instrument and then baked either by being sun-dried or in a kiln.[517] Sun-dried clay did not last forever, whilst kiln-baked clay formed a more permanent record. It turns out that many of the sun-dried clay tablets have been lost to us through poor preservation, whilst some of these have been rescued through accident! Many clay tablets have only survived because they were "fired" in a fire that destroyed the building they were housed in! Writing tablets were made from wood and covered with wax.[518] The scribe would then mark the wax with a sharp point or "iron pen" to form the letters and words of text.[519] This form of writing was obviously only temporary. The Egyptians discovered the use of papyrus as a writing material. In the New Testament the term translated "book" in the KJAV is the Greek word "***biblos***" which is the inner bark from the papyrus plant. Papyrus reeds were dried and cut into strips and laid side by side. More strips were laid across these at right angles to the first layer. The whole collection of strips forming a square were glued together and pressed to dry. Sheets of papyrus could be glued together to form a scroll or codex (book). Papyrus was susceptible to damage from water but if it was too dry it could be very fragile and brittle. It is from the word "papyrus" that we derive our English word "paper."[520] Scrolls were

---

515   Exodus 24v12; 31v18; 32v16; Deuteronomy 5v22; Joshua 8v32; Job 19v24; 2Corinthians 3v3,7.
516   Numbers 17v2; Ezekiel 37v16-20; Luke 1v63.
517   Jeremiah 17v13; Ezekiel 4v1.
518   Proverbs 3v3; Jeremiah 17v1; Isaiah 30v8; Habakkuk 2v2; Luke 1v63.
519   Job 19v23,24.
520   2John 1v12

formed by gluing several papyrus sheets together and winding them around a stick.[521] Rolls of parchment skins or vellum were more durable, however, and could be written on both sides.[522] Parchment was essentially prepared animal skins and thus provided for a much more durable product. The preparation included removal of hair, scraping, treatment with lime, more scraping whilst stretched on a frame, wetting, chalking and rubbing with pumice before being allowed to dry whilst still stretched across a frame. Parchment was smoother than leather and papyrus and because of its toughness it endured writing on both sides. The process used to make parchment meant that it was expensive. Since parchment comes from animal skins it was difficult to get large numbers of sheets the same size and colour. It was also denser than papyrus and so tended to be heavier to carry. Reed pens were used with ink to write on parchment and papyrus.[523] The ink was often kept in a "writer's inkhorn" that was carried in a girdle around the waist.[524] Mistakes could be erased with water.[525]

Letter-writing was common even in very ancient times.[526] Seals were often applied to such letters or important documents to protect the privacy of their contents.[527] An "open letter," therefore, could be taken as an insult.[528] Often the seal (or, signet) was worn as a ring.[529] It represented the authority of the one to whom it belonged, and if the ring was given to another, the authority behind it was transferred as well.[530] Often because parchment and papyrus were not available, notes, bills, and other forms of writing were done on "ostraca" or broken bits of pottery. In times when pots were used for all sorts of reasons it is not surprising that they often broke and so good use was made of these left-over shards. It would be a little like our use of the back of an envelope or a paper serviette to write things down!

The Bible was written from earliest times.

It is vital that we understand the importance of accepting the revealed will of God as *written* material. This may seem to be far too obvious a statement to make, yet we must do this partly to refute the erroneous idea that written Scripture depends heavily upon a long line of oral

---

521　　Revelation 5v1.
522　　Ezra 6v1,2; Isaiah 34v4; Jeremiah 36v2,14,20,21,23,25,27,29; Ezekiel 2v9; 3v1,2; Zechariah 5v1,2; Luke 4v17,20; 2Timothy 4v13.
523　　Jeremiah 8v8.
524　　Jeremiah 36v18; 2 Corinthians 3v3; 2 John v12; 3 John v13; Ezekiel 9v2.
525　　Numbers 5v23.
526　　2 Samuel 11v14; 1 Kings 21v8; 2 Kings 5v5-7; 10v1; Nehemiah 6v5; Esther 8v10.
527　　Genesis 38v18; 1 Kings 21v8; Esther 3v10-12; 8v2,8,10; Isaiah 8v16; 29v11; Daniel 12v4,9; Haggai 2v23; Revelation 5v4,9; 10v4; 22v10.
528　　Nehemiah 6v5.
529　　Genesis 41v42; Esther 3v10-12; 8v2, 8,10; Jeremiah 22v24.
530　　1 Kings 21v8; Esther 8v2,8,10.

transmission. Such a process is often thought to have occurred in the formation of the Scriptures, because of the supposed backward and "primitive" nature and conditions of ancient people and times. Along with such an idea comes the problem of purity of transmission, it being supposed that stories handed down by word of mouth must undoubtedly have altered considerably with time, a kind of "chinese-whispers" effect. That this sort of thing did occur in the myths of ancient peoples is certain, yet when such reasoning is applied to the origin of the Scriptures, we demand proof. The prevailing opinion of men (which is quite contrary to the testimony of the Bible itself), is that stories and events were rehearsed and related from father to son for many generations before being written down. The Scriptures themselves teach rather differently, but even if it were true that generations of oral transmission occurred, this would be no problem for the omnipotent Creator God who would surely be able to preserve intact His will through such a means if He so desired.

Why is a consideration of the Scriptures as written material so important? The answer arises from the fact that many in our day would seek to disparage the written word viewing it as dead and meaningless without some external input. The most common of these inputs is personal subjective experience, often claimed to be the work of the Holy Spirit. Now, of course, without the Spirit the natural man cannot receive the things of God.[531] Yet it remains true still that the Bible itself is a living book.[532] Furthermore, others (particularly in the past) have sought to denigrate Scripture by imposing an evolutionary straight-jacket upon the way it has been formed. At one time it was considered utterly impossible for Moses to have written the Pentateuch, because *Modern Scholarship* fuelled by the archaeology of the day did not believe that the ancients began writing until quite late on in human history. When archaeological evidence was unearthed that clearly demonstrated the fact that the earliest of the great Middle Eastern civilisations had the ability to write, the idea that Moses could not have written the Pentateuch fell to pieces. Whilst we may rejoice that archaeological evidence has been found corroborating the Bible, we ought never to be influenced in this way. Our faith must never rest on such chance archaeological discoveries.[533] It is shameful that Christians were ever deflected by the theories of men from believing that God revealed His pure word and that Moses wrote down all as instructed. We must beware in our present day that we are not kowtowing and bowing to any modern-day ideas which the Scriptures cannot sanction. We can assert full confidence in the Scriptures, for they are not simply the writings of mere men, but the product (in its entirety) of an awesome, holy, but merciful Creator God. We shall

---

531   1Corinthians 2v14.

532   Hebrews 4v12. Philip Mauro has written a wonderful essay entitled: "Life in the Word" which appears in "The Fundamentals" edited by R. A. Torrey and updated by Charles L. Feinberg (Chapter 20, PP239-248). Published by Kregel Publications. Grand Rapids, Michigan, USA. 1990.

533   These discoveries are provided by the grace of God, I believe, to challenge the ridiculous theories of men.

consider the divine nature of Scripture later but for the moment we shall pay some attention to the human instruments used by the Lord for His great work. Those people who may have been disturbed by the insistence of "scholars" that Moses couldn't possibly have written the Pentateuch because writing was unknown in his time, should have paid heed to the Scriptures alone. For, from Genesis to Deuteronomy, within the entire Pentateuch, there is abundant evidence of these books having been written or compiled by Moses. They are not the product of oral transmission like the myths and legends of the ancient pagan nations. No! Rather are they the carefully collated and chosen words of godly scribes, and yet, at the same time, they are also the infallibly inspired words from the living God written down for all generations. Let it never be thought that Scripture is simply man's record of an inspired prophecy. As we have already discussed, the Scriptures themselves are inspired.

Evidence for the Bible being written early can be gleaned by looking at the text closely. In Genesis chapter 5v1 we read the following:

> *This is the book of the genealogy of Adam. In the day that God created man, He made him in the likeness of God.*

The Hebrew word "book" in the above verse literally means "writing," and is derived from the word which means "to score with a mark" or "to inscribe."[534] So here right at the beginning of human history we have reference to written material. The genealogy of Adam is something written down. It would appear from the text that Adam was the one responsible for this early history. Wiseman and others have argued that the contents of Genesis were written by the patriarchs from Adam, Noah, Shem and so on, and these were then used by Moses as he compiled the book as we know it.[535] This idea is based on the fact that the Hebrew word behind our English word "genealogy" represents the idea of a history, (the Hebrew word *toledoth* can also be rendered "history"). The historical records including the genealogical lists were written down by each of the patriarch as listed in table 7.1 Whether or not this is true, we know for certain that writing and books were written from the time of Adam, and the pre-flood and post-flood patriarchs were very much concerned with their family history and the details of God's dealings with them.

The Hebrew word translated usually as "genealogy" also occurs in other books too. Thus in Exodus 6v16,19 we find that the same word is used in connection with the lineage and history of Levi. In Numbers 3v1 we have the same word in connection with Aaron and Moses and there are

---

534   Strong's code number 5612.
535   P. J. Wiseman. Clues to Creation in Genesis. Marshall, Morgan and Scott. 1977.

other uses in Numbers, Ruth and 1Chronicles, indicating the running theme that theses works are all historical in nature.[536] It would appear also that Moses gave the written law to the Levites for safe keeping in the ark of the covenant [537] Given the fact that Moses gave the Levites such responsibility it is not unreasonable to assume that Levi also had written records of his family affairs.

Table 7.1: The histories of Genesis.

The history of ….	'Author'	Text
The history of the heavens and the earth	The Lord	1v1 - 2v4a
The history according to Adam	Adam	2v4b - 5v1a
The history according to Noah	Noah	5v1b - 6v9a
The history according to the sons of Noah	Sons of Noah	6v9b - 10v1a
The history according to Shem	Shem	10v1b - 11v10a
The history according to Terah	Terah	11v10b - 11v27a
The history according to Isaac*	Isaac	11v27b - 25v19a
The history according to Jacob**	Jacob	25v19b - 37v2a

* This would include the history according to Ishmael (25v12).

** This would include the history according to Esau (36v1,9).

In Genesis 11v1f we find reference to language and speech. At this point in the history of the world all people spoke just one language. The text of Genesis 11v1f indicates that there was not only a single lip, or speech,[538] but also a unique set of words.[539] The implication of this is that there was probably a written grammar and dictionary (set of words) as well as a unique dialect (sound of speech) understood by all.

But there is further evidence in favour of the idea that Scripture was written early on from the Pentateuch, for we find that Moses was given instruction from God to write down what he had received. The following eight Scriptures show that throughout the Pentateuch the Lord instructed Moses to make accurate records of His commands:

---

536   Numbers 1v20,22,24,26,28,30,32,34,36,38,40,42; Ruth 4v18, and; 1Chronicles 1v29; 5v7; 7v2,4,9; 8v28; 9v9,34; 26v32.
537   Deuteronomy 31v9,24,26; Leviticus 10v8-11; Deuteronomy 31-9-13; 33v8,11; 2Chronicles 17v8-10; Nehemiah 8v9.
538   Strong's code number: 8193.
539   Strong's code number: 1697.

*Then the LORD said to Moses, "**Write** this for a memorial in the book and recount it in the hearing of Joshua, that I will utterly blot out the remembrance of Amalek from under heaven." (Exodus 17v14).*

*3 So Moses came and told the people all the words of the LORD and all the judgements. And all the people answered with one voice and said, "All the words which the LORD has said we will do." 4 And Moses **wrote** all the words of the LORD. And he rose early in the morning, and built an altar at the foot of the mountain, and twelve pillars according to the twelve tribes of Israel. (Exodus 24v3,4).*

*1 These are the journeys of the children of Israel, who went out of the land of Egypt by their armies under the hand of Moses and Aaron. 2 Now Moses **wrote** down the starting points of their journeys at the command of the LORD. And these are their journeys according to their starting points. (Numbers 33v1,2).*

*Also it shall be, when he sits on the throne of his kingdom, that he shall **write** for himself a copy of this law in a book, from the one before the priests, the Levites. (Deuteronomy 17v18).*

*Also every sickness and every plague, which is not **written** in this Book of the Law, will the LORD bring upon you until you are destroyed. (Deuteronomy 28v61).*

*if you obey the voice of the LORD your God, to keep His commandments and His statutes which are **written** in this Book of the Law, and if you turn to the LORD your God with all your heart and with all your soul. (Deuteronomy 30v10).*

*So Moses **wrote** this law and delivered it to the priests, the sons of Levi, who bore the ark of the covenant of the LORD, and to all the elders of Israel. (Deuteronomy 31v9).*

*24 So it was, when Moses had completed **writing** the words of this law in a book, when they were finished, 25 that Moses commanded the Levites, who bore the ark of the covenant of the LORD, saying: 26 Take this Book of the Law, and put it beside the ark of the covenant of the LORD your God, that it may be there as a witness against you. (Deuteronomy 31v24-26).*

Then also we find that twelve times we read the phrase "by the hand of Moses" indicating that what was penned was written by Moses.[540] The terms "write," "written," and "book" can also be found in the book of Job.[541]

In the New Testament, the Old Testament is referred to as "Scripture"[542] and "Scriptures"[543] in a variety of places. The term "Scripture" points to a particular reference as in the case below:

---

540   Leviticus 8v36; 10v11; 26v46; Numbers 4v37,45,49; 9v23; 10v13; 15v23; 16v40; 27v23; 36v13.
541   Job 13v26; 19v23; 31v35.
542   Occurs 31x at: Mark 12v10; 15v28; Luke 4v21; John 2v22; 7v38,42; 10v35; 13v18; 17v12; 19v24,28,36,37; 20v9; Acts 1v16; 8v32,35; Romans 4v3; 9v17; 10v1; 11v2; Galatians 3v8,22; 4v30; 1Timothy 5v18; 2Timothy 3v16; James 2v8,23; 4v5; 1Peter 2v6; 2Peter 1v20.
543   Occurs 22x at: Matthew 21v42; 22v29; 26v54,56; Mark 12v24; 14v49; Luke 24v27,32,44,45; John 5v39: Acts 17v2,11; 18v24,28; Romans 1v2; 15v4; 16v26; 1Corinthians 15v3,4; 2Timothy 3v15; 2Peter 3v16.

> *So the Scripture was fulfilled which says, "And He was numbered with the transgressors."*
> *(Mark 15v28).*

In contrast, the term "Scriptures" refers to several texts or to the whole:

> *And beginning at Moses and all the Prophets, He expounded to them in all the Scriptures*
> *the things concerning Himself. (Luke 24v27).*

The word "Scripture(s)" literally means "writing(s)" in English. The Bible, then, must never be considered as stories handed down by word of mouth, but as writings. On top of this, the New Testament characters often referred to the Old Testament Scriptures by using the phrase: "it is written," especially when they want to clinch an argument.[544] The Old Testament, therefore, is a collection of written material. For example when the Lord Jesus was tempted by Satan the Lord responded by saying:

> *It is written, 'Man shall not live by bread alone, but by every word of God.' (Luke 4v4).*

This idea of an appeal to what was "written" can also be found throughout the Old Testament too. For example:

> *As Moses the servant of the LORD commanded the children of Israel, as it is written in the*
> *book of the law of Moses. (Joshua 8v31).*

At least two New Testament Scriptures refer to other parts of the New Testament as being "Scripture." Thus in 1Timothy 5v18, Paul quotes Deuteronomy 25v4 and then Luke 10v7 which he refers to as "Scripture."

> *For the Scripture says, "You shall not muzzle an ox while it treads out the grain," and, "The*
> *labourer is worthy of his wages." (1Timothy 5v18).*

The first of Paul's quotes is from Deuteronomy 25v4, whilst the second phrase comes from Luke 10v7:

> *You shall not muzzle an ox while it treads out the grain. (Deuteronomy 25v4).*

---

544   Matthew 2v5; 4v4,6,7,10; Mark 9v12,13; Luke 3v4; 19v46; John 6v31; 12v14; Acts 1v20; 7v42; Romans 8v36; 1Corinthians 1v19; Galatians 3v10,13; Hebrews 10v7.

And remain in the same house, eating and drinking such things as they give, for <u>the labourer</u> <u>is worthy of his wages</u>. Do not go from house to house. (Luke 10v7).

It will be seen from all this that the apostle Paul considered the gospel according to Luke on the same level as he did the book of Deuteronomy. In the second instance, we note that the apostle Peter refers to Paul's epistles as "Scripture":

> *15 And account that the longsuffering of our Lord is salvation; even as our beloved brother Paul also according to the wisdom given unto him hath written unto you; 16 As also in all his epistles, speaking in them of these things; in which are some things hard to be understood, which they that are unlearned and unstable wrest, as they do also the other Scriptures, unto their own destruction. (2Peter 3v15,16, KJAV).*

Thus in 2Peter 3v15,16 Peter indicates that Paul's writings are misunderstood just as "other Scriptures" are by certain men. It is quite clear here that Peter considered that Paul's writings were on a par with the Old Testament Scriptures.

There is clear teaching with regard to the term "Scriptures" (or "writings") that they are especial. They are referred to as "holy," as giving "comfort," and as "prophetic."[545] Seven important teachings connected with this term "Scripture" are as follows:

[1] If you don't know the Scriptures you will be mistaken (Matthew 22v29; Mark 12v24).

[2] The Scriptures must be fulfilled (Matthew 26v54,56; Mark 14v49).

[3] The Scriptures speak of Christ (Luke 24v27,44; John 5v39; Acts 18v28).

[4] The Scriptures need to be "opened" to you (Luke 24v32,45).

[5] Reason must start from a Scriptural base (Acts 17v2).

[6] Scripture cannot be broken (John 10v35).

[7] All Scripture is inspired by God and is profitable (2Timothy 3v16).

So all in all, the writings (or Scriptures), and that which was "written," are the authority for the saints. Throughout the Bible those to whom the Lord revealed Himself were given the charge to write down the message for all to heed. He gave this charge to Moses:

> *And the LORD said unto Moses, Write ... (Exodus 17v14, KJAV).*

And a similar one was also given to Isaiah, Jeremiah, and Habakkuk :

---

545   Holy (Romans 1v2; 2Timothy 3v15); Comfort (Romans 15v4); Prophetic (Romans 16v26).

> *Moreover the LORD said unto me, Take thee a great roll, and write in it with a man's pen ...*
> *(Isaiah 8v1, KJAV).*

> *Thus speaketh the LORD God of Israel, saying,* **Write** *thee all the words that I have spoken*
> *unto thee in a book. (Jeremiah 30v2, KJAV).*

> *And the LORD answered me, and said, Write the vision ... (Habakkuk 2v2, KJAV).*

Then at the end of the Bible we find a similar call to the apostle John:

> *"... What thou seest, write in a book ..." (Revelation 1v11, KJAV)*

There can be no doubt therefore, that from Genesis through to Revelation, the Lord not only revealed His will and word to men, but further that He instructed it to be written down as soon as was practically possible.

Chapter 8.

Pure and right.

Pure as precious silver.

We have an incredible witness to the veracity of Scripture, and one which is far better than that which may be provided by mere men, for He who can never tell a lie has given us His promise that His word is pure:

> *The words of the Lord are pure words, as silver tried in a furnace of earth, purified seven times. (Psalm 12v6, KJAV)*

The words of the Lord are not just pure words; they are absolutely 100% completely pure. In human understanding pure often means partially contaminated, but with respect to God's infallible, inerrant word, pure means absolute purity. We have two indications of the absolute purity of God's word in Psalm 12v6. First of all, the Hebrew word used in this verse for "pure" is derived from the Hebrew verb which means "to be clear," "to be bright," "to be pure, unmixed," and has the sense of "uncontaminated," "unadulterated," or "unmixed."[546] Then, we note that in the second half of this verse God's word is likened to silver that has been purified seven times. The number seven in Scripture signifies that which is complete, or that which is perfect.[547] Thus silver that has been purified seven times signifies silver that is completely 100% pure. Purifying another time would not increase its purity any more, because seven times purified implies completely purified. God's word is just like that – completely pure.

When it comes to extracting metals from the ground and refining or purifying them, modern industries use a range of sophisticated chemical and physical techniques. However the basic method for a precious metal (i.e. one that is relatively non-reactive) is to start from the fact that each element or compound in the ore has a precisely defined melting temperature. If the metal you want is found in an ore with other elements and compounds then by heating the mixture to the metal's melting point the metal is separated from the rest of the ore. Because metals have a higher density

---

546   Strong's number: 2891.
547   Genesis 2v1,2; Exodus 20v10; Revelation 1v4.

than most of the compounds in the ore, the solid un-melted parts will float to the surface of the molten metal. This unwanted material is called "dross" and is scooped away leaving the pure metal behind. However because the heated metal liquid is vigorously in motion you can never be sure that all of the solid components are fully removed to the surface. So, by repeatedly heating, melting and removing the dross, you have more chance of purifying the metal. If you want to extract a reactive metal you need to do more by way of chemical reactions and this has added problems for producing pure metals.

Now, no metal on earth has ever really been purified to 100% purity. The metals provided by such companies as Johnson Matthey Metals for the purpose of scientific research are probably the purest that have ever been attained.[548] These rarely get beyond 99.99% pure. Even if they could reach 99.999999% pure, (the cost would be astronomical), they could never reach total purity, since you only need one impure atom in a million to reduce the impurity level to 99.9999% pure. But a million atoms is a mere trifle! If we take silver as an example, then a million atoms of this precious metal would weigh only 1.8×10^{-16} g, or 0.00000000000000018g. Suppose, however, that we were to consider a normal everyday object of silver, like a ring for instance. Assuming that this ring weighed 10 grams, then it would contain slightly more than 5.5×10^{22}, (or fifty five thousand, million, million, million = 55,000,000,000,000,000,000,000), atoms of silver. Clearly the chance of making this ring 100% pure is nil, since we would have to ensure that all the atoms would be silver atoms. God's word is not like this, since it is like silver that has been purified seven times. In other words, it is like silver that has been so completely purified, that there are absolutely no impurities of any kind left whatsoever. Of course, God's word did not have to go through any process in order to be so pure. It is pure because it has come from the pure one – God Himself.

Although the precious word of God has endured many trials and vigorous assaults throughout the ages, it remains as pure as ever. C. H. Spurgeon once noted in commenting on Psalm 12v6:

> The Bible has passed through the furnace of persecution, literary criticism, philosophic doubt, and scientific discovery, and has lost nothing but those human interpretations which clung to it as alloy to precious ore.[549]

The true Christian who loves his/her Lord will cling to the Biblical doctrine of inerrancy, and will continue to accept as binding every word of the Bible to be the pure, unadulterated word of God. As we turn the pages of Scripture we find that we must agree with the proverb writer Agur son of

---

548   I used this company's reagents for my research work as a PhD student.
549   C. H. Spurgeon. Treasury of David. Volume 1, P161.

Jakeh, when he stated that:

> *Every word of God is pure. (Proverbs 30v5, KJAV)*

Furthermore, we accept wholeheartedly the words penned, under the inspiration of the Holy Spirit, by David:

> *"Thy word is very pure: therefore Thy servant loveth it." (Psalm 119v140, KJAV)*

Commenting on these words C. H. Spurgeon said of God's word, that:

> It is truth distilled, holiness in its quintessence. In the word of God there is no admixture of error or sin. It is pure in its sense, pure in its language, pure in its spirit, pure in its influence, and all this to the very highest degree – "very pure."[550]

That which is described as very pure, and moreover, as completely pure, is something which can confer its purity on those who seek out its treasures, for:

> *7 The law of the Lord is perfect, converting the soul: the testimony of the Lord is sure, making wise. 8 The statutes of the Lord are right, rejoicing the heart: the commandment of the Lord is pure, enlightening the eyes. (Psalm 19v7,8 – KJAV)*

God's word in its purity, therefore, enlightens the eyes of men, brings understanding to their souls, and leads them to salvation.[551] The word "pure" in Psalm 19v8 is derived from the Hebrew word which means "to separate that which is impure or drossy," or "to make clean and pure."[552] It has the sense of choosing or selecting that which is good from that which is impure. To those who are being saved, the elect or chosen of God, His word is a delight and a joy, pure and spotless wherein dwelleth no bad or evil thing. God's word, therefore, is absolutely pure. In Psalm 19v7 we are also told that God's law is perfect. C. H. Spurgeon interpreted the word "law" to mean:

> .... not merely the law of Moses but the doctrine of God, the whole run and rule of sacred writ.[553]

Thus we can say without fear of contradiction that not only is the entire word of God pure, but it is

---

550   C. H. Spurgeon. Treasury of David. Volume 6, P298.
551   Psalm 119v9; James 1v18.
552   Strong's number: 1262.
553   As for footnote 550. Volume 1, P87.

also perfect. Matthew Henry's comments on this verse are also worth repeating:

> It is perfectly free from all corruption, perfectly filled with all good, and perfectly fitted for
> the end for which it is designed; and it will make the man of God perfect, 2Timothy 3v17.
> Nothing is to be added to it nor taken from it.[554]

So that from Genesis 1v1 to Revelation 22v21, God's word is absolutely perfect. The Hebrew word
for "perfect" in Psalm 19v7 means "to complete," "to make full, perfect, entire," "to finish,"
"without blemish," "sound," or "uninjured." Thus the pure word of God which is utterly
uncontaminated by any impurity, is also perfect, complete, and finished. It cannot be added to, so
that there can be no more prophetic revelation of the type claimed by the likes of Joseph Smith,
Mary Baker Eddy, Charles Taze Russell, or modern day prophets, such as the Kansas City Prophets
who blew to prominence in 1991.[555] Thus we can concur with C. H. Spurgeon's further comments
on Psalm 19v7, when he said that:

> There are no redundancies and no omissions in the Word of God, ... The gospel is perfect in
> all its parts, and perfect as a whole: it is a crime to add to it, treason to alter it, and felony to
> take from it.[556]

The Bible is Holy.

The theme of purity naturally leads to the idea of holiness. Holiness implies absolute purity
and is a quality of God alone, who on fifteen occasions is called the "Holy One."[557] Holiness is that
characteristic of God which means that He cannot abide sin and evil. God is often described in
terms of being unapproachable, or of being a bright and glorious light, or of being an all-consuming
fire.[558] This is why in order to be a friend of God holiness is a pre-requisite.[559] The thought of any
sin or evil entering heaven, for example, is absurd. Now the Bible itself is described twice as being
"holy":

> *Which he had promised afore by his prophets in the holy Scriptures. (Romans 1v2, KJAV).*

> *And that from a child thou hast known the holy Scriptures, which are able to make thee wise*

---

554   Matthew Henry. Volume 3. P302.
555   Jospeh Smith founder of the Mormons, Mary Baker Eddy founder of Christian Science, Charles Taze Russell
founder of the Jehovah's Witnesses.
556   C. H. Spurgeon. Treasury of David. Volume 1. P308.
557   Psalm 71v22; 78v41; Isaiah 29v23; 30v15; 43v3; 48v17; 54v5; 55v5; 60v9; Jeremiah 51v5; Hosea 11v9;
Habakkuk 1v12; 3v3; Mark 1v24; Luke 4v34.
558   1Timothy 6v16; Hebrews 12v29.
559   Hebrews 12v14.

unto salvation through faith which is in Christ Jesus. (2Timothy 3v15, KJAV).

The fact that the Scriptures are holy is another vital truth which we must take hold of. Thus, we must recognise the essential link between a holy God and that which He has said, which must also be holy. Since the Scriptures are holy they must be free from error in the sense of sin and evil. It is imperative, therefore, that we ought to treat it as if it were in very fact *exactly* what God is saying out of His holy character. Remember the words of the Lord in the gospel of Matthew we have referred to frequently in this work:

> *But concerning the resurrection of the dead, have you not read what was spoken to you by God, saying. (Matthew 22v31).*

This statement comes at a point where the Lord is rebuking the Sadducees when they posed a "teaser" to Him. The phrase, "have you not read what was spoken to you" serves to indicate that when we read the Scriptures, we must take it as the Lord "speaking" to us. We have got into a dreadful situation these days because we only take a Scripture as "speaking to us" if we *feel* it is. How often do you hear some say "oh that Scripture doesn't speak to me"? We should remember that the Scriptures are holy and whenever we read them we are letting the holy God speak to us. We ought to tremble! We are not to treat the Bible as a mere human production or as a literary piece akin to Shakespeare, it is the very words *to us* from a holy God.

Right and true.

Having determined that the word of God is perfectly pure we could easily rest content at this point, and build upon this foundation. But David in Psalm 19 stipulates two other qualities of God's word, namely its righteousness, and, its truthfulness or faithfulness. The God of the Bible is a righteous God and there is no other beside Him. Furthermore, we know that all in the world, (except the Lord Jesus Christ), were born in sin and were totally depraved, devoid of any righteousness or righteous intent. But God's word, left in the world as a witness, is righteous through and through. It declares, without proof:

> *The statutes of the Lord are right, rejoicing the heart. (Psalm 19v8, KJAV).*
>
> *I know, O Lord, that Thy judgements are right .... (Psalm 119v75, KJAV).*
>
> *137 Righteous art Thou, O Lord, and upright are Thy judgements. 138 Thy testimonies that Thou hast commanded are righteous and very faithful. (Psalm 119v137,138, KJAV).*

Mike Viccary

The righteousness of Thy testimonies is everlasting .... (psalm 119v144, KJAV).

.... all Thy commandments are righteousness. (Psalm 119v172, KJAV).

God is righteous, and all that He declares and says is righteous in nature and in intent. In fact, our definition of righteousness must stem from the character of God as the Righteous One, which, in turn, we derive from His unadulterated word. What God has said therefore in His word is "right." Of course we must interpret it correctly, but the main point is that what is contained in Scripture is all correct and above board. It is "right."

Another characteristic of God's word is that it is true. We have so far considered the testimony that God's word is pure and that it is perfect. The fact that God's word is *pure* means that we have the words that God intended, and nobody else's, but the idea that God's word is *perfect* signifies that we have all that we need of God's word in the Bible, and there is no more to add. We must now add that God's pure and perfect word is all true. As with the definition of righteousness, the definition of truth must stem from the Lord Himself. He alone is true, (whilst all men have been found to be liars), and thus His word is true and even called "the truth."[560]

.... the judgements of the Lord are true and righteous altogether. (Psalm 19v9, KJAV).

All Thy commandments are faithful. (Psalm 119v86, KJAV).

The testimonies that Thou hast commanded are righteous and very faithful. (Psalm 119v138, KJAV).

.... Thy law is the truth. (Psalm 119v142, KJAV).

.... all Thy commandments are truth. (Psalm 119v151, KJAV).

I warm to C. H. Spurgeon's comments on Psalm 119v142. They are worth repeating here, since God's word is utterly discredited in this modern age:

> As God is love, so his law is the truth, the very essence of truth .... We hear great disputes about, "What is truth?" The holy Scriptures are the only answer to that question. Note, that they are not only true, but the truth itself. We may not say of them that they contain the truth, but that they are the truth: "thy law is the truth." There is nothing false about the law ....[561]

We read elsewhere in Scripture about the truth of God's word. Where better to turn, having

---

560   Romans 3v4.
561   C. H. Spurgeon. Treasury of David. Volume 6. P298,299.

considered David's testimony given and guided by the Holy Spirit, than to the great Son of David Himself? Speaking to His disciples during the week before He died, Jesus said:

> *Heaven and earth shall pass away, but My words shall not pass away. (Matthew 24v35, KJAV).*

And then a little later, on the night before He died, Jesus prayed to His Father and uttered these eternal words:

> *.... Thy word is truth. (John 17v7, KJAV).*

We can be sure, then, that God's word is true, if we believe the testimony given by David and the Lord Jesus Christ. If you have faith in Christ for salvation, you must also have faith in Him for His words. Believe then that God's word is 100% pure, completely perfect and absolutely true.

Truth that endures.

There may be some, however, who still question the veracity of Scripture in today's modern age. Surely the people of 2000 years ago and more, could not have anticipated today's modern ways and difficulties? How can the Bible speak to us in our modern world? It may have been truth back then in New Testament times, but surely is it relevant for today? Such questions as these and many others abound at a time when belief in the Bible is falling dramatically. How short sighted our hearts, and how shallow is our thinking and view of God when we say these things? God's word is, quite simply, God's word, written by Him using human agents. It is not the words of mere changeable men, for although God employed human beings to pen the words, He so overruled the work, that everything written or said and now contained in Scripture was exactly what God wanted to be written. Have a low view of God and you can mangle and distort Scripture to say whatever you wish. Increase your view of God and understand how awesome He is and you will respect His word as pure, perfect and true. If you do not believe that God's word is pure, perfect and true, you will never come to faith in Christ. There will always be the nagging doubt that something written may not be true or binding. It is true to say that only the truly converted, truly regenerate men, women and children will accept the absolute trustworthiness of the word of God. To these I say have faith to believe that God's word is utterly right. Always appeal to the word of God, for it is not the words of men trapped in a so-called backward culture and age, but the eternal words of the living God who created all things and is sovereign over all. To demonstrate the fact that God's word is not time-bound, and is applicable throughout the ages, let us turn once again to its own testimony concerning itself. This is God's word, remember, not just words uttered by ancient human beings, but the very words the Creator intended for us to hear and consider:

> *For the Lord is good; His mercy is everlasting; and His truth endureth to all generations. (Psalm 100v5, KJAV).*

> **89** *For ever, O Lord, Thy word is settled in heaven.* **90** *Thy faithfulness is unto all generations... (Psalm 119v89,90, KJAV).*

> *Concerning Thy testimonies, I have known of old that Thou hast founded them for ever. (Psalm 119v152, KJAV).*

> *Thy word is true from the beginning: and every one of Thy righteous judgements endureth for ever. (Psalm 119v160, KJAV).*

God's truth endures throughout all generations. His word is settled in heaven, and it can never be altered. Therefore, although it was written so long ago, the Bible has been preserved intact so that you and I can read what God wants us to know for today. Since God was so careful in the compilation of His word, surely He would also take pains in its preservation? If He went to such great lengths to provide people with His will in days long gone by, would He not see to it that that same will, plan, and purpose is kept intact for each new generation to discover? Imagine an author writing his life's work. He puts down the pen at the last word and sends it off to the publishers. Would he not fight tooth and nail for his work to be faithfully reproduced in printed form? I cannot believe that God is any less concerned about how His word appears in each new generation. I believe that God has so preserved His word that people of all generations can come to a knowledge of that which is pleasing unto Him through His word. What right, then, do we have in disbelieving it, or altering it by addition or subtraction? The whole counsel of God contained in Scripture is absolute truth, being pure and perfect. God has spoken from the very beginning of time.[562] In times past He spoke through the prophets, but in the last days, (that is, in between the first and second advents of the Lord Jesus Christ), He has spoken to us in His own precious Son.[563] Now the last of the four verses quoted above is a very precious verse for the Christian. It has a direct bearing on the first eleven chapters of the book of Genesis, for it states that right, from the beginning, God's words are true. Thus Genesis 1v1 is just as true as any other part of Scripture. Indeed Genesis chapters 1 to 11 are just as true as the gospels. Now modern translations have altered this verse, (Psalm

---

562   Isaiah 48v16.
563   Hebrews 1v1,2.

119v160), by changing the word, "beginning", to "sum" or "all." Thus the NASB has:

The sum of Thy word is truth .... (Psalm 119v160, NASB).

Whilst the NIV states:

All your words are true .... (Psalm 119v160, NIV).

The Hebrew word translated in these three different ways is: **"rô'sh."**[564] It has the following meaning, according to Strong's Exhaustive Concordance:

.... from an unused root apparently meaning to shake; the head (as most easily shaken) ....[565]

It is therefore most usually translated "head," "chief," "top," or "beginning" in the KJAV, (see table 8.1). The translation of **"rô'sh"** as "sum" is very interesting. It is translated in this way ten times in the KJAV, but eight of these have been changed in the NKJV to "census," (i.e. "head count"), or "count," an example followed by most other modern translations, as shown in table 8.2. We are left, therefore, with only two legitimate examples of **"rô'sh"** being translated as "sum."

Now where the KJAV translates **"rô'sh"** as "beginning" in Psalm 119v160, modern translations (as we have already noted), seem to have a problem. Three change it to "sum," the NKJV picks up the amplified meaning of the AMP, translating it "entirety," whilst the NIV abandons translation by substituting "all" (see table 8.2). Concerning Daniel 7v1, where we have the word **"rê'sh"**[566] translated as "sum" in the AJKV, other translations differ (see table 8.2). Interestingly enough, the NKJV which translates it as "main fact" has a marginal note pointing out the literal meaning of **"rê'sh,"** that is, "head." The NASB, which has "summary" has an alternative translation in the margin, namely, "beginning," whilst the AMP and the NIV go for "gist" and "substance" respectively. Only the RSV sticks with the KJAV translation "sum." Clearly there is some confusion. In view of the fact that in the overwhelming majority of cases **"rê'sh"** is translated "head" (twelve out of fourteen times – see table 8.1), it seems absurd to me to supply "sum" just for Daniel 7v1. The only other place where we have "sum" in the KJAV then, is Psalm 139v17, which reads:

---

564   Strong's number: 7218.
565   Strong's number: 7218.
566   Strong's number: 7217.

Table 8.1: English translations of the Hebrew word "rô'sh" [7218] in the KJAV[567].

%	English	No. in singular	No. in plural	Total	Notes[568]
58.9	Head	259	83	342	7217x12[569]
16.9	Chief	97	1[570]	98	7225x6; 7223x4; 7217x1
12.9	Top	67	8	75	--
2.4	Beginning	12	2	14	7225x18; 7223x4; 7221x1[571]
1.7	Captain	4	6	10	--
1.5	Sum[572]	9	--	9	7217x1[573]
1.0	First	6	--	6	7223x128; 7225x23[574]
0.9	Principal	5	--	5	7225x1
0.9	Company	5	--	5	--
0.9	High	3	2[575]	5	--
0.7	Chapiters	--	4	4	--
0.3	Band	--	2	2	--
0.3	End	--	2	2	--
0.3	Ruler	--	2	2	--
0.2	Excellent	1	--	1	--
0.2	Forefront	1	--	1	--
			TOTAL	581	

---

567   Following Strong's notation.
568   Similar Hebrew words translated the same as 7218. The table refers strictly to the use of 7218. Strong's entries for 7217, 7218, 7221, 7223 an 7225 are given below. The words underlined show how the Hebrew has been translated in the KJAV.

7217: **"rê'sh"** - (Chaldee). Corresponding to 7218: the head; fig. The sum: <u>Chief, Head, Sum.</u>

7218: **"rô'sh"** - from an unused root apparently meaning to shake; the head (as most easily shaken), whether lit. or fig. (in many applications, of place, time, rank, etc.): See table 1.

7221: **"rî'shâh"** - from the same as 7218; a beginning: <u>Beginning.</u>

7223: **"rî'shôn"** - from 7221; first in place, time or rank (as adjective or noun): <u>Ancestor, Before, Beginning, Eldest, First, Forefather, Foremost, Former, Of old time, Past.</u>

7225: **"rê'shî'yth"** - from the same as 7218: the first in place, time, order or rank (especially a firstfruit): <u>Beginning, Chief, First, Firstfruits, Principal thing</u>

569   Once in plural.
570   "Chiefest".
571   7221 in plural.
572   Scripture references for "sum": Exodus 30v12; Numbers 1v2,49; 4v2,22; 26v2; 31v26,49; Psalm 139v17.
573   Daniel 7v1.
574   7225 - "Firstfruits" (x12, once in singular).
575   "Highest" and "Height".

> *How precious also are Thy thoughts unto me, O God! How great is the sum of them! (Psalm 139v17, KJAV).*

Here in Psalm 139v17 we have the Hebrew word **"rô'shêhem"**[576] which, according to Davidson's Lexicon, is a masculine plural noun with third person masculine plural suffixes. Hence the universal translation "sum of them" (see table 8.2), rather than "heads, chiefs, or beginnings of them." I suspect that the translation of **"rô'shêhem"** in Psalm 139v17 as "sum" is probably correct in view of the fact that we have a plural form. It is difficult, though not impossible, to consider a vast number of the "beginnings" of God's thoughts towards man, but taking account of the context of verse eighteen, ("if I should count them"), "sum" meaning "the total inclusive sum" is probably a better choice.

Table 8.2: A comparison of the use of "rô'sh" [7218] as "sum" in various modern translations.

Scripture	KJAV	NKJV	RSV	NIV	NASB	AMP
Exodus 30v12	sum	census[577]	census	census	census[578]	census
Numbers 1v2	sum	census	census	census	census	census
Numbers 1v49	sum	census	census	census	census	census
Numbers 4v2	sum	census	census	census	census	census
Numbers 4v22	sum	census	census	census	census	census
Numbers 26v2	sum	census	census	census	census	census
Numbers 31v26	sum	count	count	count	count	count
Numbers 31v49	sum	count	count	counted	census	counted
Psalm 139v17	sum	sum	sum	sum	sum	sum
Psalm 119v160	beginning	entirety	sum	all	sum	sum[579]
Daniel 7v1[580]	sum	main fact[581]	sum	substance	summary[582]	gist

Going back to Psalm 119v160, however, there seems to be no reason whatsoever to translate **"rô'sh"** as "sum." This gives the distinct impression that God's word is only partially true, for the

---

576   From 7218.
577   That is, "head" count.
578   Literally, "sum" in margin.
579   [the total of the full meaning of all your individual precepts] – these words added by AMP to expand the meaning.
580   7217 Chaldee for 7218.
581   Margin: literally, "the head (or chief) of the words".
582   "Beginning" in margin.

"sum" of something could be taken to mean the summary or synopsis, and not the entirety. It should be remembered that Psalm 119 has been cleverly constructed. There are a total of 176 verses arranged in 22 groups or sections of eight. The beginning of each verse in any particular group starts with the same Hebrew letter. Each verse in the first group of 8 begins with the first letter of the Hebrew alphabet, א ("aleph"). The verses in the next group all begin with the second letter of the Hebrew alphabet, ב ("beth"). This continues through the 22 letters of the Hebrew alphabet, making a total of 176 verses. Now Psalm 119v160 is the last verse in the group of eight that begins with the Hebrew letter ר, ("resh"), which is equivalent to our letter "r." The word **"rô'sh"** was therefore selected by the Psalmist partially because it began with this particular Hebrew letter, ר, "resh." The verse in the KJAV states that from the beginning, God's word is true. We will expand on this thought later, but for the moment let us note that this verse is telling us that from its own beginning God's words are true. Thus the right or correct word is used here in the beginning of this verse. That is, the word **"rô'sh"** is the right word. Since its primary meaning is "head," and since it is the first word in the verse, then the correct rendition of this word should clearly be "head" in the sense of "beginning," (rather like at the "head" or beginning of the page). We note furthermore that **"rô'sh"** is not in the plural form, (cf. Psalm 139v17), so that "sum" is not implied. In view of all of these considerations, I propose that the KJAV rendering for **"rô'sh"** is Psalm 119v160 is preeminently preferable to the renderings given in the modern translations.

Verse 160 of Psalm 119 is a particularly interesting verse. The Hebrew is as follows:

$$\text{רֹאשׁ-דְּבָרְךָ אֱמֶת; וּלְעוֹלָם, כָּל-מִשְׁפַּט צִדְקֶךָ}$$

There is a clever symmetry in this verse. It consists of two clauses, each of which contain three Hebrew words, and is balanced by the central Hebrew word of the verse translated "for ever" in most translations. (NASB has "everlasting," NIV has "eternal"). We have an opening phrase: רֹאשׁ-דְּבָרְךָ אֱמֶת, a middle "fulcrum" word: וּלְעוֹלָם, and a final phrase: כָּל-מִשְׁפַּט צִדְקֶךָ. My translation is shown below in table 8.3.

Table 8.3: Translation of Psalm 119v160.

Hebrew phrase	Translation
רֹאשׁ-דְּבָרְךָ אֱמֶת	The beginning[583] of Your word [is] truth.
וּלְעוֹלָם	And to forever.
כָּל-מִשְׁפַּט צִדְקֶךָ	All judgements of Your righteousness [endure].

The middle or "fulcrum" word becomes a focus. The emphasis here is therefore, eternity. Thus we have two statements which pivot about the fulcrum. The first clause of three Hebrew words states:

The beginning of Thy word is[584] truth

The second clause (also with three Hebrew words), adds that:

all judgement of your righteousness endureth[585]

In between these two clauses we have the fulcrum word, which is simply translated "for ever" in the text.[586] In actual fact, however, a literal rendering of this Hebrew word reads: "and to for ever". Putting all this together we get:

The beginning of Thy word is truth

and to for ever

all judgement of your righteousness endureth

This translation seems to imply that the connecting fulcrum, (and to for ever), fits only with the second clause thus:

and to for ever all judgement of your righteousness endureth

---

583   The Hebrew word רֹאשׁ has been chosen to open this verse as it fits in the section in which all verses begin with the letter ר. The literal translation of this Hebrew word is "head" taken to mean at the start of something, (e.g. at the head of a letter). It is used in Genesis 1v1.
584   This verb is not in the original and must be supplied by the translator to make sense of the words in English. Often it is the verb "to be".
585   This verb is not in the original and must be supplied by the translator to make sense of the words in English. In this case it could be translated as simply "is" but the KJAV translators have supplied "endureth".
586   From 5769.

However, we could translate the conjunction (and) on our pivotal Hebrew word (for ever) as "even." Altering the fulcrum word to "eternity," which is identical in meaning to "for ever," this verse would then read:

> *The beginning of Thy word <u>is</u> truth*
> *even to eternity*
> *all judgement of your righteousness <u>endureth</u>*

The fulcrum now fits in with both clauses. We have:

> *The beginning of Thy word <u>is</u> truth even to eternity*

That is, from the beginning of thy word to the end, all is truth. Alternatively we could equally well say that the very beginning of God's word is always true, even until eternity. The second clause with the fulcrum reads:

> *even to eternity all judgement of your righteousness <u>endureth</u>*

Thus until the end of time and beyond, all of God's righteous judgements endure. So that from the beginning to the end, God's word and His judgement can be trusted as accurate and true, faithful and sure. Let us accept God at His word and lay all of our own ideas in the rubbish bin where they belong!

Now there are those who adulterate and mutilate Scripture by amalgamating it with other ancient documents in order to get at what they consider to be the "truth" concerning our origins, or other related matters.[587] What a Christian should say, however, is:

> *I understand more than the ancients because I keep Thy precepts. (Psalm 119v100, KJAV).*

It is so important to guard jealously the Scriptures. If we start to think that the Scriptures are wrong in certain parts and need the help of other documents, be they ancient Babylonian or modern scientific, we will shipwreck our faith. Remember what the Lord Jesus said: "the Scripture cannot

---

[587]   Fasold in his book: "The Discovery of Noah's Ark" used Babylonian accounts to modify and alter the Biblical record of the flood. Wiseman in his book: "Clues to Creation in Genesis" trusted to the Babylonian creation account in his interpretation of Genesis one. Ramm in his book (and many others besides): "The Christian view of Science and Scripture" appeals to modern science as a tool for interpreting Genesis one to eleven.

be broken."[588] If every word of God is pure, and all of His words are perfect, righteous and true, why should we turn to other stories, phrases or words which differ in detail from the Bible? Let every man be found a liar and God's word upheld as the truth.[589]

---

588   John 10v35.
589   Romans 3v4.

Chapter 9.

Universal (scope).

Introduction.

As a young man my chosen career path was as a research scientist. In my conversations with colleagues I was often the butt of people's jokes for trusting Scripture. How could I believe that old book when we have modern science? Surely modern science has made the Bible totally irrelevant and outmoded? Some would say to me things like: "the Bible is a pre-science ancient document" or "the Bible is not a textbook of science" or "the Bible has been abrogated by modern science." Sadly such statements have been accepted by many Christians. The Bible certainly does precede modern science but what does this really mean? I think this type of thinking is fuelled by an undercurrent of belief and acceptance of an evolutionary world view. It is almost by nature that people accept that what is modern or new must be better and more developed than what is older and ancient. The Bible is old – very old – and so must be primitive in its view point and teaching. It simply cannot compete with us moderns with our great modern science! Well if we reject the evolutionary world view and take the Biblical view of creation followed by the fall and the history enumerated by the Bible, we will take a different view point of such a statement that the Bible is pre-science. Remembering that the Bible is God's word and that he speaks truth for all ages we must conclude that whatever new-comer arrives through history the Bible is more than its equal. Just because modern science has risen from nothing over the last four hundred years, this is nothing to shout home about. There have been religions and philosophies which have come and then gone into oblivion. The Bible stands tall and defeats all.

The other oft quoted phrase – that the Bible is not a textbook of science – is equally lame when considered in light of the Bible's truths. The implied claim is that the Bible is not a rigorous set of discovered truths which have experimental and observational weight. The science textbook writer claims that he (or she) has put together a series of truths and systems which are the pinnacle of modern knowledge. No one has come up with these discoveries until now and therefore they cannot be bettered by anything in the past. For example, no one really considers Rutherford's model of the atom as being correct today as there has been one hundred years of experiments and study which has dug deeper than Rutherford was able to. So how can the Bible compete? Well what these scientists forget is that the Bible is God's word to man for all ages. The Creator who made what scientists call atoms and so on is the one who has revealed what we ought to know.[590] So clearly the Bible is over and above whatever science may describe or pronounce. It stands supreme above all things and is in a class of its own because it alone is the word of God. To develop this idea that Scripture covers all things we shall consider the following general themes:

> Statements of faith.
>
> Where do you cut the text.
>
> Who should be believed? God cannot lie?
>
> Some Scriptural proof.
>
> Wisdom comes from God not man.
>
> A look at particular disciplines.
>
> What God has given covers all areas of life.
>
> We have a new (world) view governed by Scripture.
>
> The world never satisfies.
>
> God is an abundant giver.

Statements of faith.

One of the unfortunate features of modern churches and their operation is the way in which certain things are done and carried out. It is sad that the church reflects the spirit of the modern age which is too fast and more inclined to consider the present rather than either the past or the future. Nothing is built to last and we seem to lurch from one fashion to the next in a stream of text and vision. But, as believers we must hold onto the beauties of the past and prepare our generations for what they will face. After all, the church is a continuum through time. This problem is nowhere more evident than in modern statements of faith. Before we proceed we need to establish exactly why we have such things. Isn't it sufficient to simply say: we believe the Bible? Well in many ways that would be sufficient. The problem arises when we consider the commission we have been given, which is to make fully known all that Christ has made know to us, and to make disciples of all peoples throughout the world. In keeping to this mission perspective we find that we must explain the details we have in Scripture and especially where the teachings conflict sharply with what the world holds dear. Our task is twofold. We must declare the truth as it is found in Scripture. This is why preaching – a declarative act – is so important. But there is another equally important task and that is to seek to persuade people of the truth of what we hold dear. We ought to be compassionate

---

590   They have not really got to the essence of what stuff we are made of if the truth be told.

and patient with our students, even when they give every appearance of being anything but studious and willing to learn. It is for such reasons that we ought to prepare statements of faith which set out clearly what we believe and why. Sadly what passes for such is often cut-and-pasted from elsewhere, or simply copied from a larger grouping, be it an agency or denominational organisation. Now of course, we ought to look at a variety of statements of faith, but unless we are expressing in our own words that which we believe and why, we are failing in our mission.

When it comes to many modern statements of faith, they not only reflect summarised versions of older statements, but crucially they also often limit the scope of the inspiration of Scripture to "matters of faith and practice," or "matters of salvation." I observed this when I was a deacon in a church we had been serving in shortly after leaving Bible College when our children were all young. At the same time I discovered that the older confessions like the Westminster Confession and the Baptist confession of 1689 were much fuller and deeper and seemed to have been constructed to counter the problems of the day. Modern statements, as I have said, are not like this. They are hurried documents usually constructed by very busy people who have so many other things to do! It would also seem that the simplifying of modern statements of faith, particularly with regard to the doctrine of Scripture, has been done in order to sit in both camps, as-it-were. The camp of the orthodox who believe the Bible to be God's word, and the camp of the modern scholar who believe that men can discover some truths (e.g. origins through science). However, although the Bible is mainly about Christ and his work, it does have a lot to say about many other subjects as well.[591]

It is pertinent to state at this point that we ought to be preparing statements of faith which address the problems and difficulties we face today. This is precisely what the framers of the Westminster confession did all those years ago. Top of the list of doctrines that ought to be clarified today is the doctrine of man. How the world is in a sea of confusion over man's make-up and constitution! Young people are being led astray in droves as they are being taught that identity is a matter of personal choice. The church ought to be issuing a clear message about exactly who man is. Man is, made by God and not evolved, made in His image, made male and female, and made with a spiritual component as well as a physical one. Since God made us, we have no right to determine who or what we should be! Then further we ought to be answering the many questions posed by genetics and genetic engineering. There are other burning issues which we ought to be facing and our statements of faith should reflect these issues with a clear and compassionate representation of the gospel as it applies to these things.

---

591   Luke 24v27; John 5v39.

Mike Viccary

Where do you cut the text?

The doctrine of inspiration cannot be limited merely to statements of salvation or faith or religious practice. This is because it is impossible to disentangle statements about salvation from statements that mention history, geography or science. For example, our Lord Jesus Christ does not hesitate to refer to Adam and Eve as historical people when talking about divorce. By laying down teaching on divorce and adultery using such a passage of Scripture, He is making use of a document which teaches about our origins which is in flat denial with what science currently teaches. As another example He refers to Jonah's experiences in the belly of a large fish as being typical of His death and resurrection. The fact of His death and resurrection is made certain and sure (in the mind of Christ and thence to His hearers) by this reference to Jonah. Christ clearly accepted the historicity and actuality of Jonah's experience and made use of this to teach concerning His death and resurrection.

The whole history of Israel is used to teach about salvation. If the history of Israel is wrong then why believe the teaching about salvation derived from it? Much salvation doctrine is taught using the example of Noah and his experiences. If the historical details of this story are wrong what about the teaching derived from the events? If the flood was local this must mean that some people escaped the catastrophe (living away from that region). If this is so, then salvation is possible outside the ark! In New Testament terms this means that the exclusivity of the gospel (by grace through faith in Christ alone) falls. Further, it would mean that the next great catastrophe (fire) culminating in the final judgement can be escaped also.[592] Clearly these conclusions make nonsense of what these writers intended for us to understand. One writer who concluded that the flood was a local affair suggested that it was then possible to reconstruct the Genesis genealogies to make then accord with the "known" chronologies as derived from archaeology.[593] Such thinking flies in the face of the whole nature of Scripture. Dare we ever say that God needs our help? Of course not! Why then do we stoop to such nonsense of suggesting that God's word needs our help and reconstruction?

Who should be believed? God cannot lie!

We come to the point of asking who should be believed? Why should we believe men's ideas and discoveries over and above what God has said? We remind ourselves that the Almighty God cannot lie. This is not only self-evident from a consideration of God's character, but also

---

592　See 2Peter 3.
593　David I Dye. Faith and the Physical World. Paternoster Press. 1966.

explicitly stated in Scripture.[594] It is an impossibility for God to lie! Think of the consequences of a God who could lie. Such a thought leads to the destruction of holiness, purity, truth, honour, wisdom and so on. The Scriptures make abundantly clear that it is the devil, Satan, who was the father of lies.[595] That being the case, if God revealed by inspiration all of the books (or sections) of the One Book the Bible, it must all be true and pure, as the Scriptures affirm.[596] Given these unassailable facts the question of whom to believe is resolved very simply. We must believe God! We must believe what He has said.

People probably believe in man's ideas rather than what God reveals for a number of reasons. Let us consider three possible suggestions. First, they do not realise that men's discoveries are actually inventions. Most people have a problem discerning what is true and factual from what is perceived or theoretical. The world has done a masterful job of destroying the simple notion that all things come from the hand of God and that our ideas and thoughts ought to be shaped by what God reveals. Somehow we seem to believe that we as human beings are independent and autonomous, as though we have a right to determine truth for ourselves. This is patent nonsense. There is no neutrality for all of us have a particular angle (or world view) which we have inherited or which we have been bullied into holding as true. What the world publishes as "truth" is nothing of the sort. Science, for example, has not "discovered" that man is an evolved creature, it has invented this story and believed in it, seeking to promote it at all costs. In many other ways the world presents as "truth" many things which are in fact the inventions of someone's mind.

A second possible reason is that they do not fully believe in the inspiration of Scripture. Perhaps one of the saddest things amongst those who own the name "Christian" is the lack of trust in the Scripture's true origins. The plethora of ideas on how the Scriptures have come about seem to be strewn with the precept and principle that they are born from man and not from God. Seeking to gain a footing in the world of academia, or trying to appease the world so that a voice can be heard, many have weakened their view of Scripture. If people really believed that Scripture is pure and all that God wanted us to know, then what a powerful thing those who hold such views would turn out to be. The Scriptures do not need our support for they, being God's word, are living and effective. However we often lament the weakness of the church in our day. If we aligned ourselves with what Scripture says about itself (that it is God's very word), we would begin to see the power of God at work. Of course we would suffer. We would be marginalised and persecuted as the word of God has been in every age. But none could stop us because we would be within the plan and purpose of

---

594   Hebrews 6v18; Titus 1v2.
595   John 8v44.
596   Psalms 12v6; 119v142,151,160; Proverbs 30v5,6; John 17v17.

God!

A third reason is that they probably have a fear of man and no fear of God. It all comes down to whom we truly fear. Whom do we give the highest honour to? When people equivocate on creation, or soften their approach to sexuality and human identity, or explain away problem areas of Scripture as they impinge on modern society, they betray their allegiance to the world. How sad. How foolish. This all comes down to whom people *see* and, therefore, worship. If we see the world and men all around with their power, their money, their influence, their support and so on, then it isn't surprising that we will defer to its authority. If, on the other hand, we see Christ and His wonderful work in all we do and experience, then surely our true sight of Him will govern our thoughts and lead us aright. How important it is to gain a sight of the Saviour daily, hourly, moment-by-moment! Can I appeal to the reader to make it of singular importance to seek Christ at all times and at all costs!

Some Scriptural proof.

In the following Scriptures we seek to show how the Bible covers all areas of life and its scope is universal. Far from just enabling us to go to heaven, it also governs how we should think about how the heavens go.[597] Our first Scripture gives us a definitive statement with regard to the scope and universal reach of the Bible:

> *I have seen an end of all perfection: but thy commandment is exceeding broad. (Psalm 119v96).*

"Broad" means "roomy in all directions." There is a contrast set up here between the "commandment" (shorthand for the word of God although focusing on what we ought to do), and what can be seen in the world where there is "an end of all perfection" (an ironic statement concerning what may be considered by men to be perfect but isn't really). The point is this: If you can see an "end" to perfection it isn't very deep and it isn't very perfect really! Spurgeon's comments on this verse are worth recalling here:

> Perfect men, in the absolute sense of the word, live only in a perfect world. Some men see no end to their own perfection, but this is because they are perfectly blind. The experienced believer has seen an end of all perfection in himself, in his brethren, in the best man's works.[598]

---

597   This is the statement Galileo made (see earlier).
598   C. H. Spurgeon. Treasury of David. Volume II. P216.

From a believing point of view the statement of Psalm 119v96 is obvious. God is omnipotent, omniscient, omnipresent whilst men are limited, mortal and depraved. Clearly the Bible does not teach everything about all subjects, but it does enough (and more) to lay the foundations for all subjects. However the Bible must be the starting point for all endeavours whatever they may be.

Wisdom comes from God not man.

One other way we can reinforce this idea that Scripture must speak as authoritative on all subjects and experiences is to consider wisdom. Where does wisdom come from? Can man be wise from himself? We shall consider again what the Bible has to say on this subject. Paul wrote these words to the Romans:

> *Oh, the depth of the riches both of the wisdom and knowledge of God! How unsearchable are His judgements and His ways past finding out! (Romans 11v33).*

Paul informs us here that God's ways are *infinitely* deep and unsearchable. That indicates not only that God is the fount of all wisdom, but further that nothing, and no one else can compare in wisdom. Our next Scripture is one of those which ought to be memorised by believers. Again we read Paul's words, this time to the Colossian Christians:

> *... of Christ, in whom are hidden all the treasures of wisdom and knowledge. (Colossians 2v2,3).*

This, to my mind, is unsurpassable. Since **all** the treasures of wisdom and knowledge are to be found in Christ, and since we only read of Christ in the Scriptures, it follows that the Scriptures contain all the treasures of wisdom and knowledge too. How then should we engage in research (of any kind)? Well if we pursue such a quest we will fail terribly if we neglect the Lord Jesus Christ. Next we shall consider some words from the prophet Isaiah:

> **8** *"For My thoughts are not your thoughts, nor are your ways My ways," says the Lord.* **9** *"For as the heavens are higher than the earth, so are My ways higher than your ways, and My thoughts than your thoughts. (Isaiah 55v8,9).*

The Lord contrasts His thoughts and ways with the distance between heaven and earth. The sense appears to be more in terms of direction as well as in degree. Thus God's thoughts are also heavenly and pure, whilst our thoughts are earthly and defiled. God's thoughts encompass the universe, ours are limited to one small planet.

The following words from the book of Proverbs need no explanation!

For the Lord gives wisdom; from His mouth come knowledge and understanding. (Proverbs 2v6).

Who else can give wisdom? James teaches us that if we lack wisdom we should ask God who gives with liberality.[599] Here the whole point is that no one else can give such a gift. Furthermore we learn that it comes from the Lord's "mouth," or what He speaks. In other words wisdom comes from hearing God speak, and we only hear God speak through His word, the Bible.

As a contrast to God having wisdom, we could look at what man has to offer. In Psalm 94 we read these searching and important words:

The Lord knows the thoughts of man, that they are futile. (Psalm 94v11).

The word translated "futile" is "breath" and signifies emptiness, that which is transitory or vain. Such are the thoughts of mankind! Even the great thoughts of Einstein, Hawking and Shakespeare are of no account. The prophet Isaiah has a similar message:

Sever yourselves from such a man, whose breath is in his nostrils; for of what account is he? (Isaiah 2v22).

Why take thought of man and his schemes? Of what value are his ideas and words? In the next Scripture, from Jeremiah, we learn not just that the wisdom of the wise is futile, but the reason for this statement:

The wise men are ashamed, they are dismayed and taken. Behold, they have rejected the word of the Lord; so what wisdom do they have? (Jeremiah 8v9).

Isn't it so true that the wise of this world reject God and His word? I think it doesn't really need establishing. However the world and its systems and ideas are never grounded in Christ and His word. Rather they are based on man-made ideas and schemes. The wise men are ashamed because they have not rescued the people or provided any means of escape. In the same way our wise men have not solved the problems we face today. In fact they have not scratched the surface of solving

---

599   James 1v5.

the difficulties we face. I will go further. They haven't even established what the main problem is! By rejecting the Lord and His word, the wise men of every age show that they have no wisdom. How wise is it to reject the One who alone can provide answers? Who in their right mind would reject the Author of all things? In Jeremiah we also learn that we cannot boast in any achievements of man. This is obvious because nothing man does has any lasting effect. Think of the Egyptians with their great buildings and exploits! Or think of the Greeks, the Romans, the British Empire, the Americans and so on. What have these great nations and empires achieved? When we look at history isn't the chief theme war?

> *8 Thus says the Lord: "let not the wise man glory in his wisdom, let not the mighty man glory in his might, nor let the rich man glory in his riches; 9 but let him who glories glory in this, that he understands and knows Me, that I am the Lord, exercising loving kindness, judgement, and righteousness in the earth. For in these I delight," says the Lord. (Jeremiah 9v23,24).*

It really isn't possible to boast except in what God is and has done. It is worth repeating Paul's words here:

> *But God forbid that I should boast except in the cross of our Lord Jesus Christ, by whom the world has been crucified to me, and I to the world. (Galatians 6v14).*

Notice that Paul claims that the world (and hence all it contains including its wisdom) has been crucified to him. In Jeremiah again we read of the great contrast between what God has done and is doing, and all that man in his idolatry does:

> *12 He has made the earth by His power, He has established the world by His wisdom, and has stretched out the heavens at His discretion. 13 When He utters His voice, there is a multitude of waters in the heavens: "and He causes the vapours to ascend from the ends of the earth. He makes lightning for the rain, He brings the wind out of His treasuries." 14 Everyone is dull-hearted, without knowledge; every metalsmith is put to shame by an image; for his moulded image is falsehood, and there is no breath in them. 15 They are futile, a work of errors; in the time of their punishment they shall perish. (Jeremiah 10v12-15).*

In this Scripture we are reminded of God's creative and sustaining power which overshadows all that man may do or think. The contrast is concluded by stating that all people are "dull-hearted" and "without knowledge." All the idols that are made, including the current idol evolution, are futile and the "work of errors."

Mike Viccary

For our final two Scriptures we turn to Paul's first letter to the Corinthians. The cross of Christ may appear foolish to the world, but it is the power of God for those being saved:

> *18 For the message of the cross is foolishness to those who are perishing, but to us who are being saved it is the power of God. 19 For it is written: "I will destroy the wisdom of the wise, and bring to nothing the understanding of the prudent." 20 Where is the wise? Where is the scribe? Where is the disputer of this age? Has not God made foolish the wisdom of this world? (1Corinthians 1v18-20).*

What God has done in sending His Son to die undoes everything attempted by man. All the "wisdom" that man may appear to have is utter rubbish when God's wisdom in Christ is revealed. Where then is the wisdom of this world? It is destroyed by the coming of Christ. It is shown up for what it is – futile. In our last Scripture we come full circle as we note Paul's quoting of Psalm 94v11:

> *18 Let no one deceive himself. If anyone among you seems to be wise in this age, let him become a fool that he may become wise. 19 For the wisdom of this world is foolishness with God. For it is written, "He catches the wise in their own craftiness"; 20 and again, "The Lord knows the thoughts of the wise, that they are futile." (1Corinthians 3v18-20).*

Paul urges us to reject the accolades of this world. Do we have this world's approbation? Are we lauded by this world for our achievements and wisdom? If true this would be a sad indictment on us. This world's wisdom is foolishness as far as God is concerned. Why then would we want to accept it, trade with it and follow it? What madness!

Since God is all-powerful and all-knowing, and since we know we are limited and sinful, we must concur with all that the Scriptures above reveal. When confronted with a call from the leaders to go to the spiritualists and mediums for guidance, the Lord instructed Isaiah to go to the law and the testimony (i.e. the word of God).[600] In the same way when people say to us to listen to the scientists, the businessmen, the great and the intellectuals of this world, our ready response is to say "But God says ..."!

A look at particular disciplines.

Our modern statements of faith, and the heritage of enlightenment thinking has convinced us that the world has something to offer. However, the Bible warns us not to drink from any other

---

600   Isaiah 8v19,20.

source, especially not the broken cisterns of this world.[601] We can see how we have limited the scope of Scripture by considering the many intellectual pursuits. For example, the physical sciences, the historical sciences, history, literature, geography/humanities, anthropology and so on. Which of these, we ask in vain, has Scripture as its basis and foundation?

Ever since the days following the Reformation and the Scientific Revolution of the sixteenth and seventeenth centuries, the pursuit of intelligent subjects has proceeded on an independent footing aside from the authority of the Bible. In the early days of the Christian church, most, if not all, of these pursuits were conducted within the church's authority. In the thirteenth century, for example, we have Thomas Aquinas attempting to meld theology with the thought and work of Aristotle. Such a pursuit, of course, was a mistake, but that it was a cleric who embarked on the work at least informs us that intellectual pursuits stemmed from some form of Biblical beginning. The Reformation saw to it that the Scriptures were given back their autonomy and rightful place at least for the Christian. Prior to this the church with its hierarchy, its traditions and so forth was ruler over man. We cannot stop here to develop how right or skewed this situation was, but merely point out that the church was, by and large, in charge. At the reformation Scripture was re-instated as authoritative, but (sadly) not in all intellectual pursuits.

At the Reformation, science was wrested from the grip of the church (a good thing) but unfortunately it was allowed complete autonomy and although the early pioneers of science held to many Christian principles and virtues (e.g. Robert Boyle) some did not, and later exponents of science rapidly departed from Christian roots. Early thinkers like Francis Bacon had an inadequate view of creation and, particularly, of the fall. Bacon believed that it was actually possible to reverse the effects of the fall through the new philosophy. We have already described how the idea of "two books," and the relationship between creation and Scripture, changed through these times. The end result was that science progressed with no sure and grounded footing. The science practised today bears little real resemblance to that initiated by such pioneers as Kepler and Boyle who held tenaciously to Scripture.

A look at some current intellectual pursuits.

We shall look briefly at a variety of intellectual pursuits and their status in connection to the word of God.

---

601   Jeremiah 2v13,

Origins.

The whole aim of scientists working in the area of origins is to deny God's existence. It was early Greek thinkers who sought to consider all things without reference to any supernatural referents. Modern science has as one of its statements of faith that the supernatural does not exist. Even though there have been attempts at challenging evolutionary thought from the likes of Halton Arp and Fred Hoyle in astronomy, and Michael Behe and other Intelligent Design followers in biology, the vast majority of scientists keep within the accepted paradigm. Opponents of evolution are dismissed and dealt with harshly by the community of scientists who are hell bent on keeping science free from what they consider to be any interference from religious belief. However such "scientists" are blind to the fact that science in every age has always had some form of belief system at its base. Currently it is the faith of secular atheistical humanism. But why should this be adequate? It seems merely a matter of choice and consensus, that is all.

Psychology.

Our current understanding of ourselves is quite literally, woeful. (We could include here the subject of anthropology – the study of man and his culture). There are as many psychotherapies and counselling styles/courses as there are people who go in for this sort of thing. When we realise how much the West has lost in allowing secular humanism to take from Biblical practice it is horrific. In the 18th and 19th centuries most counselling would occur through the family and through the local pastor. Indeed the right preaching of God's word will also counsel the people (even the unregenerate God-fearers). However, we now seem to be in a sorry state where even pastors refer the "sick of mind" to secular psychologists! This is utterly absurd and should not be allowed to continue. The Scriptures are very broad and can deal with the sickness (sin) of the mind.

Genetic engineering.

Does God not have something to say about this subject? After all He is the Creator! We seem to be at the mercy of science here. Ethical considerations are based on the pursuit of knowledge! I am extremely worried both about the developments in the relevant sciences here, and, more importantly, about the lack of a Biblical response from Christians.

History & Archaeology.

Surely the God of history (so much of salvation is historically based) has given us the world's chronology? Why do we still insist on accepting chronologies derived by men who dig in the earth, and construct a timeline based on evolutionary principles taking Egypt's data as sacred? Is not God's word to be believed here? Can not God tell us the truth about history?

Subjects covered in Scripture.

The following list is not exhaustive. It is meant to give an indication that the Bible has much to say on all subjects:

Where we have come from (origins): One Maker, One Creation, One family.

The nature of creation (it's make-up and workings).

The value of worldly philosophy.

The true nature and composition of man (starting point for counselling and for genetic engineering).

Family life.

Marriage.

Sex & sexuality.

Recreation.

National life.

Proper government.

The history of the world.

How to work for an employer.

What truly satisfies.

How we should live and behave.

How we should relate to others.

What we are to do in and with life.

How to be a steward (of time, money).

....

We remind ourselves that the central theme of the Bible is the Lord Jesus Christ, but the above subjects flow out of our knowledge of the Lord, as we ask such questions as may be posed from the topics above.

What God has given covers all areas of life.

There is one Scripture which clearly tells us that what God has given to us through the knowledge of Him is **all that we need**:

> *2 Grace and peace be multiplied to you in the knowledge of God and of Jesus our Lord, 3 as His divine power has given to us all things that pertain to life and godliness, through the knowledge of Him who called us by glory and virtue, 4 by which have been given to us exceedingly great and precious promises, that through these you may be partakers of the divine nature, having escaped the corruption that is in the world through lust. (2Peter 1v2-4).*

If He has given us all things that pertain unto living a godly life here on planet earth, then it must mean that the Scriptures are broad, and will tell us how to proceed in all the circumstances of life. Negatively it means we do not have to go to the secular humanists for help or to the scholars for wisdom. Scripture is our tool for all eventualities. It is the manual of life. How should we run our family? Scripture has the answer.

We have a new (world view) governed by Scripture.

When once we are saved by the Lord He gives us new eyes. Our world view is radically altered. No longer do we see merely the physical world in which we indulge only our own pleasures and wants. Now we see that we have wronged a holy God who actually made us and therefore owns us. Now we see that He has been so merciful and gracious to make known to us the error of our ways and to show us the reality and the truth of life and death. Now we see His incredible love to us in sending His Son! Does not this all lead us to realise that if we have been so wrong in what we once believed concerning our life's journey, that we must also be wrong about many other things as well (influenced and taught by the world, our parents, society etc.)? Furthermore, if we cannot trust the world when it comes to the most important issue of life and death, why should we trust it on the everyday things? Hear the word of the Psalmist:

> *98 You, through Your commandments, make me wiser than my enemies; for they are ever with me. 99 I have more understanding than all my teachers, for Your testimonies are my meditation. 100 I understand more than the ancients, because I keep Your precepts. (Psalm 119v98-100).*

We understand more than anyone else because we accept what is freely given to us by God.[602] Remember that Proverbs 3v6 teaches us that He will direct our paths **if** we acknowledge Him no matter what the subject ("in all thy ways"). Why then should we ever turn to the world for direction in any pursuit?

---

602   Deuteronomy 29v29; 1Corinthians 2v12.

The world never satisfies.

It is one thing to consider the infinite nature of God and all His gifts to us, but another to think about what men have to offer. The works of men, including their intellectual pursuits, never satisfies. This point is not one merely made by Christians but accepted by all who think or experience life. The man who accumulates so much wealth he cannot spend it all is left wondering what the purpose of it all is. The actor who achieves every accolade going still wants further recognition. The champion of champions is not satisfied until he makes the next final and gains the next prize. Solomon was such a man. He had wealth, fame and ability that was second to none. Here is how he sums life up:

> *1 The words of the Preacher, the son of David, king in Jerusalem. 2 "Vanity of vanities," says the Preacher; "vanity of vanities, all is vanity." (Ecclesiastes 1v1,2).*

When all is said and done, life "under the sun" (i.e. without any reference to God) is vacuous and empty. The book of Ecclesiastes is well worth considering. Solomon had it all and he tried to find out what was of true value. But as he pursued his enquiry, he found that one of the biggest problems was that he must leave all because of his coming death:

> *18 Then I hated all my labour in which I had toiled under the sun, because I must leave it to the man who will come after me. 19 And who knows whether he will be wise or a fool? Yet he will rule over all my labour in which I toiled and in which I have shown myself wise under the sun. This also is vanity. 20 Therefore I turned my heart and despaired of all the labour in which I had toiled under the sun. (Ecclesiastes 2v18-20).*

This great problem of death is hardly considered by modern man. Evolution has sought to shove it under the carpet by using it as a means of generating novel and new life. But when a man considers life the question of its end is a big problem.

That the things of earth bring very little satisfaction can be shown by looking at what the prophet Isaiah, under inspiration of the Spirit, wrote some 600 years before Christ came into our world.

> *Why do you spend money for what is not bread, and your wages for what does not satisfy? Listen carefully to Me, and eat what is good, and let your soul delight itself in abundance. (Isaiah 55v2)*

Or listen to what our Lord Jesus said when he challenged the wisdom of the age in which He came:

Mike Viccary

For what profit is it to a man if he gains the whole world, and loses his own soul? Or what will a man give in exchange for his soul? (Matthew 16v26. Cf. Mark 8v36)

That the Scriptures teach unequivocally that whatever man does and seeks will never satisfy is surely demonstrated by these verses. However we can easily demonstrate this same truth by considering the world of scientific research. Most research projects start by posing a relatively simple question defined by prior research. Tasks are designed to answer that question. This includes literature research, thought, mathematics, experimentation, analysis, computation all of which is conducted in a cyclical manner. After a period of time the result is a partial answer and a dozen more questions that were not envisaged at the start of the project. This is a great delight to the scientist because he has new research tasks to do (if he can convince the people with the money!). In passing it is also noteworthy that often scientific research is organised in such a way so as to get the money it needs, and so is never really what the *pure* scientist wishes or desires. Coming back to the main point of any research. What really results (partial answers and many more questions) is, however, very unsatisfying to the true seeker for truth, for science as a process merely diverges. It never converges towards a unifying concept that embraces all. We should remember that what appears to be unity amongst scientists is merely the dominance of personality (and money/influence) over menial servants. I will conclude this theme with a personal note. My PhD supervisor was an expert in his field. He once said to me that what he knew about the subject (solid state chemistry) amounted to merely a scratch on the surface of an iceberg (much less than the tip of the iceberg!).

In contrast God's word fully satisfies the true believer. It tells us the truth, it provides a remedy for our lost condition, it is our communion with the Lord, and it is our unfailing guide in life. All a believer's questions and worries are laid to rest. All can be seen clearly from God's perspective. This is not to say that some questions which are asked will be answered, because some aren't in fact answered at all. But this is because many questions people ask are illegitimate. The question is wrong. For example, imagine someone assumed that the moon was made of cheese and fully believed this. The question: is the moon made of Cheddar or Camembert? may be an important one for the person who believes the moon is made of cheese, but for the rest of us it is a non-question, a question that should never have been asked. We must always remember that we are at war with the world and with the tempter (Satan). We must also remember that God has put eternity in the hearts of men and yet so that they will not in and of themselves be able to find it or reach it. It is put there to frustrate them in their own self-effort and self-reliance in the hope that they will turn to the Lord for help who is the only help (but what a help!).[603]

God is an abundant giver.

The world never satisfies. The world is not enough. In stark and unimaginably wonderful contrast, God is a wonderfully abundant giver. The Scriptures give repeated testimony to this truth. On the opening pages we note first that God is abundant in His creative efforts:

> *Then God said, "Let the waters abound with an abundance of living creatures, and let birds fly above the earth across the face of the firmament of the heavens." (Genesis 1v20).*

But elsewhere we find that God is extremely liberal with His gifts. Listen first to Paul's words to the Ephesians:

> ***20** Now to Him who is able to do exceedingly abundantly above all that we ask or think, according to the power that works in us, **21** to Him be glory in the church by Christ Jesus to all generations, forever and ever. Amen. (Ephesians 3v20,21)*

The Lord wills to do "exceedingly abundantly above" that which we can ask. This is remarkable. Why ever would any person ever reject what this God can do? To Timothy Paul wrote that God's grace, His unmerited, undeserved favour is "exceedingly abundant" too:

> *And the grace of our Lord was exceedingly abundant, with faith and love which are in Christ Jesus. (1Timothy 1v14).*

Our salvation involves the work of the Holy Spirit who washes us. The Lord does not give half-heartedly, for the Lord gives us His presence by the Spirit "abundantly"!

> ***5** ... not by works of righteousness which we have done, but according to His mercy He saved us, through the washing of regeneration and renewing of the Holy Spirit, **6** whom He poured out on us abundantly through Jesus Christ our Saviour. (Titus 3v5,6).*

In this next verse we find once again that God was willing and determined to show His extravagance in giving!

> *Thus God, determining to show more abundantly to the heirs of promise the immutability of His counsel, confirmed it by an oath. (Hebrews 6v17).*

---

603   Ecclesiastes 3v11; 1John 2v15; 5v18.

God's mercy is abundant too:

> *Blessed be the God and Father of our Lord Jesus Christ, who according to His abundant mercy has begotten us again to a living hope through the resurrection of Jesus Christ from the dead. (1Peter 1v3).*

The entrance into heaven for His saints is also one of abundance too:

> *... for so an entrance will be supplied to you abundantly into the everlasting kingdom of our Lord and Saviour Jesus Christ. (2Peter 1v11).*

Then further, the Lord gives with liberality to those who ask:

> *5 If any of you lacks wisdom, let him ask of God, who gives to all liberally and without reproach, and it will be given to him. 6 But let him ask in faith, with no doubting ... (James 1v5,6).*

The Saviour pointed out that even earthly fathers know how to give good gifts. That being so then surely the Father in heaven would be better?

> *If you then, being evil, know how to give good gifts to your children, how much more will your Father who is in heaven give good things to those who ask Him! (Matthew 7v11).*

Elsewhere we read of how He gives to us:

> *The young lions lack and suffer hunger; but those who seek the Lord shall not lack any good thing. (Psalm 34v10).*

> *For the Lord God is a sun and shield; the Lord will give grace and glory; no good thing will He withhold from those who walk uprightly. (Psalm 84v11).*

The Father of His children will never let them lack what they truly need. Does this mean that God's people will always live in comfort, in peace, with health and wealth? This we cannot guarantee, for the people of God are His ambassadors and may suffer the indignities and antagonism of the country and the folk amongst whom they reside for a time. After all, the Saviour was crucified. Did not His Father give Him everthing necessary for the mission He came to carry out? Of course! The trouble is that we have such earth-focused eyes. The Lord will never fail us. Nevertheless, the representatives of Christ may be required to suffer greatly in order that their witness to God's goodness can be seen despite the rejection by men.

We cannot leave this subject of God's extravagance and abundance without considering the greatest gift of all. The Lord gave His One and Only Son:

> *He who did not spare His own Son, but delivered Him up for us all, how shall He not with Him also freely give us all things? (Romans 8v32).*

How great and all-sufficient is the Lord!

Chapter 10.

Sufficient.

Introduction.

There has been a tremendous battle over the last fifty years or so over what is required for a believer in their walk with the Lord. Charismatics place a huge emphasis on the experience of the Holy Spirit which is defined in a multitude of ways, such as, baptism in the spirit, speaking in tongues and so on. These folk include at one end of the spectrum those who lean entirely on their subjective perception of the Holy Spirit for a guide. They often ridicule anyone who points to Biblical doctrines and suggest that such folk do not have the Spirit of Christ. Then there are those who are enamoured by the academic or scholarly world and who suggest that we cannot really understand what God is saying without recourse to science or academia. How can you understand Genesis, these folk say, without understanding the Ancient Near East cultures around which Genesis was constructed? Then there are those of an ecumenical persuasion who suggest that the rich tradition of the church throughout the ages must be taken on board. These three general attitudes to how a Christian ought to proceed are what I call the "Bible and ..." brigade. However the Scriptures teach unequivocally that the only thing required by a new believer is the Scriptures.

We do not need science, nor any other secular or man-made schema to understand the Bible. Many may protest and say that without understanding something of grammar, of language and of how geography works or of how ordinary things behave, nothing in the Bible could be apprehended at all. Of course all of us are human beings who experience this world that God has created and we understand certain things by experience. If you let go of the cup you may be holding we all know that it will fall to the ground. But do we need to know the current understanding of gravity to discern Biblical teaching? Of course not! Then there are those who say that without understanding the nature of man and his mind, how can you grasp the interactions between people in Scripture. It is here where my blood begins to boil for many misguided folk have bought into the lie that psychology is a rule by which we must understand the Scriptures. A thousand times no to this poxy idea! The Scriptures reveal how man thinks and why he does so, far better and more perfectly than any psychology ever will do.

We do not need the traditions of any church or the practices of any group throughout history in order to understand and study God's word. Now let me immediately state that to ignore what other churches have come to believe and to forget church history is a very foolish thing. What I am contending for here is that the Scriptures alone are our guide and rule. No church council, no creed or confession should ever take the place of what the Scriptures say.

There are many churches today in the UK who struggle with how to bring the gospel to their local folk. Worried about compromising the faith they latch onto an old confession. For a Baptist it may be the 1689 Baptist Confession, whilst for a Presbyterian it would be the Westminster Confession, and for others some other old statement of belief. Now to my mind I fully understand why these are adhered to, but I have a problem because these confessions were worked out during the circumstances the people who wrote them faced at that time. We face very different circumstances. That is not to say we should ignore these confessions. They have some very good statements which do stand the test of time, but, and this is the vital thing, if we lean on these alone we fail to do the work that the writers of these confessions felt it important to do. What we need to do is to go to the Scriptures alone and hammer out what we believe in *today's* world and climate. We will come up with something which will agree with these older statements but we will have things in our statements which they never had to face because of the battles we face today.

What then of the charismatic movement? It is too easy to generalise so we must be careful here. Having seen many churches over the years through our movements around the country, there are charismatic groups which have the heartbeat of faith within them and then there are those which amount to heresy gone bad. On the opposite pole there are those who reject all flavours of charismatic experience who too are the very heartbeat of what it is to be a true church, and there are those whose legalism is palpable in its stench. An old dichotomous cliché has it that the charismatics have the Holy Spirit and the Reformed groups have the Bible. Well, as I have said, I have seen churches who claim the title charismatic and those who despise the term, who have the Scriptures and who love Christ demonstrably. A true believer is indwelt with the Holy Spirit and the Holy Spirit will lead that believer into all truth. Objectively all that person needs is the Bible. Experientially they need the indwelling of the Holy Spirit as well, but this is not something which can be manufactured or controlled in any way. Clearly the believer can read and study Scripture as and when they choose. Sadly there are some charismatics who state that in order to progress a believer must have some experience they designate as being "of the Holy Spirit." Equally obnoxious are the reformed groups who declare that unless you dot their "i's" and cross their "t's" you are not acceptable. In the rest of this chapter we shall continue to work out these thoughts under the following headings:

Connected with the scope of Scripture.

All truth is God's truth - or is it?

The Bible is complete   .

Nothing else is needed.

Examples of those who add to or take from the Bible.

Connected with the scope of Scripture.

Since the scope of Scripture is exceedingly broad, (i.e. it is not limited like man and his attempts are), it follows that what God has given to us is also sufficient. This also follows because God is a gracious giving Father as we noted earlier. Indeed the very nature of God Himself can be a starting point for saying that what He has given is sufficient, for are not all His ways perfect?

All truth is God's truth - or is it?

There are, of course, some who deny that Scripture is sufficient. Those who deny that Scripture is inspired (i.e. liberals) would never accept that the Scriptures have an exclusive nature about them. To these people the Scriptures are just part of the evidence for scholarly study. Some deny that the Scriptures have such a broad scope holding that they are inspired only in respect to salvation matters, and so would say that other disciplines must be bought to bear in our studies. A common expression that is used to allow for these positions is:

"ALL TRUTH IS GOD'S TRUTH"

This is one of those statements which appears perfectly all right until you start defining the terms. It is rather like a form of words which differing political sides might sign up to. Both parties can agree on the phrase, but what they mean by the phrase is very different. The problem comes when we consider the term "truth." Pilate asked the question "what is truth?" when he was faced with the whole truth (i.e. the Lord Jesus Christ).[604] However Pilate did have a point. How can we know what is true and what is not true? We know that what the Bible says is true because God cannot lie. We are taught in Scripture that men are corrupt, they lie, they go in the wrong direction, they oppose God, they seek their own ends (contrary to their design, i.e. for what they were made), they love falsehood and so on, and yet some still insist that we need some outside truth to help us in our studies etc. Lets look at two of these.

---

604   John 14v6; 18v38.

Mike Viccary

Science needed.

A number of people have taken this view. They may otherwise appear to be orthodox holding to the essential doctrines, but they fall into the medieval trap of putting theology at the top of the ladder of disciplines needed to get to the truth. Theology was thought of as the "queen of the sciences" which could only be attempted once you had mastered the Trivium and Quadrivium first).[605] A diagrammatic representation of how different people view the task of theology is shown the figure below. The Biblical approach is to take from Scripture alone. A Roman Catholic stance is that which puts tradition alongside Scripture. The New evangelical or liberal position is that which places science alongside Scripture.

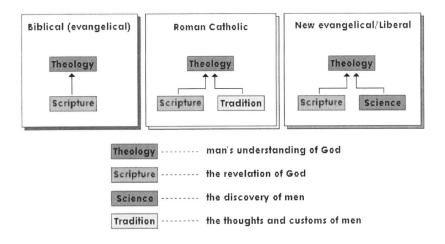

Two proponents of the idea that science is on a par with Scripture are, David I Dye (a physicist), and Bernard Ramm (a Biblical scholar who claimed to be evangelical). David I. Dye made the following assessment of how we should approach the hermeneutic task:

> ... tentativeness is another important principle of interpretation, since we may yet have acquired neither the broad view of Scripture nor the complete detailed scientific understanding needed to harmonize the data.[606]

In this statement we find the classic scientific approach expressed. Scientists are wont to appear humble and so they often speak about being "tentative" in their work all the while being dogmatic

---

605   http://classes.maxwell.syr.edu/his311/lecture%20three/trivium_and_quadrivium.htm.
606   David I. Dye. Faith and the Physical World. Paternoster Press. 1966. P123.

that those who espouse a religious or spiritual view are wholly wrong. Dye continues by outlining

this two-pronged approach which has science and Scripture as equals in the quest for understanding:

> The true Christian view offers no such alternatives: it is not a matter of either the Scriptures
> or scientific data, for when all truth is seen as God's, then one's mind is open to reinterpret
> all the available data.[607]

It can be seen from these quotes that Dye places scientific findings squarely in the "truth" camp. He

asserts that since what scientists discover must be true, we must thence also include it into our

analysis. The question is: do scientists merely discover truth? However, notice also that in a subtle

manner, we no longer are open to Scripture's gaze (a mirror) but rather have we become a judge

over all the available data which includes Scripture as well as science. There is no doubt that we

should judge science. This is paramount. But there is equally no doubt that we must never judge

Scripture, but rather be judged by it.

A second proponent of the idea that Scripture and science must be considered is Bernard

Ramm. Here is what he has to say on the subject:

> Scientific knowledge is invaluable for a knowledge of the Bible - at least to know it fully
> and completely. We do not see how it is possible to gainsay what Shields has written in this
> connection: "Without astronomical knowledge he cannot tell whether the astronomical
> Scriptures are in accord with the discovery of suns and planets. Without geological
> knowledge he cannot tell whether the order of the creative days agrees with the order of the
> earth's strata. Without ethnological knowledge he cannot tell whether the Mosaic
> genealogies include or exclude pre-Adamite and co-Adamite races of mankind. Without
> archaeological knowledge he cannot tell whether the Mosaic cosmogony was of Hebrew or
> Chaldean origin, or derived from primeval tradition still more ancient: nor whether the
> Elohist or Jehovist sections were original or compiled documents; nor whether Moses wrote
> the whole or parts of the books which have always borne his name. Without historical
> science he cannot tell whether Mosaic codes formed a logical or chronological series; nor
> whether they date before or after the Babylonian exile. And without some knowledge of
> psychology, sociology, and comparative religion he cannot even approach the higher
> problems of the soul, the Church, and the future of Christianity.[608]

Thus, in order to understand the word of God we must first have a knowledge of science! One of the

things that was instrumental in my conversion was the fact that if science was not accessible to all,

then how could it claim to be "the answer" or "the truth"? Surely all sections of society should have

access to it? How about the young? They cannot understand science so are they to be denied the

---

607   David I. Dye. Faith and the Physical World. Paternoster Press. 1966. P136.
608   Bernard Ramm. The Christian View of Science and Scripture. Eerdmans. 1954. P24.

meaning of life? Ramm and Dye's position is wholly untenable because modern science is no static thing, but a chameleon. Many historians of science have not only pointed this out but have demonstrated it by their surveys of history.[609]

Psychology needed.

Another area where some have strayed is in the realm of psychology, the study of the mind. In order to do psychology you need to have an understanding of the nature of man and the make-up of his mind. The only safe source for this is the Scriptures. It is noteworthy that none of the psychologies of the world (from whatever camp) would come up with the Biblical view of man, his make-up, his need for a relationship with God, his fall into sin, his rebellion, and so on. Why then should we go to the secular world for advice on psychological matters? One proponent who advocates the need for accepting psychology is Paul Vitz:

> Now with respect to psychology all is not bleak: there is on the intellectual horizon a new kind of psychology which is just emerging. I believe it can be best described as "Christian" psychology. It is the work of several Christian psychologists, and it offers the possibility of a real challenge to the secular stuff. Indeed, in the long run, I believe it will be possible to baptize large portions of secular psychology so as to permanently remove its anti-Christian thrust. After all, if the threat of Aristotle to the faith could be dealt with by St. Thomas Aquinas, then there is hope that this newest expression of the Greek mentality can also be defused. In any case, something like this is absolutely needed, since psychology is here to stay. Unless a Christian model of psychology is found, Christianity will continue to lose millions of souls to the message of secular psychology.[610]

Vitz's position is that Christians in psychology can "baptize" portions of this secular discipline into the Christian faith! It is very interesting that Vitz calls Thomas Aquinas as a witness. However this man melded the Christian faith with Aristotle's philosophy to create a new "organism." This is hardly what we would really want! We ought to ask a number of questions here:

[] Is that which God has provided lacking?

[] Did what Thomas Aquinas do, (the merging of Aristotle's views with the Medieval version of Christianity), prove successful?

---

609   Charles Singer pointed this out in his book: A Short History of Sceince published in 1959. He made a comment that the science of one age becomes the magic or nonsense of the next. What scientists believe today will be laughed at by the scientists of a hundred years from now.
610   Paul C. Vitz. From a secular to a Christian psychology. In Christianity confronts Modernity: A theological and pastoral inquiry by Protestant Evangelicals and Roman Catholics. Edited by P. Williamson and K. Perrotta. Ann Arbor, MI: Servant. 1981. PP121-149. P142,143. P142,143.

[] Should we be panicked by the fact that "psychology is here to stay" and that therefore we "will continue to lose millions of souls to the message of secular psychology"?

[] What happens when you "baptise" things into Christianity? Is this possible to do?

[] How can we be sure that we can remove the poison of secular thought? Who has the capability to do such a task?

These questions are really rhetorical. It is absurd to think that what God has provided in the word of God and by His Spirit is lacking! All attempts to create hybrids, such as that achieved by Aquinas, will become history at best but, more likely, do much damage in the meantime. One of the greatest problems the modern church faces is its insipid fear of man. The idea that we should kowtow to man and his ideas in order to get a hearing is utterly ridiculous when we view Christ and the mission He came to carry out. Any attempt to join secular human thinking with Biblical theology will always become something the world detests, and no true Christian will be deceived by for any length of time. The wicked hybrid known as "theistic evolution" is a case in point. Secular science which spawned the theory of evolution has no room for deity, and the problems theistic evolution establishes for the Christian are fatal. As proof of this last assertion consider the recent work of Peter Enns whose main thesis is that a belief in evolution must alter our conception of Christ's being the second Adam.[611] It is very important to realise that the sources of psychology (secular or Christian) are the polluted waters of Jung, Freud and their disciples. These were not only not Christian, but also (at least as far as Freud is concerned), anti-Christian. Another important question is, how did people survive before Freud came along? By the word of God alone! Through the preaching of this great gospel!

The Bible is complete.

When Christ died on the cross one of the seven "words" he uttered gives the Christian immense comfort. He cried out just before He gave up the ghost: "it is finished."[612] That Christ accomplished all that the Father asked of Him is nothing more nor less than we may expect from God. Such thoughts indicate that what God intends He completes. After all, creation was a finished event after 6 days. The words of Isaiah 55v11 tells us that God's word always achieves that for which it was spoken. God completes whatever project He begins. The same is so for His word. That Scripture is complete is taught by such a verse as Psalm 19v7:

---

611   Peter Enns. The Evolution of Adam. Brazos Press. 2012.
612   John 19v30.

The law of the Lord is perfect, converting the soul; the testimony of the Lord is sure, making wise the simple. (Psalm 19v7).

The word "perfect" means "complete," nothing more is to be added and nothing more is to be taken away. Now, of course, this Psalm was written before the New Testament, not to mention quite a portion of the Old Testament as well. How can a verse from about a thousand years before Christ inform us that God's word is complete and needs no more additions? Well the point is that what God speaks is always complete and perfect. When He revealed to Moses He gave the Pentateuch which was a complete unit of revelation. When He revealed to other prophets the same was true. Each revealed a whole piece of what God was revealing, complete in itself. God determined to add these newer revelations to His already revealed word. Now however we have had nothing new added to the Bible since the New Testament days. The writer to the Hebrews implies that Scripture was finished with the coming of Christ when he stated:

> *1 God, who at various times and in various ways spoke in time past to the fathers by the prophets, 2 has in these last days spoken to us by His Son, whom He has appointed heir of all things, through whom also He made the worlds; 3 who being the brightness of His glory and the express image of His person, and upholding all things by the word of His power, when He had by Himself purged our sins, sat down at the right hand of the Majesty on high, 4 having become so much better than the angels, as He has by inheritance obtained a more excellent name than they. (Hebrews 1v1-4).*

Thus whereas the Lord spoke completely through each prophet in the Old Testament in a partial way, now in these last days the Lord has spoken completely and finally in His Son, Jesus Christ. All Scripture is God-breathed, but that brought to earth as-it-were by the Son who is pre-eminent (Hebrews) is vastly superior to the Old Testament revelation even though each revelation may be complete in itself.[613]

The perfection of God's revealed word is stated in these terms at two very important times of God's revelatory activity:

> *You shall not add to the word which I command you, nor take from it, that you may keep the commandments of the Lord your God which I command you. (Deuteronomy 4v2).[614]*

> *18 For I testify to everyone who hears the words of the prophecy of this book: If anyone adds to these things, God will add to him the plagues that are written in this book; 19 and if anyone takes away from the words of the book of this prophecy, God shall take away his*

---

613   2Timothy 3v16.
614   See also Deuteronomy 12v32.

part from the Book of Life, from the holy city, and from the things which are written in this book. (Revelation 22v18,19)

Remember that an author has the right to add to his own work, so these warnings do not have any effect on the addition of God's further words through the prophets to His word written. The first Scripture was penned by Moses fourteen centuries before Christ's incarnation when the Bible was just beginning to be written. God is very careful to warn people as He publishes His work that no one is to tamper with it. He alone has the copyright. The same words are penned at the end of the New Testament before the end of the first century AD. Similar expressions can also be found in Proverbs 30v6 and Jeremiah 26v2. Remember further, that the Word of God is a living thing.[615] Thus in Moses' time the word of God was a young shoot or sapling, but by the time of John it had grown to a mature plant.

When we consider Scripture as having originated in God, it is inconceivable how anyone can think that this could be bettered. How, we ask, could God better Himself? He came in the flesh and revealed the Father. He did this openly and revealed the whole unto us. So how could He surpass that? In this way we can argue for the completion and hence the sufficiency of Scripture.

So also we must add that Christ is the end of the law.[616] After Him there can be no more revelation, for He fulfilled all that was needed, and in Him dwells "all the fullness of the Godhead bodily."[617] When Philip requested from the Lord Jesus Christ a new revelation of the Father he was rebuked because Christ Himself had fully revealed the Father.[618] Since Christ is the fullness of God, there can be no further revelation. To say the opposite implies that Christ's work of revealing the Father and His will was incomplete (we distinguish between God revealing Himself through His word – which is ongoing – and by fresh revelation of His word – which has stopped). But surely Christ completed all the tasks given Him of the Father? Did He not say that He had done His Father's business and completed the work? If so then there can be no greater revelation than that which we have in the New Testament. Just in case these considerations are not enough for the reader, then consider the following Scriptures which clinch this point:

> *I and my Father are one. (John 10v30).*

ü

> **9** *Jesus said to him, "have I been with you so long, and yet you have not known Me, Philip? He who has seen Me has seen the Father; so how can you say, 'show us the Father'?* **10** *Do*

---

615   Hebrews 4v12.
616   Romans 10v4.
617   Colossians 2v9; John 1v18.
618   John 14v8-10.

you not believe that I am in the Father, and the Father in Me? The words that I speak to you I do not speak on My own authority; but the Father who dwells in Me does the works. (John 14v9,10)

4 I have glorified You on the earth. I have finished the work which You have given Me to do. ... 6 I have manifested Your name to the men whom You have given Me out of the world. They were Yours, You gave them to Me, and they have kept Your word ... 8 For I have given to them the words which You have given Me; and they have received them, and have known surely that I came forth from You; and they have believed that You sent Me   14 I have given them Your word; and the world has hated them because they are not of the world, just as I am not of the world. (John 17v4,6,8,14).

Nothing else is needed.

Not only is the canon of Scripture closed but we must also note that nothing else is required alongside of the Bible. Of course the unregenerate will not be able to receive this truth, and believers need the Holy Spirit's aid in interpreting Scripture (illumination). But no other work, system, hierarchy, mechanism, revelation or disposition is required. What the Lord has been pleased to give us is sufficient. If we say otherwise (that we need science, tradition, new revelations or whatever), then we conclude that God is either a liar or incompetent.

Consider these points found in God's word. Peter in his second letter pointed out that we have everything we need to live a fully godly life on earth.[619] Isaiah was told to appeal to the law and God's testimony only rather than agree to contact spiritualist mediums.[620] Our Lord is the true fountain source, so why should we go to the broken cisterns of the world?[621] Paul told the Ephesian elders that he had declared unto them the whole counsel of God.[622] How could this be so unless Paul had the whole counsel of God? He must have had all he needed. Finally we refer to the passage in Jude where we here about "The Faith":

Beloved, while I was very diligent to write to you concerning our common salvation, I found it necessary to write to you exhorting you to contend earnestly for the faith which was once for all delivered to the saints. (Jude 1v3).

Here we are informed that "The Faith" was **once** delivered unto the saints, and that over 1,900 years ago. Hence no more needs to be added.

---

619   2Peter 1v3,4.
620   Isaiah 8v20.
621   Jeremiah 2v13; 17v13; Joel 3v18; Zecharaiah 13v1.
622   Acts 20v27.

Examples of those who add to or take from the Bible.

By adhering to many of the modern movements of today we are in danger of adding to or of taking from the word of God. First take note that the Nestle-Aland UBS Greek New Testament text is considerably shorter than the Textus Receptus, (by the equivalent of ~ 1 & 2 Peter). Either one is correct and the other has added to the word, or the other is correct and the former has taken from the word. (The remaining alternatives - both have taken from, or both have added to, or one has added and the other taken - render both New Testament texts to be incorrect and this leaves us in an utterly hopeless situation). We have considered this problem of the textual basis of the New Testament earlier when we reviewed the manuscript evidence. However the church as a whole does need to address this problem carefully, especially in view of the recent publications of Majority text editions of the Greek New Testament.

In what follows I will merely bring a few thoughts together. Each section really deserves greater attention which we cannot afford for now. The reader is encouraged to consider these starting points with an open Bible and to pursue the ideas further.

Charismatics.

These folk have added to the word by means of reliance on ongoing prophecy, dreams, tongues and so on. In doing this, they inadvertently take from God's word through neglect, for who would be bothered to study when you can sit back and dream a prophecy? We must get back to understanding that prophecy, tongues, visions and dreams are technical terms in Scripture. We are talking of direct communication between God and man for the benefit of all. The type of experiences going on in Charismatic circles is on a different level. The dreams and visions are not new revelation. If they were then we could argue that God is failing miserably to communicate, for where are these revelations? Why have they not been incorporated into Scripture? It should be noted that there have been many who added their dreams and visions to Scripture such as Joseph Smith, the founder of the Mormons. These however are not Christian but a new religion.

With regard to modern charismatic dreams and visions there are two possibilities for their origin. First, they may be self induced. There may be such a desire for dreams and visions that any dream or new idea may be grasped and invested with supernatural origins even though their true origin is the mind. Second, we should bear in mind that many may be influenced by demons. This is serious and needs addressing.

The revelatory gifts were given as authenticators for the New Testament writers.[623] Such

---

623 See, for example, Hebrews 2v1-4; 2Corinthians 12v12.

Mike Viccary   *In Heb the gifts were given to authenticate the gospel!*   *# Gal 12.12 – agreed! but 1 Cor 14.3 is different!*

attestations to the apostles and other inspired writers is no longer needed when Scripture is completed. However, we must reaffirm that God's revelation of Himself through the word by the Holy Spirit is definitely ongoing. It is this distinction that has been lost and is woefully misunderstood today. We may be moved by our love and experience of God and in a moment be stirred by the Spirit to sing out a spiritual song, or recite a Bible verse, but these spontaneous offerings are not revelatory. *No ?* They may be guided and moved by the Spirit but they do not have the authority and weight of Scripture. *what do they have ?*

New evangelicals.

These folk have relied on scholarship, science and so forth to interpret the Scriptures. Chief amongst these folk is John Stott, J. I. Packer, A. McGrath, Mark Noll amongst many others. By allowing secular (and even atheistic) men to have their say, these new evangelicals have added to Scripture. In actual fact, these folk are closer in alliance to liberals.[624] They accept a variety of unhelpful positions such as theistic evolution, psychology, and even ecumenism.

Church Growth.

Sadly the modern church has grown tired of trusting the gospel and has attempted to devise a whole host of methods in order to attract new blood. The use of business and pragmatic approaches has been rampant throughout the western church. Included in the gimmicks used in our day are the entertainment practices favoured in the secular world. To see what amounts to rock or pop group style worship elevated on stages with fans adoring is woeful at the very least. Let me say at once that whilst the Scriptures do teach that we may use all manner of instruments for worship, we must never ape the world. We must never elevate the worship band. It is so sad to see a new leadership role entitled "worship director" as though these were necessary. Where, we may ask, does the apostle Paul advocate music directors? He doesn't and they are not necessary for the Lord's ways are quite simple. Each of us can bring a Psalm or spiritual song when amongst the congregation. However this must be done with order and decency, not in wild abandon. But what passes for worship in our day is often base sensualism.

Other modern church growth practices are equally pernicious. Some opt for whatever may work. A kind of pragmatism is fostered. Some have even opted for asking the people what they want in a church service and then giving them this as though that would honour God. Such foolishness! Much more could be added but it is not really necessary for the Scriptures tell us all we

---

624   John Stott dialogued with one liberal by the name of Edwards even calling him a Christian. Evangelical Essentials: A Liberal Evangelical Dialogue. D. L. Edwards and J. Stott. InterVarsity Press. 1989.

need for "successful" evangelism. Of course "success" in the Bible is not measured by numbers. How often this is presented to us in Scripture. God knows the numbers necessary. We are not to go by such things. Instead we are to honour the Lord and do all that He commands. Think, for example, of Noah. Faced with great apostasy and opposition, with reluctant hearers what did Noah do? Did he entertain them? Did he ask them what they needed in worship or church so that they could be provided for? Did he seek to make use of all the available business and common means to carry out the mission of God? Of course not! What we read instead is that Noah did all that God asked him to. He built an ark. And in doing this he saved his family and condemned the world because they would not humble themselves to listen to his preaching.[625]

Ecumenism.

Many are deluded by the world's presentation of the Christian church. The world has no idea about what the true church really is. The Scriptures describe the church as victorious and of a single unified mind and mission. What the world describes is a distortion. It sees division, "separated brethren," those with curious rituals, others with strange beliefs and so on. This distortion is not something produced by Christians but by a misinterpretation offered by the world. Some Christians may be duped by the world's presentation of what the church is, and so because they are sad at the various divisions and splits, they seek a way to bring unity. Often this leads to a denial that doctrine is important. Instead these folk focus on practice with no doctrinal basis.

Liberals.

These are the ultimate "cutters" and "choppers" of God's word. Scripture is not God's word to these folk. It is just one of man's works which requires attention along with every other production of mankind. Their basis owes much to secular humanism. The implications of their views are quite devastating. With a human understanding of Scripture that has no supernatural content, the end result is an elevation of mankind and his intellectual ability. Given that modern man really has little regard for religious academia, preferring the scientific elite instead, the plight of liberals is quite a sad one.

Counselling & psychology.

I have never quite understood why those who seek to develop pastoral gifts resort to the secular streams of thought. Those who favour the new psychological and counselling routes, have

---

625　　Genesis 6v22; 7v5; Hebrews 11v7; 2Peter 2v5.

eliminated the pastoral side of Scripture, and have added man's views on the sickness of the mind. When we look back to the Puritans and other great Christian eras, we find a rich depth of Scriptural preaching and teaching. As a single example I would commend to the reader the work by William Gurnall, *A Christian in Complete Armour*. It has great depth and would do wonders for the soul.

Roman Catholicism.

Roman Catholicism is not a Christian denomination. These folk may hold to orthodox views on the trinity but their aberrations with regard to salvation, Mary, communion and the church place them well outside the Christian domain. Roman Catholics have added to God's word by their traditions, including papal statements, the apocrypha, and other teachings sanctioned by the church of Rome. The additions Roman Catholics make actually ends up taking away from God's word, because they reinterpret passages they don't like to suit their traditions.

Chapter 11.

Powerful and efficacious.

Introduction.

Here our focus will be the fruitfulness or efficacy of the word of God. In the charismatic-reformed debates there is often the charge that nothing happens except the Spirit of God is in evidence. People in all church circles like to talk of a move of the Spirit. Sometimes I wonder if the talk is steeped in mystical lore! However the Scriptures teach both that it is the Spirit who works in the hearts and minds of people, and it teaches that the Bible itself does wonderful works as well. This teaching that the Bible is efficacious and works is something we can derive clearly from the first chapter of Genesis. In this opening chapter we are taught that God created all things out of nothing using the word as his agency. In the New Testament we find that the Word of God (the Lord Jesus Christ) is the agent of creation. Clearly when God speaks, his word has effect. It does not return to him without accomplishing precisely what he intended it to do. This idea of the efficacy of the word of God is shown in many places but is, perhaps, demonstrated extensively in Psalm 19, for there, amongst other things, we see that the law and the commandments bring wisdom, restoration of heart, conversion and make the simple see.

How people today amongst the churches struggle to see things change or to see progress! I wonder if that is because there is so much talk, so much activity and so much trust in other things, with so little attention paid to the word of God? If people get into the word of God really and seek the Lord to know him what a difference that would make! Of course there are many who know the word of God in a purely intellectual sense and who could spout doctrine and wisdom that this world favours but they will do nothing but damage. Please do not get me wrong for I believe passionately in knowing doctrine but the reason for this is to know Christ – to see him!

In this section we shall consider the fruitfulness of Scripture under the following seven headings:

[1] The aim and purpose of Scripture.

[2] The Bible is not a dead letter but is living and powerful.

[3] The Bible is the means of new birth.

Mike Viccary 289 of 319

[4] Metaphors for Scripture.

[5] Descriptive phrases used for the word of God.

[6] Two key Scriptures: Psalm 19 & 2Timothy 3v16,17.

[7] Three summary effects of the word of God.

[1] The aim & purpose of Scripture.

The Scripture's primary purpose is to speak of Christ and His work.[626] In making this statement we are brought to consider that the Scriptures direct our minds away from self and self-interest, and towards the One who gave Himself up for needy sinners. The great aim of the Scriptures is summed up by John in his gospel account:

> *30 And truly Jesus did many other signs in the presence of His disciples, which are not written in this book; 31 but these are written that you may believe that Jesus is the Christ, the Son of God, and that believing you may have life in His name. (John 20v30,31).*

Clearly faith and believing are important, but the object of that faith is Jesus as the Christ, the Son of God. We remember further that the Old Testament can be summed up by the two great commandments (which are themselves a summary of the two tables of the Law the ten commandments), as the Lord Jesus Christ has said:

> *37 Jesus said to him, "'You shall love the Lord your God with all your heart, with all your soul, and with all your mind.' 38 This is the first and great commandment. 39 And the second is like it: 'You shall love your neighbour as yourself.' 40 On these two commandments hang all the Law and the Prophets." (Matthew 22v37-40).*

The great aim then is wholehearted love and devotion to God and thence also to all men. This is confirmed by the apostle Paul in his instruction to Timothy:

> *Now the purpose of the commandment is love from a pure heart, from a good conscience, and from sincere faith. (1Timothy 1v5).*

God's intention, then is that people may have love (both for Him and then for all) which stems from a pure heart and which believes in God (sincere faith). As we can see, then, the various writers of the Scriptures sometimes give us the aim for their work. How many, I wonder, can say that their work delivers on such aims? Surely in the world aim and outcome do not often show a straight forward one-to-one correspondence. In stark contrast, however, we have here not merely the

---

626   Luke 24v24,44. See also John5v46; 10v35.

writings of several human writers, but the very word of God. Consequently, because this is the word of God, we can assert with confidence that not only do the Scriptures tell us what their purpose is but also the Scriptures themselves help to bring about that very purpose.

We turn now to consider some of the ways in which the Scriptures themselves achieve the aim for which God purposed.

[2] The Bible is not a dead letter - it is living and powerful.

There is a great, and false, dichotomy proffered in some "Christian" circles whereby the Bible is considered to be a "dead" letter, in contrast to the Holy Spirit and ecstatic experiences which are considered to be as a result of the "living" Spirit. Those who suggest such a dichotomy use Paul's statements in 2Corinthians 3v6 as support. However in this Scripture Paul is contrasting the Old Testament law written in stones which, although holy and righteous, could not bring about life for those dead in trespasses and sins, with the ministry of the gospel which brings life through faith in Christ alone. It is not a case of written material being dead and spiritual experience being life, but a question of perspective. The believer responds to the Scriptures, even the Old Testament, with the eyes of gospel faith.

Now the Scriptures tell us that the gospel itself is powerful:

> *For I am not ashamed of the gospel of Christ, for it is the power of God to salvation for everyone who believes, for the Jew first and also for the Greek. (Romans 1v16).*

It is the gospel which is the "power of God" and not miracles, personalities or schemes and programmes. Paul re-emphasises this teaching when he wrote to the Corinthians:

> *For the message of the cross is foolishness to those who are perishing, but to us who are being saved it is the power of God. (1Corinthians 1v18).*

The very word or message of the cross is the power of God. However, not only is the gospel and the preaching of the gospel powerful, but the very word of God itself is said to have power:

> *For this cause also thank we God without ceasing, because, when ye received the word of God which ye heard of us, ye received it not as the word of men, but as it is in truth, the word of God, which effectually worketh also in you that believe. (1Thessalonians 2v13, KJAV)*

The Thessalonian Christians received the word of God as it was being preached by Paul, and this word worked within them "effectually" or effectively. This is wonderful news. The message we have received and which we pass on is itself effective. Then consider also these words in Hebrews:

> *For the word of God is living and powerful, and sharper than any two-edged sword, piercing even to the division of soul and spirit, and of joints and marrow, and is a discerner of the thoughts and intents of the heart. (Hebrews 4v12)*

The word of God itself is living and active and this word can penetrate the depths of the soul to reveal the intents of the heart. It is worth reminding the reader at this point of the excellent article written by the lawyer Philip Mauro in the early part of the twentieth century for the series concerning fundamental doctrines.[627] We can take enormous comfort and hope from these verses. The word of God and the preaching of the word of God are the chief tools of the Christian and these are powerful tools.

[3] The Bible is the means of new birth.

These thoughts concerning the power of God's word and message lead naturally to a consideration of both creation and re-creation or new birth. Let us remember that it was by the word of God that the "worlds were framed," or fitted and equipped.[628] Thus we find in Scripture that the word of God is indeed the means by which spiritual life (new birth) is brought into being. We read this in James:

> *Of His own will He brought us forth by the word of truth, that we might be a kind of first fruits of His creatures. (James 1v18)*

Then also we read a similar idea in Peter's first letter:

> *... having been born again, not of corruptible seed but incorruptible, through the word of God which lives and abides forever. (1Peter 1v23)*

The word of God is also the means by which spiritual life is revived in the flagging believer. The Psalmist declares seven times that it was God's word that quickened, or revived, him.[629]

---

627   "Life in the Word" which appears in "The Fundamentals" edited by R. A. Torrey and updated by Charles L. Feinberg (Chapter 20, PP239-248). Published by Kregel Publications. Grand Rapids, Michigan, USA. 1990. See also: http://www.ntslibrary.com/PDF%20Books%20II/Torrey%20-%20The%20Fundamentals%202.pdf.
628   Hebrews 11v3; Genesis 1.
629   Psalm 119v25,50,93,107,149,154,156.

[4] The metaphors for Scripture.

The Bible makes much use of metaphor. In Scripture there are at least seven metaphors used to represent the Bible. We shall look at these below.

The two-edged sword & the arrow.

We find reference to the two-edged sword in a number of places in Scripture.[630] The two-edged sword is an implement that can plunge deeply into the flesh of a man, as, for example, the dagger of Ehud the Judge which plunged into Eglon (the fat) king of Moab.[631] It is thus so described as an instrument of judgement able to distinguish and uncover the mesh and tangled web of men's thoughts and motives.[632] Thus just as the keen blade of a scalpel in a surgeon's hands can lay open to view all the intricate details of the insides of the patient, so also can God's word dissect the thoughts and plans of men. We must remember, however, that the Bible does not do this for God's benefit, (He already knows our very thoughts before we even make them), but He does it for our benefit that we might repent and turn to Him.[633]

We find reference to the Bible being an arrow in fewer Scriptures than for the two-edged sword.[634] The arrow pierces into the heart to pinpoint the error and sins of our ways. It is done to make known to us our condition. It is also done to slay the heart, for it is desperately wicked. We need new hearts, the old ones will not do. It would be worthwhile considering the places in Scripture where we read that a person was "pricked" in heart and similar ideas. We can think also of terms like "pricking", "piercing" and "convicting." Take for example the aftermath of Peter's preaching at Pentecost:

> *Now when they heard this, they were pierced to the heart, and said to Peter and the rest of the apostles, "Brethren,what shall we do?" (Acts 2v37, NASB).*

Peter's message which was the word of God, cut deep into the hearts of these folk and they turned in repentance and faith.

Fire.

The chief reference for this metaphor is found in the prophet Jeremiah:

---

630   Hebrews 4v12 and Revelation 1v16; 12v12,16. See also Isaiah 49v2; Ephesians 6v17; Revelation 19v15,21.
631   Judges 3v15f.
632   Hebrews 4v12.
633   Psalm 139v2,4,23,24.
634   Job 6v4; Psalm 38v2; Acts 2v37.

> *"Is not My word like a fire?" says the Lord ... (Jeremiah 23v29).*

Fire is an extremely effective tool for getting rid of unwanted rubbish. The word of God burns through the chaff, the stubble and the hay – all illustrations in Scripture for wicked or useless things.[635] It lays bare the very nature or essence of that which it eats up in its path.[636] Thus it is a fitting figure for the judgement aspect of God's word:

> *Therefore thus says the Lord God of hosts: "because you speak this word, behold, I will make My words in your mouth fire, and this people wood, and it shall devour them." (Jeremiah 5v14)*

As an extensive of the idea of fire, we can also think of the whole concept of refining where the true silver of faith is proved and where the dross is caused to be separated out. Yet another aspect of fire is to consider the concept of a furnace where things are baked and proved, (bread is cooked, pots are hardened).

A particularly important feature of this type of metaphor is the uncontrolled and spontaneous nature of fire. You cannot tame a fire, you can only put it out. When it rages it feeds and progresses where it will:

> *My heart was hot within me, while I was musing the fire burned; then I spoke with my tongue ... (Psalm 39v3).*

In a similar way Jeremiah found that even when he wanted to shrink back from proclaiming the word of God, he just couldn't because it burned hot within his breast:

> *Then I said, "I will not make mention of Him, nor speak any more in His name." But His word was in my heart like a burning fire shut up in my bones; I was weary of holding it back, and I could not. (Jeremiah 20v9)*

Or what of the two who unknowingly met the risen Christ on the road to Emmaus?

> *And they said to one another, "did not our heart burn within us while He talked with us on the road, and while He opened the Scriptures to us?" (Luke 24v32)*

Fire is a volatile thing, and those possessed by the word of God cannot withhold it in their breast. It

---

635   Isaiah 1v25; 5v24; Matthew 3v12; Luke 3v17; 1Corinthians 3v12.
636   2Peter 3v10-12.

is too hot to handle, and when they come near another they must spread the word of God.[637] If they happen upon a dry and parched soul that hungers and thirsts, the fire may spread and consume the drought in that beleaguered soul. Remember that God made His ministering angels flames of fire, never a damp squib![638] Also Paul told Timothy to fan into flame the gift given unto him.[639] We too ought to be on fire for God!

The hammer.

The main reference for this is in the same verse where we found the metaphor of fire:

> *"Is not My word like a fire?" says the Lord, "and like a hammer that breaks the rock in pieces? (Jeremiah 23v29).*

This metaphor may be implied in Scripture wherever we read that God strikes a blow at people especially when it tells us that He does so with the "rod of His mouth."[640] It is to be remembered that the hammer was an implement used by the craftsmen idolaters to make and fashion their idols.[641]

In Jeremiah 23v29 the hammer is used by God to fashion His creatures according to His wishes. The word "rock" in this verse means literally "fortress," or "stronghold," and is derived from the verb "to be lofty," or "craggy rocks." Thus the concept of stubbornness and pride is uppermost in thought. We ought to bear in mind that man is created from the dust of the ground and it is to dust that he shall return.[642] Now in life (under the sun) we have hardened ourselves and have become proud. Our hearts are not flesh but stone. What is required to get through is a sledgehammer to break the pride and hardness of our souls. The word of God is an effective hammer that breaks pride. In this connection, remember what the Lord Jesus Christ did to the proud Pharisees. He pronounced a series of "woes" to them in order to break up their hardened hearts and stiffened necks.[643]

We must be crushed by the word of God. We must break up the fallow ground, allowing God's word to have its deadly effect upon us, and we must yield to His saving blows which will result in contrite or broken or crushed hearts.[644]

---

637   Acts 6v7; 8v4; 12v24; 13v49; 19v20.
638   Psalm 104v4; Hebrews 1v7
639   2Timothy 1v6.
640   Psalm 110v5; Isaiah 1v5; 11v4.
641   Isaiah 41v7; 44v12.
642   Genesis 2v7.
643   Matthew 23v1f.
644   Psalm 34v18; 51v17; Isaiah 57v15; 66v2; Jeremiah 4v3; Hosea 10v12.

Mike Viccary   295 of 319

The lamp.

The main reference for this metaphor occurs in Psalm 119v105. One application of it is as a guide for life, so that the Bible is our manual for life. Another application of this image is in connection with judgement. The Scriptures teach that the whole world lies in darkness.[645] A lamp brings things into the light. An evil person's deeds are made known and revealed.[646] In passing we must ask ourselves why do Christians ever turn to the world for help? Clearly, however, given the dark and blind nature of the world we live in, we are in need of a torch by which to walk in this world. The Bible is our only guide for life.

When Christ was on this earth He was the light of the world.[647] Now that He has ascended, however, the light that remains is the Scriptures which testify exclusively of Him. The light which remains is not just the Scriptures, but those believers in whom the light of His word shines forth.[648] How vital it is for us to study the word of God.

The Bible not only shows us how to live but also it illuminates (or shows up) our lives as they truly are. We can readily see (and clearly) exactly who we are. Here the judgement aspect of light is being highlighted. Imagine some naughty children playing in a darkened room with mud and filth. When their parents enter and switch on the lights what an ugly mess is revealed! This application is at once both a judgement and a remedy. The Bible illuminates us and shows us the truth, and it highlights the errors, mistaken paths, follies and so forth. We might also mention here the mirror metaphor used by James for the word of God.[649] The Bible reflects to us exactly what state we are in. We could only see this if we had eyes and light by which to see.

Rain and snow.

This metaphor is found chiefly in the prophet Isaiah:

> *10 For as the rain comes down, and the snow from heaven, and do not return there, but water the earth, and make it bring forth and bud, that it may give seed to the sower and bread to the eater, 11 so shall My word be that goes forth from My mouth; it shall not return to Me void, but it shall accomplish what I please, and it shall prosper in the thing for which I sent it. (Isaiah 55v10,11).*

This is surely a beautiful illustration. For just as the plants and the animals (and all life) cannot do

---

645   Matthew 4v16; John 1v5; 12v46; Ephesians 6v12; Colossians 1v13; 1Thessalonians 5v4; 1Peter 2v9; 1John 5v19; Revelation 16v10.
646   John 3v18-21.
647   John 8v12; 9v5; 12v46.
648   Matthew 5v14-16; Luke 2v32; 24v27,44; John12v36; 2Corinthians 4v4-6; Ephesians 5v8,14; 1John 1v5-7
649   James 1v23.

without water so we cannot do without the word of God. Notice how the illustration is a "cover-all" and applicable to all. Thus there is no escape for anyone, for the rain drenches all, and the snow covers all the ground. There are particular areas of desert lands (in Africa for example) where some seeds lie dormant for many years. The moment the rains come, however, these areas spring back to life and become carpeted in green verdure where once they were but brown dust. The word of God is just like the rain and snow. It waters the ground, and where seeds lie they are brought to life and flourish.

We often think of the term *revival* when thinking of rain, that is, the work of conviction and conversion by the Holy Spirit.[650] Such revival, pictured as rain, will always be through the agency of the word of God preached:

> *1 Give ear, O heavens, and I will speak; and hear, O earth, the words of my mouth. 2 Let my teaching drop as the rain, my speech distil as the dew, as raindrops on the tender herb, and as showers on the grass. 3 For I proclaim the name of the Lord: ascribe greatness to our God. 4 He is the Rock, His work is perfect; for all His ways are justice, a God of truth and without injustice; righteous and upright is He. (Deuteronomy 32v1-4).*

Given these tremendous thoughts about how the word of God is like rain and snow, it is surely an even more startling fact that **we** have this word of God in our hands. What then are we doing with it? The rain has fallen.[651] The word of God does quicken. So let us trust God and preach the word!

There is, however, a warning that must be heeded. Ground that continually takes in the water and produces only thorns and briers will be condemned.[652] We must have new hearts that can yield fruit, and not the dead heart that yields destruction.[653] Beware of the thorns and thistles growing up in your garden.

The seed.

It is good to remind ourselves of the parable of the soils (sower). Here the condition of the soils is used to illustrate different conditions of people's hearts:

Pathway	Hard
Rocky ground	No deep root (superficial)
Thorns	Burdened by cares of the world
Good soil	Prepared and ready for seed

---

650   Psalm 65v9-13; 72v6,7.
651   Isaiah 30v20; Hosea 6v3; Joel 2v23.
652   John 15; Hebrews 6v7,8.
653   Matthew 12v34,35.

Mike Viccary

The word of God is the seed scattered. Growth can only proceed properly in the prepared ground. That is, in ground where the soil is turned and dug, and where stones, thorns and thistles are removed. Seeds scattered in all soil types will result in some fruit being produced. The seed scattered represents the preaching of the word in many areas and places. It is good also to attempt to remove the things which clutter and harm the seed of the word of God.

Here is one other important Scripture which make use of this metaphor:

> *Therefore lay aside all filthiness and overflow of wickedness, and receive with meekness the implanted word, which is able to save your souls. (James 1v21).*

By using the word "implanted" the writer is showing the idea of a seed planted in the heart. Here (in James) we are taught to repent from our wickedness, and to accept the word of God in humility. This word of God is part of our very heart since it is implanted there! What a privilege!

There are other Scriptures where the concept of seed and growth are evident such as:

> *Let the word of Christ dwell in you richly in all wisdom, teaching and admonishing one another in psalms and hymns and spiritual songs, singing with grace in your hearts to the Lord. (Colossians 3v16).*

We must bathe ourselves in the word of God (rain and snow metaphor) for the word of God is implanted (as a seed) in our hearts. For it to grow effectively we need to attend to it and nurture it. We do this by reading and meditating on the word, by the hearing of God's word (preaching), and by doing what we are taught (spiritual exercise). We need also to till our soils. We need (on occasion) to break up fallow ground. We need to root out thorns and briers (bitterness for example). We need to turn from evil.

Does not the lover separated from her husband treasure his every letter in her heart? Should not we also hide God's word in our hearts that not only may we not sin against the Lord, but also that we might bring forth fruit pleasing to Him.[654]

Bread.

Two key Scriptures where this metaphor is used are, Deuteronomy 8v3 and Matthew 4v4. Here we focus on the fact that the word of God must be eaten (masticated – chewed) taken into the stomach and digested (meditation). The focus is on sustenance through a process of digestion (breaking down). What we must do is to chew over the word of God and allow it to become a part

---

654   Psalm 119v11.

of our very lives. The Puritans were referred to as having the Bible in their very veins,

Notice the important "all" or "every" used in Deuteronomy 8v3. We need all the words of God, that is, every word that proceeds from His mouth. The entirety of Scripture is our need, not just a verse here and there, or a favourite book or passage. We need to have the attitude to the word of God that Job displayed:

> *I have not departed from the commandment of His lips; I have treasured the words of His mouth more than my necessary food. (Job 23v12).*

Obviously bread is efficacious to the eater and is such in a particular way. We eat to grow and sustain life. All the other metaphors have this quality of being effective or efficacious.

[5] Descriptive phrases used for the word of God.

There are many descriptive phrases for the word of God. We met some when we discussed the doctrine of inspiration. Here are some of these:

The oracles of God	(Romans 3v2).
The Word of God	(Luke 8v11).
The Word of the Lord	(Acts 13v48).
The Word of life	(Philippians 2v16).
The Word of Christ	(Colossians 3v16).
The Word of truth	(Ephesians 1v13).
The Word of faith	(Romans 10v8)

However we also have other descriptive words which indicate efficacy. Thus the word of God is described as being "holy," "righteous," "gracious," "living" and "powerful" to mention just a few. Some of these with Scripture references are shown in table 11.1.

These designations teach us that God's word is wholly fitted for its purpose and task. Not only does it have the requisite characteristics required for work on people (as created), but also for a complete work in all manner of conditions of people. By this I mean that the Bible has the proper tools as-it-were to work on the subjects in normal circumstances, and also when things go terribly wrong. Think of a new car. Mechanics have the required tools to service the car, but do they have all the tools for repair in an accident? The Bible has all the tools necessary for normal operations and maintenance and for repairs too.

Mike Viccary

Table 11.1: Descriptive words used for Scripture.

Descriptive word/phrase	Scripture references.
Holy and righteous.	Psalm 60v6; 108v7; 119v123; Isaiah 45v23; Hebrews 5v13.
Gracious.	Acts 20v32.
Living and powerful.	Philippians 2v16; Hebrews 1v3; 4v12.
Truth and faithful.	Psalm 119v43,160; John 17v17; 2Corinthians 6v7; Ephesians 1v13; Colossians 1v5; 2Timothy 2v15; Titus 1v9.
Good.	2Thessalonians 2v17; Hebrews 6v5.
Pure	Psalm 12v6; 119v140; Proverbs 30v5.
A word of promise.	Romans 9v9.
A word of reconciliation.	2Corinthians 5v19.
A word of salvation.	Acts 13v26.

[6] Two Scriptures: Psalm 19 & 2Timothy 3v16,17.

We have already considered these verses under different headings. Here we want to acknowledge that they teach quite clearly that the Bible does indeed do its work well.

Psalm 19.

Considering the second half of this Psalm there are six designations of God's word, six descriptions of God's word, and six effects which it produces:

Table 11.2: Descriptions of the efficacious word in Psalm 19.

Nature	Description	Effect
Law	Perfect	Converting the soul
Testimony	Sure	Making wise the simple
Statutes	Right	Rejoicing the heart
Commandment	Pure	Enlightening the eyes
Fear	Clean	Enduring for ever
Judgements	True	Righteous altogether

The descriptions given do not just relate to the particular aspects of God's word. Each aspect to God's word (law, testimony etc.), is used as a designation for the whole Bible. We have here in Psalm 19 six things which the Bible actually does:

(1) It is the means of conversion.

(2) It is the source of all wisdom (practical – i.e. a manual for life).

(3) It is the pathway to true joy.

(4) It is the means to understanding, (i.e. questions answered and resolved).

(5) It provides that which is enduring and lasting.

(6) It produces that which is wholesome (righteous, holy).

2Timothy 3v16,17.

This Scripture virtually speaks for itself. It is truly efficacious!

16 All Scripture is given by inspiration of God, and is profitable for doctrine, for reproof, for correction, for instruction in righteousness, 17 that the man of God may be complete, thoroughly equipped for every good work. (2Timothy 3v16,17).

Here we find that Scripture is "profitable." Such a good word for the business and economic minded amongst us! It means "helpful" "advantageous" or "serviceable" and comes from a word meaning "to heap up" (i.e. accumulate profit). The word of God then is useful for producing a righteous life through teaching, example, correction and so on. We conclude this section with a reminder from Peter's second letter that God has seen to it that we have absolutely everything we need to live godly lives here on earth:

2 Grace and peace be multiplied to you in the knowledge of God and of Jesus our Lord, 3 as His divine power has given to us all things that pertain to life and godliness, through the knowledge of Him who called us by glory and virtue, 4 by which have been given to us exceedingly great and precious promises, that through these you may be partakers of the divine nature, having escaped the corruption that is in the world through lust. (2Peter 1v2-4).

[7] Three summary effects of the word of God.

We have discussed a great variety of Scriptures which indicate that God by His word is working His purposes out. Such a work is not just wonderful, it is unsurpassed. The work of man is at the very best, weak and futile in comparison. We shall conclude this chapter by merely emphasising three important areas in which the word of God is efficacious.

First we must remember that the word of God will impart spiritual life and bring salvation to the soul.[655] Nothing else can do this. Man in his folly tinkers and plays around but has absolutely no

---

655   James 1v18,21; 1Peter 1v23.

means to bring about new birth. Second we note that Scripture has great cleansing power.[656] Just as the world cannot bring about new birth, or life in any real sense, so it cannot really do anything to make things clean and pure. In fact, whenever man dabbles in attempting to cleanse or repair a human soul, the result is usually much worse. The poor creature subjected to the efforts of a worldly attempt at making good, ends up suffering terribly. Finally, it can keep us from evil.[657] Again there is nothing in man, and certainly nothing in the world that can remove or protect from evil. This is ultimately because man is desperately wicked and evil in nature. How then can a wicked man protect or remove evil when he himself is evil?

Thus the solution to our problems, the ongoing deliverance from the pollutions of this world, and the protection from harm and the insidious encroachments of the world can only be brought about through the agency of the word of God. Nothing else will do.

---

656   Psalm 119v9; John 15v3; Ephesians 5v26.
657   Psalm 17v4; 119v11; John 17v14,17.

Chapter 12.

Authoritative.

Authority.

The Scriptures are authoritative. That is, they form the only standard of authority which a believing Christian will accept. Nothing else has this force and compulsion. We need to examine this aspect of God's word. It brings with it not just a message, but the message that God wants us to hear. There are four key themes we must consider under this heading. First we must remember that the Scriptures are God's word. Thus the Scriptures are authoritative because of inspiration. The very nature of the Scriptures is that they are "God-breathed." Secondly we must emphasise the unassailable fact that the Scriptures are a Christian's **only** authority. We must be very careful here because we do not want to lead the believer into a false sense of confidence. Many have sadly walked away with a Bible in their hands and have clung to their own views irrespective of others claiming that the Bible is their only guide. If we truly have the Scriptures as our sole authority we will do what it says and walk in fellowship and unity with other believers, including those who are now with the Lord in glory. We cannot neglect our study of church history. Notwithstanding this general caveat, we must emphasise the fact that Scripture is the sole authority because many have given other things authority besides Scripture. Thus, for example, in stating that Scripture is the "supreme" authority we open the way for subordinate guides. McGrath speaks about the many "handmaidens" which are available to guide the believer in his or her quest to grasp the Scriptures.[658] By the term "handmaidens" McGrath is referring to other sources of information and truth such as science or archaeology. Such a position leads ultimately to the downfall of faith because whatever handmaidens may be admitted into the heavenly court, they have a habit of dethroning the queen!

A third theme we shall consider is the authority of Christ. Sadly many have set Christ's authority against that of Scripture. Liberals do this when they try and acknowledge that Christ was clearly in command of His situation, but do not want to admit that what the apostles and prophets have written is binding upon us. However the Lord Jesus as the Second Person of the Holy Trinity exercises the same divine authority as that exercised by the Holy Spirit who authored Scripture.

---

658   Alister E. McGrath. A Scientific Theology: Volume 1: Nature. Edinburgh: T & T Clark, 2001. P11.

Since the Godhead works in concert we cannot set Christ's authority in opposition to any other part of Scripture. One final theme we shall investigate is the place and position of God's word in relation to His name or character, and idea which is found particularly in Psalm 138.

Authority stems from inspiration.

We begin with the truth that since the Bible is divinely inspired, it is therefore God's word, that is, a word possessed and owned by God. Furthermore because it is God's word it is thus invested with His authority. It might be objected that power and authority can be God's alone. [659] Liberals are often keen to say this. Yet we cannot separate God from His word. The Scriptures teach us of this wonderful idea that what God says must be carried through. We find this stated in Psalm 33, for example:

> *By the word of the Lord the heavens were made, and all the host of them by the breath of His mouth. ... For He spoke, and it was done; He commanded, and it stood fast. (Psalm 33v6,9).*

After recalling the history of creation as detailed in Genesis 1 in verse 6, the Psalmist then goes on to explain what this effectively meant in verse 9. Whenever God speaks, what He commands is done. This same thought is displayed in Isaiah:

> *10 For as the rain comes down, and the snow from heaven, and do not return there, but water the earth, and make it bring forth and bud, that it may give seed to the sower and bread to the eater, 11 so shall My word be that goes forth from My mouth; it shall not return to Me void, but it shall accomplish what I please, and it shall prosper in the thing for which I sent it. (Isaiah 55v10,11).*

It stands to reason, therefore, that when the infinite and perfect God speaks, what He says will be done and has this stamp of authority with it.

Sole not supreme.

Now since God has **only** spoken through His word (there is no other thing which can claim to be expressly what God has said), and since this is attested by the witness of the Lord Jesus Christ, it must therefore be the only authority for believers. Hence in submitting to Scripture a believer is therefore submitting to the Lord.

Unfortunately, the idea (expressed by many modern statements of faith) that Scripture is our "**supreme**" authority easily yields the idea that other things also hold authority in and of

---

659   Psalm 62v11; Matthew 28v18-20; John 5v27.

themselves. In stark contrast we must state categorically, however, that such things as (for example), elders or deacons, statements of faith, church meetings, or pastors can only have authority if they reflect Scriptural truth with 100% accuracy. Where such things do not reflect the Scriptures properly, they are no longer authoritative. If a statement of faith is 100% accurate with respect to Scripture at a given time, we must never consider it as having authority in and of itself. We can state this because no statement of faith can reflect Scripture in its entirety. Furthermore, the danger is that in time such a document may get altered, supplemented or added to as new controversies arise. Such a document is a *human* production, and we must be very wary of treating it as Scripture. As soon as we invest authority in something other than Scripture, we run into the problem of constructing a *hierarchy*. A hierarchy is defined as; "An organization with grades of authorities, from the highest to the lowest." In this way Scripture may be represented as the supreme authority, the highest or most important authority. In such a case, it will not be the only authority considered by a group or church. With such a diverse system the danger of developing more structural hierarchies appears. Something like this has happened in church history with the development of bishops, popes and cardinals and so on.

Holding the Bible as a supreme authority leads to the concept that it rests at the pinnacle, summit or at the top of a pile of other things which are considered important. The church of Rome may actually exalt Scripture but in order to even reach such dizzy heights you have to pass through a plethora of lesser authorities. You cannot get to Scripture unless you go through the priest, the pope and the Church of Rome. Evangelicals have fallen into this trap somewhat as well because of the tendency to elevate science, certain techniques, and especial names. You will not be accepted by some evangelicals unless you fall into certain constraints. Holding Scripture as a supreme authority also destroys the Biblical ideas of Scripture's sufficiency and scope. By using the term "supreme" this can also be made to fit in neatly with the notion that Scripture is not sufficient (we need other things like science, for example), and has only limited scope (it is only concerned with matters of faith).

We affirm that all authority must be derived directly from God. We have what He has said in the Bible. These things are faithful and true. That is our authority. And that alone! We reaffirm that there is no room for priests, bishops, cardinals, popes, house group leaders, deacons, elders, prophets, apostles, pastors, statements of faith, constitutions or any other thing to interpose between Christ and His followers. Some of these things are legitimate, (most are most certainly not), but the authority they exercise is only that authority which is vested in Scripture. Thus a deacon or an elder may only exercise authority over the flock of his care when he is doing so from Scripture's say so.

The authority is vested in Scripture alone, for "it is written".

The authority of Christ considered.

We turn now to look at the authority exercised by the Lord Jesus Christ. No one exercised authority like He did, for He alone could heal ("only say the word") and command the waves to obey Him. He alone could speak with power and raise the dead.[660] If Christ spoke with such authority, and if Christ be God, then surely the word of God, the written faithful word of God is authoritative too? Remember that the Lord Jesus Christ fully accepted the Old Testament as the authoritative word of God ("it is written"). He appealed to no other source, but castigated those who did, (for example, the Pharisees appealed to the "traditions of men").[661] He, to whom the Father gave all authority, actually submitted to the written word of God.[662] Remember further that Christ is the only head of the church (the body of believers).[663] Power, authority and control is vested in the head. It is the head that controls the body. We cannot really imagine a rival to this head.[664] A consideration of other metaphors used for the church bring similar thoughts:

The bride has but one husband (the bridegroom).

The sheep only hear the voice of their Shepherd.

The body responds to commands from only one Head.

The branches receive support and nutrients from only one Vine stock.

The temple gets its stability, strength, alignment from only one Foundation (capstone).

A country can only be ruled properly by one King

Hence our authority is God (in Christ). However, this is communicated to us exclusively by the infallible word. Men may have dreams and visions but these are not authoritative – only God's word is.

The word of God magnified above the name of God.

It comes as quite a surprise to many who want to demote the place of Scripture in the life of the church, when they read Psalms 56 and 138. Sadly in our current time many are trying a whole variety of different schemes and ideas to reach people for Christ. In many ways the heart and motivation of such people is right, but their method is all wrong. In Psalm 56 we read these words:

---

660   See Matthew 7v29; Mark 1v22,27; Luke 4v36; 9v1.
661   Mark 7v7,8.
662   Matthew 4v4,7,10; 5v17-20; 28v18-20; John 10v35.
663   Ephesians 1v22; 4v15; 5v23; Colossians 1v18; 2v10,19.
664   2Corinthians 11v3f.

4 In God I will praise his word, in God I have put my trust: I will not fear what flesh can do unto me. In God (I will praise His word), in God I have put my trust; I will not fear. What can flesh do to me? 5 All day they twist my words; all their thoughts are against me for evil. 6 They gather together, they hide, they mark my steps, when they lie in wait for my life. 7 Shall they escape by iniquity? In anger cast down the peoples, O God! 8 You number my wanderings; put my tears into Your bottle; are they not in Your book? 9 When I cry out to You, then my enemies will turn back; this I know, because God is for me. 10 In God (I will praise His word), in the Lord (I will praise His word), 11 in God I have put my trust; I will not be afraid. What can man do to me?(Psalm 56v4-11).

At the opening and ending of this section we find that the Psalmist is praising not just the Lord God, but His word as well. This is wholly understandable, for God does not waste words. What He speaks has the character of whom He is. It is good for us to pause here and consider what our words say about us. Do we think about what we say? If only we did! The Lord does not need to pause as He speaks for He speaks out of purity and holiness. His words are effective and true because He is effective and true.

And then we read these marvellous words in Psalm 138:

1 I will praise You with my whole heart; before the gods I will sing praises to You. 2 I will worship toward Your holy temple, and praise Your name for Your loving kindness and Your truth; for You have magnified Your word above all Your name. (Psalm 138v1,2).

David is concerned to praise the Lord before all supposed "gods" and towards God's holy temple. He is keen to do this for two key reasons. First the loving kindness and truth that the Lord exhibits. Second because the Lord has placed His word above all else that may be honoured. See how much God is concerned with His word! I can do no better that quote some comments on Psalm 138v2. First listen to the words of a great Puritan writer, William Gurnall (1616 – 1679):[665]

Every creature bears the name of God; but in his word and truth therein contained it is written at length, and therefore he is more choice of this than of all his other works; he cares not much what becomes of the world and all in it, so that he keeps his word, and saves his truth. Ere long we shall see the world in flames; the heavens and earth shall pass away, "but the word of the Lord endures for ever." When God will, he can make more such worlds as this; but he cannot make another truth, and therefore he will not lose one jot thereof. Satan, knowing this, sets all his wits to work to deface this and disfigure it by unsound doctrine. The word is the glass in which we see God, and seeing him are changed into his likeness by his Spirit. If this glass be cracked, then the conceptions we have of God will misrepresent him unto us; whereas the word, in its native clearness, sets him out in all his glory unto our eye.[666]

---

[665]   I commend (again) William Gurnall's excellent work "A Christian in Complete Armour" published by the Banner of Truth Trust. Every Christian should read this work on the armour of God as detailed in Ephesians chapter 6.
[666]   William Gurnall. See C. H. Spurgeon. Treasury of David. Volume VII. P211.

Gurnall has a wonderful mastery with words. If the truth expressed in God's word is distorted then all falls in disarray. God can make another world, it only takes an instant (or six days to teach man some lessons), but who can recover truth when once it is corrupted? Then we have these words from Joseph C Philpot (1802 – 1869), who left the Church of England to become a baptist pastor:

> This is one of those expressions of Scripture that seem so comprehensive, and yet so amazing. To my mind it is one of the most remarkable expressions in the whole book of God. "Thou hast magnified thy word above all thy name." The name of God includes all the perfections of God; everything that God is, and which God has revealed himself as having - his justice, majesty, holiness, greatness, and glory, and whatever he is in himself, that is God's name. And yet he has "magnified" something "above his name" - his word - his truth. This may refer to the Incarnate Word, the Son of God, who was called "the Word." "There are three that bear record in heaven, the Father, the Word, and the Holy Ghost, and these three are one" (1John 5v7). You may take the words either as meaning that God has magnified his Word, his eternal Son - above all his great name, that is he has set Jesus on high above all the other perfections of his majesty; or take it as meaning his written word, which is written in the sacred Scriptures. So, in that case, not only the Incarnate Word in the person of Jesus; but also the written word in the Scriptures of truth. He has magnified it above all his name in the fulfilment of it: God's faithfulness being so dear to him, he has exalted his faithfulness above all his other perfections. We see this in nature. Here is a man so to be depended upon, so faithful in his word, that he will sacrifice anything sooner than depart from it: that man will give up his property, or life itself, rather than forfeit his word. So God has spoken of magnifying his word above all his name. He would sooner allow all his other perfections to come to naught, than for his faithfulness to fail. He has so magnified his faithfulness, that his love, his mercy, his grace, would all sooner fail than his faithfulness - the word of his mouth and what he has revealed in the Scripture. What a firm salvation, then, is ours which rests upon his word, when God has magnified that word above all his name! What volumes of blessedness and truth are contained therein! so that, if God has revealed his truth to your soul, and given you faith to anchor in the word of promise, sooner than that should fail, he would suffer the loss of all; for, he has magnified his word above all his name.[667]

Of course when you read such words it makes sense that God would honour His word above all else because it is by these words that we meet with God, receive from Him, and have our life and being. The Scottish minister Ebeneezer Erskine (1680 – 1754) made this comment on Psalm 138:

> God has a greater regard unto the words of his mouth, than to the works of his hand: heaven and earth shall pass away, but one jot or tittle of what he hath spoken shall never fall to the ground.[668]

The word of God is our sole authority.

---

667   Joseph C Philpot. See C. H. Spurgeon. Treasury of David. Volume VII. Page 213.
668   Ebeneezer Erskine. See C. H. Spurgeon. Treasury of David. Volume VII. Page 213.

Index of headings.

76870841R00175

Made in the USA
Columbia, SC
18 September 2017